ural

ogy

∎

UME II

CLAUDE LÉVI-STRAUSS

Structural Anthropology

VOLUME II

Translated from the French by Monique Layton

The University of Chicago Press

The University of Chicago Press, Chicago 60637

Copyright © 1976 by Claude Lévi-Strauss
Reprinted by arrangement with Basic Books, Inc., New York, NY
All rights reserved. Published 1976
University of Chicago Press edition 1983
Printed in the United States of America

01 00 99 98 97 96 95   4 5 6 7

Library of Congress Cataloging in Publication Data

Lévi-Strauss, Claude.
  Structural anthropology.

  Translation of Anthropologie structurale.
  Originally published: New York: Basic Books © 1976
  Includes bibliographies and index.
  1. Structural anthropology. I. Title.
GN362.L4813   1983   306   82-16115
ISBN 0-226-47491-7 (pbk.: v. 2)

To the members of the
Laboratoire d'anthropologie sociale

*Vos quoque pectoribus nostris haeretis,
amici, dicere quos cupio nomine
quemque suo.*

Ovid, *Tristia*, III, iv.

Author's Preface

APPEARING FIFTEEN YEARS after *Structural Anthropology, Volume I*, this book remains faithful to the same formula: it brings together texts which were written both before and after the publication of the first book. Some were written in French, others directly in English; almost all are impossible to find today. They were so selected and ordered as to enable a reader unfamiliar with the problems of modern ethnology to get a bird's-eye view; to be introduced by means of a few representative examples gathered in a single volume to the way structural anthropology tackles these problems and attempts to solve them.

Part One, devoted to the past and future of the discipline, defines the field of anthropology and puts into proper perspective the questions it poses.

In Part Two, examples illustrate the way to overcome some theoretical and practical difficulties related to social organization and attitudes linked to kinship systems.

Part Three is the most developed. In it I treat that domain which I have been most concerned with for the past twenty years: mythology and ritual. I attempt to distinguish between structuralism and formalism from a theoretical point of view. Some concrete examples are used to show how variants of one myth, or several myths which appear different from one another, can be reduced to so many stages of the same group of transformations, as can their corresponding rituals among the same or among different peoples. Finally, I illustrate the manner in which a myth can degenerate into legendary tradition, romantic narrative, or political ideology.

Part Four briefly reviews the various problems which our contemporary societies face in many areas: literature, fine arts, urban life. More attention is given to the organization of research and teaching in the human and social sciences, and to certain obstacles, too often misunderstood or underestimated, against what we call progress.

This last part ends with the oldest text in this collection; a text published in 1952 and reprinted several times, but presented here in a revised version. The very wide perspective enables one to use this text as a conclusion, since it examines the relations between race and history, on the one hand, and the question of nature and the meaning of progress, on the other.

The most fashionable objection to structural anthropology is that its hypotheses cannot be "falsified." Yet, this criterion can only be applied to fully established sciences. Anthropology has not yet attained this stage. No physical or natural science could have come to maturity in the centuries it took for them to develop if they had allowed themselves to be stopped by this type of criticism.

We may even wonder if this criterion of "falsifiability" can truly be applied to human sciences. Their epistemological status is not at all like those which the physical and natural sciences can claim for themselves. These are characterized by a harmony which at all times has reigned among those who practice them at the level considered relevant to the contemporary state of the research. But such is not the case for those we call human sciences. With these, there is little or no discussion on the validity of such-and-such hypothesis. The discussion bears instead on the choice of a certain level of reference implied by this hypothesis, and not of another level which an opponent might favor.

It is exceptional for structural anthropologists to be told:

"Your interpretation of this phenomenon or group of phenomena is not the one which best accounts for the facts." Rather, they are told: "The way you break down the phenomena is not the way which interests us; we choose to break them down another way." The subject of the human sciences is man, yet the man who studies himself as he practices the human sciences will always allow his preferences and prejudices to interfere in the way he defines himself to himself. What is interesting in man is not subject to scientific decision but results and always will result from a choice which is ultimately of a philosophical order.

So we must recognize that the hypotheses of the human sciences cannot, now or ever, be falsified. In this domain, a hypothesis is never true. Consequently, it cannot be false either. Let us rather say that, in the human sciences (and thus in anthropology), a hypothesis only possesses a relative value, granted if it succeeds in accounting for more facts than those hypotheses it replaces; that is, until such times as another one makes a new step in the same direction. Thus it is proper to locate structural anthropology in relation to its predecessor and to those hypotheses which will one day replace it.

The value of the epistemological model offered by structuralism to the human sciences cannot be compared to the models available so far. Structuralism uncovers a unity and a coherence within things which could not be revealed by a simple description of the facts somehow scattered and disorganized before the eyes of knowledge. It also does this more economically, with a very small number of principles, axioms, and rules which, in a variety of domains, have proved their fecundity. But structuralism does not presume to contain the truth. It is content to say that things are a little clearer today than they were yesterday. While it hopes that its efforts, surpassed by others, have contributed to the progress made by human sciences, it knows that the nature of its study is such that this progress has no conceivable end. It also knows that we will only be able to verify or falsify the hypotheses we use on that remote day (if it ever comes) when the natural sciences are able to reach those organic foundations for progress which now we can only perceive as undefined and distorted reflections.

Claude Lévi-Strauss

Translator's Preface

I WISH TO THANK Heather Wagg, who collaborated with me through most of the translation, and Barry Pavitt, who assisted in its last stages. My thanks are also due to Francis Levy and J. Powell, who kindly gave me their help when I needed it.

May I also express my gratitude to Professor Lévi-Strauss for his constant willingness to clarify points obscure to me, and for his patient assistance.

Contents

Part Three *MYTHOLOGY AND RITUAL*

Part Four *HUMANISM AND THE HUMANITIES*

List of Figures

PART ONE

Perspective Views

The Scope of Anthropology

Mr. chairman,
My dear colleagues,
Ladies and gentlemen:

It was a little over a year ago, in 1958, that the Collège de France decided to institute a chair of social anthropology. This science is so attentive to the forms of thought we call superstitious when we encounter them among ourselves that I may be allowed, I trust, an initial homage here to superstition. Is it not in the nature of myths, which play such an important part in our re-

Chapter I was first presented as the inaugural address of the chair of social anthropology and was delivered by the author at the Collège de France on January 6, 1960. It was first published by the Collège de France under the title *Chaire d'Anthropologie sociale: Leçon inaugurale fait le 6 janvier 1960 par M. Claude Lévi-Strauss, Professor* (Paris: Collège de France, 1960). No. 31.

[*Translator's note:* A few sentences were borrowed from a previous translation of this address; see *The Scope of Anthropology*, trans. S. O. Paul and R. A. Paul (London: Jonathan Cape, 1967).]

search, to evoke a suppressed past and to apply it, like a grid, upon the dimensions of the present, and to do this in the hope of finding some meaning whereby two confronting faces—historical and structural—of man's own reality will for once coincide? On this occasion, in which I meet all the characteristics of myth, may I also be allowed to proceed on the example of myth—seeking in some past events the meaning and the lesson of the honor accorded me? The very date of your deliberation, my dear colleagues—by the strange recurrence of the number 8 already well known from Pythagorean mathematics, the periodic table of chemical elements, and the law of symmetry of the jellyfish—bears witness that the proposal, in 1958, to create a chair of social anthropology renews a tradition from which this speaker, had he even wished to, would have been powerless to escape.

Fifty years before your initial decision, Sir James George Frazer delivered at Liverpool University the inaugural lecture of the first chair in the world to be given the title of social anthropology. Fifty years earlier, in 1855—just over a century ago—Franz Boas and Emile Durkheim were born, two men whom posterity will regard as, if not the founders, at least the master builders (one in America and the other in France) of anthropology as we know it today.

It is appropriate that these three anniversaries, these three names, be evoked here. Those of Frazer and Boas give me the opportunity to attest, if only briefly, to all that social anthropology owes to Anglo-Saxon thought and to what I owe to it personally, since my first works were conceived and developed in close collaboration with it. But it should not come as a surprise that Durkheim occupies a larger place in this address: He incarnates the essence of France's contribution to social anthropology, although his centenary—lavishly celebrated in many foreign countries—passed almost unnoticed here and has not yet been marked by any official ceremony.[1]

How can we explain this injustice done to him (an injustice also to ourselves), if not as a minor consequence of this passion which moves us to forget our own history and even to hold it "in horror," in the words of Charles de Rémusat—a sentiment which leaves social anthropology in danger of "losing" Durkheim as it has already lost Gobineau and Démeunier.

And yet, my dear colleagues, those among you who share these distant memories with me will not contradict me when I recall that, around 1935, when our Brazilian friends wanted to explain to us why they were moved to choose French missions to form their first universities, they always mentioned two names: first, of course, the name of Pasteur, and next, the name of Durkheim.

But in reserving these thoughts for Durkheim, we perform another duty. No one would have been more sensitive to homage such as this than Marcel Mauss, a pupil of Durkheim and later his successor. From 1931 to 1942, at the Collège de France, Marcel Mauss held a chair devoted to the study of society. So brief was his stay in these halls of the unfortunate Maurice Halbwachs that one could truthfully assume that, by creating a chair of social anthropology, it is Mauss's chair you want to restore. This speaker, at least, owes too much to Mauss's thought not to relish this speculation.

The chair was entitled "Sociology" because Mauss, who, with Paul Rivet, worked so hard to make ethnology a science in its own right, had not quite achieved this by 1930. But to attest to the continuity between our teachings, it will suffice to recall that ethnology assumed an ever increasing place in Mauss's work; that, as early as 1924, he proclaimed the "place of sociology" to be "in anthropology"; and that—if I am not mistaken—Mauss was the first to introduce, in 1938, the words "social anthropology" into French terminology. He would not disavow them today.

Even in his boldest proceedings, Mauss never felt that he was straying from the Durkheimian line. Today we can, perhaps, perceive better than he how, without betraying an oft-affirmed loyalty, he simplified his great predecessor's doctrine and rendered it more tractable. This doctrine has not ceased to astonish us by its imposing proportions, its powerful logical framework, and the vistas it opens onto horizons where so much is yet to be explored. The mission of Mauss was to complete and fit up the prodigious edifice conjured from the earth at the passage of the demiurge. He had to exorcize a few metaphysical ghosts who were still trailing their chains there, and the edifice had to be shielded once and for all against the icy winds of dialectic, the thunder of syllogisms, the lightning flashes of antinomies. . . . But Mauss protected Durkheim's school from yet other dangers.

Durkheim was probably the first scholar to introduce this requirement for specificity into the sciences of man. He thereby opened the way for a renovation, at the beginning of the twentieth century, from which most sciences benefited, particularly linguistics. In any field of human thought and activity, one cannot ask questions regarding nature or origin before identifying and analyzing phenomena, and discovering in what measure the relations uniting such phenomena are sufficient to explain them. It is impossible to discuss an object, to reconstruct the process from which it arose, without knowing first *what it is;* in other words, without having exhausted the inventory of its internal determinants.

Yet, on rereading today *The Rules of Sociological Method* (Durkheim 1964), one cannot help but think that Durkheim has applied these principles with some partiality. He refers to them in order to constitute the social as an independent category, but without taking heed that this new category entails all sorts of specificities corresponding to the various aspects through which we apprehend it. Before maintaining that logic, language, law, art, and religion, are projections of the social, would it not have been wise to wait until the particular sciences had thoroughly examined the mode of organization and the differential function of each of these codes, thus facilitating the understanding of the nature of their interrelations?

At the risk of being accused of paradox, it seems to us that in the theory of the "total social fact" (so often praised, yet so little understood), the notion of totality is less important than the very particular manner in which Mauss conceives it. It is a foliated conception, one might say, composed of a multitude of distinct and yet joined planes. Instead of appearing as a postulate, the totality of the social is manifested in experience—a privileged instance which can be apprehended on the level of observation, in well-defined situations, and in which "the totality of society and its institutions . . . is set in motion." But this totality does not suppress the specific character of phenomena, which remain, as Mauss says in *The Gift* (Mauss 1969), "at once juridical, economic, religious, and even aesthetic, morphological." Thus totality resides finally in the network of functional interrelations among all these planes.

This empirical attitude taken by Mauss explains how he so

quickly overcame that distaste that Durkheim initially felt toward ethnographic investigations. "What counts," said Mauss, "is the Melanesian of such and such island. . . ." Against the theoretician, the observer should always have the last word, and against the observer, the native. Finally, beneath the rationalized interpretations of the native—who is often observer and even theoretican of his own society—one must seek the "unconscious categories" which, as Mauss wrote in one of his first works, are determinants "in magic, as in religion, as in linguistics." Without contradicting Durkheim (since it was to be on a new plane), this analysis in depth was to enable Mauss to reestablish ties with other sciences of man that had at times been unwisely severed: with history, since the ethnographer sets up camp in the particular, and also with biology and psychology, once social phenomena are recognized as being "first social, but also, and at the same time, both physiological and psychological." It will be sufficient, Mauss said, to take the analysis to a level where "body, soul, society, everything merges."

This lush sociology examines men as depicted by the travelers and the ethnographers who shared their existence, in either a fleeting or a lasting manner. It shows them engaged in their own historical development and set in a definite geographical space. It has, says Mauss, "as principle and as goal . . . to perceive the entire group and the entire range of its behavior."

If disembodiment was one of the perils facing Durkheimian sociology, Mauss protected it with equal success against another danger: automatism. Too often since Durkheim—and even among some who believed themselves liberated from his doctrinal domination—sociology has appeared as the product of a hasty foray into history, psychology, linguistics, economics, law, and ethnography. Sociology was content to add its recipes to the fruits of this plunder. Whatever the problem submitted to it, one could be assured of receiving a prefabricated "sociological" solution.

If we have left this stage behind, we owe it in great part to Mauss, and to Malinowski, whose names must be associated. At the same time, and no doubt aided by one another, they showed (Mauss as a theoretician, Malinowski as an experimenter) what the administration of proof can amount to in the ethnological sciences. They were the first to understand clearly that it is not enough to break down and to dissect. Social facts are not reducible to scattered fragments: they are lived by men, and this subjective consciousness is as much a form of their reality as objective characteristics.

While Malinowski was instituting the ethnographer's uncompromising participation in native life and thought, Mauss was affirming that what is essential "is the movement of the whole, the living aspect, the fleeting moment in which society, and men become sentimentally conscious of themselves and of their situation vis-à-vis others." This empirical and subjective synthesis offers the only guarantee that the preliminary analysis, carried as far as the unconscious categories, has allowed nothing to escape.

Without a doubt, the test will remain largely illusory. We shall never know whether the other person—with whom, after all, we cannot identify completely—makes from elements of his social existence a synthesis that can be exactly superimposed on the one we elaborate. But one need not go so far. It is enough—and for that the inner feeling is sufficient—that the synthesis, even approximate, arises from human experience. We must make sure of it, since we study men, and as we are ourselves men, we have that capability. The manner in which Mauss poses and resolves the problem in *The Gift* enables one to see, in the intersection of two subjectivities, the nearest order of truth to which the sciences of man can aspire when they confront the integrity of their object.

Let us make no mistake: All this, which seems so new, was implicitly present in Durkheim. He has often been reproached for having formulated, in the second part of *The Elementary Forms of the Religious Life* (1968), a theory of religion so vast and so general that it seemed to render superfluous the minute analysis of Australian religions which preceded it and—one would have hoped—paved the way for it.

The question is whether Durkheim the man could have arrived at this theory without being forced, at the outset, to superimpose upon the religious representations received from his own society those of men whom historical and geographical evidence guaranteed to have been integrally "others," and not accomplices or unsuspected acolytes. Indeed, such is the way the ethnographer proceeds when he goes into the field, for however scrupulous and objective he may want to be, it is never himself, nor is it the other person, whom he encounters at the end of his investigation. By superimposing himself on the other, he can at most claim to extricate what Mauss called facts of general functioning, which he showed to be more universal and to have more reality.

In thus completing what Durkheim envisioned, Mauss freed anthropology from the false dichotomy, introduced by thinkers such as Dilthey and Spengler between explanation in the physical sciences and explanation in the human sciences. The search for causes ends with the assimilation of an experience, but an experience at once external and internal. The famous rule to "consider social facts as things" corresponds to the first step, which the second step is left to validate. We can already discern the originality of social anthropology. Instead of opposing causal explanation and understanding, it brings to light an object which may be at the same time objectively very remote and subjectively very concrete, and whose causal explanation could rest upon that understanding which is, for us, but an additional form of proof. A notion such as empathy inspires great mistrust in us, with what it implies of compounded irrationalism and mysticism. In his demand for supplementary proof, we rather imagine the anthropologist as modeled after the engineer, who conceives and constructs a machine by a series of rational operations; it has to work, however, and logical certainty is not enough. The possibility of trying the intimate experience of "the other" with oneself is but one of the means available for obtaining this final empirical satisfaction for which both physical and human sciences feel a need, less a proof, perhaps, than a guarantee.

What, then, is social anthropology?

Although he did not specifically name it, Ferdinand de Saussure came very close to defining it when he introduced linguistics as part of a science yet to be born, for which he reserved the name "semiology." Its object of study he saw to be the life of signs at the heart of social life. Did he not, furthermore, foresee our adherence when he compared language to "writing, to the alphabet of deaf-mutes, to symbolic rites, to forms of politeness, to military signals, etc."? No one would deny that anthropology includes in its own field at least some of these systems of signs, to which it adds many others, such as mythical language, the oral and gestural signs of which ritual is composed, marriage rules, kinship systems, customary laws, and certain forms of economic exchange.

We conceive anthropology as the *bona fide* occupant of that domain of semiology which linguistics has not already claimed for its own; and this until the time when, at least for some sections of this domain, special sciences are set up within anthropology.

However, this definition must be made more precise in two ways.

First of all, one quickly recognizes that some of the subjects which have just been cited already belong within particular sciences, such as economics, law, political science. However, these disciplines address themselves to the facts closest to us, which consequently have for us a privileged interest. Let us say that social anthropology apprehends them either in their most remote manifestations or from the angle of their most general expression. From this latter point of view, anthropology can do nothing useful without close collaboration with the particular social sciences. But these sciences could not aspire to generality without the cooperation of the anthropologist, who alone can provide relatively complete accounts and inventories.

The second difficulty is more serious. One may question whether all the phenomena of interest to social anthropology can actually be characterized as signs. This is sufficiently clear for the problems which we study most frequently. When we consider some system of belief (let us say totemism) or some form of social organization (unilineal clans, bilateral cross-cousin marriages), the question we ask is "What does it all mean?" To answer it, we attempt to *translate* into our language rules originally conceived in another language.

But is this true of other aspects of social reality, such as implements, techniques, and modes of production and consumption? It would seem that we are concerned here with objects, and not with signs—the sign being, according to Peirce's famous definition, "that which replaces something for someone." What, then, does a stone axe replace, and for whom?

The objection is valid up to a certain point, and it explains why some are reluctant to include in the field of social anthropology phenomena related to other sciences, such as geography and technology. The term "cultural anthropology" is thus appropriate to distinguish this part of our studies and stress its originality.

But it is well known—and it was one of Mauss's claims to fame to have established this in agreement with Malinowski—

that, particularly in the societies with which we are concerned, but in others as well, these domains are pregnant with meaning. From this point of view, they already concern us.

Finally, the exhaustive aims which inspire our investigations greatly transform their object. Techniques taken in isolation may appear as raw fact, historical heritage, or the result of a compromise between human needs and the constraints of environment. But when one places them in that general inventory of societies which anthropology attempts to construct, they come out in a new light. For then we envisage these techniques as the equivalents of so many choices, from all the possible ones which each society seems to make. (This is a convenient language which must be stripped of its anthropomorphism.) In this sense, it is conceivable that a stone axe could be a sign. In a given context, and for the observer capable of understanding its use, it stands for the different implement which another society would use for the same purpose.

Consequently, even the simplest techniques of any primitive society take on the character of a system that can be analyzed, in terms of a more general system. The techniques can be seen as a group of significant choices which each society—or each period within a society's development—has been forced to make, whether they are compatible or incompatible with other choices.

In positing the symbolic nature of its object, social anthropology does not intend to cut itself off from *realia*. How could it, when art, in which all is sign, utilizes material media? One cannot study gods while ignoring their images; rites without analyzing the objects and substances manufactured and manipulated by the officiant; or social rules independently of the things which correspond to them. Social anthropology does not confine itself to a part of the domain of ethnology; it does not separate material culture and spiritual culture. In its own perspective—which we shall have to define—it is equally interested in each. Men communicate by means of symbols and signs. For anthropology, which is a conversation of man with man, all things are symbol and sign which act as intermediaries between two subjects.

By this deference toward objects and techniques, as well as by our certainty of working on meanings, our conception of social anthropology leads us noticeably away from Radcliffe-Brown who—until his death in 1955—did so much to give autonomy to our investigations.

According to the views (always wonderfully clear) of this English master, social anthropology would be an inductive science which, life other sciences of this type, observes facts and formulates hypotheses which can be submitted to experimental control in order to discover the general laws of nature and society. It thus sets itself apart from ethnology, which attempts to reconstruct the past of primitive societies—but by such precarious means and methods that social anthropology can learn nothing from it.

When this inductive conception, inspired by Durkheim's distinction between *circumfusa* and *praeterita*, was first formulated about 1920, it marked a healthy reaction against the excesses of the diffusionist school. But since then, "conjectural history" (as Radcliffe-Brown called it, not without some contempt) has perfected and refined its methods, thanks notably to stratigraphic excavations, to the introduction of statistics in archaeology, to the analysis of pollens, to the use of carbon 14, and especially thanks to ever-increasing collaboration between ethnologists and sociologists on the one hand, and archaelogists and prehistorians on the other. One may well wonder, then, whether Radcliffe-Brown's mistrust of historical reconstructions did not correspond to a stage of scientific development which will soon be out of date.

On the other hand, several among us hold more modest views on the future of social anthropology than those fostered by Radcliffe-Brown's great ambitions. They do not picture social anthropology modeled after the inductive sciences as they were conceived in the nineteenth century, but rather see it as a taxonomy whose purpose is to identify and to classify types, to analyze their constituent parts, and to establish correlations between them. Without this preliminary work—and we must recognize that it has barely begun—the comparative method risks remaining at a standstill. Data proposed for comparison can be, historically and geographically, either so close that one is never sure of dealing with distinct phenomena, or so heterogeneous that comparison becomes illegitimate since it brings together things which cannot be compared.

Until the last few years, we assumed that aristocratic institutions in Polynesia were recent introductions, barely a few centuries old and due to small groups of foreign conquerors. But the measure of residual radioactivity in organic remains from Melanesia and Polynesia now reveals that the difference between the dates of occupation of these two regions is not as great as was first believed. All at once, conceptions about the nature and unity of the feudal system have to be modified; for—at least in that part of the world, as the fine work done by Guiart has shown, it is possible for such a system to precede the conquerors' arrival, and for some forms of feudalism to arise in humble gardening societies.

The discovery in Africa of the art of Ife—as refined and sophisticated as the art of the Renaissance in Europe but possibly older by some three or four centuries and long preceded in Africa itself by the civilization called Nok—influences our opinion of recent art forms and corresponding cultures in black Africa. We are now tempted to see them as impoverished and almost rustic replica of higher forms of art and civilization.

The shortening of the prehistory of the Old World, and the lengthening of that of the New World—which carbon 14 enables us to postulate—may lead us to conclude that the civilizations which developed on both sides of the Pacific were even more akin to each other than first assumed, and to understand them differently when they are considered individually. We must examine facts of this type before tackling any classification or comparison. If, indeed, we hasten to postulate the homogeneity of the social field, and cherish the illusion that it is immediately comparable in every aspect and at every level, we shall overlook the essential. Then it will not be recognized that the coordinates required for defining two apparently similar phenomena are not always the same, nor always equal in number. We shall believe that we are formulating laws of a social nature while, in fact, we are only describing superficial properties or setting forth tautologies.

Neglecting the historical dimension on the pretext that there are insufficient means of evaluating it, except approximately, results in our being satisfied with an impoverished sociology in which phenomena are set loose from their context. Rules and institutions, states and processes seem to float in a void where one strains to spread a tenuous network of functional relations, and one becomes totally absorbed in this task. Men are forgotten in whose thoughts these relations are established. Their concrete culture is neglected; it is no longer known where they came from nor what they are. Indeed, anthropology should be in no hurry to claim as its own any phenomena which can be called social. Espinas, another of the masters whom we allow ourselves the luxury of forgetting, was certainly right, from the point of view of social anthropology, when he questioned whether institutions deprived of biological roots have the same coefficient of reality as the others: "The management of a great railroad company," he wrote in 1901 (p. 470), "is not at all a social reality . . . nor is an army."

The statement is excessive, since administrations are the object of thorough studies in sociology, social psychology, and other particular sciences. But it helps us to define the difference between anthropology and the preceeding disciplines. The social facts which we study are manifested in societies, each of which is a *total, concrete, and cohesive entity.* We never lose sight of the fact that existing societies are the result of great transformations of mankind which occurred at given moments of prehistory and at given points on earth, and that an uninterrupted chain of real events links these facts to facts which we can observe.

The chronological and spatial continuity between the natural order and the cultural order, which Espinas stressed so much (in a language which is no longer our own and which, for that reason, we at times find difficult to understand) also forms the basis of Boas's historicism. It explains why anthropology, even social anthropology, affirms its solidarity with physical anthropology, whose discoveries it awaits somewhat avidly.

Even if social phenomena must be provisionally isolated and treated as if they belonged to a specific level, we know very well that—de facto and even de jure—the emergence of culture remains a mystery to man. It will so remain as long as he does not succeed in determining, on the biological level, the modifications in the structure and functioning of the brain, of which culture was at once the natural result and the social mode of apprehension. At the same time, culture created the intersubjective milieu indispensable for the occurrence of transformations, both anatomical and physiological, but which can be neither defined nor studied with sole reference to the individual.

This declaration in favor of history may come as a surprise, since we have sometimes been reproached for being closed to history and for giving it a negligible place in our studies. We do not use it much, but we intend to give it its due. We just believe that nothing could be more dangerous for social anthropology in this formative period than an unmethodical eclecticism which, confusing tasks and mixing programs, would try to pose as an established science.

Yet, it happens that in anthropology experimentation precedes both observation and hypothesis. One of the peculiarities of the small societies we study is that each constitutes a ready-made experiment because of its relative simplicity and the limited number of variables required to explain its functioning. On the other hand, these societies are alive and we have neither the time nor the means to do something about them. By comparison with the natural sciences, we enjoy an advantage and suffer from a handicap: We find our experiments already set up but we cannot control them. It is therefore natural that we attempt to substitute for them models, or systems of symbols, which preserve the characteristic properties of the experiment but which (unlike the experiment) we are able to manipulate.

The boldness of such an approach, however, is tempered by the humility—one would almost say the servility—of observation as it is practiced by the anthropologist. Leaving his country, his home, for long periods of time; exposing himself to hunger, sickness, and sometimes danger; surrendering his customs, his beliefs, and his convictions to a profanation to which he becomes an accomplice when, without mental restriction or ulterior motive, he assumes the forms of life of an alien society. The anthropologist practices integral observation, observation beyond which there is nothing except—and it is indeed a risk—the complete absorption of the observer by the object of his observation.

This alternation of rhythm between two methods—the deductive and the empirical—and the rigor with which we practice each in an extreme and almost purified form give social anthropology its distinctive character among the branches of knowledge. It is undoubtedly the only science to use the most intimate kind of subjectivity as a means of objective demonstration. For it is indeed an objective fact that the same mind, which gave itself to experience and let itself be molded by it, becomes the theater of mental operations which do not abolish the preceding ones—but which yet transform the experiment into a model. This makes possible other mental operations whose logical coherence is based, in the final analysis, on the sincerity and honesty of whoever can say, like the explorer bird of the fable: "I was there, such a thing happened to me. You will believe that you were there yourself," and who, indeed, succeeds in communicating this conviction.

But this constant oscillation between theory and observation requires that the two planes always be made distinct. To return to the subject of history, it seems to me that the same holds true whether one means to devote oneself to the static or to the dynamic, to the order of the structure or to the order of the event. This history of historians does not need defending, but it is no attack on it either to say (as Braudel admits) that next to a short-scale time span there exists a long-scale time span; that some facts arise from a statistical and irreversible time and others from a mechanical and reversible one; and that the idea of a structural history contains nothing which could shock the historian. The two come together and there is no contradiction in a history of symbols and signs engendering unforeseeable developments, even though it brings into play structural combinations in a limited number. In a kaleidoscope, the combination of identical elements always yields new results. But it is because the history of historians is present in it—even if only in the successive flicks of the finger which bring about the reorganization of the structure—and because the chances are practically nil that the same configuration will appear twice.

We do not intend to take up again in its original form, the distinction, introduced in *Course in General Linguistics*,[2] between the synchronic order and the diachronic order. This is the very aspect of the Saussurian doctrine from which modern structuralism, with Trubetzkoy and Jakobson, has most resolutely diverged, and about which modern documents show that the master's thought has at times been forced and schematized by the editors of the *Course*.

For the editors of *Course in General Linguistics*, an absolute opposition exists between two categories of fact: on the one hand, that of grammar, the synchronic, the conscious; on the other hand, that of phonetics, the diachronic, the unconscious. The conscious system alone is coherent; the unconscious infrasystem is dynamic and off-balanced, made up at once of the legacy of the past and of tendencies of the future, as yet unrealized.

In fact, de Saussure had not yet discovered the presence of the differential elements behind the phoneme. His position indirectly foreshadowed Radcliffe-Brown's, with his conviction that structure is of the order of empirical observation, while in fact it lies beyond it. This ignorance of hidden realities leads the two men to opposite conclusions. De Saussure seems to deny the existence of a structure where it is not immediately given; Radcliffe-Brown affirms it, but in seeing it where it is not, he takes away from the notion of structure its strength and its significance.

In anthropology, as in linguistics, we know today that the synchronic can be as unconscious as the diachronic. In this sense already, the divergence between the two is reduced. On the other hand, the *Course in General Linguistics* posits relations of equivalence between the phonetic, the diachronic, and the individual, which pertain to speech (*parole*); and between the grammatical, the synchronic, and the collective, which pertain to language (*langue*). But we have learned from Marx that the diachronic can also occur in the midst of the collective, and from Freud that the grammatical can be achieved entirely within the individual.

Neither the editors of the *Course* nor Radcliffe-Brown have sufficiently understood that the history of systems of signs includes logical evolutions related to different levels of structuration which must first be isolated. If a conscious system exists, it can only result from a sort of "dialectical average" among a multiplicity of unconscious systems, each of which deals with one aspect or one level of social reality. However, these systems do not coincide either in their logical structure or in their historical affiliations. They are as if diffracted upon a temporal dimension, from whose density synchrony draws its consistency; and for lack of which it would dissolve into a tenuous and impalpable essence, a ghost of reality.

One would not be over-bold, then, in suggesting that the oral expression of de Saussure's teachings could not have been very far from these profound remarks by Durkheim, published in 1900 (p. 190), and which could be written today: "Without a doubt, the phenomena which concern structure are somewhat more stable than functional phenomena; but between the two orders of facts, there is only a difference of degree. Structure itself occurs in the process of development. . . . It is ceaselessly forming and breaking down; it is life which has reached a certain degree of consolidation;

and to distinguish it from the life whence it derives or from the life it determines amounts to dissociating inseparable things."

In truth, it is the nature of the facts we study which leads us to distinguish in them what pertains to the order of structure and what belongs to the order of event. Important as the historical perspective may be, we can only achieve it in due time—after a long research which (as demonstrated by the measure of radio-activity and the study of pollens) is not even always within our competence. Nevertheless, the diversity of human societies and their number—several thousand still at the end of the nineteenth century—make them appear to us as if spread out in the present. It is not so surprising, then, if, taking a cue from the object of our study, we adopt a *transformational* rather than a *fluxional* method.

A very close relationship exists between the concept of transformation and that of structure, which occupies such a large place in our work. Radcliffe-Brown, inspired by Montesquieu's and Spencer's ideas, introduced it in social anthropology. He used it to designate the lasting manner in which individuals and groups are connected within the social body. Consequently, structure for him is of the order of fact; it is given in the observation of each particular society. This view proceeds no doubt from a certain conception of the natural sciences, but one which would have been already unacceptable for a Cuvier.

Today, no science can consider the structure with which it has to deal as being no more than a haphazard arrangement of just any parts. An arrangement is structured which meets but two conditions: that it be a system ruled by an internal cohesiveness and that this cohesiveness, inaccessible to observation in an isolated system, be revealed in the study of transformations through which similar properties are recognized in apparently different systems. As Goethe wrote:

> All forms are similar, and none is like the others.
> So that their chorus points the way to a hidden law.

This convergence of scientific perspectives is very reassuring for the semiological sciences, in which social anthropology is included, since signs and symbols can only play their part insofar as they belong to systems regulated by internal laws of implication and exclusion; and since the property of a system of signs is to be transformable, in other words *translatable*, into the language of another system with the help of substitutions. That such a conception could have originated in paleontology leads social anthropology to harbor a secret dream. It belongs to the human sciences, as is clearly enough proclaimed by its name. But if it is resigned to being in a purgatory next to the social sciences, it is because it has not yet lost hope of awakening, in the hour of the last judgment, among the natural sciences.

Let us attempt to show, by two examples, how social anthropology endeavors to justify its program.

We know what function is fulfilled by the incest prohibition in primitive societies. By casting, so to speak, the sisters and daughters out of the consanguine group, and by assigning to them husbands coming from other groups, the prohibition creates bonds of alliance between these natural groups, the first ones which can be called social. The incest prohibition is thus the basis of human society; in a sense it *is* the society.

To justify this interpretation, we did not proceed in an inductive fashion. How could we have done so, with phenomena which are universally correlated, but among which various societies have invented all sorts of unusual connections? Moreover, this is a matter not of facts but of meanings. The question we asked ourselves was that of the *meaning* of the incest prohibition (what the nineteenth century would have called its "spirit") and not that of its *results*, real or imaginary. It was then necessary to establish the systematic nature of each kinship terminology and its corresponding set of marriage rules. This was only possible at the price of a supplementary effort, that of elaborating the system of these systems and putting them into a tranformational relationship. From then on, what was still nothing but chaos went on to organize itself in the form of grammar: a normative formula for all conceivable ways of setting up and maintaining a system of reciprocity.

This is where we presently stand. How, then, should we proceed to answer the next question: that of the universality of these rules in the totality of human societies, including contemporary ones? Even if we do not define incest prohibition as the Australians or the American Indians do, it still exists among us. But does it still have the same function? It may be that we are attached to it for very different reasons, such as a later discovery of the harmful consequences of consanguinal unions. It may also be—as Durkheim thought—that the institution no longer plays a positive role among us, and only remains as a vestige of obsolete beliefs, well anchored in collective thought. Or, is it not perhaps that our society—a particular instance in a broader group—depends, like all others, for its coherence and its very existence on a network (grown infinitely unstable and complicated) of ties between consanguinal families? If so, do we have to admit that the network is homogeneous in all its parts, or must we recognize in its types of structures which differ according to environment and region, and vary in function of local historical traditions?

These problems are essential for anthropology, since the answer given to them will determine the innermost nature of the social fact and its degree of plasticity. But it is impossible to settle this once and for all by using methods borrowed from the logic of John Stuart Mill. We cannot vary the complex relationships presupposed by a contemporary society on the technical, economic, professional, political, religious and *biological* planes. We cannot interrupt and reestablish them at will in the hope of discovering which are indispensable to the existence of the society as such, and which society could do without, if hard pressed.

But we could choose the most complex and least stable among the matrimonial systems whose functions of reciprocity is best established. We could construct models of them in the laboratory to determine how they would function if they involved an increasing number of individuals. We could also distort our models in the hope of obtaining models of the same type, but even more complex and unstable. . . . And we would then compare the cycles of reciprocity thus obtained with the most simple ones observable in the field (for instance, in regions characterized by small isolates). Going back and forth from the laboratory to the field and from the field to the laboratory, we would attempt to fill in progressively the gap between two series, one known, the other unknown, by the insertion of a series of intermediary forms. In the end, we would have done nothing but elaborate a language (whose sole merits would be to be coherent, like all language, and to account with a small number of rules for phenomena held until then to be very different). In the absence of an inaccessible factual truth, we would have arrived at a truth of reason.

A second example relates to problems of the same type, approached on another level; it will still be concerned with the incest prohibition, no longer in its normative form, but as a theme of mythical thought.

The Iroquois and Algonquin Indians tell the story of a young girl subjected to the amorous advances of a nocturnal visitor, whom she believes to be her brother. Everything seems to point to the culprit: Physical appearance, clothes, scratched cheek, all bearing witness to the virtue of the heroine. Formally accused by her, the brother reveals that he has a counterpart, or more exactly a double, for the tie between them is so strong that any accident befalling one of them is automatically transmitted to the other—torn garment, wound on the face. . . . To convince his incredulous sister, the young man murders his double before her, but at the same time, he pronounces his own death sentence, since their destinies are tied.

The victim's mother naturally wants to avenge her son; she is a powerful sorceress, the mistress of the owls. There is only one way of misleading her: that the sister marry her brother who passes for the double he has killed. The incest is so unconceivable that the old woman could not suspect the hoax. The owls are not deceived and denounce the culprits who will, however, succeed in escaping.

In this myth, the Western listener easily perceives a theme fixed by the Oedipus legend: the precautions taken to avoid incest make incest, in fact, inevitable. In both cases a sensational turn of events results from the fact that characters, originally introduced as distinct, are identified with each other. Is this a simple coincidence—different causes explaining that, here and there, the same motifs are arbitrarily found together? Or are there deeper reasons for the analogy? In making the comparison, have we not put our finger on a fragment of a meaningful whole?

If so, the incest between the brother and sister of the Iroquois myth would constitute a permutation of the Oedipal incest between mother and son. The contingency rendering the former inevitable—the double personality of the male hero—would be a permutation of the double identity of Oedipus, thought dead and yet alive, condemned child and triumphant hero. To complete the demonstration, one would have to discover in American myths a transformation of the sphinx episode, which is the only element of the Oedipus legend still missing.

In this particular case (this is why we have chosen it in preference to others), the proof would be truly decisive since, as Boas (1891; Boas and Hunt 1925) was first to point out, puzzles and riddles are, along with proverbs, a genre almost entirely missing among the North American Indians. If riddles were to be found in the semantic framework of the American myth, it would not, then, be the effect of chance, but proof of a necessity.

In the whole of North America, only two "riddle" situations of unquestionably native origin can be found: among the Pueblo Indians of the southwestern United States exists a family of ceremonial clowns who present riddles to an audience and whom the myths describe as having been born of an incestuous union. Next, we recall that, in the myth summarized here, the sorceress who was threatening the hero's life is a mistress of the owls; and precisely among the Algonquins, there are myths where owls (or sometimes the ancestors of owls) ask riddles which the hero must answer under pain of death. It follows that, in America also, riddles present a double Oedipal character, by way of incest on the one hand, and on the other hand, by way of the owl in which we are led to see, in a transposed form, an American sphinx.

So it seems that the same correlation between riddles and incest exists among peoples separated by history, geography, language, and culture. To set up the comparison, let us construct a model of the riddle, expressing as best we can its constant properties throughout the various mythologies, and let us define it, from this point of view, as a *question to which it is postulated that there will be no answer*. Without considering here all the possible transformations of this statement, let us simply, by way of an experiment, invert its terms. This inversion produces *an answer for which there was no question*.

Here is apparently a formula completely devoid of meaning. Yet, it is obvious that there are myths, or fragments of myths, which derive their dramatic power from this structure, one of a symmetrical inversion. Time is too limited for me to recount the American examples, so I will restrict myself to evoking, first, the death of the Buddha, rendered inevitable because of a disciple's failure to ask the expected question; and, closer to us, the old myths refashioned in the Grail cycle, in which the action depends on the hero's timidity in front of the magic vessel, of which he dare not ask "what it is used for."

Do these myths exist independently or are they to be considered in turn as a species of a wider genus, of which myths of an Oedipal type are only another species? Repeating the same procedure, we shall try to find out whether and in what measure the characteristic elements of a group can be reduced to transformations (which, here, will be inversions) of the characteristic elements of the other group. This is indeed what happens. From a hero who misuses sexual intercourse, since he carries it as far as incest, we pass on to a chaste hero who abstains from it; a clever personage who knows all the answers is replaced by an innocent who does not even know how to ask questions. In the American variants of this second type, and in the Grail cycle, the problem to be resolved is that of the "waste land," in other words, that of summer exiled. Now, all the American myths of the first or "Oedipal" type refer to an eternal winter which the hero dispels when he solves the riddles, thereby bringing on the summer. Simplifying a great deal, Percival thus appears as an inverted Oedipus —a hypothesis we would not have dared to consider if Greek and Celtic sources were to have been compared, but which is forced upon us in a North American context where both types are present in the same populations.

However, we are not at the end of our demonstration. As long as it is shown that the same homologous relation exists in a semantic system—between chastity and "the answer without question," and between an incestuous union and "the question without answer"—it must also be accepted that the two sociobiological statements are themselves in a homologous relation with the two grammatical statements. Between the solution of the riddle and incest, a relation exists, not external and of fact, but internal and of reason; and this is indeed why civilizations as different as those of classical antiquity and indigenous America can associate them independently. Like the solved riddle, incest brings together terms meant to remain separate: The son is joined with the mother, the brother with the sister, *in the same way as the answer succeeds, against all expectations, in rejoining its question.*

In the legend of Oedipus, marriage with Jocasta does not arbitrarily follow the victory over the sphinx. Besides the fact that myths of the Oedipal type (of which we are now giving precise definition) always assimilate the discovery of incest to the solution of a living puzzle personified by the hero, their various episodes are repeated on different levels and in different languages. They provide the same demonstration found in an inverted form in the old myths of the Grail. The audacious union of masked words or of consanguines unknown to themselves engenders decay and fermentation, the unleashing of natural forces—one thinks of the Theban plague—just as impotence in sexual matters (as well as in establishing a proposed dialogue) dries up animal and vegetable fertility.

To the two possibilities which could capture his imagination —a summer or a winter equally eternal, the former licentious to the point of corruption, the latter pure to the point of sterility— man must resign himself to preferring the equilibrium and periodicity of seasonal rhythm. In the natural order, the latter fulfills the same function as the exchange of women in marriage and the exchange of words in conversation do in society, provided that they are both practiced with the frank intention of communicating: in other words, without ruse or perversity, and above all without hidden motives.

We have only sketched here the broad outlines of a demonstration—which will be taken up again in detail in a future lecture [3]—to illustrate this *problem of invariance* which, like other sciences, social anthropology attempts to resolve, but which it sees as the modern form of a question with which it has always been concerned—that of the universality of human nature.

Do we not turn our backs on this human nature when, in order to extract our invariants, we replace experiential data with models upon which we perform abstract operations, as the algebraist does with equations? We have sometimes been reproached for this. The objection carries little weight with the expert, who knows with what fastidious fidelity to concrete reality he pays for the liberty of skimming over it for a few brief moments. But I would like to remind you that in proceeding as it does, social anthropology is only reassuming responsibility for a forgotten part of the program mapped out for it by Durkheim and Mauss.

In his preface to the second edition of *The Rules of Sociological Method*, Durkheim defends himself against the charge of having unjustifiably separated the collective from the individual. He sees this separation as necessary but does not exclude the possibility that in the future "we will come to conceive the possibility of a completely formal psychology, which would be a sort of common ground of individual psychology and sociology. . . ." "What would be necessary"—Durkheim goes on—"would be to seek, by the comparison of mythic themes, legends, popular traditions, and languages, in what way social representations call for each other or are mutually exclusive, merge with one another or remain distinct. . . ." He remarks, in closing, that this research pertains on the whole to the field of abstract logic. It is curious to note how close Lévy-Bruhl would have come to this aim, he had not already chosen to relegate mythical representations to the antechamber of logic, and he had not rendered the separation irrevocable when he later renounced the notion of prelogical thought. But in so doing, one might say that he was only throwing out the baby with the bathwater, denying to "primitive mentality" the cognitive character he had initially conceded to it, and casting it altogether into the midst of affectivity.

More faithful to Durkheim's conception of an "obscure psychology" underlying social reality, Mauss orients anthropology "toward the study of what men have in common. . . . Men communicate by symbols . . . but they can only have these symbols, and communicate by them, because they have the same instincts."

Such a conception (which is also our own) may well lend itself to another form of criticism. If our ultimate goal is to arrive at certain universal forms of thought and morality (for *The Gift* ends with conclusions on morals), why ascribe a privileged status to the societies we call primitive? Starting from any society, should one not arrive, in theory, at the same results? This is the last problem I would like to consider before putting an end to an address already long enough.

It is all the more necessary because, among the anthropologists and sociologists listening to me, some, who study rapidly changing societies, will perhaps challenge the ideas which I seem implicitly to have about primitive societies. They may believe that the distinctive characteristics imputed to these societies are only illusions, the effect of our ignorance of what is actually going on; objectively, these do not correspond to reality.

The character of ethnographic investigations is undoubtedly changing as the small savage tribes we used to study disappear, merging into vaster groups in which problems tend to resemble our own. But if it is true, as Mauss taught us, that ethnology is an original mode of knowledge rather than the source of some particular types of knowledge, we can only conclude that ethnology is conducted in two ways today; in the pure state and in the diluted state. A sound scientific attitude would not seek to develop ethnology where its method is mixed with other methods, where its object is confused with other objects. This chair will therefore be devoted to pure ethnology. This does not mean that its teachings cannot be applied to other ends, nor that it will be uninterested in contemporary societies which, at certain levels and in certain aspects, are directly relevant to the ethnological method.

What, then, are the reasons for the marked preference we show for these societies which, although certainly not primitive, are so-called for lack of a better word?

The first one, let us honestly admit, is of a philosophical order. As Merleau-Ponty wrote, "Each time the sociologist [*but it is the anthropologist he has in mind*] comes back to the live sources of his knowledge, to that which, in him, acts as a means of understanding the cultural formations most remote from himself, he is spontaneously indulging in philosophy" (1960, p. 138). Indeed, research in the field, by which every anthropological career begins, is mother and nurse of doubt, the philosophical attitude par excellence. This "anthropological doubt" does not only consist of knowing that one knows nothing, but of resolutely exposing what one thought one knew—and one's very ignorance—to buffetings and denials directed at one's most cherished ideas and habits by other ideas and habits best able to rebut them. Contrary to appearances, we think that it is by its more strictly philosophical method that ethnology is distinguished from philosophy. The sociologist objectifies for fear of being misled. The ethnologist does not experience this fear since the distant society he studies is nothing to him, and since he is not compelled in advance to extract all its nuances, all its details, and even its values; in a word, all that in which the observer of his own society risks being implicated.

However, in choosing a subject and an object radically distant from one another, anthropology runs the risk that the knowledge of the object does not reach intrinsic properties but is limited to expressing the relative and ever-shifting position of the subject in relation to it. It is quite possible indeed, that so-called ethnological knowledge is condemned to remain as bizarre and inadequate as the knowledge that an exotic visitor would have of our own society. The Kwakiutl Indian whom Boas sometimes invited to New York to serve him as an informant, was indifferent to the sight of skyscrapers and streets crowded with cars. He reserved all his intellectual curiosity for dwarfs, giants, and bearded ladies who were exhibited at the time in Times Square, for automats, and for the brass balls ornamenting the base of staircase banisters. For reasons which I cannot go into here, all this involved his own culture; and it was that culture alone which he was trying to recognize in certain aspects of ours.

In their own way, do not ethnologists succumb to the same temptation when they permit themselves, as they so often do, to reinterpret in a new way native customs and institutions, with the unacknowledged aim of making them square more adequately with the theories of the day? The problem of totemism, which many among us think a transparent and insubstantial one, has weighed for many years upon ethnological thinking, and we understand now that its importance stems from a certain taste for the obscene and the grotesque which is like a childhood disease of religious science, a negative projection of an uncontrollable fear of the sacred from which even the observer has not been able to disengage himself. And so, the theory of totemism was developed "for us" (*pour nous*) and not "in itself" (*en soi*). Nothing guarantees that, in its current form, it does not still proceed from a similar illusion.

The anthropologists of my generation are disconcerted by Frazer's aversion to the research to which he had dedicated his life: "tragic chronicle," he wrote "of human error and folly, of fruitless endeavour, wasted time, and blighted hopes." We are hardly less surprised to learn, from *Les Carnets*, how a Lévy-Bruhl considered myths which, according to him, "have no longer any effect on us . . . strange tales, not to say absurd and incomprehensible. . . . It costs us an effort to take an interest in them. . . ." Of course, we have acquired direct knowledge of exotic forms of life and thought, which they lacked; but is it not also true that surrealism—that is to say, a development within our society—has transformed our sensitivity, and that we owe to it having discovered or rediscovered at the heart of our studies some lyricism and some integrity?

We must then resist the appeal of a naïve objectivism, but without failing to recognize that the very precariousness of our position as observers brings us unhoped-for guarantees of objectivity. It is insofar as so-called primitive societies are far distant from our own that we can grasp in them those "facts of general functioning" of which Mauss spoke, and which stand a chance of being "more universal" and having "more reality." In these societies—I am still quoting Mauss—"one grasps men, groups and behavior . . . they are seen moving as in a piece of machinery, one sees masses and systems." This observation, which has the privilege of being distant, no doubt implies some differences of nature between these societies and our own. Astronomy not only demands that celestial bodies be far away but also that the passage of time have a different rhythm there, otherwise the earth would have ceased to exist long before astronomy was born.

Of course, so-called primitive societies belong in history; their past is as old as ours, since it goes back to the origin of the species. Over thousands of years, they have undergone all sorts of transformations, gone through periods of crisis and prosperity; they have known wars, migrations, adventure. But they have specialized in ways different from those we have chosen. They may have remained, in some respects, close to very ancient conditions of life. This is not to deny that, in other respects, they are farther from them than we are.

Although situated in history, these societies seem to have developed or retained a particular wisdom which impels them to resist desperately any modification in their structure that would enable history to burst into their midst. Those which, recently still, best protected their distinctive character appear to be societies inspired by the dominant concern to persevere in their existence. The way in which they exploit the environment guarantees both a modest standard of living and the conservation of natural resources. In spite of the diversity of their marriage rules, a demographer can recognize in them the common characteristic of rigorously limiting the birthrate and keeping it constant. Finally, a political life, based on consensus and allowing no other decisions than those taken unanimously, seems conceived to exclude that driving force of collective life which makes use of the contrasts between power and opposition, majority and minority, exploiters and exploited.

In a word, these societies, which we might define as "cold" because their internal environment borders on the zero of historical temperature, are distinguished by the limited number of their people and their mechanical mode of functioning from the "hot" societies which appeared in different parts of the world following the Neolithic revolution. In the latter, differentiations between castes and between classes are emphasized unceasingly in order to draw from them change and energy.

The value of this distinction is mainly theoretical, for there is probably no concrete society which, in its whole as well as in its components, corresponds exactly to either type. The distinction remains relative in another sense also, if it is true, as we believe, that social anthropology obeys a double motivation: a retrospective one, since primitive ways of life are on the verge of disappearing and we must hasten to draw from their teachings, and a prospective one insofar as, becoming aware of an evolution whose tempo is accelerating, we feel ourselves to be our great-grandchildren's "primitives," and we attempt to validate ourselves by drawing closer to those who were—and still are for a short while—like a part of us which persists.

On the other hand, neither do the societies which I called "hot" possess this character absolutely. When, shortly after the Neolithic revolution, the great city-states of the Mediterranean basin and the Far East imposed slavery, they built a type of society in which differential positions between men—some dominant, some dominated—could be used to produce culture at a rate until then inconceivable and unsuspected. In relation to this formula, the Industrial Revolution of the nineteenth century represents less an evolution in the same direction than a rough sketch of a different solution, which for a long time was still based on the same abuses and the same injustices, and yet made possible the transfer to *culture* of that dynamic function which the protohistoric revolution had assigned to *society*.

If—God forbid—it were expected of the anthropologist that he predict the future of humanity, he would undoubtedly not conceive it as a continuation or an extension of existing forms, but rather on the model of an integration, progressively unifying the characteristics specific to cold societies and to hot societies. His thought would resume the connection with the old Cartesian dream of putting, like automats, machines at the service of men; it would trace it back to the social philosophy of the eighteenth century, and to Saint-Simon. For, in announcing the passage "from the government of men to the administration of things," Saint-Simon anticipated both the anthropological distinction between culture and society and the conversion which advances in information theory and electronics allow us to see at least as a possibility; conversion from a type of civilization which once inaugurated historical development, but at the price of the transformation of men into machines, to an ideal civilization which would succeed in turning machines into men. With culture having integrally taken over the burden of manufacturing progress, society would be freed from a millennial curse which has compelled it to enslave men in order that there be progress. Henceforth, history would be made on its own and society, placed outside and above history, could once more assume this regular and quasi-crystalline structure which the best preserved of primitive societies teach us is not contrary to humanity. In this perspective, utopian as it may be, social anthropology would find its highest justification, since the forms of life and thought which it studies would not simply have a historical and comparative interest but would correspond to a permanent hope for mankind over which social anthropology would have mission to keep watch, especially in the most troubled times.

Our science could not stand this vigilant guard (and it would not even have conceived of its importance and necessity) if, in remote parts of the earth, some men have not obstinately resisted history and had not remained as living testimonials of what we want to preserve.

In conclusion, I would like to mention in a few words the very exceptional emotion felt by the anthropologist when he enters a house whose tradition, uninterrupted for four centuries, goes back to the reign of François I. For an Americanist especially, how many ties link him with that era in which Europe received the revelation of the New World and opened itself to ethnographic knowledge! He would have wanted to live then; indeed, he does so every day in his thoughts. And because, very remarkably, the Indians of Brazil (where I took my first steps in our science) could have adopted as a motto, "I will maintain," it happens that their study takes on a double quality: that of a journey to a distant land, and that—more mysterious still—of an exploration of the past.

But for this reason also—and bearing in mind that the mission of the Collège de France has always been to teach science in the making—the hint of a regret brushes past us. Why was this chair created so late? How does it happen that ethnology did not receive its due when it was still young, and when the facts retained their richness and their freshness? For it is in 1558 that one likes to imagine this chair established, when Jean de Léry, back from Brazil, drafted his first book and when André Thevet's *Les Singularités de la France antarctique* appeared.

Supposing, however, that it had happened that way, social anthropology would not be what it is today, a restless and fervent study harassing the investigator with moral questions as well as scientific ones. It was perhaps in the nature of our science to appear simultaneously as an effort to make up for lost time and as a meditation on a discrepancy to which some of its fundamental characteristics should be attributed.

If society is in anthropology, anthropology is itself in society, for anthropology has been able to enlarge progressively the object of its study as far as to include therein the totality of human societies—despite the fact that it has appeared at a late period in their history and in a little sector of the inhabited world. More than that, the circumstances of its appearance have a meaning understandable only in the context of a particular social and economic development. One suspects, then, that these circumstances go together with a dawning awareness—almost a remorse—that humanity could have for so long remained alienated from itself; and, above all, that the very fraction of humanity which produced anthropology should be the same one which made so many other men objects of execration and contempt. Our investigations are sometimes said to be sequels to colonialism. The two are certainly linked, but nothing could be more false than to hold anthropology as the last manifestation of the colonial frame of mind, a shameful ideology which would offer colonialism a chance of survival.

What we call the Renaissance truly marked the birth of

colonialism and anthropology. Between the two, confronting each other from the time of their common origin, an equivocal dialogue has been pursued for four centuries. If colonialism had not existed, the rise of anthropology might have been less delayed. But anthropology might not have been moved to implicate all mankind (and it has now become its role to do so) in each of its particular case studies. Our science reached its maturity the day that Western man began to understand that he would never understand himself as long as there would be on the surface on the earth a single race or a single people whom he would treat as an object. Only then was anthropology able to affirm itself as an enterprise renewing the Renaissance and atoning for it, in order to extend humanism to the measure of humanity.

Having paid tribute to the masters of social anthropology at the beginning of this address, you will allow me, my dear colleagues, to devote my last words to these savages, whose obscure tenacity still offers us a means of assigning to human facts their true dimensions. Men and women who, as I speak, thousands of miles from here, on some savannah ravaged by brush fire or in some forest dripping with rain, are returning to camp to share a meager pittance and evoke their gods together. These Indians of the tropics, and others like them throughout the world who have taught me their humble knowledge, in which is nevertheless contained the essence of the knowledge which you have entrusted me to transmit to others, soon, alas, destined to extinction through the impact of the illnesses and—to them more horrible still—the modes of life we have brought them. To them I have incurred a debt which I can never repay even if, in the place in which you have put me, I could justify the tenderness I feel for them, and the gratitude I owe them, by continuing to be as I was among them, and as, among you, I would never want to cease from being: their pupil, and their witness.

NOTES

1. A commemoration took place at the Sorbonne on January 30, 1960.
2. *Course in General Linguistics*, ed. C. Bally and A. Sechehaye, in collaboration with A. Reidlinger (London: P. Owen, 1960).
3. See our lecture report for 1960–1961, *Annuaire du Collège de France 1961–1962*, pp. 200–203.

Jean-Jacques Rousseau, Founder of the Sciences of Man

B Y INVITING an ethnologist to this celebration, you do him a signal honor, an honor for which he is personally grateful to you. You also present an opportunity for a young science to testify to the genius of a man who could be considered glorified in all aspects by an already numerous group, which includes individuals in literature, poetry, philosophy, history, ethics, political science, pedagogy, linguistics, music, botany—to mention only a few. For Rousseau was not only an acute observer of peasant life, an impassioned reader of travel books, a knowledgeable analyst of exotic customs and beliefs. Without fear of con-

Chapter II was originally presented as a speech delivered in Geneva on June 28, 1962, at the ceremonies marking the two hundred twenty-fifth anniversary of the birth of Jean-Jacques Rousseau. First published under the title "Jean-Jacques Rousseau, fondateur des sciences de l'homme," in *Jean-Jacques Rousseau* by the Université ouvrière and the Faculté des Lettres de l'Université de Genève (Neufchâtel: La Baconnière, 1962).

tradition, it can be affirmed that—a whole century before it made its appearance—he had conceived, willed, and announced this very ethnology which did not yet exist, placing it first among the already established natural and human sciences. He had even guessed at the particular form in which—thanks to individual or collective patronage—it was to take its first steps.

This prophecy, which is both a justification and a program, takes up a long note in the *Discourse on the Origin and Foundations of Inequality* (Rousseau 1964) from which I would like to quote some passages, if only to justify the presence of my discipline at today's ceremony.

"I have difficulty conceiving," wrote Rousseau, "how in a century taking pride in splendid knowledge, there are not to be found two closely united men . . . one of whom would sacrifice twenty thousand crowns of his wealth and the other ten years of his life to a celebrated voyage around the world, in order to study, not always stones and plants, but for once men and morals." He exclaimed, a little further,

> The whole world is covered with nations of which we know only the names, yet we dabble in judging the human race! Let us suppose a Montesquieu, a Buffon, a Diderot, a d'Alembert, a Condillac, or men of that stamp traveling in order to inform their compatriots by observing and describing, as they know how, Turkey, Egypt, Barbary, the empire of Morocco, Guinea, the land of the Bantus, the interior of Africa and its eastern coasts, the Malabars, the Mogul, the banks of the Ganges, the kingdom of Siam, Pegu, and Ava, China, Tartary, and especially Japan; then, in the other hemisphere, Mexico, Peru, Chile, the straits of Magellan, not forgetting the Patagonias true or false, Tucuman, Paraguay, if possible Brazil, and finally the Caribbean islands, Florida, and all the savage countries—the most important voyage of all and the one that must be undertaken with the greatest care. Let us suppose that these new Hercules, back from these memorable expeditions, then wrote at leisure the natural, moral, and political history of what they would have seen; we ourselves would see a new world come from their pens, and we would thus learn to know our own . . . (Rousseau 1964, pp. 212–213).

Is it not contemporary ethnology, with its program and methods, which we see emerging here? And the famous names cited by Rousseau remain those which today's ethnographers assign themselves as models, without presuming to be their equals, but convinced that only by following their example will they earn for their science a respect long begrudged it.

Rousseau did not restrict himself to anticipating ethnology: he founded it. First, in a practical way, by writing the *Discourse on the Origin and Foundations of Inequality*, which poses the problem of the relation between nature and culture and in which one can see the first treatise of general ethnology. Next, on the theoretical plane, by distinguishing, with admirable clarity and concision, the object proper of the ethnologist from that of the moralist and the historian: "When one wants to study men, one must look around oneself; but to study man, one must first learn to look into the distance; one must first see differences in order to discover characteristics" (Rousseau 1967, Chap. VIII).

This methodological rule which Rousseau assigns to ethnology and which marks its advent also makes it possible to overcome what, at first glance, one would take for a double paradox: that Rousseau could have, simultaneously, advocated the study of the most remote men, while mostly given himself to the study of that particular man who seems the closest—himself; and secondly that, throughout his work, the systematic will to identify with the other goes hand in hand with an obstinate refusal to identify with the self. These two apparent contradictions, which resolve themselves into a single reciprocal implication, must be resolved, at one time or other, in every ethnological career.

The ethnologist's debt toward Rousseau is increased because, not content to place a science yet unborn with extreme precision in the scheme of human knowledge, he has—by his work, by the temperament and character expressed in it, by each of his accents, by his person and his being—provided for the ethnologist the fraternal comfort of an image in which he recognizes himself and which helps him to understand himself better; not as a purely contemplative intelligence, but as the involuntary agent of a transformation conveyed through him. In Jean-Jacques Rousseau, the whole of mankind learns to feel this transformation.

Every time he is in the field, the ethnologist finds himself open to a world where everything is foreign and often hostile to him. He has only this self still at his disposal, enabling him to survive and to pursue his research. But it is a self physically and morally battered by weariness, hunger, discomfort, the shock to acquired habits, the sudden appearance of unsuspected prejudices. It is a self which, in this strange conjuncture, is crippled and maimed by all the blows of a personal history responsible at the outset for his vocation, but which will affect its future course. Hence, in ethnographic experience the observer apprehends himself as his own instrument of observation. Clearly, he must learn to know himself, to obtain, from a *self* who reveals himself as *another* to the *I* who uses him, an evaluation which will become an integral part of the observation of other selves. Every ethnographic career finds its principle in "confessions," written or untold.

But if we can throw light on this experience through that of Rousseau, is it not because his temperament, his particular past and circumstances, placed him in a situation whose ethnographic character is clear to see? A situation from which he at once draws personal consequences: "Here they are," he says of his contemporaries, "unknown strangers, non-beings to me since they so wished it! But I, detached from them and from everything, what am I? This is what remains for me to seek" (First Walk). Paraphrasing Rousseau, the ethnographer could exclaim as he first sets eyes on his chosen savages, "Here they are, then, unknown strangers, non-beings to me, since *I* wished it so! And I, detached from them and from everything, what am I? This is what I *must* find out *first*."

To attain acceptance of oneself in others (the goal assigned to human knowledge by the ethnologist), one must first deny the self in oneself.

To Rousseau we owe the discovery of this principle, the only one on which to base the sciences of man. Yet it was to remain inaccessible and incomprehensible as long as there reigned a philosophy which, taking the *Cogito* as its point of departure, was imprisoned by the hypothetical evidences of the self; and which could aspire to founding a physics only at the expense of founding a sociology and even a biology. Descartes believes that he proceeds directly from a man's interiority to the exteriority of the world, without seeing that societies, civilizations—in other words, worlds of men—place themselves between these two extremes. Rousseau, by so eloquently speaking of himself in the third person (sometimes even going as far as to split it, as in the *Dialogues*, for instance), anticipates the famous formula "I is another." Ethnographic experience must establish this formula before proceeding to its demonstration: that the other is an I. Indeed, he claims to be the great inventor of this radical reification which, he indicates during the First Walk, is his aim: "to become aware of the modifications of my soul and their successive states." He adds: "I will perform on myself in every respect the operations which physicists perform on the air to test its daily state." What Rousseau means is that there exists a "he" who "thinks" through me and who first causes me to doubt whether it is I who am thinking (a surprising truth, before psychology and ethnology made us more familiar with it). To Montaigne's "What do I know?" (from which everything stems), Descartes believed it possible to answer that "I know that I am, since I think." To this Rousseau retorts with a "What am I?" without a definite solution, since the question presupposes the completion of another, more essential one: "Am I?" Intimate experience provides only this "he" which Rousseau discovered and which he lucidly undertook to explore.

Let us not make a mistake. Even the conciliatory intention of the Savoyard vicar does not succeed in concealing the fact that for Rousseau the notion of personal identity is acquired by inference, and that its ambiguity remains unmistakable: "I exist . . . this is the first truth which strikes me and *with which I am forced to agree.* . . . Do I have a separate feeling of my existence, or do I only feel it through my sensations? This is my first doubt, which is, for the present, impossible to resolve" (italics added). But it is in Rousseau's strictly anthropological teaching—that of the *Discourse on the Origin of Inequality*—that one discovers the foundation of this doubt. It lies in a conception of man which places the other before the self, and in a conception of mankind which places life before men.

If it is possible to believe the demonstration of the *Discourse* —that a threefold passage (from nature to culture, from feelings to knowledge, from animality to humanity) occurred with the appearance of society—it can only be by attributing to man, even in his primitive state, an essential faculty which moves him to get over these three obstacles. It is a faculty which possesses originally and immediately some contradictory attributes, although not precisely within itself; which is both natural and cultural, affective and rational, animal and human; and which (provided only that it become conscious) can transform itself from one plane to the other.

This faculty—Rousseau did not neglect to repeat—is compassion, deriving from the identification with another who is not only a parent, a relative, a compatriot, but any man whatsoever, seeing that he is a man, and much more: any living being, seeing that it is living. Thus man begins by experiencing himself as identical to all his fellows. And he will never forget this primitive experience, despite demographic expansion, which plays Rousseau's anthropological thought the role of a contingent event, one which could have not happened but which we must admit did happen since society is. This demographic expansion will have forced him to diversify his ways of life, adapting himself to the different environments through which his increased numbers forced him to spread. It will also have forced him to know how to differentiate himself, but only inasmuch as a laborious apprenticeship instructed him to discern the others, that is, animals by species, humanity from animality, my self from other selves. The total apprehension of men and of animals as sensitive beings (in which identification consists) precedes the awareness of oppositions—oppositions first between common characteristics, and only later between human and nonhuman.

It is veritably the end of the *Cogito* which Rousseau proclaims in putting forward this bold solution. For until his time, the question was mostly to put man out of the question, to be assured, from humanism, of a "transcendental retreat." Rousseau is able to remain a theist, since this was the least demand made by his upbringing and his times. He unequivocally ruins his attempt by putting man in question again.

If this interpretation is correct, if by the ways of anthropology Rousseau as radically upsets philosophical tradition as we believe he does, we can better understand the underlying unity of the many aspects of his work and the really essential place of his so imperious preoccupations. (This despite the fact that they are at first glance foreign to the toil of the philosopher and the writer—I mean linguistics, music, and botany.)

As described by Rousseau in *On the Origin of Language* (1967) the process of language reproduces, in its way and on its plane, the process of humanity. The first stage is that of identification, here that of the literal sense and the figurative sense; the true name gradually comes out of the metaphor which merges each being with other beings. As for music, no other form of expression is better suited, it seems, to impugn the double Cartesian opposition between material and spiritual, body and soul. Music is an abstract system of oppositions and relations—alterations in ways of range which, when brought into play, have two consequences: firstly, the reversal in the relationship of the self and the other, since, when *I hear* music, *I listen to myself* through it. And secondly, by a reversal of the relationship between soul and body, music *lives itself* in me. A "chain of relations and combinations" (*Confessions*, Book XII) but which nature presents as incarnate in "sensitive objects" (*Rêveries*, Seventh Walk). It is in these terms, finally, that Rousseau defines botany, confirming that by this roundabout way he also aspires to rediscover the union of the sensitive and the intelligible, because it constitutes for man a first state which accompanied the awakening of consciousness and was not to survive it except in rare and precious instances.

Thus the expansion of Rousseau's thought stems from a double principle: firstly, of identification with others and even with the most "other" of all others, be it an animal; and secondly, of refusal to identify with oneself—in other words, refusal of all that can make the self "acceptable." These two attitudes complement each other, and the latter even forms the basis of the former: in truth, I am not "me," but the weakest, the most humble of "others." Such is the discovery of the *Confessions*.

What does the ethnologist write but confessions? In his own name first (as I have shown), since it is the driving force of his vocation and his work; and, through this very work, in the name of his society which, through the ethnologist, its emissary, chooses for itself other societies, other civilizations, precisely among those which appear to it the weakest and the most humble. Society does this in order to verify how "inacceptable" it is itself. It recognizes that it is not at all a privileged form, but only one of these "other" societies which have succeeded each other throughout the millennia, or whose precarious diversity still attests that—in his collective being also—man must recognize himself as a "he" before daring to lay claim to also being a "me."

Rousseau's revolution, preshaping and initiating the ethnological revolution, consists of refusing forced identifications, whether of a culture with that culture, or of an individual member of a culture with a character or social function that this same culture tries to impose on him. In both cases, the culture or the individual claims the right to free identification, which can only realize itself *beyond* man with all that is alive and, consequently, suffers; an identification also *before* the function or the character, with a being not yet shaped but given. Then, freed from an antagonism which philosophy alone sought to stimulate, the self and the other recover their unity. A primordial alliance, revived at last, enables them together to found the *we* against the *him*. It is an alliance against a society hostile to man, and which man feels all the more prepared to challenge since Rousseau, by his example, teaches him how to elude the unbearable contradictions of civilized life. For, if it is true that nature has rejected man and that society persists in oppressing him, man can at least reverse the poles of the dilemma to his benefit and *seek the society of nature to meditate there on the nature of society*. Here, it seems to me, is the indissoluble message of *Le Contrat social*, of *Lettres sur la Botanique*, and of *Les Rêveries*.

We must not see in this the manifestation of a timid will, giving a quest for wisdom as pretext for its abdication. Rousseau's contemporaries were not deceived and his successors even less. The former perceived that this proud thinking, this solitary and wounded existence, radiated a subversive force the likes of which no society had yet felt. His successors made this thought and the example of this life the levers with which to shake ethics, law, and society.

But it is today, for those of us who feel (as Rousseau predicted to his reader) "the fear of those who will have the misfortune to live after you" (*Discourse*) that his thought takes on a supreme magnitude and acquires all its significance. In this world, more cruel to man than it perhaps ever was, all the means of extermination, massacre, and torture are raging. We never disavowed these atrocities, it is true, but we liked to think that they did not matter just because we reserved them for distant populations which underwent them (we maintained) for our benefit and, in any case, in our name. Now, brought together in a denser population which makes the universe smaller and shelters no portion of humanity from abject violence, we feel the anguish of living together weighing on each of us. It is now, I repeat, by exposing the flaws of a humanism decidedly unable to establish the exercise of virtue among men, that Rousseau's thinking can help us to reject an illusion whose lethal effects we can observe in ourselves and on ourselves. For is it not the myth of the exclusive dignity of human nature, which subjected nature itself to a first mutilation, one from which other mutilations were inevitably to ensue?

We started by cutting man off from nature and establishing him in an absolute reign. We believed ourselves to have thus erased his most unassailable characteristic: that he is first a living being. Remaining blind to this common property, we gave free rein to all excesses. Never better than after the last four centuries of his history could a Western man understand that, while assuming the right to impose a radical separation of humanity and animality, while granting to one all that he denied the other, he initiated a vicious circle. The one boundary, constantly pushed back, would be used to separate men from other men and to claim —to the profit of ever smaller minorities—the privilege of a humanism, corrupted at birth by taking self-interest as its principle and its notion.

Rousseau alone rebelled against this egoism. He preferred to accept—in the note of the *Discourse* which I have quoted—that the great apes of Africa and Asia, awkwardly described by the travelers, were men of an unknown race, rather than to risk challenging the human nature of beings which could possess it. The first error would have been less serious, since respect for others knows only a natural basis, sheltered from reflection and its sophisms because anterior to it; a respect which Rousseau perceives in man in "an innate repugnance to see his equal suffer" (*Discourse*). But its discovery forces him to see an equal in any being exposed to suffering and, by the same token, indefeasibly entitled to pity. The only hope, for each of us not to be treated as an animal by his fellow men is that all his fellow men (and himself first) feel themselves immediately as suffering beings. Thus they cultivate inwardly this aptitude for pity which, in nature, takes the place of "laws, customs, and virtue," and without whose exercise we realize that there can be neither laws, customs, nor virtues.

Far from offering itself to man as a nostalgic refuge, identification with all the forms of life (beginning with the most humble ones) proposed to today's humanity—through Rousseau's voice—the principle for all collective wisdom and action. It is the only principle which, in a world so encumbered that reciprocal *consideration* is rendered more difficult but all the more necessary, can enable men to live together and to build a harmonious future.

These teachings were perhaps already contained in the great religions of the Far East. But we were confronted with an occidental tradition that held since antiquity that one could gamble on all counts and falsify the evidence that man is a living and suffering being, like all other beings before, being distinguished from them only by subordinate criteria. Who else then, except Rousseau, could have given these teachings to us? "I have a violent aversion," he wrote in the fourth letter to Malesherbes, "for the estates which dominate others. I loathe the Great, I hate their estate." Does this declaration not first apply to man himself, who claimed to dominate the other beings and to enjoy a separate estate? Did this not leave a clear field to the least worthy men, to avail themselves of the same advantage against other men, and to twist to their benefit a line of argument as exorbitant in this particular form as it already was in its general form? In an organized society there could be no excuse for the only crime which man cannot expiate: the belief in his lasting or temporary superiority and his treating other men like objects, be it in the name of race, of culture, of conquest, of mission, or simply of expediency.

We know of a minute in the life of Rousseau—a second, perhaps—whose significance in his eyes, in spite of its tenuousness, orders all the rest. It explains why at the end of his life it is that moment which obsesses him, which he lingers to describe in his last work, and to which, in his random walks, he comes back constantly. What is it, though, but a commonplace recovery of consciousness after a fall and a fainting spell? But the feeling of existing is "precious" beyond all others, undoubtedly because it is so rare and so debatable. "I felt as if I was filling with my light existence all the objects which I perceived . . . I had no distinct notion of my person . . . I felt in my whole being a ravishing calm to which, every time I recall it, I find nothing comparable in the whole experience of known pleasures." This famous text of the Second Walk is echoed by a passage from the Seventh Walk, where he gives the reason for it: "I feel ecstasies, inexpressible ravishings to melt myself, as it were, into the system of beings, to identify myself with all of nature."

Living in a society, man is denied the opportunity for this primitive feeling of identification, and, made forgetful of his essential virtue, he no longer comes to feel it, except in a fortuitous manner and by the play of paltry circumstances. Rousseau's precious moment gives us access to the very core of his works. And if we give these a special place among the great productions of human genius, it is because their author not only discovered, with identification, the real principle of the human sciences and the only possible basis for ethics. It is because he also restored for us its ardor, burning for the last two centuries and forever in this crucible, a crucible uniting beings whom the interests of politicians and philosophers are everywhere else bent on rendering incompatible: me and the other, my societies and other societies, nature and culture, the sensitive and the rational, humanity and life.

III

What Ethnology
Owes to Durkheim

AT THE TIME when he is writing *The Rules*, Durkheim mistrusts ethnology. He contrasts "the travelers' confused observations, rapidly made, and the precise texts of history." A faithful disciple of Fustel de Coulanges, it is on history that he counts to give an experimental basis to sociology. "The sociologist," he writes, "will be able to take as the principal material for his inductions the societies whose beliefs, traditions, customs, and law have taken shape in written and authentic documents. To be

Chapter III was originally published under the title "Ce que l'ethnologie doit à Durkheim," in *Annales de l'Université de Paris*, No. 1 (1960), pp. 45–50. The celebration of Durkheim's centenary took place, two years late, on June 30, 1960, in the great amphitheater of the Sorbonne, at the initiative of the University of Paris. I was able to go only as a spectator, as Mr. Georges Gurvitch, then a professor at the Sorbonne, had given his veto to my participation. The following text was requested of me by Dean Georges Davy, to appear after the addresses actually delivered. I renew my thanks to him for having made it possible for me to add my homage to those rendered to the founder of the French sociological school, to whose memory I dedicated the first volume of *Structural Anthropology*, on the very year of his centenary.

sure, he will not spurn the information offered by uncritical ethnography (there are no facts which may be disdained by the scientist), but he will put them in their true place. Instead of making this the center of gravity of his researches, he will in general utilize it as a supplement to historical data; or, at the very least, he will try to confirm it by the latter" (Durkheim 1964, p. 134).

Some years later, in 1899, Hubert and Mauss express the same opinion: "It is impossible"—they write in *Sacrifice: Its Nature and Function* (1964), originally published in the second volume of the *Année sociologique*—"to hope to glean from ethnography alone the pattern of primitive institutions. Generally distorted through over-hasty observation or falsified by the exactness of our languages, the facts recorded by the ethnographers have value only if they are compared with more precise and more complete documents."

It is clear that something has changed between the period of formation, which covers the last ten years of the nineteenth century, and the enthusiastic rallying to ethnography of 1912. This is indicated in the introduction to *The Elementary Forms of the Religious Life*, where Durkheim defines the observation of phenomena simultaneously as "historical and ethnographic." For the first time, the two methods are on an equal footing. A little further on, he claims that "the observations of ethnographers have frequently been veritable revelations which have renewed the study of human institutions." Taking a standpoint almost directly counter to his former affirmations, he disassociates himself from the historians: "So nothing is more injust than the disdain with which too many historians still regard the work of ethnographers. Indeed, it is certain that ethnology has frequently brought about the most fruitful revolutions in the different branches of sociology" (Durkheim 1968, pp. 18–20).

Obviously, the attitude of Durkheim and his collaborators toward ethnography was transformed between 1892 and 1912. How can we explain this conversion?

Its principal cause is, no doubt, the change which the foundation of *l'Année sociologique* imposed on Durkheim's work methods and on his readings. Having resolved to judge and comment, in the name of his doctrine, on all the sociological literature published in the world, he could not fail to come into contact with ethnographers working "in the field." Boas, Preuss, Wilken, Hill Tout, Fison and Howitt, Swanton, Roth, Cushing, Hewitt, Strehlow, Spencer and Gillen, and others are revealed to him, while his initial mistrust was inspired by compilers or theoreticians like Wundt, Mannhardt, Hartland, and Tylor. Properly speaking, Durkheim has not changed his attitude toward ethnography. The discipline he had first criticized was not that one; at least, it was not the same as the ethnography to which he was to rally. Perhaps the first and greatest service that he rendered ethnological theory was to teach it that, in the absence of the facts themselves, one can reflect with validity only on the sources, and examine them with the same rigor, the same scrupulous care as an experimenter working on his notes. Beside his truly ethnological works—*Incest: the Nature and Origin of the Taboo* (1963) and *Primitive Classification* (Durkheim and Mauss, 1963)—Durkheim made a capital contribution to ethnology in his reviews, scattered throughout the *Année sociologique*. They testify to such lucidity in the choice of the works reviewed! The spirit which inspires these reports is so modern that one would still wish to see them published today.

In going back to the sources, however, Durkheim makes one discovery: the opposition he first imagined between history and ethnography is largely illusory—or, rather, he had improperly interpreted it. Indeed, he reproached the theoreticians of ethnology not for their ignorance of history, but their elaborating a historical method which could not bear comparison with the method of true historians. On this point, at a decisive moment in the evolution of the Durkheimian doctrine, Hubert and Mauss throw some light on the master's thought when, in *Sacrifice: Its Nature and Function*, they undertake to substitute for the opposition between history and ethnography an underlying opposition between two concepts of history: on the one hand, that of historians, and, on the other, that which Radcliffe-Brown, faithful to Durkheim's inspiration, was to qualify a quarter of a century later as "conjectural history." "Robertson Smith's error," wrote Hubert and Mauss, "was above all one of method. Instead of analyzing in its original complexity the Semitic ritual system, he set about classifying the facts genealogically, in accordance with the analogical connections that he believed he saw between them. This is a characteristic common to English anthropologists. . . . In this category of facts all purely historical investigations are fruitless. The antiquity of the texts or of the facts recounted, the comparative barbarity of the peoples, and the apparent simplicity of the rites are deceptive chronological indications" (Hubert and Mauss 1964, pp. 7–8).

Hence the real opposition lies between two different manners of looking at history. One relies directly on documents, "written by the actors themselves, in their language," or on monuments decorated with figures. The other—which is practiced at this time by most of the theoreticians of ethnology—is a form of ideological history which consists in putting observations in chronological order, in any manner found intellectually satisfactory.

But here is the crucial point. Once freed from its pretentions and brought back to the particular data of observation, ethnography reveals its true nature. For, if these data are not the reflections of a false history, the scattered projections into the present of hypothetical "stages" of the evolution of the human mind, if they do not pertain to the order of the event, what can they teach use? Durkheim, protected by his rationalism against the temptation (which was to attract Frazer in his last works) of seeing in these data the product of rambling thought, was almost necessarily led to the interpretation he gives in the introduction to *The Elementary Forms:* "Primitive civilizations offer privileged cases . . . because they are simple cases . . . the relations between events are more apparent." They provide us, then, with "a means of discerning the ever-present causes upon which the most essential forms of religious thought and practice depend" (Durkheim 1968, pp. 19–21).

Today, of course, we ask ourselves the question (which did not concern Durkheim much) whether this prerogative of ethnographic knowledge is due to the properties of the object, or whether it is not rather explained by the relative simplification of a mode of knowledge when it is applied to a very distant object. The truth is probably halfway between the two interpretations, and the one chosen by Durkheim is not inaccurate, even if the arguments he proposes are no longer those we would retain. It is nevertheless true that, with Durkheim, the goal and methods of ethnographic research undergo a radical upheaval. It can henceforth escape its confining alternatives: either to satisfy an antiquarian's curiosity (its value measured by the strange and bizarre character of its finds); or to illustrate *a posteriori,* by means of complacently chosen examples, speculative hypotheses on the origin and evolution of mankind. The role of ethnography must be defined in other terms. Each of its observations presents, absolutely or relatively, a value of experience and makes possible the discernment of general truths.

Nothing is more moving or convincing than to read this message throughout the works of Radcliffe-Brown, to whom—as well as to Boas, Malinowski, and Mauss—ethnology owes the acquisition of its autonomy at the turn of the first quarter of this century. Although English, and consequently heir to an intellectual tradition with which the very history of ethnology merges, the young Radcliffe-Brown turns toward France and toward Durkheim when he undertakes to make ethnology (until then a historical or philosophical science) an experimental science comparable to the other natural sciences. "This conception," he wrote in 1923, "is by no means novel. Durkheim and the important school of the *Année sociologique* have insisted upon it since 1895" (Radcliffe-Brown 1958, p. 16).

And if, in 1931, he expresses regret that the new field-work methods did not originate in France, he is still taking into account the fact that "France led the way in the development of the theoretical study of comparative sociology" (Radcliffe-Brown 1958, pp. 69–70).

The paradox that Radcliffe-Brown emphasizes is more apparent than real. The first generation formed by Durkheim would have yielded field workers, had it not been decimated by World War I. The generation which followed devoted itself largely to direct observation. And, although Durkheim himself did not practice it, *The Elementary Forms of the Religious Life* (1968) by no means ceased to be a source of theoretical inspiration for Australian researchers. This is because, for the first time, methodically analyzed and classified ethnographic observations ceased to appear either as a collection of curiosities of aberrations, or as relics of the past. An attempt was now made to situate them in a systematic typology of beliefs and behaviors. From the distant marches where it was stationed, ethnography was thus brought back within the walls of the scientific city. All those who have since helped to keep it there have wholeheartedly acknowledged themselves as Durkheimians.

CHAPTER IV

The Work of the Bureau of American Ethnology and Its Lessons

Among my many cherished recollections of the years I spent in the United States, the one which remains outstanding is a casual discovery, one day in 1941, in New York, on lower Broadway. It was of a bookstore which specialized in secondhand government publications, where one could buy most of the *Annual Reports* of the Bureau of American Ethnology (if in a rather tattered condition) for two or three dollars apiece.

Chapter IV is based on a speech delivered on September 17, 1965, in Washington, D.C., at the bicentennial celebration commemorating the birth of James Smithson, founder of the Smithsonian Institution.

[*Translator's Note:* This chapter was published under the title "Anthropology: Its Achievements and Future," in *Knowledge among Men,* ed. P. H. Oehser (New York: Simon and Schuster, 1966). Copyright © 1966 by Simon & Schuster, Inc. Reprinted by permission of the Publisher and the Smithsonian Institution. It is reproduced here with the few minor additions from Professor Lévi-Strauss's French adaptation of the text he originally wrote in English.]

I can hardly describe my emotion at this find. That these sacrosanct volumes, representing most of our knowledge about the American Indians, could be found for sale alongside commonplace books was something I had never dreamed of. To my mind they belonged rather to a prestigious past where they merged with the beliefs and customs of which they spoke. It was as though the American Indian cultures had suddenly come alive and become almost tangible through the physical contact that these books, written and published before these cultures' definite extinction, established between their times and me. My financial resources were scant; three dollars represented all I had to spend on food for the same number of days. Yet this sum seemed negligible compared to the value of these marvelous publications which enabled me to acquire Mallery's *Pictographs*, Matthew's *Mountain Chant*, Fewkes's *Hopi Katcinas;* or such troves of knowledge as Stevenson's *Zuni Indians*, Boas and Hunt's *Tsimshian Mythology*, Roth's *Guiana Indians*, and Curtin and Hewitt's *Seneca Legends*.

Thus it happened that, volume after volume, at the cost of some privations, I succeeded in building up an almost complete set of *Annual Reports,* from Volume 1 to Volume 48, all belonging to the "great period" of the Bureau of American Ethnology. At that time, I was far from imagining that a few months later, I would be invited by the same Bureau to come to Washington and become a contributor to one of its major undertakings: the seven-volume *Handbook of South American Indians*.

In spite of this close association and the years that have since elapsed, the work of the Bureau of American Ethnology has lost for me none of its glamour. I still feel toward it an admiration and respect shared by innumerable scholars the world over. Since it so happens that in the same year that marks the two hundredth anniversary of James Smithson, the life of the Bureau has come to an end (though its activities are now carried on under a new name), it seems only fitting here to pay tribute both to the memory of the founder of the Smithsonian Institution and to the Bureau, which has been one of its greatest achievements.

Founded in 1879, the Bureau first emancipated ethnology from geography and geology, with which it had until then been merged. Above all, the Bureau availed itself fully of the amazing opportunity provided by the presence of scores of native tribes at a few hours' or days' travel from the great cities. It did this in such a way that a modern ethnologist could write that "the accounts of custom and culture published by the Bureau compare in thoroughness and quality of reporting with modern ethnographic studies" (Lienhardt 1964, p. 24). We are indebted to the Bureau for instituting standards of scholarship that still guide us, even though we but rarely succeed in attaining them.

The collection of native texts and factual observations contained in the forty-eight major *Reports* (and certain of the subsequent ones), in the two hundred or so *Bulletins*, and in the *Miscellaneous Publications* is so impressive that, after nearly a century of use, only its surface has been scratched. This being the case, one can only wonder at the neglect into which this invaluable material has temporarily fallen. The day will come when the last primitive culture will have disappeared from the earth, compelling us to realize only too late that the fundamentals of mankind are irretrievably lost. Then, and for centuries to come—as happened in the case of our own ancestral civilizations—hosts of scholars will devote themselves to reading, analyzing, and commenting upon the publications of the Bureau of American Ethnology. These publications preserve so much more of American Indian cultures than has been preserved of other bygone cultures—and this is not to mention the unpublished manuscripts placed in the Bureau's custody. If we succeed one day in enlarging our narrow-minded humanism to make it include each and every expression of human nature, thereby perhaps ensuring to mankind a more harmonious future, we shall owe much to undertakings such as those of the Bureau of American Ethnology.

However, nothing could be farther from my mind than the notion that the work of the Bureau belongs to the past. I believe, on the contrary, that all of us, together with its legal successor, the Department of Anthropology,[1] should seek in these achievements a living inspiration for the scientific task ahead of us.

It has become fashionable in certain circles to speak with condescension of anthropology as a science on the wane on account of the rapid disappearance of its traditional subject matter, the so-called primitives. Or else it is claimed that in order to survive, anthropology should abandon fundamental research and become an applied science, dealing with the problems of developing countries and the pathological aspects of our own society. I should not want to minimize the obvious pertinence of these new fields of research. But I nevertheless feel that there is, and will remain for a long time to come, much to be done along more traditional lines. It is precisely because the so-called primitive peoples are sooner or later threatened with extinction that their study should now be given absolute priority.

It is not too late for anthropologists to set to work. As early as 1908, Sir James Frazer, in his inaugural lecture at Liverpool University, stated that classical anthropology was nearing its end. What have we witnessed instead? Two great wars, together with scientific and technical development, have shaken the world and destroyed physically or morally a great many native cultures. But this process, however disastrous, has not been entirely one-way. World War I indirectly gave rise to Malinowski's new anthropology by obliging him to share the life of the Trobriand Islanders in a more durable and intimate manner than, perhaps, he would have done otherwise. And as an indirect consequence of World War II, anthropologists were given access to a new world: the New Guinea highlands, with a population of 600,000 to 800,000 souls whose institutions are changing our traditional outlook on many theoretical problems. Likewise, the establishment of the new federal capital of Brazil and the building of roads and airports in remote parts of South America have led to the discovery of small tribes in areas where no native life was thought to exist.

Of course, these opportunities will be the last. Moreover, the compensation they afford is small indeed, compared with the feelings of horror and indignation inspired by the extinction (directly or indirectly caused by these events) of primitive tribes the world over. There are about 40,000 natives left in Australia, as opposed to 250,000 at the beginning of the nineteenth century. Most, if not all, of them are hungry and disease-ridden, threatened in their deserts by mining plants, atomic testing grounds, and missile ranges. Between 1900 and 1950, over ninety tribes were wiped out in Brazil. There are now barely thirty tribes still living there, precariously and in a state of relative isolation. During the same period, fifteen South American languages have ceased to be spoken. Scores of similar examples could be given.

Yet, anthropology should not lose heart. It is certainly true that we have less and less material to work with. But we are able to compensate to some extent for this diminishing volume by putting what there is to better use—thanks to our greater theoretical and factual knowledge and more refined techniques of observation. We are left with less and less to study, but our study will take more time and will yield richer results than before. We have learned how to look for the cultural "niches" in which traditional lore finds a temporary refuge from the impact of industrial civilization, such as language, kinship, ethnobotany, ethnozoology, and the like.

To be sure, the physical disappearance of the last populations that remained faithful until the very end to their traditional way of life does, indeed, constitute a threat to anthropology. Curiously enough, however, a more immediate threat comes from an evolution that has been taking place in such parts of the world as Asia, Africa, and the American Andes, areas which used to be considered within the realm of anthropological studies. The population density of these regions was always high, and it shows no sign of decreasing—quite the contrary. The new threat to our studies is not, then, so much quantitative as qualitative. These large populations are changing fast, and their culture is more and more resembling that of the Western world. Like the latter, it tends to fall outside the field of anthropology. But this is not all, for the mere fact of being subjected to ethnographical investigation seems more and more distasteful to these peoples, as if they suspected that by studying the ways in which their old beliefs and customs differed from our own, we were granting these differences an absolute status and conferring upon them a more enduring quality.

Contemporary anthropology thus finds itself in a paradoxical situation. It was out of a deep feeling of respect toward cultures other than our own that the doctrine of cultural relativism evolved. It now appears that this doctrine is deemed unacceptable by the very people on whose behalf it was upheld, while those ethnologists who favor unilinear evolutionism find unexpected support from peoples who desire nothing more than to share in the benefits of industrialization; peoples who prefer to look at themselves as temporarily backward rather than permanently different.

Hence the distrust in which traditional anthropology is held nowadays in some parts of Africa and Asia. Economists and sociologists are welcome, while anthropologists are tolerated at best—and from certain areas are simply banned. Why perpetuate, even in writing, old usages and customs which are doomed to die? The less attention they receive, the faster they will disappear.

And even should they not disappear, it is better not to mention them lest the outside world realize that one's culture is not as fully abreast with modern civilization as one deludes oneself in believing it to be. There have been periods in our own history when we, too, have yielded to the same delusion, only to find ourselves struggling to regain balance after eradicating so recklessly the roots that joined us to our past. Let us hope that this dire lesson will not be lost on others. The question is, in effect: What can we do to keep the past from being lost? Is there a way of making peoples realize that they have a tremendous responsibility toward themselves and toward mankind as a whole, a duty not to let their past perish before they have become fully aware of its originality and its value and have fully recorded it? This is generally true, but even more so in the case of peoples whose unprecedented privilege it is to experience their past even as they are meeting their incipient future.

The suggestion has been made that in order to render anthropology less distasteful to its subjects, it will suffice to reverse the roles and occasionally allow ourselves to be "ethnographized" by those for whom we were once solely the ethnographers. In this way, each in turn will get the upper hand, so to speak. And since there will be no permanent privilege, nobody will have grounds to feel inferior to anybody else. At the same time, we shall get to know more about ourselves through the eyes of others, and human knowledge will derive an ever-growing profit from this reciprocity of perspective.

Well-meant as it undoubtedly is, this solution appears to me naïve and difficult to practice in a systematic manner. It implies that the problems are as simple and superficial as those of children unaccustomed to playing together, whose quarrels can be settled by making them follow the elementary rule: "Let me play with your dolls and I shall let you play with mine." A formulated understanding between people who are not merely estranged from one another by their physical appearances and their peculiar ways of life, but who also stand on an unequal footing to one another, is a different question altogether.

Anthropology—although it would like to—will never succeed in being a dispassionate science like astronomy, which springs from the contemplation of things at a distance. It is the outcome of a historical process which has made the larger part of mankind subservient to the other. During this process millions of innocent human beings have had their resources plundered and their institutions and beliefs destroyed, whilst they themselves were ruthlessly killed, thrown into bondage, and contaminated by diseases they were unable to resist. Anthropology is daughter to this era of violence. Its capacity to assess more objectively the facts pertaining to the human condition appropriately reflects, on the epistemological level, a state of affairs in which one part of mankind treated the other as an object.

A situation of this kind cannot be soon forgotten, much less erased. It is not because of peculiar mental endowments that the Western world gave birth to the science of anthropology. Rather, it occurred because exotic cultures, treated by us as mere things, could be studied, accordingly, as things. We did not feel concerned by them, whereas we cannot help their feeling concerned by us in the most direct manner. Between our attitude toward them and their attitude toward us, there is and can be no parity.

Therefore, if cultures—which until recently were called native—are ever to look at anthropology as a legitimate pursuit and not as a sequel to the colonial era or that of economic domination, it cannot suffice for the players simply to change camps while the anthropological game remains the same. Anthropology itself must undergo a deep transformation in order to carry on its work among those cultures which, lacking a written record of their history, most need it.

Instead of (as in the past) making up for this gap through the application of special methods, the new aim will be to fill it in. Anthropology, whenever it is practiced by members of the culture it endeavors to study, loses its specific nature and becomes rather akin to archaeology, history, and philology. For anthropology is the science of culture as seen from the outside, and the first concern of people made aware of their independent existence and originality must be to claim the right to observe their culture themselves, from the inside. Anthropology will survive in a world undergoing such transformations by allowing itself to perish in order to be born again under a new guise.

Anthropology is thus confronted with tasks which would prove contradictory were they not undertaken simultaneously in the same field. Wherever native cultures, though disappearing physically, have remained to some extent morally intact, anthropological research should be carried out along traditional lines. The means at its disposal should be increased to the utmost. And wherever populations have remained physically strong or are even increasing while their culture is rapidly veering toward our own, anthropology, progressively taken over by local scholars, should adopt aims and methods similar to those which, from the Renaissance on, have proved fruitful for the study of our own culture.

From the very beginning, the Bureau of American Ethnology has had to face this twofold necessity by reason of the peculiar situation of the American Indians, who allied cultural remoteness, physical proximity, and—despite all the orders they have been subjected to—a tremendous will to live. Thus the Bureau was compelled from the start both to carry out ethnographic surveys and to encourage the natives themselves to become their own linguists, philologists, and historians. The cultural riches of Africa, Asia, and Oceania can only be saved if, following this example, we succeed in raising dozens (and they themselves hundreds) of such men as Francis La Flesche, son of an Omaha chief; James Murie, a Skidi Pawnee; George Hunt, a Kwakiutl; and many others, some of whom, like La Flesche and Murie, were on the staff of the Bureau. We can but marvel at their maturity and foresight, and hope for the worldwide extension of what a handful of resolute and enlightened men and women knew should be done in the field of American studies.

This does not mean that we should be content merely to add similar material to that which is already available. There remains so much to be saved that the urgency of the task may make us overlook the present evolution of anthropology, which is changing in quality and increasing in quantity as the mass of material accumulates. This evolution itself should make us more confident in the future of our studies. New problems have arisen which can still be solved, even though they have received but scant attention. Until recently, for instance, anthropologists have neglected to study the elasticity of the yield of crops and the relationship between yield and the amount of work involved. Yet one of the keys to the understanding of the social and religious importance of yams throughout Melanesia can probably be found in the remarkable elasticity of the yield. The farmer who may harvest far less than he needs must plant for more in order to be reasonably certain to have enough. Conversely, if the harvest is plentiful, it may so widely exceed expectations that to consume it all becomes impossible. This leaves no other use for it than competitive display and social food presentation. In such cases, as in many others, we can see more fully the significance of the observed phenomena by learning to translate in terms of several different codes phenomena that we have been apprehending in terms of one or two codes only.

A broad system of equivalents could then be established between the truths to which anthropology can aspire and those of neighboring sciences which have been progressing at a similar pace. I am thinking not only of economics, but of biology, demography, sociology, psychology, and logic. It is through a number of such confrontations and adjustments that the originality of our field will best appear.

There has been much question lately as to whether anthropology belongs among the humanities or among the natural sciences. In my opinion, this is a false problem. Anthropology is unique in not lending itself to such a dichotomous distinction. It has the same subject matter as history, but for lack of time perspective it cannot use the same methods. Its own methods tend rather toward those of sciences which are synchronically oriented but not devoted to the study of man. As in every other scientific undertaking, these methods aim at discovering invariant properties beneath the apparent particularity and diversity of the observed phenomena.

Will this assignment deter anthropology from a humanistic and historical outlook? Quite the opposite. Of all the branches of our discipline, physical anthropology is probably the one most akin to the natural sciences. For this very reason, it is worth noting that by refining its methods and techniques, it has been getting ever closer to—not farther from—a humanistic outlook.

For the physical anthropologist, to look for invariant properties traditionally meant to look for factors devoid of adaptive value from the presence or absence of which something could be learned about the racial divisions of mankind. Our colleagues are less and less convinced, though, that any such factors really do exist. The sickle-cell gene, formerly held to be such a factor, can no longer be so considered if—as is now generally accepted—it carries a certain amount of immunity to a pernicious form of malaria. However, as Livingstone brilliantly demonstrated, what appears to be an irretrievable loss (from the point of view of long-range conjectural history as historians conceive it) is, in fact, both concrete and at close range. For, by reason of the adaptive value of the sickle-cell gene, a map showing its distribution throughout Africa would make it possible for us to read, as it were, African history in the making. The knowledge thus obtained could be correlated with that acquired from language and other cultural maps. What can we conclude from this example? Invariant properties which have vanished at the superficial level, where they were originally sought out, reappear at a deeper functional level. Instead of becoming less informative in the process, these properties turn out to be more meaningful.

This remarkable process is actually taking place everywhere in our field. Foster has recently injected new life into what most of us held to be an exhausted question—that of the origin of the potter's wheel. He has done so by pointing out that such an invention is neither simply a new mechanical device nor a material object that can be described objectively (and from the outside). Rather, it is a manner of proceeding, one which may avail itself of a number of different devices, some crude and others more elaborate. In the field of social organization, I myself have tried to show that kinship systems should not be described by their external features—such as the number of terms they use or the way they classify, merge, and distinguish all possible ties between individuals. In so doing, all we can hope to obtain is a long, meaningless list of types and subtypes; whereas if we try to find out how they work— that is, what kind of solidarity they help to establish within the group—their apparent multiplicity is reduced to a few basic and meaningful principles.

Similarly, in the field of religion and mythology, an attempt to reach beyond external features (which can only be described and arbitrarily classified by each scholar according to preconceived ideas) shows that the bewildering diversity of mythical motifs can be reduced to a very small number of schemes, each of which appears endowed with a specific operational value. At the same time, there emerge for each culture certain sets of transformation rules which make it possible to include in the same group myths previously held to be markedly different.

These few examples, chosen among many others, tend to show that anthropology's traditional problems are assuming new forms, and that none of these problems can be said to be exhausted.

Anthropology is distinctive among the human sciences in that it looks at man from the very point where, at each period of history, it was considered that anything like man had ceased to exist. During antiquity and the Middle Ages, this point was too close to permit observation, since each culture or society was inclined to locate it on its neighbor's doorstep. Within a century or so, when the last native culture will have disappeared from the earth and our only interlocutor will be the electronic computer, the point will have become so remote that we may well doubt whether the same kind of approach will deserve to be called "anthropology." Between these limits lies the only chance that man ever had or will have to look at himself in the concrete forms of his historical experience. He will still remain a problem unto himself, but one he knows can be solved since it is already certain that the outer differences conceal a basic unity.

Let us suppose, for a moment, that astronomers should warn us that an unknown planet is nearing the earth and will remain at close range for twenty or thirty years, thereafter receding and disappearing forever. In order to avail ourselves of this unique opportunity, neither effort nor money would be spared to build specially designed telescopes and satellites. Should not similar study be made of one half of mankind—only recently acknowledged as such—still so close to the other half that except for the lack of money, its study raises no problem, although it will soon become impossible forever? If the future of anthropology could be seen in this light, no study would appear more urgent and more important. Native cultures are disintegrating faster than radioactive bodies. The Moon, Mars, and Venus will still be at the same distance from the earth when that mirror which other civilizations still holds up to us will have so receded from our eyes that, however costly and elaborate the instruments at our disposal, we may never again be able to recognize and study this image of ourselves, which will be lost and gone forever.

NOTES

[1. *Translator's note:* The Office of Anthropology was later reorganized and continues to operate as the Department of Anthropology, National Museum of Natural History, Smithsonian Institution.]

CHAPTER V

Comparative Religions of Nonliterate Peoples

1888	October 20	Creation of a noncredit course called "Religions of Uncivilized Peoples," entrusted to Leon Marillier.
1890	March 13	Transformation of this noncredit course into a lecture course, entrusted to Leon Marillier, titular lecturer, with the same title: "Religions of Uncivilized Peoples."
1901	October 15	Death of Leon Marillier.
	December 5	Marcel Mauss is appointed titular lecturer, to replace Mr. Marillier.
1907	August 20	Marcel Mauss is appointed assistant director.
1940	October 31	Professor Marcel Mauss retires.
1941	March 22	Maurice Leenhardt is appointed professor in Marcel Mauss's place.
1950	September 30	Mr. Leenhardt retires.
1951	January 25	Claude Lévi-Strauss is appointed professor to replace Mr. Leenhardt.
1954	February 9	The lecture takes its present title.

Chapter V was originally published under the title "Religions comparées des peuples sans écriture," in *Problèmes et méthodes d'histoire des religions: Mélanges publiés par la section des sciences religieuses à l'occasion du centenaire de l'École practique des hautes études* (Paris: Presses universitaires de France, 1968), pp. 1–7.

THE FACT THAT, almost as soon as I was called upon to occupy this chair in 1951, I felt the need to change its title should not imply on my part a lack of deference or faithfulness to the memory of my illustrious predecessors Leon Marillier, Marcel Mauss, and Maurice Leenhardt. But it happened that, as a sign of the times to which we could not be insensitive, and as early as my first year of teaching, papers read by me or by researchers back from a mission elicited remarks, commentary, or criticism from overseas students. These students were anxious to have it known that they themselves belonged to the population spoken of, and that they did not agree with such and such an interpretation.

Under these conditions, it would have been paradoxical to encourage such precious collaboration under cover of a title which attributed the religions under study to "uncivilized peoples," even if this epithet did not matter much fifty years ago, since none of those concerned were there to give it, rightly or wrongly, a pejorative interpretation. It would also have been questionable to plead that no culture whatever is to be defined by what is denied it but, instead, by what characterizes it as worthy of attention. It is true that the new title, referring to nonliterate peoples, also evinces a privative character. But, even disregarding that it is a statement of fact which does not imply a value judgement, the absence of writing in the societies we study seems to us—and this is indeed an essential theme of our thinking—to exercise a sort of regulatory influence on a tradition which is to remain oral. Better than our traditions, whose transformation accelerates with the ever increasing mass of knowledge accumulated in books, these traditions lend themselves to an experimental research which requires a relative stability in its object.

It can be said of teachings which have gone on for eighteen years that they already have their own history. Looking back on ours, we discern three phases of approximately the same length. During the first period, one course took up one of the two weekly hours (the other was reserved for seminar work, generally in the form of presentations given by colleagues, students, or guests, and followed by a discussion). These lectures made it possible to elaborate progressively—to try out, as it were, on an indulgent audience —the principles and methods of analysis to which mythical representations and religious practices have been submitted in several books published since then. A second phase marked the evolution of the conference into a true seminar, and also a broadening which allowed the inclusion of seemingly marginal problems. But the place increasingly accorded ethnology among the sciences of man prohibits it from overlooking topical questions, such as modern techniques of documentation (which also proved to be indispensable) and the relevant positions of contemporary philosophy.

The years 1959–1962 were thus largely devoted to discussing the use of descriptive codes, punched cards, and computers in our disciplines, as well as the relationship between ethnology and philosophy in the light of recent works. One should not overlook the cardinal role played at the time by young and brilliant scientists, like Jean-Claude Gardin, who later founded and directed the *Section d'Automatique documentaire* of the CNRS; [1] and the late Lucien Sebag, whose tragic disappearance will not soon obliterate a sense of the promise in his work. My appointment to the *Collège de France* in 1954 finally led us to focus on the teaching material in the lectures and to reserve the sessions at *l'École* [2] for seminar work—most often reports of missions presented by researchers from the *Laboratoire d'anthropologie sociale* (founded in 1960) or from neighboring institutions.

Since the beginning of this third phase, around the year 1962, we have determinedly attempted to reduce the number of auditors, so that our weekly seminar can become the meeting place for a team whose members, already united by other ties, can thus keep each other informed of their individual work. It goes without saying that this collaboration supposes a certain unity of views without, however, excluding a doctrinal independence. The unity results from the fact that, whether to get inspiration from them or to combat them, the participants readily take as terms of reference the ideas that we, ourselves, continue to develop in both our lectures at the *Collège* and the discussions—often very lively—which occupy the last part of each seminar. It is thus not superfluous to sum up these themes.

Our first researches in Brazil led us to take exception to the notion of "primitive." If the societies observed by ethnographers are no more "primitive" than others, and if they therefore do not give us access to knowledge about the archaic stages of humanity's development, of what use is their study? Certainly not to reveal the primitive beneath the civilized. But to the extent to which these societies offer man an image of his social life—reduced on the one hand (because of their small population) and balanced on the other (due both to their entropy from the absence of social classes and a true, albeit illusory, repudiation of history by those societies themselves)—they constitute privileged cases. In the domain of social facts, they make it possible to perceive the model through the reality; or, more precisely, to construct with the least effort the model *from* the reality.

This privileged status does not result, however, from properties inherent in societies considered primitive so much as from our particular situation with regard to them. These are the societies which present (in relation to that of the observer) the most considerable differences. Vis-à-vis the other human sciences, the ethnologist is in a position rather comparable to that of the astronomer among the physical and natural sciences. Astronomy was for a long time restricted to crude and superficial knowledge because of the remoteness of the celestial bodies, their magnitude being egregiously unamenable to the very size of the observer and to his paltry means of observation. Yet it is no accident that astronomy discovered the ground on which the exact sciences were to take their first steps.

Likewise, the obstacles met by ethnological knowledge may present a means of approaching reality. The ultimate goal is not to know what the societies under study "are"—each on its own account—but to discover how they differ from one another. As in linguistics, the study of *contractive features* constitutes the object of anthropology.

Here again, pertinent phenomena, because they consist of relations, would escape an investigation concerned only with empirically observable facts. In our teaching at the *École pratique des hautes études*, as well as at the *Collège de France*, our goal is essentially to carry the method of models into a little-exploited domain where our ethnographic orientation led us: that of mythology, and more particularly the mythology of the two Americas.

As early as the first year, and later on (1950–1951, 1958–1959), we showed that ceremonial behaviors marked by an ostensible lack of restraint were grouped in America and elsewhere in the world around three poles. They were illustrated, respectively, by the characters of the "glutton," the "fool," and the "cannibal." Each of these ritual functions, and all the intermediate forms, seem correlative with certain attitudes toward the dead. With the deceased, the society of the living endeavors to maintain relationships, peaceful or aggressive but ideal; or else real—but in that case transposed to the plane of relationships between fellow countrymen and foes.

To the typology of ritual behavior, we then added a typology of representations of the soul (1956–1957). These are grouped between two poles: a "'sociological" pole where the souls, gathered in a society after the fashion of the living, generally keep "out of the way" and are periodically invited to renew their ties with the latter; and, secondly, a "naturalist" pole where the soul, considered from the point of view of the individual, breaks down into an organic society of functional souls, each presiding over a particular vital activity. The problem—a symmetrical inversion of the previous, ceremonial one—consists in warding off the permanent tendency of the souls to disperse. This falling into place of great mythical concepts has moved us to reconsider the theoretical interpretation of certain controversial rites: *couvade*, initiation, and double inhumation (1954–1955, 1958–1960).

From 1951 to 1953, we worked on an analysis of the complex functions illustrated by the pantheons of the Pueblo tribes in the southwestern United States. These pantheons seem to be answerable to the typology which includes groups also found elsewhere. Their study promised to be fruitful from the point of view of comparative mythology. We thus established the pre-Columbian character of a mediator, which had generally been held to be a recent importation. This phallic god is consecrated to ashes and refuse, is master of wild animals, fog, dew, and precious garments, and is witnessed from Mexico to Canada. It presents, even in detail (in spite of a systematic inversion of all the terms, which excludes borrowing), a regular correspondence with a character reduced to a minor role on the European and Asiatic scene: Cinderella.

If functions and terms are initially defined in an unequivocal manner (subject of the 1959–1961 lectures), structural analysis—far from constraining one to formalism—opens perspectives on the field of geography and history. This conviction still guides our later research on mythical representations, even in its most abstract phases.

Rather than undertake hasty comparisons and rush into speculations on origins, it is better to proceed to the methodical analysis of myths, defining each one by the totality of its demonstrated variants, eliminating any preconceived ideas. Only in this way can we hope to reach a stage where man and his works take their place as subjects of positive knowledge. But to do so, one should apply a very strict method, which is reducible to three rules:

> 1. A myth must never be interpreted on one level only. No privileged explanation exists, for any myth consists in an *interrelation* of several explanatory levels.
> 2. A myth must never be interpreted individually, but in its relationship to other myths which, taken together, constitute a transformation group.
> 3. A group of myths must never be interpreted alone, but by reference: (*a*) to other groups of myths; and (*b*) to the ethnography of the societies in which they originate. For, if the myths transform each other, a relation of the same type links (on a transversal axis) the different levels involved in the evolution of all social life. These levels range from the forms of technoeconomic activity to the systems of representations, and include economic exchanges, political and familial structures, aesthetic expression, ritual practices, and religious beliefs.

Myths of various types are created from the transformations of the relatively simple structures reached in this manner. In this way, anthropology is a modest collaborator in the elaboration of that *logic of the concrete*, a logic which seems to be one of the major concerns of modern thought, and which shows us to be closer to—rather than farther from—forms of thought very foreign to ours in appearance.

These myths can no longer be described as prelogical. Their logic is alien, but only to the extent that Western thinking has been dominated by too narrow a logic. The anthropologist, without claiming to have a share in the development of the mathematics designated as qualitative (which has broadened our logic by making the concern for rigor prevail over the concern for measure), can submit to the logician and the mathematician materials of a type original enough to retain their attention.

In the same perspective, an attempt has also been made to integrate the study of myth and that of ritual. The current theory, according to which a term-to-term correspondence exists between two orders (whether the rite acts out the myth, or the myth explicates the rite), is reducible to the particular case of a more general relation. The study of individual cases makes myths and rites appear as different transformations of identical elements (lectures from the years 1954–1955 and 1959–1960). Thus the mythology of the Pawnee, who are plains Indians, presents a symmetrical and inverted image of their ritual, the direct symmetry being reestablished only in relation to the ritual of neighboring tribes.

Myth and ritual do not always correspond to each other. Nevertheless, they complete each other in domains already presenting a complementary character. The value of the ritual as meaning seems to reside in instruments and gestures: it is a *paralanguage*. The myth, on the other hand, manifests itself as *metalanguage;* it makes full use of discourse, but does so by situating its own significant oppositions at a higher level of complexity than that required by language operating for profane ends.

Our method comes down, then, to postulating an analogy of structure among various orders of social facts and language, an analogy which constitutes the social fact *par excellence.* They all appear to us as the same type of phenomena, and we have sometimes wondered (lectures of the years 1955–1956, 1958–1959) whether the kinship systems or mythical representations of two neighboring populations do not interrelate in the manner of dialectal differences.

Parallel studies, pursued on different levels, suggest the outlines of a general theory of society implying a vast system of communication among individuals and groups with several perceptible levels: that of kinship, perpetuated by exchange of women among groups of affines; that of economic activities, wherein goods and services are exchanged between producers and consumers; and that of language, which permits the exchange of messages among speaking subjects. Inasmuch as religious facts have their place in such a system, it can be seen that one aspect of our attempt consists in stripping them of their specificity.

Indeed, myths and rites can also be treated as modes of the communication from gods to men (myths) or from men to gods (rites). With this difference, however: that divine interlocutors are not partners, like others, within the same system of communication. Man conceives them as the images or the (total or partial) projections of this system, introducing in the theory an additional constraint—but not impairing its economy or its principles.

Ethnographers tend to believe too readily that they have succeeded in grasping, beyond their own preconceptions, the ideas of the indigenous people. Their descriptions are too often reduced to a phenomenology. We hope to introduce an additional exigency into our disciplines: to discover, beyond men's idea of their society, the hinges of the "true" system. We hope to carry the investigation beyond the limits of consciousness.

One is led finally to treat the various forms of social life within a given population, and the forms on the same level in different populations, as the elements of a vast combinatory system submitted to rules of compatibility or incompatibility. This makes certain arrangements possible, excludes others, and brings about a transformation of the general balance each time that an alteration or a substitution affects any of the elements. It can be said that Marcel Mauss was the initiator of this enterprise from the time when he first occupied this chair in 1902 until he relinquished it in 1940. Maurice Leenhardt's work, in part at least, keeps the same orientation. The commitment has been pursued without interruption for almost three-quarters of a century in the same building —and often in the same lecture hall. Taking into account the results and what remains to be accomplished, it is safe to venture that the task will occupy our successors for a long time to come.

NOTES

[1. *Translator's note:* French National Center for Scientific Research.]
[2. *Translator's note:* École pratique des hautes études, linked to the Sorbonne.]

PART TWO
Social Organization

The Meaning and Use of the Notion of Model

I N HIS INTERESTING PAPER, Mr. Maybury-Lewis takes me to task on two grounds. I am accused of misrepresenting the ethnographical data, at least in two instances. More generally, my methodological approach is said to be "morally" wrong. The first criticism has no real basis and results from his mistaking a theoretical reconstruction for a description of actual facts. As to the value judgement, it is, as such, irrefutable, and I can only try to clarify the line of reasoning which I have followed.

Let us first consider what I shall call, for brevity's sake, the

Chapter VI was originally written in English and appeared under the title: "On Manipulated Sociological Models," in *Bijdragen tot de Taal-, Land- en Volkenkunde*, CXVI, No. 1 (1960), pp. 17–44, in answer to D. Maybury-Lewis's article published in the same issue, "The Analysis of Dual Organisations: A Methodological Critique." This itself was written as a criticism of my article: "Les Organisations dualistes existent-elles?" ibid., CXII, No. 2 (1956), pp. 99–128, republished in *Structural Anthropology*, Vol. 1, Chapter VIII.

[*Translator's note:* We have reproduced most of Professor Lévi-Strauss's original English version of this chapter, while trying to respect some slight modifications made by him when he later translated the original essay into French.]

Winnebago discrepancy (See *Structural Anthropology*, Vol. 1 [hereafter referred to as *S.A.*], pp. 133–135). Are we to believe that it can be overcome by admitting that one category of informants—those of the lower phratry—simply omitted the dual division because it was not contextually relevant? But it was not enough simply not to mention it. While they did away with it in their description of the ancient village, they introduced another dual division—admittedly not a social one, but not merely ecological either, since it emerges as a substitute for, and a transformation of, the other division.

To reconstruct the village layout, it would not be sufficient to put one diagram on top of the other, as if each offered a "true" picture, although in its way an incomplete one. In so doing, one would be doing the very thing for which I am reproached, i.e., "manipulating" models. The only empirical data given us consist of two drawings of the ancient Winnebago village, each of which bears a complementary relation to the other, if not the one suggested to us. These drawings not only present a fragmentary image of a total configuration (so that all we have to do is to supplement one with the other) but they also stand in opposition to each other, and this relation of opposition cannot be lightly dismissed since it is itself part of the ethnographical data.

In other words, if the distinction between the inhabited village and the cleared ground (as well as the one between the cleared ground and the surrounding woods) is not relevant in one diagram, why does it become so in the other? What we have here is nothing more than a curious fact, the true interpretation of which probably will never be known. This is all the more reason to follow each and every line of interpretation.

I have taken up one, which at least offers the advantage of being novel. What would be the theoretical consequences, if the social distinction between the two moieties, on the one hand, and the ecological (but also philosophical) distinction between cleared ground (pertaining to culture) and the wilderness beyond the timberline (pertaining to nature), on the other hand, should be recognized as two different codes, codes used to carry the same message, but at the cost of complementary distortions?

Let us recapitulate briefly. In the first place, a tribe whose social organization and religious thought are strongly marked with a principle of dual division displays another form of dualism, one which is no longer diametric but, as it were, concentric. In the second place, this concentric dualism manifests itself openly and in isolation in populations such as the Trobriand, where one can observe it independently from the other type. To object that the Trobriand have no dual organization in the classical sense of the term would therefore be to miss the point. For it is precisely the exclusive presence of the concentric dualism that permits its identification and its definition as an ethnographic phenomenon. Thirdly, one could examine societies where the two types coexist in a particularly clear manner: Bororo, Timbia, and so many Indonesian groups. It is easier to present a syncretic model than to consider them one after the other. Three conclusions were reached: (1) where the two types coexist, there is a functional relation between them; (2) the concentric pattern is logically more essential than the diametric one; and (3) since this concentric pattern covers a ternary pattern, the latter can be said to underlie—at least in a latent manner—the diametric dualism itself.

It would then be futile to establish an empirical opposition between the two types of dualism. One of them could scarcely be reduced to a reflection of symbolic values in the village layout, with the other—the only "true" dualism—being said to involve the real segments of the social group. The latter type also has a symbolic value, and the former entails rights and obligations no less than the latter. What I have tried to do is to transcend these partial views of a selfsame reality, and put to the test a kind of common language into which the two forms of dualism could be translated. This would, I feel, enable us to reach—not on the level of observation, of course—a "generalized" interpretation of all the phenomena of dualism. I hope to have shown that such an interpretation is not only possible, since all the considered instances of dualism can be reduced, despite their apparent heterogeneity, to the various combinations of only five binary oppositions (*S.A.*, p. 160); but that this common language reveals an important and hitherto undetected fact. It is that social dualism exists not only in the form which we described but assumes and covers a triadic system, of which each individual case of dualism (taken in a broad sense, but including among other forms, dual organizations) should be considered as a simplification and as a limit.

Admittedly, this marks a departure from the thesis put forward in *Les Structures élémentaires de la parenté*, as I have myself taken care to explain (*S.A.*, p. 150). But it does not do away with the distinction between dyadic and triadic structures which occupied such an important place in that work, since, for practical purposes, that distinction remains as useful as it was. But it seems that—as mathematicians with whom the problem was discussed agreed—by treating dyadic systems as a special case of the triadic formula, the general theory of reciprocity becomes greatly simplified. Moreover, this manner of formulating the problem seems to be more convenient for the purpose of historical reconstruction, since there are cases when the triadic "core" appears to be not only logically more simple, but older than the dyadic "upper crust" which covers it.

Now let us get down to the supposed ethnographical distortions, and first to the question of the Bororo north-south axis.[1] If its presence contradicted the observations of the Salesian Fathers to the extent that has been maintained, I would suspect that I misunderstood my informants, whose statements were quite clear in that particular respect. But (1) these observations were made in a different part of the Bororo country, where the villages were not necessarily structured in the same manner; (2) there are similar indications recorded in Colbacchini's first publications; and (3) Albisetti's more recent descriptions show something which looks like the north-south axis inside the men's house, dividing the sectors allocated to each moiety; then a north-south axis ideally present inside of each clan, and resulting in independently attested correlation between "lower" and west, on the one hand, and "higher" and east, on the other hand. Thus, the difference between the two accounts is that, in one case, the north-south axis has a positive existence inside the men's house, and a relative one outside; while in the other case, the north-south axis is objectively present both inside and outside.

In order to see there an insurmountable contradiction, one would have to postulate two things: first, that the Bororo social structure was perfectly identical throughout their vast territory; second, that the north-south axis, as recorded on the Rio Vermelho, did serve to separate the clans according to status distinction.

With regard to the first point, such a homogeneity does not seem very likely. The Bororo once occupied a territory as big as half of France; in historical times, it was still a quarter of the earlier area. The rate of growth and extinction could not be the same for each clan and in each village, especially when losses due to wars against or by neighboring tribes are taken into account. Each village was probably confronted with demographic problems of its own, and the number of clans and their distribution on the village circle must have varied considerably. The Salesians could hardly have given us a description of a situation which once existed in the whole territory. It did not even exist where they were working themselves, as their earlier, more empirical descriptions show. Rather, many years of patient work enabled them to construct an ideal formula, the theoretical model which was most suitable in accounting for numerous local variations. It is not surprising, then, if the actual pattern recorded at one time in a village is slightly different from that recorded at another time (in villages belonging to a distinct group). Finally, it is obvious that, when we work on the invaluable documents which the Salesian Fathers have left us after many years of painstaking reconstruction, we are not confronted with empirical data. Rather, we are manipulating a sociological model. Like it or not, this is what we all do when we engage in that type of discussion.

Will it be said that the two descriptions are incompatible and that one should have chosen between them, instead of using them both concurrently? Incompatibility would result if the terms *xobbuguiugue, xebbeguiugue* were given the same meaning in the earliest descriptions of the Salesians, in their later ones, and in my own; that is, if these terms always meant "superior" and "inferior" and connotated absolute differences. For, then, instead of having "superior" and "inferior" families inside each clan, the West clans would be absolutely inferior, the East clans absolutely superior, and it would be impossible to merge the two systems into one.[2] But such was not the case on the Rio Vermelho, nor on the Rio das Garças, according to Colbacchini's earlier account. For him, as well as for me, the native terms referred to the topography and meant "uphill" and "downhill" for Colbacchini's informants, and "upstream" and "downstream" for mine. It just so happens that, in Bororo, as in many other languages, the same term has all three connotations. It was all the more easy for the Bororo to avoid equivocation when they had two couples of contrasted terms to express status distinction: between "great" and "small," on the one hand, and "red" and "black," on the other.

Was I wrong to write that two clans in each moiety represent the two legendary heroes of the Bororo? It is true that two clans belonging to one moiety do so at present and that, in the past, two clans of the other moiety did so. However, if this merging of a synchronic analysis with a diachronic analysis is an ethnographical mistake, does my critic not commit the same mistake when, in trying to explain the Winnebago discrepancy, he puts forth a mythical account according to which the lower phratry may once have held or shared the chieftainship—a story of exactly the same type as the Bororo one that I relied on?

This is not all. In neither case are we confronted with an opposition between the synchronic and the diachronic order. Here, the past referred to is mythical, not historical. And, as a myth, the content is actually given to the native consciousness. When the Bororo myth tells us about a time when two Tugare clans, instead of the two Cera clans, were connected with the cultural heroes, it may refer to past events. Of the truth of these events, we will remain for ever ignorant. But we are made quite sure that, in the present, some kind of connection is felt to exist, between the dispossessed clans and the cultural heroes.

Coming now to the Winnebago, it is a mistake to attribute to me the notion that the Winnebago village actually comprised twelve clans distributed into three groups. This statement, as I made it, did not claim to be an ethnographical description of the Winnebago village as it existed in the past. It merely described a theoretical diagram, purporting to reorganize ethnographical data which, at the observation level, do not clearly exhibit those properties (or else, my undertaking would have been useless).

Thus, there is no claim that the Winnebago village was ever distributed into three groups of four clans each. What is being suggested here is quite different; namely, that on purely deductive grounds, the three cases taken from different societies may be treated as transformations one of the other under several conditions, one of them being that the Winnebago village be analyzed in such and such a way.

This inference being deductively drawn, it is highly gratifying that the ethnographical data should give it independent support. There is evidence in Radin's material that this interpretation of the village structure existed not only in the anthropologist's mind but also in the minds of some of the natives themselves. If it were imposed on us by the manifest content of the ethnographical data, there would be nothing to demonstrate—it would be sufficient to describe what one sees or what one is being told. On the other hand, a theoretical hypothesis which deviates from the manifest content of the ethnographical data is substantially upheld if we are to discover, in the latent content supplied by the myths, the religious representations, etc. Some data show a remarkable parallelism between the native categories, and they are arrived at by the way of theoretical reconstruction. In the Winnebago case, Radin says (1923, p. 241), "One informant . . . said . . . that the clans were arranged in three groups, one over which the Thunderbird clan ruled, another over which the Water-spirit ruled, and a third over which the Bear clan ruled." This is proof enough that a ternary system existed at least in a latent state. This is more than could be expected, especially as it comes from a part of the world where the operation of such ternary systems had remained hitherto unsuspected.

The argument that the ternary system would be irrelevant in consideration of the Winnebago marriage system appears, along these lines, out of order. The point made in Figure 13 of *S.A.* (p. 155) is that, even if the system should be considered as ternary, this would not affect the dualistic marriage system. As a matter of fact, the usefulness of the diagram lies in its enabling us to "see" the social structure either as ternary (sky, water, earth) or as binary (higher, lower). Also, the northwest-southeast axis, "spatial referent of Winnebago dualism," is not "omitted," since the diagram makes clear that marriage possibilities are between higher (= sky), on the one hand, and lower (= water + earth), on the other.

As to the village circle, which is claimed to be "irrelevant in a diagram of marriage relations," there are two comments to be made. In the first place—and contrary to what is maintained—the diagrams do not concern marriage relations alone. Rather, they are intended to show how marriage relations, social structure, village layout, religious representations, and so forth are all part of a system. The difference is that, in each case, they are assigned different functions; or—to express it in diagramatic terms—they are permuted in different topological positions. To put it yet differently, what a given society "says" in terms of marriage relations is being "said" by another society in terms of village layout, and in terms of religious representations by a third, and so on.

In the second place (and to limit myself to the Winnebago ethnographical material which I have been reproached as having misrepresented), it is enough to refer the reader to Radin's enlightening comments on the relationship between village and clan structure. If there are Winnebago myths representing the whole tribe as having once consisted of one village, the overall social structure cannot be thought of as independent of the residential unit. Radin raises the question—wisely, I believe—whether the "band" or village, "setting off one group against another," is not an early form of social grouping, so that, as elsewhere in North America, village organization may have preceded the clan (Radin 1923, p. 184–185).

I shall not dwell at length on the discussion of the other diagrams since it follows the same erroneous line: that of confusing a theoretical analysis of models, intended to explain the ethnographical data (by reducing them to a small number of common factors) with an actual description of the data as they appear to the empirical observer. Many Southeast Asian societies make the useful and often true statement that women circulate, not men; this does not invalidate the truth (to be covered by a generalized model) that nothing would be changed in the formal properties of the structure, if the situation were described the other way around, as some tribes actually do. The "tripod" in Figures 13 to 15 (*S.A.*, pp. 155–158) only expresses the fact that, in an asymmetrical marriage system as well as in a symmetrical one, there is a rule of exogamy in operation; but that, in the first case, it creates a sociological opposition between the sexes, whatever group they belong to, while in the second case, the opposition exists between the groups, whatever sexes they include.

It is equally inaccurate to state that the east-west axis does not appear in the Bororo diagram. It is true that it does not appear where the natives put it, since it has been demonstrated that in so doing, they let themselves be mystified by their own system. For that reason, it has been represented, as it should, by the tripod, each branch of which bisects the three otherwise fully endogamous groups. On the other hand, the hypothesis that the north-south axis provides the unifying factor is admittedly weak. This is so, not because the existence of this axis results from an ethnographical error—a charge which has already been shown to be gratuitous (see p. 81, n. 1)—but because I have myself so qualified it, and have explained that it first requires a careful testing in the field.

Obviously, the Bororo diagram is not exhaustive—none of the diagrams are and none are meant to be. It nevertheless represents quite satisfactorily what is essential and was asked of us: on the one hand, a pair of moieties, on the other hand, a triad of endogamous groups. A diagram does not pretend to show everything, but only the functions which are recurrent in all the cases diagramatically exemplified (and despite the fact that these functions do not manifest themselves, each time, on the same level of social reality).

We reach here a major point of disagreement. Should the only conclusion of my paper be that disparate elements drawn from different societies can be represented in identical patterns, I would not consider such a demonstration devoid of sociological implications. For we may have found a way of showing that what appears superficially disparate may not be so, and that behind the bewildering diversity of empirical data, there may exist a small number of recurrent, identical properties, although they are combined differently.

To sum up, may I point out to what extent my critic remains the prisoner of the naturalistic misconceptions that have so long pervaded the British school. He claims to be a structuralist. He even claims to defend structuralism against my reckless manner of handling it. But he is still a structuralist in Radcliffe-Brown's terms in that he believes the structure to lie at the level of empirical reality and to be a part of it. When, therefore, he is presented a structural model which departs from empirical reality, he feels cheated in some devious way. To him, social structure is like a kind of jigsaw puzzle, and everything is achieved when one has discovered how the pieces fit together. But, if the pieces have been arbitrarily cut, there is no structure at all. On the other hand, if—as is sometimes done—the pieces were automatically cut in different shapes by a mechanical saw, the movements of which are regularly modified by a camshaft, the structure of the puzzle exists, though not at the empirical level (since there are many ways of recognizing the pieces which fit together). Its key lies in the mathematical formula expressing the shape of the cams and their speed of rotation. This information does not correspond in any perceptible manner to the puzzle as it appears to the player, but it alone can explain the puzzle and provide a logical method to solve it.

But Maybury-Lewis writes: "Social relations cannot be formally represented by symbols in the same way as mathematical relations can. Accordingly, sociological models are not manipulable in the sense that mathematical equations are." Should he not explain, first, what he means by "social relations"? (1960, p. 35). If he refers to concrete social relations, as seen by the empirical observer, we cannot but agree with Maybury-Lewis's statement, while remembering that already in primary school, we were taught the impossibility of adding pears to apples. But if a distinction is made between the level of observation and symbols to be substituted for it, I fail to see why an algebraic treatment of, say, symbols for marriage rules, could not teach us, when aptly manipulated, something of the way a given marriage system actually works, and bring out properties not immediately apparent to the empirical observer.

Of course, the final word should rest with experiment. However, the experiment suggested and guided by deductive reasoning will not be the same as the unsophisticated one with which the whole process had started; the latter will remain as alien as ever to the deeper analysis.

The ultimate proof of the molecular structure of matter is provided by the electronic microscope, which enables us to see actual molecules. This achievement does not alter the fact that henceforth the molecule will not become any more visible to the naked eye. Similarly, it is hopeless to expect a structural analysis to change our way of perceiving concrete social relations. It will only explain them better. If the structure can be seen, it will not be at the earlier, empirical level, but at a deeper one, previously neglected; that of those unconscious categories which we may hope to reach by bringing together domains which, at first sight, appear disconnected to the observer: on the one hand, the social system as it actually works, and on the other, the manner in which, through their myths, their rituals, and their religious representations, men try to hide or to justify the discrepancies between their society and the ideal image of it which they harbor.

To give, from the start, an absolute value to the distinction between those two domains is to beg the question. For the problem originally raised in my paper on dual organization (*S.A.*, Chapter VIII) is precisely that of the absolute value of such a distinction. The problem can be phrased in the following terms: Do these organizations always belong to the domain of real social segments, or are they not sometimes reduced to symbolic representations of this reality? If the descriptions of the Bororo social structure are correct, then, as I have shown elsewhere (*S.A.*, Chapter VII), dual organization among the Bororo belongs to the domain of symbolic representations, since its operative value is canceled, so to speak, by actual rules of endogamy. On the other hand, the concentric dualism of the Bororo village, opposing the profane circle to the sacred center, should be endowed with a higher coefficient of objective truth, since there is nothing in the system to contradict it, and since it is permitted to unfold all its consequences, on both the religious and the social levels.

But the same thing cannot be said of other examples of dual organization elsewhere. Hence the conclusion that actual social segments and symbolic representations may not be as heterogeneous as it seems. To some extent, they may correspond to codes whose functions and fields of application are permutable. Herein lies one's right to deal with social segments and symbolic representations as parts of an underlying system endowed with a better explanatory value, although—or rather, because—empirical observation never apprehends it as such.

NOTES

1. The following paragraphs now seem superfluous, as the question has been categorically settled. The controversial north-south axis, which I was accused of having invented, has been independently found by J. C. Crocker, working in the Sao Lourenço region thirty years later, in 1965: "My informants corroborated those of Lévi-Strauss in saying that for some purposes the village was formerly divided into 'upper' and 'lower' halves on a north-south axis running through the middle of the village. This division is certainly not utilised among contemporary Bororo" (J. C. Crocker, "Reciprocity and Hierarchy among the Eastern Bororo," *Man*, n.s., IV, No. 1 (March 1969), pp. 44–58).

2. This is the error of interpretation made by the *Encyclopedia Bororo*, I, pp. 443–444.

CHAPTER **VII**

Reflections on the Atom of Kinship

In a recent book *Pourquoi l'épouser?*, Luc de Heusch takes up again the text of a study previously published in *Critique* (Nos. 219–220, 1965). On the basis of a new example, the book renews the objections formulated by our colleague (as early as 1958) to the notion of the atom of kinship I introduced in 1945 in an article (later to become the second chapter of the first volume of my book *Structural Anthropology*). Occupied by other tasks, I was able neither in 1958 nor in 1965 to pay his arguments the attention they deserved. But it is not too late, and the publication of *Pourquoi l'épouser?* gives me the opportunity to do so now. I will attempt to show that—except for a material inaccuracy which he pointed out to me and which I corrected (*S.A.*, p. 46, n. 48)—the objections made by Luc de Heusch rest on misunderstandings; and that they are also explained by the momentary

Chapter VII was originally published under the title "Réflexions sur l'atome de parenté," in *L'Homme, revue française d'anthropologie*, XIII, No. 3 (1973), pp. 5–30.

omission of a fundamental rule of structural analysis which, in other circumstances, he knows very well how to use. The rule is that the analysis can never consider the terms only but must, beyond the terms, apprehend their interrelations. These alone constitute its true object.

What was the purpose of my 1945 article? The point was to show—*contrary* to Radcliffe-Brown and most of the ethnologists of his generation—that even the simplest structure can never be constructed from the biological family made up of a father, a mother, and their children, but that it always implies a marriage relationship. This last relationship stems from a practically universal fact of human societies. For a man to obtain a wife, she must be directly or indirectly given to him by another man who, in the simplest cases, is posited as father or brother. This double contingency alone would have sufficed to show that the maternal uncle of children produced by the marriage (that is, the brother of the woman initially given away) appeared in my diagrams because he had the position of wife-giver, and not because of his particular place in a genealogy. This was further shown in a later text: "We reduce the kinship structure to the simplest conceivable element, the atom of kinship, if I may say so, when we have a group consisting of a husband, a woman, a representative of the group which has given the woman to the man . . . and one offspring" (*Conference of Anthropologists and Linguists*, Bloomington, Indiana, 1952; *S.A.*, p. 72). Far from maintaining, as Leach does (1961, p. 56) that a girl's matrimonial fate is always and everywhere controlled by her agnates, I showed in *The Elementary Structures of Kinship* (1969a, pp. 261–262, 301–304, 436–437) that this control often falls to her mother's brother, thus to the representative of a matrilineal tree. This phenomenon—the structural meaning and the full significance of which I had also brought out—was later described in Australia by several authors (Meggitt, Hiatt, and Shapiro) who believed it to be something new; and it was even said (Shapiro 1969, pp. 71–75) to be the means to separate the Australian systems completely from those of Southeast Asia, where I had, however, first spotted it.

Even in societies where the marriage control falls to the agnates, it is conceivable for the wife's father to assume it instead of her brother (or a more distant relative if the system is more complex than those we have chosen to support the demonstration) precisely because of the very simple structure which can be seen in some societies. The existence of such simple structures, immediately resulting in formalized attitudes between brother and sister, husband and wife, father and son, maternal uncle and nephew—paired attitudes which can be expressed by two positive relations and two negative relations—all this constituted a number of particularly strong arguments in support of the thesis. In the framework of an article, these examples seemed to be sufficient. But I expressly reserved the case of more complex systems, and asked that in each particular case two hypotheses be considered: "First, one in which the kinship system operates through the simple juxtaposition of elementary structures, and where the avuncular relationship therefore remains constantly apparent; second, a hypothesis in which the building blocks of the system are already of a more complex order. . . . In this type of structure, the avuncular relationship . . . is no longer the predominant one. In structures of still greater complexity, the avunculate may be obliterated or may merge with other relationships" (*S.A.*, pp. 48–49).

What I suggested calling the atom of kinship (i.e., the quadrangular system of relationships between brother and sister, husband and wife, father and son, maternal uncle and nephew) was thus in my mind the most easily conceivable and at times the most easily observable structure. But I carefully anticipated other structures, deriving with some transformations from the simplest one. It is, to pursue the metaphor, a little like the atom of hydrogen (the simplest observable one in the physical world because it is composed of a single electron gravitating around a single proton) which does not preclude the existence of heavier atoms, which are recognized as such under the sole condition that their particles be of the same nature and that the same links exist between them.

Two reasons led me to consider from the start a rudimentary structure. First, it alone was implied by the problem of the avunculate, as Radcliffe-Brown had formulated it and as I intended to argue it. Second, in a larger perspective, this structure made it possible to articulate in the most economical way possible the three constituent kinship relations: "a relation of consanguinity, a relation of affinity, and a relation of filiation" (*S.A.*, p. 46).[1] These relations must always be present, but the terms they unite may change or multiply. Yet, from the three examples invoked by Luc de Heusch, I would say that the first one (the Lambumbu example) is not conclusive; and that if it is, it confirms rather than weakens my thesis. As for the other two (taken from the Mundugomor and the Lele), they illustrate those complex cases which I certainly had not forgotten. It is then particularly interesting to try and find out whether and how the atom of kinship can be constructed for these societies and the fundamental properties I had set forth be respected.

As Luc de Heusch (1958, p. 234) points out, little is known of the Lambumbu, a population who live in the centre of Malekula Island, in the New Hebrides. The indications left by Deacon are so summary that the case cannot be easily discussed. However, it can be admitted as a first approximation and in agreement with Luc de Heusch, that "the father-son relationship is familiar, since the son may disobey his father, while the maternal uncle-nephew relationship is rigid, the latter owing obedience to the former" (Heusch 1958, p. 236). The difficulty starts with the attempt to qualify, in their reciprocal relationship, the prevailing attitudes between brother and sister, on the other hand, and husband and wife, on the other.

We freely concede that the brother-sister relationship is a negative one. Deacon contrasts the reserve imposed on these siblings with the familiar friendliness observable among the Seniang, in the south. A Lambumbu does not enter a house in which his sister is alone: he speaks to her from the door. It would not be thought proper for a brother and a sister to go about together. Should they walk along a path in each other's company, they are uneasy and afraid to be observed. Yet, the brother is, to a certain extent, responsible for his sister and, in the event of the father's death, it is he who must arrange her marriage (Deacon 1934, pp. 101–102).

This being so, the behavior between husband and wife will have the value of a test. If, as is maintained, it is also negative, the system I postulated is not applicable since it requires two pairs of attitudes, positive and negative, respectively, whose relation of correlation and opposition keeps the structure in balance. But, before going any further, we must open a parenthesis.

By reproaching me with rigging up relationships often tinged with ambivalence in negative or positive signs Luc de Heusch (1958, p. 236–237) ignores the same warnings which I had myself given: "The positive and negative symbols . . . represent an over-simplification, useful only as a part of the demonstration. . . . In many systems the relationship between two individuals is often expressed not by a single attitude, but by several attitudes which together form, as it were, a 'bundle' of attitudes" (*S.A.*, p. 49). Here as elsewhere, the contents which can be assigned to such and such an attitude are less important than the relations of opposition discernible between coupled pairs of attitudes. What these attitudes are in themselves, the affective contents they mask, does not have, from the particular point of view of our argument, any intrinsic meaning. In the extreme case, we would not even need to know what these contents are. It would be enough to perceive among them, directly or indirectly, a relation of opposition which the signs "+" and "–" would be enough to connote.

Yet, among the Lambumbu, a very clear opposition is seen between the brother-sister relationship and the husband-wife relationship. We know that the first is characterized by a reserve such that brother and sister fear to be seen together. We can say, with Luc de Heusch, that the husband and wife relationship is also negative, on the basis of the husband's violent jealousy, on the one hand, and on the other hand, of a name taboo between spouses (less strict however among the Lambumbu than among the Seniang). But the conjugal relation is especially marked by a *lack of reserve* and this is the manner in which it forms, with the brother-sister relation, an oppositional pair. A young woman in love with a man can make the first step by sending her father or her brother to get the feel of things through the sister of that man. If the woman is a widow, the intermediary becomes unnecessary; the advances are then up to the interested parties.

Some men have such strong feelings for one or two women that they refuse to have other wives. Even in the case of numerous wives, one of them is described as being "close up" to her husband. If he is polygamous, he must share himself equally among all his wives. Should he neglect one, she would wreak her wrath on him by telling everyone that there is no lack of men who can satisfy her. Wives are passionately jealous of one another and are not afraid of venting their disputes in public. Nor is it unusual for a husband to make a fool of himself in a fit of obsessive jealousy and draw down on himself the raillery of his friends (Deacon 1934, pp. 103–104, 159–171). The relations between spouses are thus dominated by a strong reciprocal jealousy, which they exhibit on any pretext and without the slightest discretion. "A wife will not infrequently beat her husband's genitals with the very painful leaves of the nettle-tree if he is remiss in doing his duty by her" (Deacon 1934, p. 170; and not "whip her own genitals . . . as a sign of protest," Heusch 1958, p. 235).

We can see that the brother-sister relationship can be defined by a great reserve, and the husband-wife relationship by a total lack of reserve. As for the two other relationships, which are established between men, they are qualified by rigidity in one case, and absence of rigidity in the other, or by reciprocal dependence or independence. These latter characteristics correspond best to Deacon's description: "A boy has the privilege of appropriating his maternal uncle's goods for his own needs during the lifetime of the latter; in return, he owes him strict obedience. Contrary to the practice of the Seniangs, a man is more or less free to obey or disobey his father, but the commands of his mother's brother are law. Thus, should the latter say to his nephew, 'Come, let us go and fight,' the boy will go with him, even though his father should forbid him to do so. If the father were determined to prevent his boy going off with his wife's brother, he would have to use drastic methods. On the other hand, were the father to tell his son to join him in a fight, and the maternal uncle to forbid him to go, the lad would desist and stay at home. But although a man owes great obedience to his mother's brother, their relations are those of mutual friendship, rather than of authority, on the one hand, and subservience, on the other. The attitude of the nephew is that though his uncle must be obeyed, he is at the same time a "good sport" (Deacon 1934, p. 101).

So it appears that, in the emotional register, the relationship between brother and sister is to the relationship between husband and wife as—perhaps in another emotional register (although it is not certain that they differ)—the relationship between father and son is to the relationship between maternal uncle and nephew. With the reservations already drawn up to keep us from hasty simplifications, the system of attitudes can be represented by the diagram in Figure 1 in keeping with the initial hypothesis:

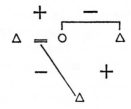

FIGURE 1

The case of the Mundugomor of the Yuat River, an affluent of the Sepik in northwestern New Guinea, presents other problems. According to Luc de Heusch, the brother-sister, husband-wife, father-son relationships would all be negative, the only positive one being the relationship between maternal uncle and nephew. However, one has only to follow step by step the descriptions given by the admirable field ethnographer Margaret Mead to note that the Mundugomor illustrate the case of one of these complex structures of which—precisely with them in mind (*S.A.*, p. 41, n. 30—I foresaw the possibility: adding the father's sister to his left and distinguishing according to sex the child produced by the marriage in the following generation (*S.A.*, p. 48), at the same time as the grandparents appear in the previous generation. It is only when the total structure is considered—instead of its being mutilated in order to reduce it—that its architecture appears and its features come out clearly.

We know that the Mundugomor have an original system of descent. A man belongs to the same line (the Mundugomor say "rope") as his mother, his mother's father, his mother's father's mother, etc., while a woman belongs to the same line as her father, her father's mother, her father's mother's father, etc. In other words, the descent rule is matrilineal for the boys, patrilineal for the girls, and brother and sister have different genealogical statuses. Consequently, particularly intimate ties prevail between the father and his daughter on the one hand, and the mother and her son on the other, to the extent that each parent can sleep with the child of the opposite sex in the mosquito-proof basket in which every Mundugomor spends the night.

Normally, marriage is by exchange. The mother, bound to her son, sees her daughter as the means of providing him with a wife. But, as the father wishes to keep his daughters to obtain by exchange supplementary wives for himself, an acute feeling of rivalry, bordering on hostility, arises between him and his son—a feeling which the mother stirs up in her remarks to her son. The same rivalry exists between brothers as each tries to monopolize his sisters to provide wives for himself. In such a system, consequently, brother and sister feel separated from each other from childhood; the son also feels separated from his father, and the daughter from her mother. As for the husband and wife, they harbor contradictory designs on the future of their children, which find expression in the efforts that each exerts in exciting in the child of the opposite sex (but who is directly linked to him by the rule of descent) feelings of distrust toward the other parent.

On the other hand, a boy has a cordial relationship with his mother's brother, with whom he takes refuge in the event of conflict with his father. So, in opposition to several negative relationships—between father and son, mother and daughter, brother and sister, husband and wife—it seems that, with the exception of the mother and son, and father and daughter relationships which had no place in our first diagrams, one can only bring forth a single positive relationship: between maternal uncle and nephew. But, with this type of reasoning, other relationships would be neglected which Margaret Mead's descriptions have pointed out and which cannot be overlooked.

In the first place, the relationship between maternal uncle and nephew does not present a strictly normative character. "Between a boy and his mother's brother there are often friendly relations. It is true that he does not belong to either the same rope as his mother's brother or the same land-owning group. But the mother's brother is always willing to shelter his nephew if the boy gets into trouble with his father" (Mead 1950, p. 132). This occasional solidarity stems from the tension between the brothers-in-law: "Giving his nephew help against the latter's father is congruent with the other attitudes of the mother's brother. A boy's own mother's brother is felt to be a very close relative, so close that he will perform the scarification ceremony without pay" (Mead 1950, p. 132).

The relation between maternal uncle and nephew is a derivative one. It is of the same type, but not as clear-cut as the one which sometimes exists between the maternal uncle and his niece: "Sometimes a man who has several sons and no daughters, and a wife who is unwilling to adopt daughters, will bespeak the child of a sister by undertaking part of its care. Under the influence of the theory that girls are very difficult to obtain, this petition for a sister's child is usually made before birth. The petitioner then sends food regularly to the pregnant woman, but the child turns out to be the wrong sex half of the time and the father of sons finds himself in the uncomfortable position of having assumed a quasi-paternal responsibility for still another boy" (Mead 1950, p. 138).

It will be at once noted that this boy, who at birth spoils his uncle's hopes and is for him, in a way, a disaster, is none other than his sister's son, this very nephew with whom under normal circumstances he has a friendly relationship. Nothing demonstrates better that this relationship has a subsidiary place in comparison with the one existing between a maternal uncle and his "reserved" niece, since she will be as his daughter and since the ties between father and daughter are the most intimate ones known to a Mundugomor. In this system, the relationship maternal uncle–sister's daughter is thus of the same type as the relationship maternal uncle–nephew, but offers more possibilities than the latter.

Secondly, the relationship of the uncle and the nephew can be inscribed in the system only if the system also features the relationship with the father's sister, which the ethnographic description puts on exactly the same plane: "A Mundugumor child is taught that everyone who is related to it as mother's brother, father's sister, sister's child of a male, brother's child of a female, and their spouses, is a joking relative with whom one engages in roughhouse, accusations of unusual and inappropriate conduct, threats, mock bullying, and the like" (Mead 1950, p. 143, cf. also p. 146). The parallelism between father's sister and mother's brother is further reinforced by the fact that, in the previously considered case when, before her birth, a man reserves his sister's daughter in view of making her his own daughter, his consenting wife will be the sister of this girl's father if—as is theoretically the rule among the Mundugomor—the marriages have resulted from a sister exchange between the two men. We have seen that the true maternal uncle makes the ritual scarifications upon the person of his nephew without claiming the considerable payments that are the rule when the officient is a more distant relative. The father's sister fulfills a parallel function for her nephew and niece, as it is her responsibility in the course of a ceremony to break the food taboos imposed on children until they are about two years old (Mead 1950, p. 141).[2]

Finally, neither can one neglect Margaret Mead's testimony on the particularly close bonds existing between distant members of the same "rope," that is, from father's mother to female grandchild, and from mother's father to male grandchild. Each of these grandchildren bears the name of his grandparent in the same rope. He is "socially identical" with him; and each, when addressing members of his own generation, uses the same kinship terms as his ascendant would. The system of terminology takes on a cyclical form: it makes a loop every three generations. The father's mother and the mother's father thus have their place marked in the Mundugomor atom of kinship, as well as the father's sister opposite the mother, and the daughter opposite the son. One ends up with Figure 2.

In this diagram, the vertical and horizontal links are all nega-

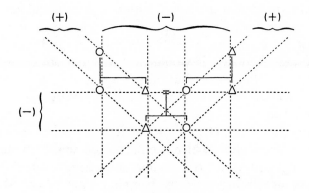

FIGURE 2

tive: from father to son, from mother to daughter for the former; from brother to sister, from husband to wife, from brother-in-law to brother-in-law for the latter. Conversely, all the oblique links are positive: the ones corresponding to the ropes which go from father's mother to son's daughter, and from mother's father to daughter's son; and also those which, without being ropes, link the father's sister to the brother's son, and the mother's brother to the sister's daughter. Furthermore, we have seen that the latter two can come closer together and, in extreme cases, merge, since the maternal uncle has the right to retain his yet unborn niece to serve him as daughter, and the father's sister performs the rites for lifting the food taboo on both her niece and nephew. We have also seen that the maternal uncle himself, wishing to act as a father to his niece if he does not himself have a daughter, performs the scarification rites on his nephew free of charge. He also has an affectionate relationship with him, a weaker counterpart of the feelings he has toward the boy's sister when she becomes his daughter.

This manner of analyzing and representing the system offers two advantages. First, the Mundugomor descent rule, said to be "teratological and aberrant" (Heusch 1958, p. 240–241), becomes clearer when it is placed in a global structure where it forms a logical and coherent whole with the system of attitudes. It does this also with the other Mundugomor rule according to which marriage can only take place between individuals belonging to the same age set (Mead 1950, p. 145). This is indispensable if the straight links are to remain always distinct from the oblique links. In the last analysis, it is on the opposition between these two types of links that the economy of the system rests, for attitudes as well as for descent. (Actually, it would be enough to know whether two related individuals are situated on a straight line or on an oblique line to determine the fundamentally positive or negative character of their relationship.)

Second, the interpretation proposed here makes it possible to transcend this dualism which would be too simple in the case of the Mundugomor, and to account immediately for the three types of attitudes distinguished by Margaret Mead: "The Mundugumor divide the kin up into those persons with whom one jokes, those whom one avoids in shame, and those whom one treats with varying shades of ordinary intimacy" (1950, p. 142). We know that these last feelings prevail between members of the same rope and that the distant reserve expresses tension (which can go as far as hostility) that characterizes belonging to straight links. This is the case with siblings and brothers-in-law, but also with husband and wife, father and son, and mother and daughter.

What about the third type? As we have seen, it covers the relation between nephew and niece, on the one hand, and father's sister or mother's brother, on the other; that is to say, relatives united by oblique links like the ropes to which these links are parallel without being themselves ropes. They are pseudo-ropes, as it were, if one considers only their formal properties. From this point of view, they occupy an intermediate place—as do the attitudes corresponding to them—between the true ropes and the rectangular links. One could then call the latter antiropes since they imply attitudes diametrically opposed to those existing between members of the same rope.

One single difficulty seems to stand in the way of our interpretation. Two women whom their brothers have exchanged as respective wives are united by a horizontal link. However, a certain intimacy exists between them: "They are spoken of as the 'return' one of the other, and there is no emphasis upon rivalry or injury, as there is so often between brothers-in-law." (Mead 1950, p. 147–148). This particular case would then be an exception to the native theory, according to which "a natural hostility . . . exists between all members of the same sex" (p. 127). It would also contradict the rule, illustrated by Figure 2, which affects all horizontal relationships with a negative coefficient.

Two remarks are in order at this point. First, no system is ever strictly symmetrical for both sexes since, in every society, their respective positions are not commutative. Margaret Mead herself notes (1950, p. 147–148) that, among the Mundugomor, the relations between women are on the whole less difficult than the relations between men. Next and most important, the rapport established between two women exchanged by their brothers derives from two types of previous relationships: those between brother and sister, on the one hand, and, on the other, those between men who, through sister exchange, have become each other's brother-in-law. Furthermore, these two types of relation are negative and it is conceivable that, as in arithmetic, their product take a positive value. Anyway, here one goes beyond the limits of the elementary structure envisaged in its synchronic dimension. The same is true—reascending the temporal axis (since one is then placed before the conclusion of the alliance and not afterward)—if one takes into account the grossly scatological jokes that a young bachelor exchanges with his classificatory "sisters," that is, first or second cousins whom in theory he cannot marry (Mead 1950, p. 146).

All the preceding considerations suggest that, in a periodical table of kinship systems and attitudes, the Mundugomor would illustrate the case of a "heavy" atom. However, this atom continues to fulfill the three conditions required by our initial hypothesis: (1) that an elementary kinship structure rest on an alliance relation to the same extent as on consanguine relations; (2) that the content of the avuncular relation is independent from the rule of descent; and (3) in the midst of this structure, that the attitudes which are opposed to one another (and which can thus, to simplify, be called positive or negative) form a balanced whole.

Let us now consider a third example: that of the Lele of the Kasai, studied by Mary Douglas. Luc de Heusch feels that, like the previous ones, this example fails to verify the thesis I had put forward: "The Lele kinship system yields three negative relationships (brother/sister; father/son; maternal uncle/sister's son) against one single positive relationship (husband/wife). The only positive masculine relationship is situated outside the kinship elements: it establishes a solidarity and a relation of great familiarity between the grandfather and the grandson" (Heusch 1971, p. 20).

We will easily agree that the brother-sister relationship is negative, on the basis on Mary Douglas's observations: "A woman had to learn to avoid her brothers, not to stay in the same hut with them, not to speak to them face to face, to place their food respectfully on the ground near them, not to touch them" (Douglas 1963, p. 124). We will also admit that the husband-wife relationship is positive: "There was nothing uncertain or ambiguous about the relations of husband and wife. Lele recognized that their cooperation laid the basis for all social life. They would speak approvingly of a happy couple that 'they had made their marriage well'. . . . Husband and wife were bound to stay with one another in sickness as well as in health. To care for one another in illness was one of the major responsibilities of marriage" (1963, pp. 120–121).

On the other hand, the affirmation that the father-son relation is negative seems singularly hazardous when one reads this description given by Mary Douglas, which I quote in full to rule out any suspicion of my having—quite unnecessarily—twisted the meaning of her text:

> Between Lele father and son there is a close personal tie. The talk of young men and boys suggests a highly emotional attitude to their fathers. Orphaned men love to recall their father's companionship and teaching. They have no word which correspond to "respect" as Professor Radcliffe-Brown uses it. *Heki* is to show honor, and it is significant that it is supposed to be a reciprocal attitude between father and son. Each honors the other, with generosity and consideration. This close tie between father and son is supposed to endure throughout life. In the father's old age, the son has a duty to live with and cherish him, and this duty conflicts effectively with the interest which the boy has in joining his mother's brothers, who can pay blood compensation for his crimes and allocate him a wife. It is remarkable how many men do not leave their natal village to join their maternal uncles until after the father's death. Whatever light discipline the father may have exercised in the childhood of his son is sanctioned in adult life only by his power to curse his disobedient child. There is no other ritual sanction he can employ, and no way of desinheriting or otherwise enforcing his authority over his grown son" (Douglas 1952, p. 61–62).

Further on, the author underlines "the conspicuous lack of strict discipline from the parents' generation. . . . There is little enough [authority] displayed by the father over his young children and still less when they are adult" (p. 62). According to Mary Douglas, this relation is one of tenderness and indulgence on the father's part, of love and reverence on the son's part; it contrasts radically with the relation prevailing between the sister's son and his maternal uncles:

> The authority which a group of mother's brothers have over a man has little to compare with the close intimacy of father and son. They wield important sanctions by their control of negotiations over blood debts and the allocating of wives, but their au-

thority is diffuse. Maternal uncles weaken their own solidarity by competing with each other in the disposal of brides to favorite nephews. A man may easily transfer his loyalty from one of his own mother's brothers to another or to a more distant clansman, since personal ties built up by common residence or mutual services and gifts count for more than strict genealogical relationship" (Douglas 1952, p. 62).

The author notes further that the preferential rights to marry women from other clans, transmitted from mother's brother to sister's son, are the best illustration among the Lele of what elsewhere would be called successorial right (p. 64).

What comes out of these analyses is that the attitudes between father and son on the one hand, and maternal uncle and nephew, on the other, are diametrically opposed; and that the Lele kinship element, were it reduced to the brother, the sister, the husband, the wife, the father, and the son, would manifest in the most simple and typical manner a well-known system of attitudes in matrilineal societies: negative between sister and brother, positive between husband and wife, positive between father and son, and negative between maternal uncle and nephew. In these societies, as we have just seen with the Lele, it is the men from the mother's clan who have jurisdiction over their sister's sons, who are members of their clan.

The situation being such, how can Luc de Heusch have defined the system in a very different manner? It is because he has paid special attention to other aspects, which Mary Douglas did not bring to the fore in her 1952 article, but which are brought to light in the book she published in 1963.

As far as the father-son relationship is concerned, however, her book confirms her earlier article. Witness the following passages: "They [the Lele] rhapsodized about what a man should do for his father, what a father should do for his son" (p. 73). And further: "Lele honored fatherhood. Boys were taught: 'Your father is like God' . . . that the debt which they owed him for his care of them in infancy was unrepayable, immeasurable" (p. 114). But the author adds a detail to the picture: "It was very shameful for a man to show disrespect to his father. Fathers were expected to avoid their grown sons, so that the latter should not feel bowed down with the burden of respect" (p. 114). This indication is corroborated by another remark: "*Cin*, to avoid, was the way to show respect. A man had to avoid his elder brothers and, by implication, his younger brothers too, his mother's brother, his father, and his wife's father, mother, and mother's brother. It was a serious injunction" (p. 103).

It seems that Luc de Heusch's affirmation that the father-son relationship is negative overlooks the observations to the contrary which we have first noted. It rests only on the last two passages quoted in the preceding paragraph.[3] Admittedly, it is not much, but they must not be overlooked either. Before coming back to it, we must look into other considerations which could lead to the same interpretation.

In her 1952 article, Mary Douglas stresses the special position of maternal uncles as wife-givers. Some examples have already been referred to. Nevertheless, from a passage (p. 64) explaining that a man gives the women for whom he has a preferential right "to one of his sisters' sons," i.e., clan juniors ("clan juniors" is opposed on the same page to "senior clansmen"), it turns out that the author does not mean—by the terms "mother's brother," "sister's son"—to designate exclusively the holders of certain genealogical positions. Probably following the native usage, she designates in a looser manner males belonging to different age sets in the same clan. The 1963 book is all the more explicit in this respect in that it denies the true maternal uncle's ability (in practice) to give a wife to the sister's son. In effect, Lele men get married on the average some fifteen or twenty years later than their sisters, which brings about a clear discrepancy between the age of men and women belonging to the same age set: ". . . a man could claim by right his daughter's daughter. He could marry her himself if he wished . . . or he could give her to his brother . . . or to his sister's daughter's son. He was not supposed to give her to his own sister's son, although the latter might occasionally be allowed to inherit her as a widow. In the old days, before monogamous Christian marriage had restricted the range of possible partners, a man could hardly have hoped to marry a girl as close to his own age as his mother's brother's daughter" (p. 115). Anyway, it comes out clearly from the context that, in marriage exchanges, it is not the boy's mother's brother, but his mother's mother's brother who plays a determinant role. Thus it is surprising that

Luc de Heusch can write that "the only positive masculine relationship . . . establishes a solidarity and a relation of great familiarity between the grandfather and the grandson" (1971, p. 20). He should have added, "and between the mother's mother's brother and the sister's daughter's son," which would have shown the way to a solution.

In effect, Mary Douglas gives this relationship as an example of those existing between relatives who have a reciprocal intimacy and treat each other as equals: "So the relation of a man to his old mother's mother's brother was treated in kinship terminology as if they were in one sense brothers, in another sense, age-mates. The child calling his mother's mother's brother 'my big brother' did not have to avoid him as he would have avoided an elder brother. He could call him *mbai*, "age-mate" (1963, p. 104), the term connoting one of the most warm and intimate relationships known to the Lele (p. 73).

On what basis could one reduce the kinship element always and everywhere to the simplest forms it may take in certain societies? Contrary to what some have chosen to understand, we have never suggested that these simple forms were universal, but only that they appear often enough to give significance to their recurrence (*S.A.*, p. 39; Lévi-Strauss 1972a). Our critics fail to appreciate that the element of kinship, as we have described it, does not consist in *positions* defined once and for all, but in a system of *relations* which alone is pertinent. The choice of the maternal uncle (brother of the father's wife) is justified when it allows for the definition of the function of wife-giver with the greatest economy of means. There is no reason to want to have recourse to it with the Lele, where the maternal uncle cannot play this role—incumbent not on him but on the mother's mother's brother in whose benefit the avunculate is reestablished.

Thus we will first seek to entrench the mother's mother's brother firmly in his position as a wife-giver. This function is somewhat obscured by two orders of fact. Firstly, there are among the Lele two types of takers; and secondly, each of these takers can play on three different marriage formulae. According to Mary Douglas's striking formula, the whole philosophy of life of the Lele rests upon a postulated identity: wife, life (1963, p. 36). For this ostensibly matrilineal people, the birth of a daughter, who will later give birth to other daughters, ensures the perpetuation of the clan. Consequently, if a man married to a woman of the clan has a daughter, he will have the right to claim the daughter born to that daughter for his own clan. The same privilege exists for the benefit of the father who has the right to claim his daughter, not for his clan, but for his father's.

One may wonder why the Lele formulate these two rival claims so differently. In one case, they leave it to the mother's father to claim her directly for his own clan, and in the other case to the daughter's own father, who acts not on behalf of his clan but of his father's clan, to which he himself does not belong. There are two reasons for this, one practical and one theoretical.

In the first place, the father is on the spot. But this is not necessarily the case with the father's father because of the great freedom of residence, patrilocal in theory, commonly practiced among the Lele (Douglas 1963, p. 88). In the second place, and in particular, the two claims cannot be put on the same footing. Only in the first case can the argument be fully applied according to which a man who gave a daughter to his wife's clan can claim another daughter of that clan (in the present case his granddaughter) for the benefit of his own clan. Logically, the father could only make the same claim on his second daughter. He has already given one and claims another; the first daughter appears all the less claimable in that she is the juridical cause of a subsequent claim. But as the man acts in this case on behalf of the clan of his father, paternal grandfather of the young woman, it can be said that the true taker is the father's father, as, in the first case, the taker was officially the mother's father. The two grandfathers are thus the wife-takers among the Lele.

But we have seen that they can dispose in either of three ways of these women who are their granddaughters. They can either marry them themselves, or give them to a younger brother, or again to their sister's daughter's son, a member of their clan and of the same age set as the girl to be married. If, as everywhere else, the relation of wife-giver to wife-taker is an integral part of the element of kinship, these three types of marriage must be reduced to a single one in order that the position of giver be defined without ambiguity.

The first type seems to have become the most rare (Douglas 1963, p. 118). But there is an even better reason to eliminate it from the system. A maternal grandfather cannot have a granddaughter if he has not first had a daughter and he cannot have a daughter if he is not already married. However, this marriage must necessarily be of another type than the one with a grand-daughter, otherwise one would be locked in a circle. No doubt the same argument does not apply to the second type, where the grandfather foregoes his privilege for a younger brother. But, from a structural point of view, the latter occupies in the system the same position as his elder brother, in virtue of the principle of sibling equivalence, well known in kinship theory, and accord-ing to which a single position suffices to represent all the brothers or all the sisters, except in the sometimes verified hypothesis where the distinction of siblings into older and younger implies for all of them, or for a third party, different marital statuses. This cannot be the case when the younger brother contracts the same type of marriage as the one renounced in his favor by his elder brother. On the formal plane, which alone interests us here, the second type of marriage is thus reducible to the first, which logic has already led us to eliminate, so that, to give a schematic representation of the system, the third type alone ap-pears to be pertinent.

Having admitted this much, we will get back to the problem set by Luc de Heusch's interpretation. As we have said, it over-looks the indications, although very meaningful, in support of an intimate and warm relationship between father and son, and only retains from Mary Douglas's analyses two brief references to mutual avoidance. Coming from an observer of the caliber of Mary Douglas, these indications cannot contradict each other; so they must complement each other, and they do so all the more clearly in that they correspond to succeeding phases of individual life.

The first data we have used oppose the attitude toward the father to the attitude toward the mother's brothers; the second data oppose the attitude (apparently inverted from positive into negative) toward the father to the attitude toward the mother's mother's brother. This at a time when the great-nephew/great-uncle relationship predominates over that of nephew-uncle, be-cause the young man has become an adult and is interested in obtaining a wife, whom he can only expect from the former (the latter being as we have seen excluded as potential wife-giver). One would then be in the presence of two "activating states" of the system, one corresponding to Ego's childhood and youth, of a strictly classical type, and the other, which manifests itself when Ego reaches the age of marriage constituting a transformation of the previous one, illustrated by Figure 3.

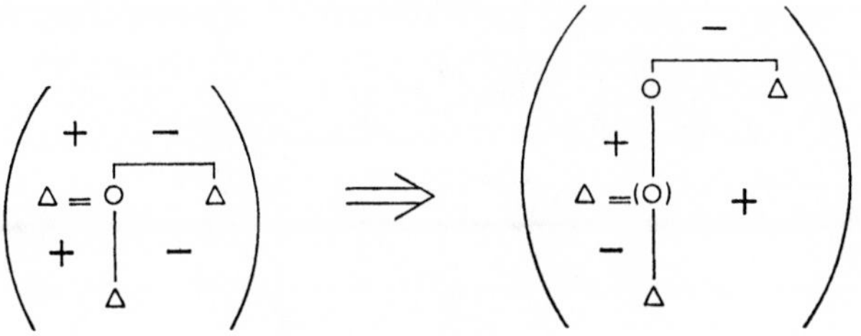

FIGURE 3

In the course of this transformation, the positive father-son relationship becomes negative, while the negative relationship between sister's son and mother's brother gives way to a positive relationship between sister's daughter's son and mother's mother's brother, who is still a "maternal uncle," but one generation removed. Concerning the Ashanti, Meyer Fortes (1949, pp. 54–84) has indeed shown how a structural model can develop in the course of the life of individuals, in function of the successive statuses each is called on to fill.

In the present case, the first state of the system presents no problem. It is thus to the second that we must direct our attention.

We have just seen that this state is characterized by a negative attitude between brother and sister, positive between husband and wife, negative between father and son, positive between mother's mother's brother and sister's daughter's son (Douglas 1963, pp. 52, 69, 88, 104, 120–121, 124).[4] The element of kinship remains comparable to those for which we noted the simplest forms prolonged vertically to cover two generations. This lengthening corresponds, in the case of the Lele, to the principle of antagonism between consecutive generations and solidarity between alternate ones. This principle is immediately observable at the level of village organization, that is, the members of generations I and III live side by side, and an imaginary diagonal separates them from the members of generations II and IV similarly grouped on the other side (pp. 78–79). The result is that the elements overlap and partly cover each other, and are always staggered from one generation to the next, a little like the tiles on a roof, as represented in Figure 4.

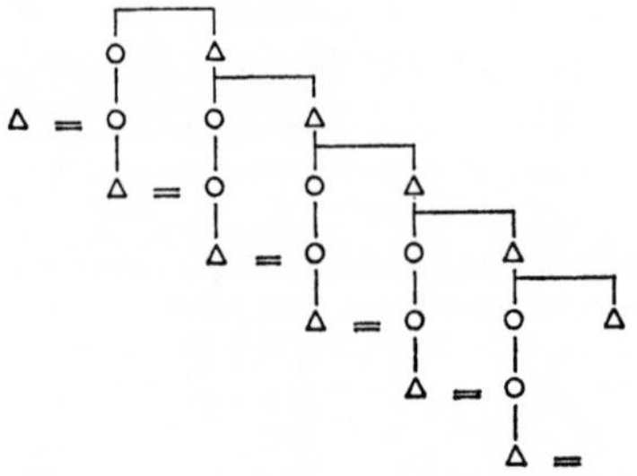

FIGURE 4

This is in the case where the taker, acting on behalf of his great-nephew, is the young girl's mother's father. As we have seen, a different case occurs when the girl's father acts as taker on behalf of his own father's clan. We have shown (p. 99) that this latter case cannot be put on the same footing as the former, but the diagram of Figure 5 shows that it does not contradict the former. The diagram has the same form, except that an additional link appears—due to the fact that this solution involves four clans instead of three—in the person of the father acting on behalf of a clan different from his own, and whose role is explained from the functional point of view.

These diagrams by no means exhaust the complexity of the system which Luc de Heusch made obvious, on the basis of Mary

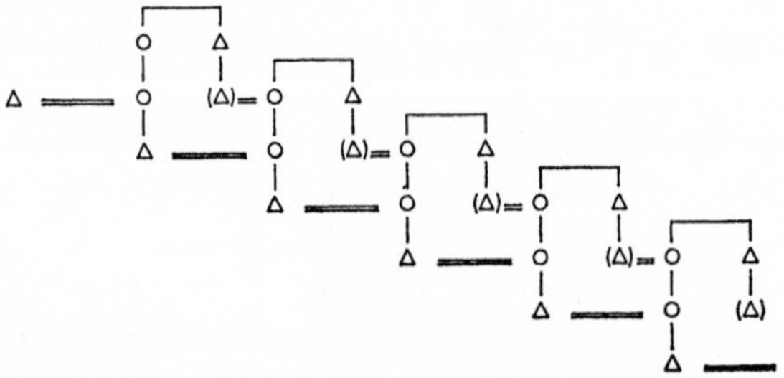

FIGURE 5

Douglas's indications. They simply attempt to show that a representation of the system based on the "atoms of kinship," to the exclusion of any other factor, does not contradict the given data in any way.

Thus, if someone were to object that diagrams do not regularly take into account matrilineal descent, we would first answer that we are only dealing with a scriptural simplification. Diagrams more scrupulous in this regard would be less easy to read, but their general appearance would be unchanged. Moreover, the liberty which we have taken is justified by our 1945 article (Chapter II of *S.A.*), which sought to prove that the mode of descent does not intervene in determining the structure of the element of kinship (*S.A.*, p. 41). In effect, this article attempted to show that the relationship with the maternal uncle stands out immediately in such a structure, apprehended in its simplest form, without the necessity of referring to a patrilineal or matrilineal rule of descent the way Radcliffe-Brown does. This is what Adler and Cartry seem to forget when they write: "Lévi-Strauss, while considering that filiation is irrelevant, nevertheless keeps it as a criterion to designate the systems which he takes as examples" (1971, p. 11). But, besides the fact that these rules of descent exist as objective properties of these systems, I had to put myself on the same ground as the authors I wanted to discuss (Lévi-Strauss 1972*a*). Likewise, Pierre Étienne declares in an otherwise very interesting article: "The concept of the atom of kinship elaborated by Lévi-Strauss, in spite of the confidence which its inner coherence could inspire, has not been much help to us for the interpretation of the concrete phenomena which we were facing" (1970, p. 35). He adds further on, in a footnote: "However, we entirely subscribe to Lévi-Strauss's point of view when he maintains that the maternal uncle is an immediate given of the structure of kinship and marriage" (p. 37, n. 5). But the only purpose of the notion of atom of kinship, a "false synthesis" according to Étienne, was to be of use in founding this affirmation, new at the time; one cannot help being delighted if some people refer to it now in passing, as a matter of course.

In the case of the Lele, it seems significant that the matrilineal links are not relevant—or that they are not regularly so—in giving an adequate representation of the marriage system, and we would like to end this study with some rapid considerations on this subject. If the preceding analyses are well founded, it means that Luc de Heusch has too narrow a conception of the Mundugomor and Lele systems. However, it may be that a double error is resting on a common truth, and that the same unduly restrictive interpretation of systems seemingly very different one from the other, could be explained by the fact that at a deeper level their properties are close enough to raise the same type of difficulties, thus inciting the too-hurried analyst to conclude by giving them the same false solution.

The reader will recall that the Mundugomor system implies particularly warm and intimate ties between father and daughter, on the one hand, mother and son, on the other. This is a consequence of an original mode of descent which puts in the same line or "rope" the father, the daughter, the daughter's son, the daughter's son's daughter, and so forth, and in another "rope" the mother, the son, the son's daughter, the son's daughter's son, and so forth.

We saw that with the Lele, warm and intimate ties also exist, but between father and son (see p. 95). Similarly, Mary Douglas points out the even closer ties existing between mother and daughter:

> A girl was supposed to have no secrets from her mother, and men would express amazement at their lack of reserve. Mother and daughter would go to the river together, see each other naked, scrub each other's backs; one might even ask the other to shave her head, pluck her eyebrows, anoint her, or administer an anal injection, intimate services which men of different generations could not conceive of performing for each other (1963, p. 126).

No doubt these attitudes only carry to the extreme those normally prevailing between sisters and, generally, among women: "Women spent most of their time with other women, and developed their strong emotional ties with their mothers, sisters, and daughters" (Douglas 1963, p. 124). On the other hand, these feminine attitudes were not exactly comparable to those prevailing between father and son who "honored" each other; or between brothers, also united by very strong ties founded, however, on the voluntary abstention of any type of rivalry "which might spoil their affection" (Douglas 1963, p. 100); on the responsibility of the elder one toward the younger, one to whom he owes aid in all occurrences; and on the respect of the younger for the elder one, which is manifested by presents of food and manufactured objects (p. 99). Masculine relations thus pertained to culture, feminine relations—at least in the eyes of the men—rather to nature: "The informality of their relations, which had an almost instinctive air about it, caused the men to marvel at women, and to compare them to animals because their behavior conspicuously lacked the formality shown between men, even men of the same family" (p. 126–127). Despite these differences, it remains that, among the Lele, the relations which were the most marked with emotion were those between father and son, on the one hand, and mother and daughter, on the other.

It is as if the Lele, who conceived their rule of descent according to a matrilineal mode, lived it in fact according to a different mode, that is, sentimentally uniting the son with the father in the same line, and the daughter with her mother in another line. This is a system symmetrical to that of the Mundugomor and, like it, characterized by the implicit or explicit recognition of two lines of descent, but in the form of two privileged filiations—one entirely feminine, the other entirely masculine. Among the Mundugomor, the sexes alternated in each line in the course of the generations. In practice, this duality was made manifest by the recognition of the father's patrilineal line to the same extent as that accorded the mother's matrilineal one. "The bilateral emphasis in Lele kinship flowed from the importance of fatherhood, a valve inevitable in a society of men competing for the control of women" (Douglas 1963, p. 114).

Let us now consider another aspect. Each Mundugomor man is supposed to obtain a wife only by exchanging his sister for another man's sister. "Theoretically," writes Margaret Mead, "there is no other way in which he can legally obtain a wife" (1950, p. 128). It is a condition reinforced even more by the theoretical rule that marriage can only take place between members of the same generation. The marriage exchanges thus run along a horizontal axis, as opposed to the Lele doctrine, which takes as a model the marriage with the daughter's daughter (based on the principle that a man who fathers a daughter and thus gives her to his wife's clan has the right to claim in return the daughter born to that daughter): "This custom of giving back girls to be married into the clan of their mother's father is a key institution of Lele society. . . . It is the institution of which they are most proud, and which they seek to honor whenever possible" (Douglas 1952, p. 64). In reverse to the Mundugomor custom, we are dealing here with an exchange taking place on the vertical axis (see Figure 6).

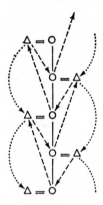

FIGURE 6

This is not all, for the Lele, whose marriage system theoretically rests on the vertical exchange, derive from it in practice a horizontal system of exchange. The maternal great-uncle most often yields his conjugal right on his granddaughter to his sister's daughter's son, that is; to a man who is an age-mate of the granddaughter. When the wife-taking grandfather is the father of the mother of the beneficiary, the marriage takes place between the sister's daughter's son and the daughter's daughter; when the grandfather is the father's father, the marriage takes place between the sister's daughter's son and the daughter's daughter. According to the formula of generalized rather than restricted exchange, these marriages are then in reality made by horizontal exchange at the level of cross-cousins' daughters and sons.

With the Mundugomor, where the sister's and the brother's belonging to separate lines always threatens to jeopardize the mechanism of exchanges, one observes a symmetrical reversal of the system, swinging this time from the horizontal to the vertical.

Margaret Mead (1950, p. 131) draws attention to a network of reciprocal obligations between the descendants of two brothers who have exchanged their sisters. The sister's son ritually scarified the grandson of the brother, who in turn scarified his scarificator's grandson and, at the fourth generation, the children issued from the two lines were supposed to marry (see Figure 7).

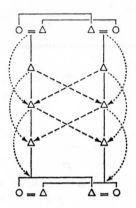

FIGURE 7

Although the system was too complicated to work in practice, it reconstitutes the model of the vertical exchange, for the right ritually to scarify a boy—also like the right to pierce a girl's ears, which was transmitted among women according to the same rule—involved considerable material advantages in the form of payment in pigs and in ornaments. To permit the comparison with the Lele marriage system, the common point we must remember is that between two lines already allied by a marriage, a duty rendered by one line in the generation following the one in which the marriage took place results in a similar duty rendered by the other line in the following generation. In the case of the Lele, this duty materializes in the begetting of daughters; in the case of the Mundugomor, it materializes, not in the begetting of sons, but in their initiation, which is a second birth. In both cases, this interweaving of obligations down a vertical axis brings about, on the horizontal axis, the periodical return of alliance between the two lines, renewing the initial alliance—every three generations among the Lele, every five among the Mundugomor. On the whole, the Lele opposition between consecutive generations and alternate generations is similar to the opposition formulated by the Mundugomor in terms, if one may say so, of "consecutive sexes" and "alternate sexes."

One could pick up other points of comparison between the two societies, consisting sometimes of similarities and sometimes of contrasts. The Mundugomor had no clans, and those of the Lele offered no consistency: "an amorphous collection of individuals who never assembled or took common action of any kind. Its members did not know each other" (Douglas 1963, p. 85). In both cases, the unit of residence—village or hamlet—provided the only basis of social organization. There was no clan-centered cult among the Lele and no local cult among the Mundugomor.

Both societies had a system founded on the identification of alternate generations and the opposition of consecutive generations. Here and there, names repeated themselves every other generation (Mead 1950, p. 144; Douglas 1952, p. 63). In these circumstances, and taking into account our remarks on the rule of descent, officially characterized by the alternation of man and woman in each "rope" among the Mundugomor and—in an implicit or at least embryonic manner—on the continuous succession of men in one line and of women in the other line among the Lele, one may wonder whether the principle of alternate generations is not, here and there, structurally linked to a mode of filiation which in both cases assigns different statuses to the brother and the sister. Indeed, it is to the principle of alternate generations that the two lines owe their ability to rejoin each other periodically, even if it is only to cross each other before diverging until some future return. With regard to this, the Mundugomor and the Lele would essentially differ in the great functional efficiency of the kinship system for the former, while for the latter—as Mary Douglas repeatedly points out—"the kinship organization is weak and unstable, suffering competition from other forms of social grouping" (1952, p. 61; cf. p. 64, where "the weaknesses of the kinship structures" is stressed). The same author also insists on "a complete lack of interest in genealogical reckoning and a general ignorance of the relations among members of the grandparents' or even the parents' generation" (p. 62). It is hardly surprising, then, that a system with so little effectiveness, where three possible types of marriage make the noticeable kinship bonds between two individuals so complicated as to be practically un-resognizable (Douglas 1963, p. 112), does not respond well to efforts of formalization.

On the other hand, the possible correlation between the principle of alternate generations and the attribution of different statuses to siblings of both sexes ought to be thoroughly examined. One knows that this latter phenomenon was given the name of "sex affiliation" by F. E. Williams, to whom credit must be given for identifying it as an original institution among the Idutu-bia of the Gulf of Papua, where its distinctive characteristics are far from clearly manifest. The notion of the alternate generation remains very clouded, because of the past tendency to extend it to all the systems which apply the same kinship term to individuals occupying symmetrical positions and separated by two or three generations. However, it does not seem that this notion is applicable to the Dobu kinship terminology, which also goes along with a marriage prohibition between cross cousins. The fact that all the masculine and feminine members of the second generation, ascending and descending, are called by the same term *tubuna*, seems to signal only one limit of the system. It is the point at which terminological distinctions cease to be relevant, without it resulting that the grandchildren and grandparents are held to be "socially identical" (as in the Mundugomor), or that the grand-father appears again mystically in the person of his grandson, or the grandmother in the person of her granddaughter, in the absence noted by Fortune (1963, p. 127) of beliefs related to reincarnation. The same can be said about the Kapauku kinship system, where special terms group together, respectively, the relatives of the fourth, third, and second generations in ascending or descending order (Pospisil 1959–1960). It is not a question of alternate generations, but of a representation of kinship, having the form of concentric circles in relation to Ego.

On the other hand, alternate generations and sex affiliation seem structurally linked in Brazil, among the populations of the Gé linguistic family. The Kayapo have a complex system of transmitting proper names, attributed by the grandfather or the mother's brother to the grandson or maternal nephew, and by the grandmother to the granddaughter or paternal niece. Further-more, the morphemes that go into the making of the term *tab-djuò*, designating among others the sister's children and the grand-children, seem to imply that these individuals are socially identical to the speaker (Turner 1966, pp. 170–176 and Appendix II, p. xxxv). The Timbira, who alternate age sets on an East-West axis, give names of the paternal line to the girls, and names of the maternal line to the boys (Nimuendaju 1946, pp. 78, 90–91). Among the Apinaye, the names are transferred from maternal uncle to sister's son and from maternal aunt to sister's daughter (Nimuendaju 1939, p. 22); but in this case it is the membership rules in the groups called *kiyé* which follow sex affiliation, from father to son and from mother to daughter (Nimuendaju 1939, p. 31). Finally, among the Sherente, the rules of transmission of masculine and feminine names differ, for this transmission takes place either in the framework of the moieties, or in that of the associations. Moreover, the principle of alternate generations rules both the transfer of masculine names and the membership to masculine societies (Nimuendaju 1942, pp. 43–44, 52, 59–64). Hence in all these cases, a principle of alternating generations is at work, not necessarily in the kinship terminology, but in parallel institutions; and it seems directly or indirectly linked to the principle of sex affiliation, which is itself at work in the same or other institutions.

The same observations can be made in Africa. The Ashanti have a system of alternate generations with mystical identification of the grandfather with the grandson in whose person the former has a possibility of reincarnation, and ancient testimonies suggest that the food taboos, called *tcina*, are transmitted from father to son for the men, and from mother to daughter for the women (cf. Lévi-Strauss 1969a, p. 131).

If these rapid indications, which are valuable only as sug-gestions, were to be corroborated by other examples, it would show that—independently from the subjective functions fulfilled in a particular society by the systems with alternate generations—these systems could be in a first approximation the effect of a phenomenon of convergence. As the case may be, they would find their origin either in a double dichotomy into respectively patri-lineal and matrilineal moieties, or in the preferential marriage with the patrilateral cross cousin (Lévi-Strauss 1969a, Chapter XXVII), or, finally, in a mode of transmission of certain elements of personal status separating the brother and sister and linking each, in an elective manner, to one or the other of their ascendants. In the three cases, the system insures that regarding the personal status or any of its elements, the lines issued from a brother and a sister, respectively,—provided that the marriage exchange represents an ideal model—can only crisscross at the end of two generations.

Among these three possible origins of the systems with alternate generations, a structural relation would also be perceived. On either side of the patrilateral marriage formula, where the opposition of the other two formulae is annulled, the double dichotomy of the moieties would force the lines of descent to respect a principle of duality constituting a general framework, property of the system imposed to each from the outside. The sex affiliation would insure the automatic respect of the same principle, but act within each line and, thus, as it were, from the inside (see Figure 8).

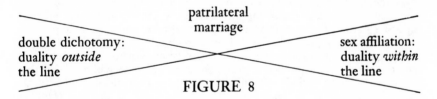

patrilateral
marriage

double dichotomy: sex affiliation:
duality *outside*   duality *within*
the line   the line

FIGURE 8

The three formulae would thus represent the states of a same group of transformation, and the patrilateral marriage would indicate the precarious point of balance where the differential characters of the other two states, symmetrical and inverted in relation to each other, would be neutralized.

NOTES

1. One can judge the carelessness of Leach's attacks. Using a faulty translation and not taking the trouble to check the original (the American edition mistranslates the word *"filiation"* in the sentence above by "descent"

(in French *descendance*), Leach makes, among others, the criticism—"in his view, the most important one" (*sic*)—that I had confused the two notions: He maintains that my thesis "presumes that unilineal descent systems are universal, which," he adds, "is wholly untrue" (1970, pp. 101–102); but he doesn't at all take into account that I had written: "First, the avunculate does not occur in all matrilineal or all patrilineal systems, and we find it present in some systems which are neither matrilineal nor patrilineal" (*S.A.*, p. 41). No wonder some young researchers, inspired by such an example, find it in order to refute texts without checking the original, basing their work on inaccurate translations and fallacious reviews.

2. In a personal letter, Margaret Mead is willing to be more precise: gift of a skull by the mother's brother, ear piercing by the brother's sister, and gift of a pig in return to both of them.

3. However, Luc de Heusch himself felt that there is a problem, as the doubts expressed in the following passage show: "In a matrilineal tribe of the Kasai, the Lele, the term *heki* (to honor) characterizes the father-son relationship, and "it is significant that it is supposed to be a reciprocal attitude" (Douglas 1952, p. 61). This term expresses less respect than reserve. But the same term *heki* also applies to the avuncular relation. According to a personal communication from Mrs. Douglas, avoidance exists between the maternal uncle and the sister's son, on the one hand, and between the father and the son, on the other. These two relations appear to be homologous and not inverted. However, this reserve is tempered with great tenderness in the father-son relation, which is not so clear-cut in the maternal uncle-nephew relation. The inverted sentimental polarity noted by Radcliffe-Brown thus comes into play only imperfectly. However, from the structural point of view, the maternal uncle and the father are assigned opposite signs in the patrilineal and matrilineal cultures, and a new problem is now manifestly present" (Heusch 1958, pp. 212–213).

4. If one wants to introduce the two relations—mother-daughter at the anterior generation, mother-son at the posterior one—one will note that they are also opposite: intimate familiarity and reciprocal collaboration in the second case, marked distance and asymmetrical duties in the first (Douglas 1963, pp. 35, 52, 53, 57, 74–75).

PART THREE
Mythology and Ritual

CHAPTER VIII

Structure and Form: Reflections on a Work by Vladimir Propp

THE SUPPORTERS of structural analysis in linguistics and in anthropology are often accused of formalism. This is to forget that formalism exists as an independent doctrine from which structuralism—without denying its debt to it—separated because of the very different attitudes the two schools adopt toward the concrete. Contrary to formalism, structuralism refuses to set the concrete against the abstract and to recognize a privileged value in the latter. *Form* is defined by opposition to material other than itself. But *structure* has no distinct content; it is content itself, apprehended in a logical organization conceived as property of the real.

Chapter VIII was originally published in *Cahiers de l'Institut de science économique appliquée*, No. 9 (Series M, No. 7) (Paris: ISEA, March 1960), pp. 3–36. It was published simultaneously under the title "L'Analyse morphologique des contes russes," in *International Journal of Slavic Linguistics and Poetics*, III (1960). The reader may refer to the two French editions of Propp's book, *Morphologie du conte* (Paris: Gallimard, 1970; Éditions du Seuil, 1970).

This difference deserves to be examined more thoroughly by means of an example. We can now do so, thanks to the publication in an English translation of an early work by Vladimir Propp, *Morphology of the Folktale*,[1] whose thinking remained very close to that of the Russian formalist school during the short period in which it flourished, roughly from 1915 to 1930.

The author of the introduction, Svatava Pirkova-Jakobson, the translator, Laurence Scott, and the Research Center of the University of Indiana, have rendered a tremendous service to the social sciences with the publication of a far too neglected work, in a language accessible to new readers. Indeed, in 1928, the date of the Russian edition, the formalist school finds itself in a crisis, officially condemned in the Soviet Union and lacking communication with the outside. In his subsequent works, Propp himself was to abandon formalism and morphological analysis to devote himself to historical and comparative research on the relationships of oral literature to myths, rituals, and institutions.

The message of the Russian formalist school was not, however, to be lost. In Europe itself, the Linguistic Circle of Prague first took it up and spread it. Since about 1940, Roman Jakobson's personal influence and teachings have been carrying it to the United States. I do not mean to insinuate that structural linguistics, and modern structuralism within and outside linguistics, are only an extension of Russian formalism. As I have already mentioned, they differ from it in the conviction that, if a little structuralism leads away from the concrete, a lot of structuralism leads back to it. But although his doctrine cannot in any way be called "formalist," Roman Jakobson has not lost sight of the historical role of the Russian school and its intrinsic importance. In dealing with the antecedents of structuralism, he has always reserved a prominent position for it. Those who have listened to him since 1940 remained indirectly marked by this remote influence. If, as Mme Pirkova-Jakobson writes, the author of these words seems to have "applied and even extended Propp's method" (p. vii, *p. xxi*), it cannot have been consciously, since he had no access to Propp's book until the publication of this translation. But through Roman Jakobson, some of its substance and inspiration had reached him.

It is to be feared that, even today, the form in which the English translation was published will not help the diffusion of

Propp's ideas. I would also add that printing mistakes make it difficult reading, and so do the obscurities which may perhaps exist in the original but seem rather to result from the translator's difficulty with the author's terminology. It is thus not unhelpful to follow the work closely while attempting to condense its theses and conclusions.

Propp begins with a brief history of the problem. Works on folktales consist mostly of collections of texts, systematic studies remain scarce and rudimentary. Some invoke insufficient documents as a justification for this situation. The author rejects such an explanation because, in every other field of knowledge, the problems of description and classification have been laid down very early. Moreover, there is no failure to discuss the origin of folktales, but "one can speak about the origin of any phenomenon only after it has been described" (p. 4, *p. 5*).

The usual classifications (Miller, Wundt, Aarne, Veselovskij) have a practical utility. They always run into the same objection, namely, that it is always possible to find tales which come under several categories. This remains true, whether the classification is founded on the *types* of tales or on the *themes* brought into play. Indeed, the delineation of themes is arbitrary; it does not rest on real analysis, but on the intuitions or the theoretical positions of each author (the former being, as a general rule, better founded than the latter, as Propp remarks, pp. 5–6, 10; *pp. 5–6, 11*). Aarne's classification provides an inventory that is most helpful to researchers, but the delineation is purely empirical, so that it is only arbitrarily that a tale belongs under a particular heading.

The discussion of Veselovskij's ideas is particularly interesting. For him, the theme can be split up into motifs, to which the theme adds only a unifying, creative operation by integrating motifs which constitute irreducible elements. But in this case, Propp remarks, each sentence constitutes a motif, and the analysis of tales must be taken to a level which, today, would be called "molecular." However, no motif can be said to be indivisible, since an example as simple as "a dragon kidnaps the king's daughter" may be decomposed into at least four elements, each of which is commutable with others ("dragon" with "sorcerer," "whirlwind," "devil," "eagle," etc.; "abduction" with "vampirism," "putting to sleep," etc.; "daughter" with "sister," "bride," "mother," etc.; and finally "king" with "prince," "peasant," "priest," etc.). Smaller units than motifs are thus obtained, according to Propp, with no independent logical existence. If we have lingered in this discussion, it is because in this affirmation of Propp's, which is only half true, lies one of the main differences between formalism and structuralism. We will come back to it later.

Propp gives Joseph Bédier full credit for the distinction between variable and constant factors within the folktales, with the invariants constituting the elementary units. However, Bédier was unable to define what these are exactly.

If the morphological study of tales has remained rudimentary, it is because it has been neglected in favor of research into origins. Too often, so-called morphological studies come down to tautologies. The most recent one (at the time of Propp's writing), that of the Russian R. M. Volkov in 1924,[2] would demonstrate nothing except that "similar tales give similar schemes" (p. 13, *p. 15*). Yet, a good morphological study is the basis of all scientific investigation. Moreover, "as long as no correct morphological study exists, there can also be no correct historical study" (p. 14, *p. 15*).

As formulated by Propp at the beginning of the second chapter, his whole undertaking rests on a working hypothesis, namely, the existence of "fairy tales" as a special category of folktales. At the beginning of the study, "fairy tales" are empirically defined as those tales classified by Aarne under numbers 300 to 749 in the following manner:

Given the statements

1. A king gives the hero an eagle, which carries him away to another kingdom.
2. An old man gives Sučenko a horse, which carries him away to another kingdom.
3. A sorcerer gives Ivan a little boat which takes him to another kingdom.
4. The princess gives Ivan a magic ring. Young men appearing from out of the ring carry Ivan away into another kingdom.

These statements contain both variables and constants. The dramatis personae and their attributes change, but the actions and the functions do not. The property of folktales is to attribute identical actions to various personages. It is the constant elements which will be used as a base provided that it can be shown that the number of these functions is finite. Now, we see that they recur very often. Thus it can be stated that "the number of functions is startlingly small, compared with the great number of dramatis personae. This explains the twofold quality of a folktale: it is amazingly multiform, picturesque, and colorful, and, to no less a degree, remarkably uniform and recurrent" (p. 19, *pp. 20–21*).

In order to define the functions, considered as the basic components of the tale, the dramatis personae will first be eliminated, their roles being only to "support" the functions. A function will be expressed simply by the name of an action: "interdiction," "flight," and so forth. Secondly, in defining a function, its place in the narrative must be taken into account. A wedding, for instance, can have different functions, depending on its role. Different meanings are given to identical acts, and vice versa; and this can only be determined by replacing the event among others, i.e., by situating it in relation to preceding and succeeding events. This presupposes that the *sequence of functions is constant* (p. 20, *p. 22*); it is subject (as will be shown later) to the possibility of certain deviations which constitute secondary phenomena, exceptions to a norm which it must always be possible to restore (pp. 97–98, *pp. 107–108*). It is also taken for granted that each tale, taken individually, never shows the totality of the functions enumerated but only some of them without the order of succession being modified. The total system of functions—the empirical realization of which may well not exist—therefore seems to present, in Propp's thinking, the character of what would be called today "metastructure."

The preceding hypotheses lead to one last consequence (which will later be verified), although Propp admits that it seems at first glance "absurd or perhaps even savage": *All fairy tales are of one type in regard to their structure* (p. 21, *p. 22*).

Winding up the question of method, Propp wonders whether the research needed to verify or infirm his theory must be exhaustive. If so, it would be practically impossible to take it to its end. Yet, if one admits that functions constitute the subject of the study, the latter will be seen as ended only when its pursuit brings about the discovery of no new functions—provided, of course, that the sampling be random and as if "dictated from without"

(p. 22, *p. 23*). Linking up with Durkheim—no doubt unintention-ally—Propp stresses that "we are not interested in the quantity of material but, rather, in the quality of the analyses of it" (p. 22, *p. 24*). Experience shows that a hundred tales constitute more than enough material. Consequently, the analysis will bear on a selection of the tales numbered 50 to 151 in Afanasyev's collection.

We will skim more rapidly over the inventory of functions, impossible to enumerate, and which forms the topic of Chapter III. Each function is summarily defined, then abridged into a single term ("absence," "interdiction," "violation," etc.), and finally given a coded sign, a letter or symbol. For each function, Propp distinguishes the "species" from the "genera," the former being sometimes subdivided into "varieties." The general scheme of the fairy tale goes as follows:

After the "initial situation" has been explained, a character goes away. This absence leads to some misfortune, either directly or indirectly (through the violation of an interdiction or obedience to an injunction). A villain enters the scene, receives information about his victim, and deceives him in order to cause him harm.

Propp analyzes this sequence into seven functions, coded with the first letters of the Greek alphabet to distinguish them from the subsequent functions (coded with capital Roman letters and diverse symbols). These seven functions are indeed preliminary in two ways. First, they set the action going and, secondly, they are not universally present, as some tales start directly with the first main function, which is the action of the villain himself: abduction of a person, theft of a magical agent, bodily injury, casting of a spell, substitution, murder (pp. 29–32, *pp. 30–35*). A "lack" results from this "villainy," unless the initial situation links up directly with the state of lack. The lack is perceived and a hero is solicited to remedy it.

There are now two possible paths. The victim may become the hero of the tale, or the hero may be distinct from the victim and come to his help. The hypothesis of the uniqueness of the tale is not thereby infirmed, because no tale follows both characters simultaneously. Consequently, there is only one "hero-function," which either one of the characters can "support." Nevertheless a choice is offered between two sequences: (1) appeal to the seeker-hero, his departure on a quest; or (2) distancing of the victim-hero, and perils to which he is exposed.

The hero (victim or seeker) meets a "donor," willing or unwilling, eager or reticent, helpful at once or hostile at first. He tests the hero (in many varied ways, which can go as far as engaging him in combat). The hero reacts negatively or positively, on his own or by means of a supernatural intervention (there are many intermediate forms). The acquisition of supernatural help (object, animal, person) is an essential trait of the function of the hero (p. 46, *p. 50*).

Transferred to the place of his intervention, the hero joins in combat with the villain (struggle, competition, game). He receives a mark of identification, physical or other; the villain is defeated, and the initial need is liquidated. The hero starts on his way home, but is pursued by an enemy from whom he escapes through help received or some stratagem. Some tales end with the hero's return and his subsequent marriage.

But other tales go on to what Propp calls another "move." Everything begins anew—villain, hero, donor, tests, supernatural help—after which the narrative follows another direction. So a series of *"bis-functions"* must first be introduced (pp. 53–54, *p. 59*), which are then followed by new actions. The hero comes back in disguise and a difficult task is proposed to him which he successfully accomplishes. He is then recognized, and the false hero (who has usurped his place) is unmasked. At last, the hero receives his reward (bride, kingdom, etc.) and the tale ends.

The inventory we have just summarized leads Propp to several conclusions. In the first place, the number of functions is very limited: thirty-one altogether. In the second place, the functions implicate one another "with logical and artistic necessity"; they belong to the same axis so that any two functions are never mutually exclusive (p. 58, *p. 64*). On the other hand, some functions can be grouped in pairs ("prohibition"–"violation"; "struggle"–"victory"; "persecution"–"deliverance", etc.) and others in sequences (e.g., the group "villainy"–"dispatch"–"decision for counteraction"–"departure from home"). Pairs of functions, sequences of functions, and independent functions are organized in an unchanging system. This is a real touchstone, permitting the appreciation of each particular tale and the assigning of its place in a classification. Indeed, each tale receives its formula, analogous to chemical formulae, which enumerates in the natural order of succession the letters (Greek or Roman) and the symbols used to code the various functions. Letters and symbols can receive an exponent denoting one variety within a specific function. For instance, the formula for a simple tale summarized by Propp will be:

$$a^1 \, \delta^1 \, A^3 \, B^1 \, C \uparrow H^1 - I^1 \, K \downarrow W^0$$

The eleven symbols assigned to it read, in order: "A king (father of) three daughters"—"the daughters go walking"—"stay late in the garden"—"a dragon kidnaps them"—"call for help"—"quest of three heroes"—"battles with the dragon"—"victory"—"rescue of the maidens"—"return"—"rewarding" (p. 114, *p. 128*).

The rules of classification being thus defined, Propp devotes the following chapters (IV and V) to the solution of various difficulties. The first of these, already mentioned, refers to the apparent resemblance of two functions. Thus, "the testing of the hero by the donor" may be told in a way that makes it indistinguishable from the "assignation of a difficult task." In such cases, the identification takes place—not by considering the intrinsic content of the function, which is ambiguous—but in relation to the context, that is, to the uncertain function among those which emcompass it. Conversely, a statement that appears to be equivalent to a single function, can in fact overlay two really distinct functions, as, for instance, when the future victim allows himself to be "deceived by the villain" and at the same time "breaks an interdiction" (pp. 61–63, *pp. 69–70*).

A second difficulty stems from the fact that, once the tale is analyzed into functions, some residual material is left to which no function corresponds. This problem troubles Propp, who suggests dividing what is left into two nonfunctional categories: the "connectives," on the one hand, and the "motivations," on the other.

The connectives consist most often of episodes explaining how character A learns what character B has just done, which he must know in order to act in turn. More generally, the connective serves to establish some immediate relation between two characters, or between a character and an object, whereas circumstances in the story would have made possible only an indirect relation. This theory of connectives is doubly important. It explains how the functions may seemingly be connected in the tale despite the fact that they are not consecutive; and it makes it possible to reduce the phenomenon of trebling to a single function, in spite of connectives which do not have the nature of independent functions but serve only to make trebling possible (pp. 64–68, *pp.* 74–75).

By motivations are meant "all reasons and aims of characters which give rise to their deeds" (p. 68, *p. 75*). But it often happens in the tales that the actions of the characters are not motivated. Propp concludes that when the motivations exist, they may result from a secondary formation. In fact, the motivation for a state or for an action sometimes takes the form of a real tale, developing within the main tale and acquiring an almost independent existence. "The folktale, like any living thing, can only generate forms that resemble itself" (p. 70, *p. 78*).

We have seen that the thirty-one functions, to which all fairy tales are reducible, are "supported" by a certain number of dramatis personae. When the functions are classified according to their "supports," each character is discovered bringing together several functions in a "sphere of action" which characterizes him. Thus, the functions "villainy"–"struggle"–"pursuit" form the sphere of action of the villain. The functions "transference of the hero"–"liquidation of lack"–"rescue"–"solution of a difficult task"–"transfiguration of the hero" define that of the magical agent, and so forth. It results from this analysis that the dramatis personae of the tale, like the functions, are limited in number. Propp notes seven protagonists: the villain, the donor, the magical agent, the sought-for person, the dispatcher, the hero, and the false hero (pp. 72–73, *pp. 79–80*). Other characters exist, but they are part of the "connectives." Between each protagonist and his sphere of action, the correspondence is rarely unequivocal. The same protagonist can intervene in several spheres and a single sphere can be shared among several protagonists. Thus the hero can do without a magical agent if he himself has supernatural power; and in certain tales, the magical agent assumes functions which are elsewhere the attributes of the hero (pp. 74–75, *pp. 82–83*).

If the tale is to be conceived of as a whole, is it not possible all the same to distinguish several parts of it? Reduced to its most abstract formula, the fairy tale can be defined as a development which starts with villainy and ends with a wedding, a reward, a liquidation of lack or harm, the transition being made by a series of intermediate functions. Propp designates such a whole by a term which the English translator renders as "move" and which we prefer to call *"partie"* in French, which means both the principal division of a tale and a card or chess game. We are indeed dealing with both things at once, since, as we have seen, the tales containing several *"parties"* are characterized by the non-immediate recurrence of the same functions, as in successive card games one periodically shuffles, cuts, deals, calls, plays, and takes the tricks. In other words, *one repeats the same rules* in spite of *different deals.*

A tale can comprise several moves. But do these not constitute as many tales? This question can only be answered once the relations among the moves are morphologically analyzed and defined. The moves may follow each other, or one be inserted in another, momentarily interrupting its development while it is itself subjected to the same type of interruption. Two moves may also be introduced simultaneously and one held over shortly until the other is ended. Two successive moves can also reverse a single conclusion. Finally, it does happen that certain dramatis personae are split into two, the transition between the two being effected by a recognized sign.

Without going into details, we will just note here that for Propp, there is one single tale (in spite of the plurality of the moves), when a functional relation exists among these latter, if they are logically disjointed, the narrative is analyzed as several distinct tales (pp. 83–86, *pp. 92–96*).

After giving an example (pp. 86–87, *pp. 96–98*), Propp comes back to the two problems he formulated at the beginning of his book: the relationship between the fairy tale and the folktale in general; and the classification of fairy tales, constituted as an independent category.

We have seen that a fairy tale is nothing more than a narrative that puts into words a limited number of functions in a constant order of succession. The formal differences between several tales result from the choice, made by each, among the thirty-one functions available and the possible repetition of some of them. But nothing prevents the making up of tales where fairies have a role, without the narrative's conforming to the previous norm. This is the case with fabricated tales, of which examples are found in Andersen, Brentano, and Goethe. Conversely, the norm may be respected in the absence of fairies. The term "fairy tale" is thus improper on two counts. For lack of a better definition and not without misgivings, Propp accepts the formula "tale with seven protagonists," as he feels he has shown that these seven protagonists form a system (pp. 89–90, *pp. 99–100*). But if one day we were able to give the investigation a historical dimension, the term "mythical tales" would then be suitable.

An ideal classification of tales would be based on a system of incompatibilities among functions. But Propp has recognized a principle of reciprocal implication (p. 58, *p. 64*) which, on the contrary, presupposes an absolute compatibility. Now—and with one of the second thoughts so frequent in his book—he reintroduces incompatibility, restricted to two pairs of functions: "struggle with the villain"–"hero's victory," on the one hand; "assignation of a difficult task"–"solution," on the other. These two pairs are so rarely encountered within the same move that the cases contrary to the rule can be considered as exceptions. It results from this that four classes of tales can be defined: those using the first pair; those using the second pair; those using them both; and those rejecting them both (pp. 91–92, *pp. 101–102*).

As the system reveals no other incompatibility, the classification is to be pursued according to the varieties of specific functions everywhere present. Only two functions present this universality: "villainy" and "lack." The tales will thus be distinguished according to the forms taken by this function within each of the four categories previously isolated.

The problem becomes yet more complex when one attempts to classify the tales into several moves. However, the privileged case of the tales in two moves makes it possible, according to Propp, to solve the apparent contradiction between the morphological unity of fairy tales (postulated at the beginning of the work) and the incompatibility of the two pairs of functions (introduced at the end) as offering the only possible basis for a structural classification. In effect, when a tale comprises two moves (of which one includes the pair "struggle"–"victory," and the other "difficult task"–"solution") these pairs are always in the order in which they have just been cited, i.e., "struggle" $\longrightarrow$ "victory" in the first move, "difficult task" $\longrightarrow$ "solution," in the second. Moreover, the two moves are linked by an initial function, common to both (p. 93, *p. 103*).

By integrating all the typical formulae, a canonical formula is obtained:

$$A \ B \ C \uparrow D \ E \ F \ G \ \frac{H \ J \ I \ K \downarrow Pr\text{–}Rs^0 \ L}{L \ M \ J \ N \ K \downarrow Pr\text{–}Rs} \ Q \ Ex \ T \ U \ W$$

from which the four fundamental categories are easily drawn, corresponding, respectively, to:

1. First group + upper group + last group.
2. First group + lower group + last group.
3. First group + upper group + lower group + last group.
4. First group + last group.

The principle of morphological unity is thus intact (p. 95, *p. 105*).

The principle of the invariable succession of functions is equally intact, subject to the permutation of the function (L): "claims of a false hero," in the final or in the initial position, depending on the choice between two incompatible pairs (HI) and (MN). Furthermore, Propp accepts other permutations of isolated functions, and even sequences.

The typological unity and the morphological kinship of all fairy tales is not brought into question by these permutations, since they imply no difference in the structure (p. 97–98, *p. 106*).

The most striking aspect of Propp's work is the vigor with which it anticipates further developments. Those among us who first approached the structural analysis of oral literature around 1950, without direct knowledge of Propp's attempts a quarter of a century earlier, recognize there, to their amazement, formulae —sometimes even whole sentences—which they know well enough they have not borrowed from him: the notion of an "initial situation"; the comparison of a mythological matrix with the rules of musical composition; the necessity of a reading that is at once "horizontal" and "vertical" (p. 107, *p. 119*); the constant use of the notion of a group of substitutions, and of transformation, in order to resolve the apparent antinomy between the constancy of the form and the variability of the content (*passim*); the effort—at least sketched by Propp—to reduce the apparent specificity of functions to pairs of oppositions; the privileged case of myths in structural analysis (p. 82, *p. 90*); and, finally and above all, the essential hypothesis that there exists, strictly speaking, but a single tale (pp. 20–21, *p. 22*)—that the collection of known tales must be treated as a series of variants of a unique type (p. 103, *p. 113*) so that one may one day discover, through calculations, vanished variants or unknown ones, exactly as one can infer the existence of invisible stars as functions of the laws of astronomy.

These are so many intuitions, the penetration of which—the prophetic character of which—compel our admiration. They earn for Propp the devotion of all those who, unknown to themselves, were his followers. Then, if in the following discussion we are led to formulate certain reservations and to offer some objections, they can in no way diminish Propp's tremendous merit, nor contest the right of priorities of his discoveries.

This made clear, one can wonder about the reasons which made Propp choose folktales, or a certain category of tales, to test his method. These tales should not be classified as separate from the rest of oral literature. Propp writes that, from a certain point of view ("historical" according to him, but we think also psychological and logical), "the fairy tale, in its morphological bases, amounts to a myth. We, of course, realize," he adds immediately, "that, from the point of view of contemporary science, we are stating a totally heretical idea" (p. 82, *p. 90*).

Propp is right. There is no serious reason to isolate tales from myths; although a difference between the two is subjectively felt by a great many societies; although this difference is objectively expressed by means of special terms to distinguish the two genres; and finally, although prescriptions and prohibitions are sometimes linked with one and not the other (recitation of myths at certain hours, or during a season only, while tales, because of their "profane" nature, can be narrated any time). These native distinctions present a great interest for the ethnographer, but it is not at all certain that they are founded on the nature of things. On the contrary, it is observed that tales, which have the character of folktales in one society, are myths for another, and vice versa. This is a first reason to beware of arbitrary classifications. Moreover, the mythographer almost always realizes that, in an identical or transformed form, the same tales, the same characters, the same motifs reappear in the tales and myths of a given population. In constituting the complete series of transformations of a mythical theme, one can seldom limit oneself to the myths (so qualified by the natives); some of these transformations must be sought in the tales, although it is possible to infer their existence from the myths proper.

One cannot question, however, that almost all societies perceive the two genres as distinct, and that the constancy of this distinction can be explained by some cause. We believe that this foundation exists, but reduced to a difference of degree which is twofold. In the first instance, the tales are constructed on weaker oppositions than those found in myths. The latter are not cosmological, metaphysical, or natural, but, more frequently, local, social, and moral. In the second place—and precisely because the tale is a weakened transposition of the myth—the former is less strictly subjected than the latter to the triple consideration of logical coherence, religious orthodoxy, and collective pressure. The tale offers more possibilities of play, its permutations are comparatively freer, and they progressively acquire a certain arbitrary character.

But if the tale works with minimized oppositions, these will be so much more difficult to identify. And the difficulty increases because the already very small oppositions indicate a lack of precision which allows the shift to literary creation.

Propp saw this latter difficulty very clearly. He saw "that the purity of folktale construction"—indispensable for the application of his method—"is peculiar only to the peasantry—to a peasantry, moreover, little touched by civilization. All kinds of foreign influences alter and sometimes decompose a folktale." In this case, "it is impossible to make provision for all details" (p. 90, *p. 100*). Nonetheless, Propp admits that the teller has a relative freedom in the choice of certain characters, in the omission and repetition of such and such a function, in determining the modalities of retained functions, and, finally, in a more complete manner still, in the nomenclature and the attributes of the characters, who are themselves imposed: "a tree may show the way, a crane may give a steed a gift, a chisel may spy, and so forth. This freedom is a specific peculiarity of the folktale alone" (pp. 101–102, *pp. 112–113*). Elsewhere, he mentions the attributes of these characters, such as "their age, sex, status, external appearance (and any peculiarities of same), and so forth," which are variable because they "provide the folktale with its brilliance, charm and beauty." Thus, external causes alone can explain why, in a tale, one attribute is substituted for another: transformation of real-life conditions, influence of foreign epic literature, of scholarly literature, of religion and superstitions. "The folktale has gradually undergone a metamorphic process, and these transformations and metamorphoses are subject to certain laws. These processes create a multiformity which is difficult to analyze" (p. 79, *p. 87*).

All this really means that the tale lends itself imperfectly to structural analysis. This is no doubt true to a certain extent, but less so than Propp believes, and not exactly for the reasons he gives. We shall come back to this. But we must first find out why, in these conditions, it is the folktale which he chose to test his method. Should he not rather have used myths, the privileged value of which he recognizes several times?

The reasons for Propp's choice are many, and are of varying importance. As he is not an ethnologist, one can suppose that he had no access to mythological material collected by him or among peoples known to him, and which he knew fully how to handle. In addition, he started on a path on which others immediately preceded him. It is precisely tales, rather than myths, which constituted his predecessors' topic of discussion and which provided the ground where certain Russian scholars had sketched the first plans of morphological studies. Propp takes up the problem where they left it, using the same material: Russian folktales.

But we believe that Propp's choice can also be explained by his lack of knowledge of the true relationship between myth and folktale. If he has the great merit of seeing in them *species* of a same *genus*, he nonetheless remains faithful to the historical priority of the former over the latter. He writes that, to be able to start studying myth, one would have to add to the morphological analysis "a historical study which, for the present, cannot enter into our task" (p. 82, *p. 90*). A little further on, he suggests that "very archaic myths" constitute the realm where folktales have their distant origin (p. 90, *p. 100*). "Everyday life and religion die away, while their contents turn into a folktale" (p. 96, *p. 106*).

An ethnologist will beware of such an interpretation, because he knows that, in present times, myths and folktales coexist side by side. One genre cannot then be held to be a survival of the other, unless it is postulated that tales preserve the memory of ancient myths, themselves fallen into oblivion.[3] But, besides the fact that the proposition could not be demonstrated most of the time (since we are ignorant of all, or almost all, of the ancient beliefs of the peoples we are studying, and call them "primitive" precisely for this reason), the usual ethnographic experience leads one to think that, on the contrary, myth and folktale exploit a common substance, each in its own way. Their relationship is not that of anterior to posterior, of primitive to derived. It is rather a complementary relationship. Tales are miniature myths, where the same oppositions are transposed to a smaller scale, and it is this which makes them difficult to study in the first place.

The preceding considerations certainly must not make one wave away the other difficulties evoked by Propp, although one could formulate them in a slightly different manner. Even in our contemporary societies, the tale is not a residual myth, but it certainly suffers from subsisting alone. The disappearance of myths has broken the balance. Like a satellite without a planet, the tale tends to get out of orbit, to let itself be caught by other poles of attraction.

These are added reasons for calling upon civilizations where myth and tale have coexisted until a recent period, and sometimes continue to do so; where, consequently, the system of oral literature is total and can be apprehended as such. The point is not to choose between tale and myth, but to understand that they are the two poles of a field that also includes all sorts of intermediate forms and that morphological analysis must be considered in the same way, if one does not want to leave out elements belonging, like the others, to one and the same system of transformations.

Thus, Propp reveals himself torn between his formalist vision and the obsession with historical explanations. One can, to some degree, understand the regret which made him give up the former to return to the latter. As soon as he had settled on the folktales, the antinomy became overpowering. Clearly, there is history in the tales, but a practically inaccessible history, since we know very little about the antehistoric civilizations where they originated. But is it really history which is lacking? The historical dimension appears rather as a negative modality, resulting in the lack of correspondence between the present tale and a missing ethnographic context. The opposition is resolved when one envisages an oral tradition still "in situation," like those studied by ethnography. Then, the problem of history is irrelevant, or only relevant in exceptional cases, since the external references are just as present as the oral tradition to whose interpretation they are indispensable.

Thus, Propp is the victim of a subjective illusion. He is not torn, as he thinks, between the demands of synchrony and those of diachrony. *It is not the past that he lacks, it is context.* Formalist dichotomy, which opposes form and matter and which defines them by antithetic characters, is not imposed on him by the nature of things, but by the accidental choice which he made in a domain where form alone survives while matter is abolished. Reluctantly, he resigns himself to dissociating them and at the most decisive moments of his analysis, he reasons as if what escapes him de facto also escapes him de jure.

Except for certain passages—prophetic, but how timid and hesitating, and to which we will come back—Propp divides oral literature in two: a form, which constitutes the essential aspect because it lends itself to morphological study; and an arbitrary content to which, because it is arbitrary, I think he only gives an accessory importance. We will be permitted to insist on this point which sums up the whole difference between formalism and structuralism. For the former, the two domains must be absolutely separate, since form alone is intelligible, and content is only a residual deprived of any significant value. For structuralism, this opposition does not exist. There is not something abstract on one side and something concrete on the other. Form and content are of the same nature, susceptible to the same analysis. Content draws its reality from its structure and what is called form is the "structural formation" of the local structure forming the content.

The limitation, which we believe to be inherent in formalism, is particularly striking in the main chapter of Propp's work, dealing with the protagonists' functions. The author categorizes them in *genera* and *species*. It is clear, however, that whereas the former are defined by exclusively mythological criteria, the latter are only partly so; unwittingly, no doubt, Propp uses them to reintroduce some aspects pertaining to content, such as the generic function "villainy." It is subdivided into twenty-two species and sub-species, such as: the villain "abducts a person," "steals a magical agent," "plunders or spoils the crops," "steals the daylight," "makes a threat of cannibalism," (pp. 29–32, *pp. 31–34*). The whole content of the tales is thus progressively reintegrated, and the analysis oscillates between formal terms—so general that they can be indistinctly applied to all tales (this is the generic level)—and a simple restitution of the raw material, the formal properties of which alone have an explanatory value (as mentioned at the beginning).

The ambiguity is so flagrant that Propp desperately seeks a middle position. Instead of systematically cataloguing what he maintains are "species," he is content to isolate some, putting together, pell-mell, in a single "specific" category all those not frequently encountered. "It is technically more useful," he writes, "to isolate several of its most important forms while, on the other hand, generalizing about those remaining" (pp. 29, 33, *pp. 31–32, 35*). But either one deals with specific forms and cannot formulate a coherent system without cataloguing and classifying them all, or there is nothing there but content and—according to the rules set by Propp himself—one must exclude it from the morphological analysis. In any case, a drawer where one is content to pile up unclassified forms does not constitute a "species."

Why, then, this compromise, which seems to satisfy Propp? For a very simple reason, which explains another weakness of the formalist position. Unless the content is surreptitiously reintegrated into the form, the latter is condemned to remain at such a level of abstraction that it neither signifies anything any longer nor has any heuristic meaning. *Formalism destroys its object.* With Propp, it results in the discovery that there exists in reality but one tale. Henceforth, the problem of explanation is only displaced. We know what *the tale* is, but as experience puts before us not an archetypal tale but a great number of concrete tales, we do not know how to classify them anymore. Before formalism, we were certainly unaware of what these tales had in common. Since formalism, we have been deprived of any means of understanding how they differ. One has passed from concrete to abstract, but can no longer come down from the abstract to the concrete.

Concluding his work, Propp quotes an admirable page from Veselovskij:

> Is it permissible in this field also to consider the problem of typical schemes . . . schemes handed down from generations as ready-made formulae capable of becoming animated with a new mood, giving rise to new formations? . . . The Contemporary narrative literature, with its complicated thematic structure and photographic reproduction of reality, apparently eliminates the very possibility of such a question. But when this literature will appear to future generations as distant as antiquity (from prehistoric to medieval times) seems to us at present—when the synthesis of time, that great simplifier, in passing over the complexity of phenomena, reduces them to the magnitude of points receding into the distance, then their lines will merge with those which we are now uncovering when we look back at the poetic traditions of the distant past—and the phenomena of schematism and repetition will then be established across the total expanse" (quoted by Propp, p. 105, *p. 116*, from A. N. Veselovskij, *Poetika*, Vol. II).

These views are very profound but, at least in the passage quoted, one cannot perceive on what basis the differentiation will take place when, beyond the unity of literary creation, one will want to determine the nature of and the reason for its modalities.

Propp sensed this problem and the last part of his work consists of an attempt, as fragile as it is ingenious, to reintroduce a principle of classification. There is but one tale, but this tale is an archtale, composed of four groups of functions, logically articulated. If we call them 1, 2, 3, 4, the concrete tales will be divided into four categories, depending on their concurrent use of the four groups; or into three groups, which can only be (because of their logical articulation) 1, 2, 4 or 1, 3, 4; or into two groups, which must then be 1, 4 (see p. 126).

But this classification into four categories leaves us practically as far from real tales as does the single category, since each category still includes dozens or hundreds of different tales. Propp knows this so well that he continues: "Further classification can also be made according to the varieties of this obligatory element. Thus at the heading of each class will come the folktales about the kidnapping of a person, then folktales about the stealing of a talisman, etc., on through all the varieties of element A (villany). Folktales with *a* (i.e., folktales about the quest for a bride, for a talisman, etc.) appear thereafter" (p. 92, *p. 102*). What does it mean, if not that morphological categories do not exhaust reality, and that the content of the tale, after being banished as unfit to form a classification, is reintegrated because the morphological attempt has failed?

There is a more serious matter still. We saw that the fundamental tale, of which all tales only offer a partial realization, is formed of two moves, certain functions of which are recurrent —some being simple variants of others and others belonging specifically to each move (see p. 125). These specific functions are (for the first move) "struggle," "branding of the hero," "victory," "liquidation of lack," "return," "pursuit of the hero," "rescue"; and (for the second move) "the hero's unrecognized arrival," "difficult task," "success," "recognition of the hero," "exposure of the false hero," and "transfiguration of the hero."

What is the basis for differentiating these two series? Could one not treat them, as well, as two variants, where the "assigning of a difficult task" would be a transformation of the "struggle," [4] the "false hero," a transformation of the "villain," the "success" a transformation of the "victory," and the "transfiguration," a transformation of the "branding"? In this case, the theory of the fundamental tale in two moves would collapse and, with it, the weak hope of beginning a morphological classification. There would be then, truly, a single tale. But it would be reduced to such a vague and general abstraction that nothing would be learned from it about the objective causes of a multitude of particular tales.

The proof of the analysis is in the synthesis. If the synthesis is shown to be impossible, it is because the analysis is incomplete. Nothing can be more convincing of the inadequacy of formalism than its inability to reconstitute the very empirical content from which it was itself drawn. What then has it lost on the way?

Precisely the content. To his great credit, Propp discovered that the content of tales is *permutable*. But he too often concluded that it was *arbitrary*, and this is the reason for the difficulties he encountered, since even permutations conform to rules.[5]

In the myths and tales of the Indians of North and South America, the same actions are attributed—depending on the tales—to different animals. To simplify, let us consider birds: eagle, owl, raven. Will we distinguish, as Propp does, between the function (constant) and the characters (variable)? No, because each character is not given in the form of an opaque element, confronted with which structural analysis should come to a stop, telling itself to go no further. When, after the fashion of Propp, the narrative is treated as a closed system, one could no doubt believe the opposite. In effect, the narrative does not contain any information about itself, and the character is comparable to a word encountered in a document but not appearing in the dictionary, or even to a proper noun, i.e., a term deprived of context.

But to understand the meaning of a term is always to change it in all its contexts. In the case of oral literature, these contexts are at first provided by the totality of the variants, that is, by the system of compatibilities and incompatibilities that characterize the permutable totality. That the eagle appears by day and that the owl appears by night in the same function already permits the definition of the former as a diurnal owl and of the latter as a nocturnal eagle, and this signifies that the pertinent opposition is that of day and night.

If the oral literature considered is of an ethnographic type, other contexts exist, provided by the ritual, the religious beliefs, the superstitions, and also by factual knowledge. It is then to be noticed that the eagle and the owl together are put in opposition to the raven, as predators to scavenger, while they are opposed to each other at the level of day and night; and that the duck is in opposition to all three at the new level of the pairs sky–land and sky–water. Thus, a "universe of the tale" will be progressively defined, analyzable in pairs of oppositions, diversely combined within each character who—far from constituting a single entity—is a bundle of differential elements, in the manner of the phoneme as conceived by Roman Jakobson.

In the same manner, the American narratives sometimes mention trees, designating them, for example, as "plum tree" or as "apple tree." But it would be equally false to believe that only the concept "tree" is important and that its concrete realizations are arbitrary, or again that one function exists of which a tree is regularly the "support." The inventory of contexts reveals that, philosophically speaking, what interests the native about the plum tree is its fecundity, while the apple tree attracts his attention because of the strength and depth of its roots. The one introduces a positive function, "fecundity," the other a negative function, "earth-sky transition"; and both are a function of vegetation. The apple tree, in its turn, is opposed to the wild turnip (a removable plug between the two worlds), itself realizing the function: positive "sky-earth transition."

Inversely, by carefully examining the contexts, we can eliminate false distinctions. Among the Plains Indians, mythical narratives about eagle hunts refer to an animal species sometimes identified as "wolverine," sometimes as "bear." One can decide in favor of the former, after noticing that, of the wolverine's habits, the natives especially remember the fact that it makes game of traps dug into the ground. The eagle hunters, however, hide in pits, and the opposition eagle-wolverine becomes that of a celestial prey and a chthonic hunter, the strongest one conceivable in the order of hunting. By the same token, this maximum amplitude between terms generally less remote explains why eagle hunting is subjected to a particularly exacting ritual.[6]

To maintain, as we do, that the permutability of contents is not arbitrary comes down to saying that, unless the analysis is carried to a sufficiently deep level, constancy reappears through diversity. Inversely, the so-called "constancy of form" must not hide from us the fact that functions are also permutable.

The structure of the folktale, illustrated by Propp, is seen as a chronological succession of qualitatively distinct functions, each constituting an independent "genre." One can wonder whether— as in the case of dramatis personae and their attributes—he does not stop the analysis too soon, seeking the form too close to the level of empirical observation. Among the thirty-one functions which he distinguishes, several appear reducible, i.e., assimilable to the *same* function, reappearing at *different* moments of the narrative, but after undergoing one or a number of *transformations*.

We have suggested that this could be the case with the false hero, a transformation of the villain; with the assigning of a difficult task, a transformation of the test, etc. (see p. 000); and that, in this case, the two moves constituting the fundamental tale would themselves be a transformation of each other.

There is nothing to prevent pushing this reduction even further, and analyzing each part, taken separately, in such a way that several of Propp's functions would in reality constitute the grouping of transformations of one and the same function. Thus one could treat the "violation" as the reverse of the "prohibition," the latter as a negative transformation of the "injunction." The "departure" of the hero and his "return" would appear as the same function of disjunction, negatively or positively expressed. The "quest" of the hero (he pursues someone or something) would become the converse of his "pursuit" (he is pursued by something or someone), etc. In other terms, instead of Propp's chronological scheme—where the order of succession of events is a property of the structure

$$A,B,C,D,E,\dots\dots\dots\dots\dots M,N,H,\dots\dots\dots\dots T,U,V,W,X,$$

another scheme should be adopted, which would present a model of structure defined as the group of transformations of a small number of elements. This scheme would appear as a matrix with two or three dimensions or more:

$$
\begin{array}{cccccc}
w & -x & \dfrac{1}{y} & 1-z & \cdots \\[2ex]
-w & \dfrac{1}{x} & 1-y & z & \cdots \\[2ex]
\dfrac{1}{w} & 1-x & y & -z & \cdots \\[2ex]
1-w & x & -y & \dfrac{1}{z} & \cdots \\
\end{array}
$$

$$\dots\dots\dots\dots\dots\dots\dots\dots\dots\dots\dots\dots$$

and where the system of operations would be closer to Boolean algebra.

In Vol. I of *Structural Anthropology*, p. 209, I have shown that this formulation alone can give an account of the double aspect of time representation in all mythical systems: the narrative is both "in time" (it consists of a succession of events) and "out of time" (its significant value is always current). But in confining ourselves here to the discussion of Propp's theories, this formulation offers another advantage, which is to conciliate—much better than Propp himself succeeds in doing it—his theoretical principle of the permanence of the order of succession, with the empirical evidence of the shifting among certain functions or groups of functions observed from one tale to the next (pp. 97–98, *p. 108*). If our conception is adopted, the order of chronological succession is reabsorbed into an atemporal matrix structure, the form of which is indeed constant. The shifting of functions is then no more than one of their modes of permutation (by vertical columns or fractions of columns).

These criticisms are no doubt valid for the method used by Propp and for its conclusions. However, it cannot be overemphasized that he himself raised them, and that in certain passages he formulates with perfect clarity the solutions which we have just suggested. Let us take up again, from this view point, the two essential themes of our discussion: constancy of content (in spite of its permutability) and permutability of functions (in spite of their constancy).

Chapter VII of *Morphology of the Folklore* is entitled: "On the Attributes of Dramatis Personae *and Their Meaning*" (italics added). In rather obscure terms (at least in the English translation), Propp reflects upon the apparent variability of elements, which does not exclude repetition. Thus one can recognize some fundamental forms, and other, derived or heteronomous forms. On this basis, one distinguishes an "international" model, "national" or "regional" models, and finally models characteristic of certain social or professional groups. "By grouping the material of each heading, we are able to define all methods, or, more precisely, all aspects of transformation" (p. 80, *p. 89*).

But in reconstituting a typical tale from fundamental forms peculiar to each group, one sees that this tale harbors certain abstract representations. The tests imposed by the donor on the hero can vary, depending on the tales. Nevertheless, they imply a constant intention of one dramatis persona toward another. The same applies to the tasks imposed on the kidnapped princess. Among these intentions, expressible in formulae, a common trait can be seen. In comparing "these formulae with other attributive elements, we unexpectedly come upon a connective link in both the logical and the artistic plans. . . . Even such details as the golden hair of the princess . . . acquire a completely special meaning and may be studied. The study of attributes makes possible a scientific interpretation of the folktale" (pp. 81–82, *p. 90*).

As he does not have at his disposal an ethnographic context (which ideally an historic and prehistoric inquiry could alone procure), Propp gives up this program as soon as he has formulated it or postpones it until better times (which explains his return to the search for survivals and to comparative studies): "Everything we state, however, is in the form of a supposition." Nevertheless, "the study of the attributes of dramatis personae, as we have outlined it, is of great importance" (p. 82, *p. 90*). Even if it is reduced provisionally to an inventory (of little interest in itself), the study is an incentive to look at "the laws of transformation and the abstract notions which are reflected in the basic forms of these attributes" (p. 82, *p. 90*).

Here Propp gets to the bottom of the problem. Behind the attributes, at first disregarded as arbitrary, residual, and deprived of significance, he foresees the intervention of "abstract notions" and a "logical plan," the existence of which (if it could be established) would allow us to treat the tale as a myth (p. 82, *p. 90*).

As far as the second theme is concerned, the examples gathered in Appendix II show that Propp does not hesitate at times to introduce notions such as the negative function or the reverse function. He even uses a special symbol for the latter (===). We have seen (p. 125) that certain functions are mutually exclusive. There are others which implicate each other, such as "interdiction" and "violation," on the one hand, "deception" and "submission" on the other; these two pairs are most often incompatible [7] (p. 98, *p. 108*). Thence the problem explicitly stated by Propp: "Are the varieties of one function necessarily linked to the corresponding varieties of another function?" (p. 99, *p. 109*). Always, in some cases ("interdiction" and "violation," "struggle" and "victory," "branding" and "recognition," etc.); in other cases, only sometimes. Certain correlations can be univocal, others reciprocal (the act of throwing down a comb always appears in the context of flight, but the reciprocal is not true): "in this light, unilaterally and bilaterally substitutable elements would appear to exist" (p. 99, *p. 110*).

In a previous chapter, Propp studied the possible correlations between the different forms of "testing" of the hero by the donor and the forms which the "transmission of the magical agent" to the hero can take. He concluded that two types of correlations exist, depending on whether or not bargaining characterizes the transmission (pp. 42–43, *pp. 46–47*). In applying these rules and others like them, Propp foresaw the possibility of verifying all his hypotheses experimentally. To apply the system of compatibilities, of implications and correlations (total or partial) to the making of synthetic tales would be sufficient. One would then see these creations "come alive and become folktales" (p. 101, *p. 112*).

Obviously, Propp adds, that would only be possible if the functions were distributed among dramatis personae borrowed from tradition or invented, and if motivations, connections "and other auxiliary elements" were not omitted, the creation of which is "absolutely free" (p. 102, *p. 112*). Let us insist, once more, that it is not, and that Propp's hesitations on this subject explain that his attempt first appeared—and appeared to himself as well—unsuccessful.

The origin myths of the western Pueblo Indians start with the account of the first men's emergence from the depths of the earth where they lived at first. This emergence must be motivated, and it is in two ways: Either the men become conscious of their miserable condition and wish to escape from it, or the gods discover their own loneliness and call the men to the surface of the earth in order to have these men address their prayers to them and worship them. One recognizes the "situation of lack" described by Propp, but one motivated either from the point of view of the men or from that of the gods. But this change of motivation from one variant to the other is so far from being arbitrary that it entails the correlative transformation of a whole series of functions. In the last analysis, it is linked to different ways of posing the problem of the relationship between hunting and agriculture.[8] But it would be impossible to reach this explanation if the ritual, the technique, the knowledge, the beliefs of the peoples concerned could not be studied sociologically and independently from their mythical incidence. Otherwise, one would be trapped in a closed circle.

The error of formalism is thus twofold. By restricting itself exclusively to the rules which govern the grouping of propositions, it loses sight of the fact that no language exists in which the vocabulary can be deduced from the syntax. The study of any linguistic system requires the cooperation of the grammarian and the philologist. This means that in the matter of oral tradition the morphology is sterile unless direct or indirect ethnographic observation comes to render it fertile. Imagining that the two tasks can be dissociated, that the grammatical study can be undertaken first and the lexical study postponed until later, one is condemned to produce nothing but an anemic grammar and a lexicon in which anecdotes replace definitions. In the end, neither would accomplish its purpose.

This first error of formalism is explained by its misunderstanding of the complementarity of signifier and signified, which has been recognized since Saussure in all linguistics systems. But to this error another one is added in formalism; namely, the treating of oral tradition as a linguistic expression similar to all the others—in other words, unequally propitious to structural analysis, depending on the level considered.

It is currently accepted that language is structural at the phonological stage. We are gradually becoming convinced that it is also structural at the level of the grammar, but less convinced about the vocabulary stage. Except perhaps for certain privileged domains, we have not yet discovered the angle under which vocabulary would give a handle to structural analysis.

The transposition of this situation to oral tradition explains Propp's distinction between a single, truly morphological level—that of functions—and an amorphous level where characters, attributes, motivations, and connections all pile up; this latter level being amenable only (as it is believed of vocabulary) to historical investigation and literary criticism.

This assimilation disregards the fact that, as its modes, myths and tales use language "hyper-structurally," it could be said that they form a "metalanguage" in which structure operates at all levels. They owe to this property their immediate perception as folktales or myths (and not as historical or romantic narratives). As language, they naturally use grammatical rules and words. But another dimension is added to the usual one, because rules and words are used in narratives to build images and actions which are both "normal" signifiers, in relation to what is signified in the text, and elements of signification, in relation to a supplementary signifying system located at another level. Let us say, to clarify this thesis, that in a tale a "king" is not only a king and a "shepherdess" a shepherdess, but that these words and what they signify become tangible means of constructing an intelligible system formed by the oppositions: *male/female* (with regard to *nature*) and *high/low* (with regard to *culture*), as well as all possible permutations among the six terms.

The language and metalanguage which, united, constitute folktales and myths can have certain levels in common. These levels are, however, displaced in them. While remaining terms of the narrative, the words of myth function in it as sheaves of differential elements. From the point of view of classification, these mythemes are not located at the level of the vocabulary but at the level of the phonemes, with the difference that they do not operate on the same *continuum* (resources of perceptible experience, in one case, and of the phonatory apparatus, in the other); and with this similarity also: that the *continuum* is decomposed and recomposed according to the rules—binary and ternary—of opposition and correlation.

The problem of the vocabulary is then not the same, depending on whether language or metalanguage is considered. The fact that in American tales and myths the function of the trickster can be "carried out" sometimes by the coyote, sometimes by the mink, or sometimes by the raven, poses an ethnographic and historical problem comparable to a philological investigation of the current form of a word. And yet, it is altogether a different problem from that of knowing why a certain animal species is called *vison* in French and "mink" in English. In the second case, the result can be considered as arbitrary; all that is involved is the reconstruction of the development that led to such and such a verbal form. In the first case, the constraints are much stronger because the constituent elements are few and their possible combinations limited. The choice is thus limited to a few existing possibilities.

If one looks a little more closely, however, one perceives that this apparently quantitative difference is not really related to the number of constituent units—which is not of the same order of magnitude, according to whether phonemes or mythemes are considered—but to the nature of these constituent units, qualitatively different in both cases.

According to the classical definition, phonemes are elements deprived of signification, but the presence or absence of which serves to differentiate terms—the words—which themselves have a signification. If these words seem arbitrary in their phonetic form, it is not only because they are the product—to a great extent problematical (although possibly less than it is believed)—of possible combinations between phonemes, of which a considerable number are allowed by every language. The contingency of verbal forms comes mostly from the fact that their constituent units (phonemes) are themselves undetermined with regard to signification. Nothing predisposes certain combinations of sounds to convey such and such a meaning. As we have tried to show elsewhere (*S.A.*, Chapter V), the structuralization of vocabulary appears at another stage: a posteriori and not a priori.

It is a different matter with mythemes, since they result from a play of binary or ternary oppositions (which makes them comparable to phonemes). But they do so among elements which are already full of signification at the level of the language—the "abstract representation" of which Propp speaks—and which can be expressed by words of the vocabulary. Borrowing a neologism from the building technique, one could say that, unlike words, mythemes are "prestressed." Of course, they are still words, but with a double meaning of *words of words*, which operate simultaneously on two levels: that of language, where they keep on having their own meaning, and that of metalanguage, where they participate as elements of a supersignification that can come only from their union.

If this is true, it is then understandable that there is nothing in folktales and myths which can remain foreign or refractory to structure. Even the vocabulary—i.e., the content—is seen there stripped of this character of "naturing nature" in which one feels authorized (wrongly perhaps) in seeing something being made in a contingent and unforeseeable manner. Through the tales and the myths, the vocabulary is apprehended as "natured nature." It is a given fact, with its laws which force a certain delineation of contours upon the real and mythical vision itself. For the latter, there only remains to find out what coherent arrangements are possible between the pieces of a mosaic for which number, meaning, and shapes have been determined beforehand.

We have denounced the error of formalism, which is the belief that the grammar can be tackled at once and the dictionary postponed. But what is true for some linguistic systems is even more true for myths and tales. This is so because in this case grammar and vocabulary are not only closely linked while operating at distinct levels; they virtually adhere to each other on all surfaces and cover each other completely. As opposed to language, where the problem of vocabulary still exists, metalanguage has no level where elements do not result from well-determined operations, effected according to the rules. In this sense, everything in it is syntax. But in another sense everything in it is vocabulary, since the differential elements are words. Mythemes are still words; functions—these mythemes to the second power—are denoted by words (as Propp perceives very well). And it is likely that languages exist in which an entire myth can be expressed in a single word.

Postscript

In the Italian edition of his work,[9] Propp had responded to the text which has just been read with an offended harangue. Invited by the Italian publisher to answer, but concerned not to prolong what seemed to me to be a misunderstanding, I restricted myself to a brief comment. Not having kept the original, I can reconstruct the text approximately from the translation on page 164.

> All those who read the essay which I wrote in 1960 about Propp's prophetic work, included in this volume by the Italian publisher, cannot have failed to take it for what it was meant to be: a homage rendered to a great discovery which preceded by a quarter of a century all the attempts made by others and myself in the same direction.
>
> This is why I note with surprise and regret that the Russian scholar, to whose deserved fame I thought I had modestly contributed, saw something quite different in my words: not a cour-

teous discussion on some theoretical and methodological aspects of his work, but a perfidious attack.

I do not wish to engage with him in a polemic on this subject. It is clear that, treating me as a philosopher, he shows that he ignores all my ethnological work, whereas a profitable exchange of views could have been founded on our respective contributions to the study and the interpretation of oral traditions.

But, whatever conclusions better informed readers can draw from this confrontation, Propp's work will, to them and to me, forever keep the merit of having been the first.

NOTES

1. See V. Propp, "Morphology of the Folktale," Part III, trans. L. Scott, *International Journal of American Linguistics*, XXIV, No. 4 (October 1958); also published, under the same title, for the American Folklore Society and the Indiana University Research Center for the Language Sciences, Publication 10 (October 1958). A second edition was revised and edited by L. Wagner (Austin: University of Texas Press, 1968).

   [*Translator's note:* The page numbers in Prof. Lévi-Strauss's text refer to the first edition (1958). As the second edition (1968) is now more commonly used, we have added in italics the page references to this latter edition when it is cited in the text.]

   On the Russian formalist school, see: V. Erlich, *Russian Formalism* (The Hague: Mouton, 1955); B. Tomashevsky, "La Nouvelle École d'histoire littéraire en Russie," *Revue des études slaves*, VIII (1928).

2. R. M. Vólkov, *Skazka: Rozyskanija po sjužetosloženiju narodnoj skazki* [The tale: investigations on the theme composition of the folktale] (Kiev: 1924), Vol. I, Skazka velikorusskaja, ukrainskaja, belorusskaja [The Great Russian, Ukrainian, and Belorussian Tales].

3. For the discussion of a definite example of hypotheses of this type, see Chapters X and XIV.

4. Or, rather, of the "testing" of the hero, which takes place before.

5. For an attempt at joint restitution of form and content, see Chapter IX.

6. On these analyses, see *Annuaire de l'École pratique des hautes études* (Sciences religieuses), *1954–1955*, pp. 25–27 and *1959–1960*, pp. 39–42; see also *La Pensée sauvage*, 1962, pp. 66–71.

7. This second system of incompatibilities pertains to functions that Propp called preparatory, because of their contingent character. Let us remember that, for Propp, the main functions have only one pair of incompatibilities.

8. *Structural Anthropology*, Chapter XI; see also *Annuaire de l'École pratique des hautes études* (Sciences religieuses), *1952–1953*, pp. 19–21, *1953–1954*, pp. 27–29.

9. V. Propp, *Morfologia della fiabra*, ed. G. L. Bravo, with a commentary by C. Lévi-Strauss and a reply by the author (Turin, 1966).

CHAPTER IX

The Story of Asdiwal

Thisstudy of a native myth from the Pacific coast of Canada has two aims. First, to isolate and compare the *various levels* on which the myth evolves: geographic, economic, sociological, and cosmological—each one of these levels, together with the symbolism proper to it, being seen as a transformation of an underlying logical structure common to all of them. And, second, to compare the *different versions* of the myth and to look for the meaning of the discrepancies between them, or between some of them; for, since they all come from the same people (but are recorded in different parts of their territory), these variations

Chapter IX was originally published under the title "La Geste d'Asdiwal," in *Annuaire 1958-1959*, École pratique des hautes études. Section des sciences religieuses (Paris, 1958), pp. 3-43. It was republished in *Les Temps Modernes*, No. 179 (March 1962).

[*Translator's note:* "The Story of Asdiwal" was published in *The Structural Study of Myth and Totemism* (London: Tavistock, 1968), translated by N. Mann. When Prof. Lévi-Strauss added his "Postscript," he brought a few modifications to the French text of *Asdiwal;* while respecting these modifications, we have used as much of Mann's translation as possible.]

cannot be explained in terms of dissimilar beliefs, languages, or institutions.

The story of Asdiwal, which comes from the Tsimshian Indians, is known to us in four versions, collected some sixty years ago by Franz Boas and published in the following books: *Indianische Sagen von der Nord-Pacifischen Küste Amerikas* (Berlin, 1895); *Tsimshian Texts*, Smithsonian Institution, Bureau of American Ethnology, Bulletin No. 27 (Washington, 1902); *Tsimshian Texts* (G. Hunt, co-author) Publications of the American Ethnological society, n.s., III, (Leyden, 1912); and *Tsimshian Mythology*, Smithsonian Institution, Bureau of American Ethnology 31st Annual Report, 1909–1910, (Washington; 1916).

We shall begin by calling attention to certain facts which must be known if the myth is to be understood.

The Tsimshian Indians, with the Tlingit and the Haida, belong to the northern group of cultures on the Northwest Pacific coast. They live in British Columbia, immediately south of Alaska, in a region which embraces the basins of the Nass and Skeena rivers, the coastal region stretching between their estuaries, and, further inland, the land drained by the two rivers and their tributaries. Both the Nass in the north and the Skeena in the south flow in a northeast-southwesterly direction, and they are approximately parallel. The Nass, however, is slightly nearer north-south in orientation, a detail which, as we shall see, is not entirely devoid of importance.

This territory was divided among three local groups, distinguished by their different dialects: in the upper reaches of the Skeena, the Gitskan; in the lower reaches and the coastal region, the Tsimshian themselves; and in the valleys of the Nass and its tributaries, the Nisqa. Three of the versions of the myth of Asdiwal were recorded on the coast and in Tsimshian dialect (Boas 1895*a*, pp. 285–288; Boas and Hunt 1912, pp. 71–146; Boas and Hunt 1916, pp. 243–245, and the comparative analysis, pp. 792–824); the fourth was recorded at the mouth of the Nass, in Nisqa dialect (Boas and Hunt 1902, pp. 225–228). It is this last which, when compared with the other three, reveals the most marked differences.

Like all the people on the northwest Pacific Coast, the Tsimshian had no agriculture. During the summer, the women's work was to collect fruit, berries, plants, and wild roots, while the men hunted bears and goats in the mountains and sea lions on the coastal reefs. They also practiced deep-sea fishing, catching mainly cod and halibut, but also herring nearer the shore. It was, however, the complex rhythm of river fishing that made the deepest impression upon the life of the tribe. Whereas the Nisqa were relatively settled, the Tsimshian moved, according to the seasons, between their winter villages, which were situated in the coastal region, and their fishing places, either on the Nass or the Skeena.

At the end of the winter, when the stores of smoked fish, dried meat, fat, and preserved fruits were running low, or were even completely exhausted, the natives would undergo periods of severe famine, an echo of which is found in the myth. At such times they anxiously awaited the arrival of the candlefish, which would go up the Nass (which was still frozen to start with) for a period of about six weeks in order to spawn (Goddard 1935, p. 68). This would begin about March 1, and the entire Skeena population would travel along the coast in boats as far as the Nass in order to take up position on the fishing grounds, which were family properties. The period from February 15 to March 15 was called, not without reason, the "month when Candlefish is Eaten," and that which followed, from March 15 to April 15, the "Month when Candlefish is Cooked" (to extract its oil). This operation was strictly taboo to men, whereas the women were obliged to use their naked breasts to press the fish. The oil-cake residue had to be left to become rotten from maggots and putrefaction and, despite the pestilential stench, it had to be left in the immediate vicinity of the dwelling houses until the work was finished (Boas and Hunt 1916, pp. 44–45, 398–399).

Then everyone would return by the same route to the Skeena for the second major event, which was the arrival of the salmon fished in June and July (the "Salmon Months"). Once the fish was smoked and stored away for the year, the families would go up to the mountains, where the men would hunt while the women laid up stocks of fruit and berries. With the coming of the frost in the ritual "Month of the Spinning Tops" (which were spun on the ice), people settled down in permanent villages for the winter. During this period, the men sometimes went off hunting again for a few days or a few weeks. Finally, toward November 15, came the

"Taboo Month," which marked the inauguration of the great winter ceremonies, in preparation for which the men were subjected to various restrictions.

Let us remember, too, that the Tsimshian were divided into four nonlocalized matrilineal clans, which were strictly exogamous and divided into lineages, descent lines, and households: the Eagles, the Ravens, the Wolves, and the Killer Whales; also, that the permanent villages were the seat of chiefdoms (generally called "tribes" by native informants); and, finally, that Tsimshian society was divided into three hereditary castes with bilateral inheritance of caste status (each individual was supposed to marry according to his rank): the "Real People" or reigning families, the "Nobles," and the "People," which comprised all those who (failing a purchase of rank by generous potlatches) were unable to assert an equal degree of nobility in both lines of their descent (Boas and Hunt 1916, pp. 478–514; Garfield 1939, pp. 173–174; Garfield, Wingert, and Barbeau 1951, p. 134; Garfield and Wingert 1966).

Now follows a summary of the story of Asdiwal taken from Boas and Hunt (1912) which will serve as a point of reference. This version was recorded on the coast at Port Simpson in Tsimshian dialect. Boas published the native text together with an English translation.

> Famine reigns in the Skeena valley; the river is frozen and it is winter. A mother and her daughter, both of whose husbands have died of hunger, both remember independently the happy times when they lived together and there was no dearth of food. Released by the death of their husbands, they simultaneously decide to meet, and they set off at the same moment. Since the mother lives down-river and the daughter up-river, the former goes eastwards and the latter westwards. They both travel on the frozen bed of the Skeena and meet halfway.
>
> Weeping with hunger and sorrow, the two women pitch camp on the bank at the foot of a tree, not far from which they find, poor pittance that it is, a rotten berry, which they sadly share.
>
> During the night, a stranger visits the young widow. It is soon learned that his name is Hatsenas,[1] a term which means, in Tsimshian, a bird of good omen. Thanks to him, the women start to find food regularly, and the younger of the two becomes the

wife of their mysterious protector and soon gives birth to a son, Asdiwal (Asiwa, Boas 1895a; Asi-hwil, Boas 1902).[2] His father speeds up his growth by supernatural means and gives him various magic objects: a bow and arrows, which never miss, for hunting, a quiver, a lance, a basket, snowshoes, a bark raincoat, and a hat— all of which will enable the hero to overcome all obstacles, make himself invisible, and procure an inexhaustible supply of food. Hatsenas then disappears and the elder of the two women dies.

Asdiwal and his mother pursue their course westward and settle down in her native village, Gitsalasert, in the Skeena Canyon (Boas and Hunt 1912, p. 83). One day a white she-bear comes down the valley.

Hunted by Asdiwal, who almost catches it thanks to his magic objects, the bear starts to climb up a vertical ladder. Asdiwal follows it up to the heavens, which he sees as a vast prairie, covered with grass and all kinds of flowers. The bear lures him into the home of its father, the sun, and reveals itself to be a beautiful girl, Evening-Star. The marriage takes place, though not before the Sun has submitted Asdiwal to a series of trials, to which all previous suitors had succumbed (hunting wild goat in mountains which are rent by earthquakes, drawing water from a spring in a cave whose walls close in on each other, collecting wood from a tree which crushes those who try to cut it down, a period in a fiery furnace). But Asdiwal overcomes them all, thanks to his magic objects and the timely intervention of his father. Won over by his son-in-law's talents, the Sun finally approves of him.

Asdiwal, however, pines for his mother. The Sun agrees to allow him to go down to earth again with his wife, and gives them, as provisions for the journey, four baskets filled with inexhaustible supplies of food, which earn the couple a grateful welcome from the villagers, who are in the midst of their winter famine.

In spite of repeated warnings from his wife, Asdiwal deceives her with a woman from his village. Evening-Star, offended, departs, followed by her tearful husband. Halfway up to heaven, Asdiwal is struck down by a look from his wife, who disappears. He dies, but his loss is at once regretted and he is brought back to life by his celestial father-in-law.

For a time, all goes well. Then, Asdiwal once again feels a twinge of nostalgia for earth. His wife agrees to accompany him as far as the earth, and there bids him a final farewell. Returning to his village, the hero learns of his mother's death. Nothing remains to hold him back, and he sets off again on his journey downstream.

When he reaches the Tsimshian village of Ginaxangioget, he seduces and marries the daughter of the local chief. To start with, the marriage is a happy one, and Asdiwal joins his four brothers-in-law on wild goat hunts which, thanks to his magic objects, are crowned with success. When spring approaches, the whole family moves, staying first at Metlakatla, and then setting off by boat for the river Nass, going up along the coast. A head wind forces them to a halt and they camp for a while at Ksemaksén. There, things go wrong because of a dispute between Asdiwal and his brothers-in-law over the respective merits of mountain-hunters and sea-hunters. A competition takes place—Asdiwal returns from the mountain with four bears that he has killed, while the brothers-in-law return empty-handed from their sea expedition. Humiliated and enraged, they break camp, and, taking their sister with them, abandon Asdiwal.

He is picked up by strangers coming from Gitxatla, who are also on their way to the Nass for the candlefish season.

As in the previous case, they are a group of four brothers and a sister, whom Asdiwal wastes no time in marrying. They soon arrive together at the River Nass, where they sell large quantities of fresh meat and salmon to the Tsimshian, who have already settled there and are starving.

Since the catch that year is a good one, everyone goes home: the Tsimshian to their capital at Metlkatla and the Gitxatla to their town Laxalan, where Asdiwal, by this time rich and famous, has a son. One winter's day, he boasts that he can hunt sea lions better than his brothers-in-law. They set out to sea together. Thanks to his magic objects, Asdiwal has a miraculously success-ful hunt on a reef, but is left there without food or fire by his angry brothers-in-law. A storm gets up and waves sweep over the rock. With the help of his father, who appears in time to save him, Asdiwal, transformed into a bird, succeeds in keeping him-self above the waves, using his magic objects as a perch.

After two days and two nights the storm is calmed, and Asdiwal falls asleep exhausted. A mouse wakes him and leads him to the subterranean home of the sea lions whom he has wounded, but who imagine (since Asdiwal's arrows are invisible to them) that they are victims of an epidemic. Asdiwal extracts the arrows and cures his hosts, whom he asks, in return, to guarantee his safe return. Unfortunately, the sea lions' boats, which are made of their stomachs, are out of use, pierced by the hunter's arrows. The king of the sea lions therefore lends Asdiwal his own stomach as a canoe and instructs him to send it back without delay.

When he reaches land, the hero discovers his wife and his son inconsolable. Thanks to the help of this good wife (but bad sister, for she carries out the rites which are essential to the success of the operation), Asdiwal makes killer whales out of carved wood and brings them to life. They break open the boats with their fins and bring about the shipwreck and death of the wicked brothers-in-law.

But once again Asdiwal feels an irrepressible desire to re-visit the scenes of his childhood. He leaves his wife and returns to the Skeena valley. He settles in the town of Ginadâos, where he is joined by his son, to whom he gives his magic bow and arrows, and from whom he receives a dog in return.

When winter comes, Asdiwal goes off to the mountains to hunt, but forgets his snowshoes. Lost, and unable to go either up or down without them, he is turned to stone with his lance and his dog, and they can still be seen in that form at the peak of the great mountain by the lake of Ginadâos (Boas and Hunt 1912, pp. 71–146).

Let us keep provisionally to this version alone in order to attempt to define the essential points of its structure. The narrative refers to facts of various orders: first, the physical and political geography of the Tsimshian country, since the places and towns mentioned really do exist; second, the economic life of the natives which, as we have seen, governs the great seasonal migrations between the Skeena and Nass valleys during the course of which Asdiwal's adventures take place; third, the social and family organizations, for we witness several marriages, divorces, widow-hoods, and other connected events; and lastly, the cosmology, for, unlike the others, two of Asdiwal's visits, one to heaven and the other below the earth, are of a mythological and not of an experiential order.

First of all, let us consider the geographical aspects.[3]

The story begins in the Skeena Valley, when the two heroines leave their villages, one upstream, the other downstream, and meet halfway. In the version that Boas recorded at the Nass estuary, it is stated that the meeting place, this time on the Nass, is called Hwil-lê-ne-hwada, "Where-They-Meet-Each-Other" (Boas 1902, p. 225).

After her mother's death, the young woman and her son settle in her native village (i.e., her father's, where her mother had lived from the time of her marriage until her husband's death, the downstream village. It is from there that the visit to heaven takes place. This village, called Gitsalasert, "People of the [Skeena] Canyon," is situated not far from the modern town of Usk (Garfield 1939, p. 175; Boas and Hunt 1912, pp. 71, 276; cf. Krause

1956, pp. 214–215: "Kĭtselāssin," on the Skeena River). Although the Tsimshian dialect was spoken there, it was outside the "nine towns" which, strictly speaking, formed the Tsimshian province (Boas and Hunt 1912, p. 225).

On his mother's death, Asdiwal continues his journey downstream, that is to say, westward. He settles in the town of Ginaxangioget, where he marries. This is in Tsimshian country proper on the lower reaches of the Skeena. Ginaxangioget is, in fact, a term formed from the root of *git* = "people" and *gi.k* = "hemlock tree," from which comes *Ginax-angi.k*, "the people of the firs" (Garfield 1939, p. 175). Ginaxangioget was one of the nine principal towns of the Tsimshian (Boas and Hunt 1916, pp. 482–483).[4]

When Asdiwal leaves with his in-laws for the Nass to fish candlefish there, they go first to the Skeena estuary, then take to the sea and stop at the capital city of the Tsimshian, Metlakatla. A recent town of the same name, founded by natives converted to Christianity, is to be found on Annette Island in Alaska (Beynon 1941; Garfield, Wingert, and Barbeau 1951, pp. 33–34). Old Metlakatla is on the coast, north of Prince Rupert and halfway between the Skeena and the Nass estuaries. Ksemaksén, where the first quarrel takes place, and where Asdiwal is first abandoned by his brothers-in-law, is also on the coast, a little further north.

The Tsimshian-speaking tribe called Gitxatla, which is independent of those centers around Metlakatla, forms a group of islanders living on McCauley, Porcher, and Dolphin islands, across and south of the Skeena estuary. Their name comes from *git*, "people," and *qxatla*, "channel" (Garfield 1939, p. 175; Boas and Hunt 1916, p. 483).[5] Having traveled from east to west, Asdiwal accompanies them to the Nass, that is to say in a south-north direction, then in the opposite direction, to "their town," offshore from which (and probably to the west, since it was a deep-sea expedition) the visit to the sea lions takes place.

From there, Asdiwal returns to the Skeena—this time from west to east. The story ends at Ginadâos (or perhaps Ginadoiks from *git*, "people," *na*, "of," *doiks*, "rapid current"; the name of a torrent which flows into the Skeena. (Garfield 1939, p. 176).[6]

Let us now consider the economic aspect. The economic activities brought to notice by the myth are no less real than the geographical places and the populations evoked in the preceding paragraphs. Everything begins with a period of winter famine such

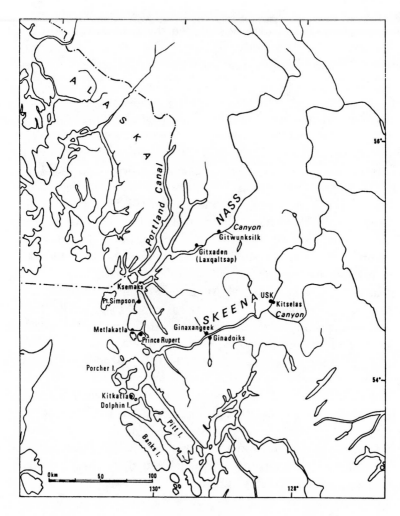

FIGURE 9

as was well known to the natives in the period between mid-December and mid-January, before the moment when, theoretically, the spring salmon arrived, which was just before the arrival of the candlefish, the period called the interval" (Boas and Hunt 1916, pp. 398–399). After his visit to the heavens, Asdiwal takes part in the spring migration to the Nass for the candlefish season; then we are told of the return of the families to the Skeena in the salmon season.

These seasonal variations—to use Marcel Mauss's expression—are on a par with other, no less real differences emphasized by the myth, notably that between the land hunter (personified by Asdiwal, born on the river and upstream, i.e., inland) and the sea hunter (personified first by the People of the Firs who live downstream on the estuary, and then, still more clearly, by the inhabitants of Porcher and Dolphin islands.

When we move on to the sociological aspects, there is a much greater freedom of interpretation. It is not a question of an accurate documentary picture of the reality of native life, but a sort of counterpoint which seems sometimes to be in harmony with this reality, and sometimes to part from it in order to rejoin it again.

The initial sequence of events evokes clearly defined sociological conditions. The mother and daughter have been separated by the latter's marriage, and since that time each has lived with her own husband in his village. The elder woman's husband was also the father of the younger woman, who left her native village to follow her own husband upstream. We can recognize this as a society in which, while having a system of matrilineal filiation, residence is patrilocal, the wife going to live in her husband's village; and one in which the children, although they belong to their mother's clan, are brought up in their father's home and not in that of their maternal kin.

Such was the situation among the Tsimshian. Boas emphasizes it several times: "In olden times it was customary for a great chief to take a princess from each tribe to be his wife. Some had as many as sixteen or eighteen wives. . . ," which would clearly be impossible if a man had to live in his wife's native village. More generally, says Boas, "There is ample evidence showing that the young married people lived with the young man's parents," so that "the children grew up in their father's home" (Boas and Hunt 1916, pp. 355, 529, 426; cf. p. 420, 427, 441, 499–500).

But, in the myth, this patrilocal type of residence is quickly undermined by famine, which frees the two women from their respective obligations and allows them, upon the death of their husbands, to meet (significantly enough) halfway. Their camping at the foot of the tree on the bank of the frozen river, equidistant from up-river and down-river, presents a picture of a matrilocal type of residence reduced to its simplest form, since the new household consists only of a mother and her daughter.

This reversal, which is barely hinted at, is all the more remarkable because all the subsequent marriages are going to be matrilocal, and thus contrary to the type found in reality.

First, Hatsenas's marriage with the younger woman. Fleeting though this union between a human being and a supernatural being may be, the husband still lives in his wife's home, and therefore in her mother's home. The matrilocal trend is even more apparent in the version recorded on the Nass. When his son Asi-hwil has grown up, Hatsenas (who here is called Hôux) says to his wife: "Your brothers are coming to look for you. Therefore I must hide in the woods." Shortly thereafter, the brothers come, and leave again, laden with supplies of meat given to the women by their protector. "As soon as they left, Hôux returned. The [women] told him that their brothers and uncles had asked them to return home. Then Hôux said, 'Let us part. You may return to your home; I will return to mine.' On the following morning, many people came to fetch the women and the boy. They took them to Gitxaden. The boy's uncles gave a feast and his mother told them the boy's name, Asi-hwil . . ." (Boas 1902, p. 227).

Not only does the husband seem an intruder—regarded with suspicion by his brothers-in-law and afraid that they might attack him—but, contrary to what happens among the Tsimshian and in other societies characterized by the association of matrilineal filiation and patrilocal residence (Boas and Hunt 1916, p. 423; Malinowski 1922) the food gifts go from the sister's husband to the wife's brothers.

Matrilocal marriage, accompanied by antagonism between the husband and his in-laws, is further illustrated by Asdiwal's marriage to Evening-Star; they live in her father's home, and the father-in-law shows so much hostility toward his son-in-law that he sets him trials which are deemed to be fatal.

Matrilocal, too, is Asdiwal's second marriage in the land of the People of the Firs, which is accompanied by hostility between the husband and his brothers-in-law because they abandon him and persuade their sister to follow them.

The same theme is expressed in the third marriage in the land of the People of the Channel, at any rate to start with. After Asdiwal's visit to the sea lions, the situation is reversed: Asdiwal recovers his wife, who has refused to follow her brothers and was wandering in search of her husband. What is more, she collaborates with him to produce the "machination"—in the literal and the figurative sense—by means of which he takes revenge on his brothers-in-law. Finally, patrilocality triumphs when Asdiwal abandons his wife (whereas in the previous marriages it had been his wife who had abandoned him) and returns to the Skeena where he was born, and where his son comes alone to join him. Thus, having begun with the story of the *reunion of a mother and her daughter*, freed from their affines or *paternal kin*, the myth ends with the story of the *reunion of a father and his son*, freed from their affines or *maternal kin*.

But if the initial and final sequences on the myth constitute, from a sociological point of view, a pair of oppositions, the same is true, from a cosmological point of view, of the two supernatural voyages which interrupt the hero's "real" journey. The first voyage takes him to the heavens and into the home of the Sun, who first tries to kill him and then agrees to bring him back to life. The second takes Asdiwal to the subterranean kingdom of the sea lions, whom he has himself killed or wounded, but whom he agrees to look after and to cure. The first voyage results in a marriage which, as we have seen, is matrilocal, and which, moreover, bears witness to a maximal exogamous separation (between an earth-born man and a woman from heaven). But this marriage will be broken up by Asdiwal's infidelity with a woman of his own village. This may be seen as a suggestion of a marriage which, if it really took place, would neutralize matrilocality (since husband and wife would come from the same place) and would be characterized by an endogamous proximity which would also be maximal (marriage within the village). It is true that the hero's second supernatural voyage, to the subterranean kingdom of the sea lions, does not lead to a marriage. But, as has already been shown, this visit brings about a reversal in the matrilocal tendency of Asdiwal's successive marriages, for it separates his third wife from her brothers, the hero himself from his wife, their son from his mother, and leaves only one relationship in existence: that between the father and his son.

In this analysis of the myth, we have distinguished four levels: the geographic, the techno-economic, the sociological, and the cosmological. The first two are exact transcriptions of reality; the fourth has nothing to do with it; and in the third real and imaginary institutions are interwoven. Yet in spite of these differences, the levels are not separated out by the native mind. It is rather that everything happens as if the levels were provided with different codes, each being used according to the needs of the moment, and according to its particular capacity, to transmit the same message. It is the nature of this message that we shall now consider.

Winter famines are a recurrent event in the economic life of the Tsimshian. But the famine that starts the story off is also a cosmological theme. All along the northwest Pacific Coast, in fact, the present state of the universe is attributed to the havoc wrought in the original order by the demiurge Giant or Raven (Txamsen, in Tsimshian) during travels which he undertook in order to satisfy his irrepressible voracity. Thus Txamsen is perpetually in a state of famine, and famine, although a negative condition, is seen as the *primum mobile* of creation.[7] In this sense we can say that the hunger of the two women in our myth has a cosmic significance. These heroines are not so much legendary persons as incarnations of principles which are at the origin of place names.

One may schematize the initial situation as follows:

mother	daughter
elder	younger
downstream	upstream
west	east
south	north

The meeting takes place at the halfway point, a situation which, as we have seen, corresponds to a neutralization of patrilocal residence and to the fulfillment of the conditions for a matrilocal residence which is as yet only hinted at. But since the mother dies on the very spot where the meeting and the birth of Asdiwal took place, the essential movement, which her daughter begins by leaving the village of her marriage "very far upstream" (Boas and Hunt 1912, p. 71), is in the direction east-west, as far as her native village in the Skeena Canyon, where she in her turn dies, leaving the field open for the hero.

Asdiwal's first adventure presents us with an opposition—that of heaven and earth—which the hero is able to surmount by virtue of the intervention of his father, Hatsenas, the bird of good omen. The latter is a creature of the atmospheric or middle heaven and consequently is well qualified to play the role of mediator between the earth-born Asdiwal and his father-in-law the Sun, ruler of the highest heaven. Even so, Asdiwal does not manage to overcome his earthly nature, to which he twice submits, first in yielding to the charms of a fellow countrywoman and then in yielding to nostalgia for his home village. Thus there remains a series of unresolved oppositions:

low	high
earth	heaven
man	woman
endogamy	exogamy

Pursuing his course westward, Asdiwal contracts a second matrilocal marriage which generates a new series of oppositions:

mountain hunting	sea hunting
land	water

These oppositions, too, are insurmountable, and Asdiwal's earthly nature carries him away a third time, with the result that he is abandoned by his wife and his brothers-in-law.

Asdiwal contracts his last marriage not with the river dwellers, but with islanders, and the same conflict is repeated. The opposition continues to be insurmountable, although at each stage the terms are brought closer together. This time it is in fact a question of a quarrel between Asdiwal and his brothers-in-law on the occasion of a hunt on a reef on the high seas; that is, on land and water at the same time. In the previous incident, Asdiwal and his brothers-in-law had gone their separate ways, one inland and on foot, the others out to sea and in boats. This time they go together in boats, and it is only when they land that Asdiwal's superiority is made manifest by the use he makes of the magic objects intended for mountain hunting: "It was a very difficult hunt on account of the waves which swept past [the reef] in the direction of the open sea. While they were speaking about this, [Asdiwal] said: 'My dear fellows, I have only to put on my snowshoes and I'll run up the rocks you are talking about.' He succeeds in this way, whilst his brothers-in-law, incapable of landing, stay shamefacedly in their boats" (Boas and Hunt 1912, pp. 125–126).

Asdiwal, the earth-born master of the hunt finds himself abandoned on a reef in high seas. He has come to the furthest point in his westward journey; so much for the geographic and economic aspects. But from a logical point of view, his adventures can be seen in a different form—that of a series of impossible mediations between oppositions which are ordered in a descending scale: high and low, water and earth, sea hunting and mountain hunting, and so forth.

Consequently, on the spatial plane, the hero is completely led off his course, and his failure is expressed in this *maximal separation* from his starting point. On the logical plane, he has also failed because of his immoderate attitude toward his brothers-in-law, and because of his inability to play the role of a mediator, even though the last of the oppositions which had to be overcome—between the types of life led by the land hunters and sea hunters—is reduced to a *minimal separation*. There would seem to be a dead end at this point; but from neutral the myth goes into reverse and its machinery starts up again.

The king of the mountains (in Nass dialect, Asdiwal is called Asi-hwil, which means "Crosser of Mountains") is caught on a caricature of a mountain, one that is doubly so because, on the one hand, it is nothing more than a reef and, on the other, it is surrounded and almost submerged by the sea. The ruler of wild animals and killer of bears is to be saved by a she-mouse, a caricature of a wild animal.[8] She makes him undertake a *subterranean journey*, just as the she-bear, the supreme wild animal, had imposed on Asdiwal a *celestial journey*. In fact, the only thing that is missing is for the mouse to change into a woman and to offer the hero a marriage which would be symmetrical to the other, but opposite to it. Although this element is not to be found in any of the versions, we know at least that the mouse is a fairy: Lady Mouse-Woman, as she is called in the texts, where the word *ksem*, a term of respect addressed to a woman, is prefixed to the word denoting a rodent. Following through the inversion more systematically than had been possible under the preceding hypothesis, this fairy is an old woman incapable of procreation—an "inverse wife."

And that is not all. The man who had killed animals by the hundreds goes this time to heal them and win their love.[9] The bringer of food (who repeatedly exercises the power he received from his father in this respect for the benefit of his family) becomes food, since he is transported in the sea lion's stomach.[10]

Finally, the visit to the subterranean world (which is also, in many respects, an "upside-down world") sets the course of the hero's return; for from then onward he travels from west to east, from the sea toward the mainland, from the salt water of the ocean to the fresh water of the Skeena.

This overall reversal does not affect the development of the plot, which unfolds up to the final catastrophe. When Asdiwal returns to his people and to the initial patrilocal situation, he takes up his favorite occupation again, helped by his magic objects. But he *forgets* one of them, and this mistake is fatal. After a successful hunt, he finds himself trapped halfway up the mountain side: "Where might he go now? He could not go up, he could not go to either side" (Boas and Hunt 1912, p. 145). And on the spot he is changed to stone, that is to say, paralyzed, reduced to his earthborn nature in the stony and unchangeable form in which he has been seen "for generations."

The above analysis leads us to draw a distinction between two aspects of the construction of a myth: the sequences and the schemata.

The sequences form the apparent content of the myth, the chronological order in which things happen: the meeting of the two women, the intervention of the supernatural protector, the birth of Asdiwal, his childhood, his visit to heaven, his successive marriages, his hunting and fishing expeditions, his quarrels with his brothers-in-law, and so forth.

But these sequences are organized on planes at different levels of abstraction in accordance with schemata, which exist simultaneously, superimposed one upon the other; just as a melody composed for several voices is held within bounds by two-dimensional constraints: first by its own melodic line, which is horizontal, and second by the contrapuntal schemata, which are vertical. Let us then draw up an inventory of such schemata for this present myth.

1. *Geographic schema.* The hero goes from east to west, the returns from west to east. This return journey is modulated by another one, from the south to the north and then from the north to the south, which corresponds to the seasonal migrations of the Tsimshian (in which the hero takes part) to the River Nass for the candlefish season in the spring, then to the Skeena for the salmon fishing in the summer.

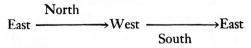

$$\text{North}$$
$$\text{East} \longrightarrow \text{West} \longrightarrow \text{East}$$
$$\text{South}$$

2. *Cosmological schema.* Three supernatural visits establish a relationship between terms thought of respectively as "below" and "above": the visit to the young widow by Hatsenas, the bird of good omen associated with the atmospheric heavens; the visit by Asdiwal to the highest heavens in pursuit of Evening-Star; and his visit to the subterranean kingdom of the sea lions under the guidance of Lady Mouse-Woman. The end of Asdiwal, trapped in the mountain, then appears as a *neutralization* of the intermediate mediation established at his birth but which even so does not enable him to bring off two further extreme mediations (the one between heaven and earth considered as the opposition low/high and the other between the sea and the land considered as the opposition east/west).

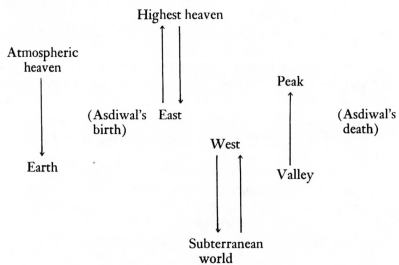

3. *Integration schema.* The above two schemata are integrated in a third consisting of several binary oppositions, none of which the hero can resolve, although the distance separating the opposed terms gradually dwindles. The initial and final oppositions, high/low and peak/valley, are "vertical" and thus belong to the cosmological schema. The two intermediate oppositions, water/land and sea hunting/mountain hunting, are "horizontal" and belong to the geographic schema. But the final opposition, peak/valley, which is also the narrowest contrast, brings into association the essential characteristics of the two preceding schemata: it is "vertical" in form, but "geographical" in content.[11] Asdiwal's failure (he is trapped half way up the mountain because he forgot his snowshoes) thus takes on a significance geographical, cosmological, and logical.

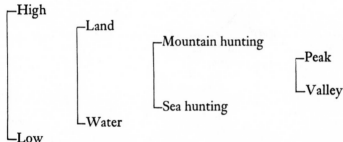

When the three schemata are reduced in this way to their bare essentials, retaining only the order and amplitude of the oppositions, their complementarity becomes apparent.

> *Schema 1* is composed of a sequence of oscillations of constant amplitude: east–north–west–south–east.
> *Schema 2* starts at a zero point (the meeting halfway between upstream and downstream) and is followed by an oscillation of medium amplitude (atmospheric heavens–earth), then by oscillations of maximum amplitude (earth-heaven, heaven-earth, earth-subterranean world, subterranean world-earth) which die away at the zero point (halfway up, between peak and valley).
> *Schema 3* begins with an oscillation of maximum amplitude (high-low) which dies away in a series of oscillations of decreasing amplitude (water–land; sea hunting–mountain hunting; valley-peak).

4. *Sociological schema.* To start with, the patrilocal residence prevails. It gives way progressively to the matrilocal residence

(Hatsenas's marriage), which becomes deadly (Asdiwal's marriage in heaven), then merely hostile (the marriage in the land of the People of the Firs), before weakening and finally reversing (marriage among the People of the Channel) to allow a return to patrilocal residence.

The sociological schema does not have, however, a closed structure like the geographic schema, since, at the beginning, it involves a mother and her daughter; in the middle, a husband, his wife, and his brothers-in-law; and, at the end, a father and his son.[12]

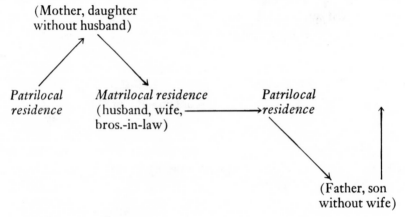

5. *Techno-economic schema.* The myth begins by evoking a winter famine; it ends with a successful hunt. In between, the story follows the economic cycle and the seasonal migrations of the native fishermen:

Famine ⟶ Fishing for candlefish ⟶ Salmon fishing ⟶ Successful hunt

6. *Global integration.* If the myth is finally reduced to its two extreme propositions, the initial state of affairs and the final, which together summarize its operational function, then we end up with a simplified diagram:

Female / East-west / Famine / Movement   axis ⟩ —————— ⟨ Male / High-low / Repletion / Immobility   axis

Having separated out the codes, we have analyzed the structure of the message. It now remains to decipher the meaning.

In Boas's *Tsimshian Mythology*, there is a version of the story of Asdiwal that is remarkable in several respects. First, it brings a new character into play: Waux, the son of Asdiwal's second marriage, who seems to be a double of his father, although his adventures take place after those of Asdiwal. In chronological order, they form supplementary sequences of events. But these *later* sequences are organized in schemata which are at the same time *homologous* to those which have been described before and more *explicit*. Everything seems to suggest that, as it draws to its close, the apparent narrative (the sequences) tends to approach the latent content of the myth (the schemata). It is a convergence which is not unlike that which the listener discovers in the final chords of a symphony.

> When Asdiwal's second wife (his first earth-born wife) bore him a son, he was called Waux. That means "very light," for this son used to fly away like a spark.[13]
> The father and son loved each other very much and always hunted together. And thus it was a cause of great sorrow to Waux when his uncles forced him to follow them after they had left his father (Asdiwal) at Ksemaksén. The mother and son had even secretly tried to find Asdiwal and had only abandoned the attempt when they were convinced that he must have been devoured by some wild animal.
> Waux, following in his father's footsteps, became a great hunter. Before his mother died, she made him marry a cousin, and the young couple lived happily. Waux continued to hunt on his father's hunting grounds, sometimes in company with his wife, who gave birth to twins.
> Soon Waux's children went hunting with him, as he had formerly done with his father. One day he went with them into an unexplored region. The children slipped on the mountain and were both killed. The following year, Waux returned to the same place to hunt, armed with all the magic objects he had inherited from his father, except the lance, which he forgot. Taken unawares by an earthquake, he tried in vain to make his wife (whom he saw in the valley) understand that he needed her ritual help. He shouted to her to sacrifice fat to the supernatural powers in order to appease them. But the wife could not hear and misunderstood, repeating not what her husband had said but what she

wanted to do herself: "You want me to eat fat?" Discouraged, Waux agreed, and his wife sated herself with fat and cold water. Satisfied, she lay down on an old log. Her body broke apart and was changed into a veined flint which is still found all over that place today.

Waux, because he had forgotten the lance which enabled him to split the rock and open a way through the mountain, and having lost his last chance of placating the elements because of the misunderstanding which had arisen between his wife and himself, was turned to stone, as were his dog and all his magic objects. They are still here to this day (Boas and Hunt 1916, pp. 243–245).

Several significant permutations will be noticed if this is compared with the version which we have taken as a point of reference.

Asdiwal had an only son (in fact, as we have seen, two only sons, born of consecutive marriages and confused into one single one in the story), whereas Waux has twins. We do not know much about these twins, but it is tempting to set up a parallel between them and the two magic dogs that Asi-hwil was given by his father in the River Nass version, one red, the other spotted; that is, marked by a contrast which suggests (when compared with the symbolic color systems so common among the North American Indians) divergent functions.

Moreover, the existence of twins already provides a pointer. In the American series of mediators, twins represent the weakest term, and come at the bottom of the list, after the Messiah (who unites opposites), and the trickster (in whom they are in juxtaposition). The pair of twins brings opposites into association but at the same time leaves them individually distinct.[14]

The change from a single mediator to a pair of twins is thus a sign of a weakening in the function of the mediator. This is all the clearer from the fact that, only shortly after their appearance on the mystical scene, the twins die in unexplored territory without having played any part.

Like Asdiwal, Waux ends by being turned to stone as a result of forgetting a magic object. The identity of this object, however, changes from one version to another. In Asdiwal, it is the snowshoes, in Waux the lance. The magic objects are the instruments of mediation given to the hero by his supernatural father. Here again there is a gradation. The snowshoes make it possible to climb up and down the steepest slopes. The lance enables its owner to go straight through walls of rock. The lance is thus a more radical means than the snowshoes, which come to terms with the obstacle rather than doing away with it. Waux's omission seems more serious than Asdiwal's. The weaker mediator loses the stronger instrument of mediation and his powers are doubly diminished as a result.

Thus the story of Waux follows a dialectic regression. But, in another sense, it reveals a progression, since it is with this variant that a structure which had remained open in certain respects is finally closed.

Waux's wife dies of *repletion*. That is the end of a story which opened by showing Asdiwal's (or Asi-hwil's) mother a victim of *starvation*. It was this famine which set her in *motion*, just as, now, abuse of food brings Waux's wife to a *halt*.

Before leaving this point let us note that in fact two characters of the initial sequence were two women who were *single*, *unfed*, and *on the move*, whereas those of the final sequence were a *couple* composed of a husband and his wife, one a *bringer of food* (who is not understood) and the other *overfed* (because she does not understand), and both *paralyzed* in spite of this opposition (but also perhaps because of the negative complementarity that it expresses).

The most important transformation is that represented by the marriage of Waux. It has been seen that Asdiwal contracted a series of marriages, all equally unsuccessful. He cannot choose between his supernatural bride and his fellow countrywoman; he is abandoned (though against her will, it is true) by his Tsimshian spouse. His Gitxatla wife remains faithful to him and even goes so far as to betray her brothers; it is he who abandons her. He ends his days, having joined forces with his son again, in a celibate state.

Waux, on the other hand, marries only once, but this marriage proves fatal to him. Here, however, it is a case of a marriage *arranged* by Waux's mother (unlike Asdiwal's *adventurous* marriages) and a marriage with a *cousin* (whereas Asdiwal marries complete *strangers*); or more precisely, with his cross-cousin, his mother's brother's daughter (which explains the intermediary role played by his mother).[15]

As Boas explains in the text quoted in the footnote above,

there was a preference for marriage with the mother's brother's daughter among the Tsimshian, especially in the noble classes from which our heroes are drawn. Garfield doubts whether the practice was strictly in accordance with mythical models (1939, pp. 232–233), but the point is of secondary importance, since we are studying schemata with a normative function. In a society like that of the Tsimshian, there is no difficulty in seeing why this type of marriage could be thought ideal. Boys grew up in their fathers' homes, but sooner or later they had to go over to their maternal uncle when they inherited his titles, prerogatives, and hunting grounds.[16] Marriage with the matrilineal cousin provided a solution to this conflict.

Furthermore, as has often been found to be the case in other societies of the same type, such a marriage made it possible to overcome another conflict: that between the patrilineal and matrilineal tendencies of Tsimshian society, which, as we have seen above, is very deeply conscious of the two lines. By means of such a marriage, a man ensures the continued existence of his hereditary privileges and of such titles as he might have within the limits of a small family circle (Swanton 1909a; Wedgewood 1928; Richards 1914).

I have shown elsewhere that it is unlikely that this interpretation may be seen as the universal origin of cross-cousin marriage (Lévi-Strauss 1969a, pp. 123–124). But in the case of a society which has feudal tendencies, it certainly corresponds to real motives which contributed to the survival or the adoption of the custom. The final explanation of this custom must, however, be sought in those characteristics which are common to all societies which practiced it.

The Tsimshian myths provide, furthermore, a surprising commentary on the native theory of marriage with the matrilateral cross-cousin in the story of the princess who refused to marry her cousin (her father's sister's son).

> No less cruel than she was proud, the princess demands that her cousin prove his love by disfiguring himself. He slashes his face and then she rejects him because of his ugliness. Reduced to a state of despair, the young man seeks death and ventures into the land of Chief Pestilence, master of deformities. After the Hero has undergone rigorous trials, the chief agrees to transform him into a Prince Charming.

Now his cousin is passionately attracted to him, and the young man, in his turn, demands that she sacrifice her beauty, but only in order to heap sarcasm upon her head. The now hideous princess tries to move Chief Pestilence to pity, and at once the maimed and deformed race of people who make up his court set upon the unfortunate woman, break her bones and tear her apart (Boas and Hunt 1916, pp. 185–191).

Boas' informant sees in this tale the myth which lies at the origin of the rites and ceremonies celebrated at the marriages of cross-cousins.

There was a custom among our people that the nephew of the chief had to marry the chief's daughter, because the tribe of the chief wanted the chief's nephew to be the heir of his uncle and to inherit his place after his death. This custom has gone on, generation after generation, all along until now, and the places of the head men have thus been inherited.

But, the informant goes on, it is because of the disaster that struck the rebellious princess that it was decided that on such occasions "no young woman should have any say about her marriage. . . . Even though the young woman does not want to marry the man, she has to consent when the agreement has been made on both sides to marry them" (that is to say, after negotiations between the maternal-descent groups of the young people):

When the prince and princess have married, the tribe of the young man's uncle mobilize. Then the tribe of the young woman's uncle also mobilize and they have a fight. The two parties cast stones at each other, and the heads of many of those on each side are hit. The scars made by the stones on the heads of each chief's people are signs of the marriage pledge (Boas and Hunt 1916, pp. 185–191).[17]

In his commentary Boas notes that this myth is not peculiar to the Tsimshian, but is found also among the Tlingit and the Haida, who are likewise matrilineal and likewise faithful to the same type of marriage. Thus it is clear that it portrays a fundamental aspect of the social organization of these peoples, which consists in a hostile equilibrium between the matrilineal lineages of the village chiefs. In a system of generalized exchange, such as results in these feudal families from the preferential marriage with the mother's brother's daughter, the families are, so to speak, ranged around a more or less stable circle, in such a way that each family occupies (at least temporarily) the position of "wife-giver" with respect to some other family and of "wife-taker" with respect to a third. Depending on the society, this lopsided structure (lopsided because there is no guarantee that in giving one will receive) can achieve a certain equilibrium—more apparent, however, than real—in any of several ways. It can achieve this democratically, by following the principle that all marriage exchanges are equivalent; or, on the contrary, by stipulating that one of the positions (wife-giver, wife-taker) is, by definition, superior to the other. But given a different social and economic context, this amounts in theory, if not in practice, to the same thing, since each family must occupy both positions (Lévi-Strauss 1949; *S.A.*, p. 305). The societies of the northwest Pacific Coast could not, or would not, choose one of these points of balance, and the respective superiority or inferiority of the groups involved was openly contested on the occasion of each marriage. Each marriage, along with the potlatches which accompanied and preceded it, and the tranfers of titles and property occasioned by it, provided the means by which the groups concerned might simultaneously gain an advantage over each other and end former disputes. French mediaeval society offers, in terms of patrilineal institutions, a symmetrical picture of a situation which had much in common with the one just described.

In such circumstances, is there anything amazing about the horrid little story in which the natives see the origin of their marriage institutions? Is there anything surprising in the fact that the ceremony of marriage between first cousins takes the form of a internecine battle? When we believe that, in bringing to light these antagonisms which are inherent in the structure of Tsimshian society, we are "reaching rock bottom" (in the words of Marcel Mauss), we express in this geological metaphor an approach that has many points of comparison with that of the myths of Asdiwal and Waux. All the paradoxes conceived by the native mind, on the most diverse planes—geographic, economic, sociological, and even cosmological—are, when all is said and done, assimilated to that less obvious yet so real paradox, the dilemma which marriage with the matrilateral cousin attempts but fails to resolve. But the failure is *admitted* in our myths, and there precisely lies their function.

Let us glance at them again in this light. The winter famine which kills the husbands of the two original heroines frees them from patrilocal residence and enables them first to meet and then to return to the daughter's native village, which corresponds, for her son, to a matrilocal type of residence. Thus a shortage of food is related to the sending out of young women, who return to their own descent groups when food is scarce. This is symbolic of an event which is illustrated in a more concrete fashion each year— even when there is no famine—by the departure of the candlefish from the Nass and then of the salmon from the Skeena. These fish come from the open sea, arrive from the south and the west, and go up the rivers in an easterly direction. Like the departing fish, Asdiwal's mother continues her journey westward and toward the sea, where Asdiwal discovers the disastrous effects of matrilocal marriage.

The first of his marriages is with Evening-Star, who is a supernatural being. The correlation of female heaven and male earth which is implicit in this event is interesting from two points of view.

First, Asdiwal is in a way fished up by the She-Bear who draws him up to heaven, and the myths often describe grizzly bears as *fishing for salmon* (Boas and Hunt 1916, p. 403).[18] Like a salmon, too, Asdiwal is fished up in a net by the compassionate Sun after he has crashed to earth. (Boas and Hunt 1912, pp. 112–113).[19] But when Asdiwal returns from his symmetrically opposite visit to the subterranean kingdom of the sea lions, he travels in one of their stomachs, like food—comparable to the *candlefish* which are scooped up from the bed of the River Nass, the "Stomach River." Furthermore, the hero now goes in the opposite direction, no longer from the east to west like the food disappearing, but from west to east like the food returning.

Second, this reversal is accompanied by another: that from matrilocal to patrilocal residence. This latter reversal is in itself a variable of the replacement of a celestial journey by a subterranean one, which brings Asdiwal from the position of earth/male/dominated to that of earth/male/dominant.

Patrilocal residence is no more successful for Asdiwal. He gets his son back but loses his wife and his affines. Isolated in this new relationship and incapable of bringing together the two types of filiation and residence, he is stuck halfway at the end of a successful hunt: he has reconquered food but lost his freedom of movement. Famine, which causes movement, has given way to abundance, but at the price of paralysis.

We can now better understand how Waux's marriage with his matrilateral cousin, following that of his father, symbolizes the last futile attempts of Tsimshian thought and Tsimshian society to overcome their inherent contradictions. For this marriage fails as the result of a *misunderstanding* added to an *omission*. Waux had succeeded in staying with his maternal kin while at the same time retaining his father's hunting grounds. He had managed to inherit in both the maternal and paternal lines at the same time. But, although they are cousins, he and his wife remain alienated from one another, because cross-cousin marriage, in a feudal society, is a palliative and a decoy. In these societies, women are always objects of exchange, but property is also a cause of battle.

The above analysis suggests an observation of a different kind: it is always rash to undertake, as Boas wanted to do in his monumental *Tsimshian Mythology*, "a description of the life, social organization and religious ideas and practices of a people . . . as it appears from their mythology" (Boas and Hunt 1916, p. 32).

The myth is certainly related to given facts, but not as a *representation* of them. The relationship is of a dialectic kind, and the institutions described in the myths can be the very opposite of the real institutions. This will always be the case when the myth is trying to express a negative truth. As has already been seen, the story of Asdiwal has landed the great American ethnologist in no little difficulty, for there Waux is said to have inherited his father's hunting grounds. Other texts—as well as eyewitness observation—reveal that a man's property, including his hunting grounds, went to his sister's son, that is, from man to man in the maternal line.[20]

But Waux's paternal inheritance no more reflects real conditions than do his father's matrilocal marriages. In real life, the children grew up in the patrilocal home. Then they went to finish their education at their maternal uncle's home. After marrying, they returned to live with their parents, bringing their wives with them, and they settled in their uncle's village only when they were called upon to succeed him. Such, at any rate, was the case among the nobility, whose mythology formed a real "court literature."

The comings and goings were some of the outward signs of the *tensions* between lineages connected by marriage. Mythical speculations about types of residence which are exclusively patrilocal or matrilocal do not therefore have anything to do with the reality of the structure of Tsimshian society, but rather with its inherent possibilities and its latent potentialities. Such speculations, in the last analysis, do not seek to depict what is real, but to justify the shortcomings of reality, since the extreme positions are only *imagined* in order to show that they are *untenable*. This step, which is fitting for mythical thought, implies an admission (but in the veiled language of the myth) that the social facts when thus examined are marred by an insurmountable contradiction. A contradiction which, like the hero of the myth, Tsimshian society cannot understand and prefers to forget.

This conception of the relation of the myth to reality no doubt limits the use of the former as a documentary source. But it opens the way for other possibilities; for, in abandoning the search for a constantly accurate picture of ethnographic reality in the myth, we gain, on occasions, a means of reaching unconscious categories.

A moment ago it was recalled that Asdiwal's two journeys— from east to west and from west to east—were correlated with types of residence, matrilocal and patrilocal, respectively. But in fact the Tsimshian have patrilocal residence, and from this we can (and indeed must) draw the conclusion that one of the orientations corresponds to the direction implicit in a real-life "reading" of their institutions, the other to the opposite direction. The journey from west to east, the return journey, is accompanied by a return to patrilocality. Therefore the direction in which it is made is, for the native mind, the only real direction, the other being purely imaginary.

That is, moreover, what the myth proclaims. The move to the east assures Asdiwal's return to his element, the earth, and to his native land. When he went westward it was as a bringer of food, putting an end to starvation; he made up for the absence of food while at the same time traveling in the same direction as that taken by food when it departed. Journeying in the opposite direction, in the sea lion's stomach, he is symbolically identified with food, and he travels in the direction in which the food returns.

The same applies to matrilocal residence. It is introduced as a negative reality, to make up for the nonexistence of patrilocal residence caused by the death of the husbands.

What then is the west-east direction in native thought? It is the direction taken by the candlefish and the salmon when they arrive from the sea each year to enter the rivers and race upstream. If this orientation is also that which the Tsimshian must adopt in order to obtain an undistorted picture of their concrete social existence, is it not because they see themselves as being *sub specie piscis;* that they put themselves in the fishes' place—or rather, that they put the fish in their place?

This hypothesis, arrived at by a process of deductive reasoning, is indirectly confirmed by ritual institutions and mythology.

Fishing and the preparation of the fish are the occasion for all kinds of ritual among the natives of the northwest Pacific Coast. We have already seen that the women must use their naked breasts to press the candlefish in order to extract the oil from it, and that the remains must be left to rot near the dwellings in spite of the smell. The salmon does not rot, since it is dried in the sun or smoked. But there are other ritual conditions which must be observed; for instance, the salmon must be cut up with a primitive knife made of a mussel shell, and any kind of stone, bone, or metal blade is forbidden. Women set about this operation sitting on the ground with their legs apart (Boas and Hunt 1916, pp. 449–450, 919–932, Nootka).

These prohibitions and prescriptions seem to represent the same intention: to bring out the "immediacy" of the relationship between fish and man by treating fish as if it were man, or at any rate by ruling out, or limiting to the extreme, the use of manufactured objects which are part of culture; in other words, by denying or underestimating the differences between fish and men.

The myths, for their part, tell of the visit of a prince to the kingdom of the salmon, whence he returns—having won their alliance—himself transformed into a fish. All these myths have one incident in common: the hungry prince is welcomed by the salmon and learns that he may under no circumstances eat the same food as they. But he must not hesitate to kill and eat the fish themselves, regardless of the fact that they thenceforth appear to him in human form (Boas and Hunt 1916, pp. 192–206, 770–778, 919–932).

It is at this point that the mythical identification hits upon the only real relationship between fish and men: one of food. It persists, even in the myth, as an alternative: either to eat like salmon (although one is a man) or to eat salmon (although they are like men). This latter solution is the right one, provided that the ritual requested by the salmon is observed and thanks to it they are re-born from their bones, which had been carefully collected and then immersed or burned.[21] But the first solution would be an *abuse of identification*, of man with salmon, not of salmon with man. The character in the myth who was guilty of this was trans-formed into a root or a rock—like Asdiwal—condemned to im-mobility and perpetually bound to the earth.

Starting with an initial situation characterized by irrepressible movement and ending in a final situation characterized by perpetual immobility, the myth of Asdiwal expresses in its own way a funda-mental aspect of the native philosophy. The beginning presents us with the absence of food; and everything which has been said above leads us to think that the role of Asdiwal, as bringer of food, consists in a negation of this absence, but that is quite another thing from the presence of food. In fact, when this presence is finally obtained, with Asdiwal taking on the aspect of food itself (and no longer that of bringer of food), the result is a state of inertia.

But starvation is no more a tolerable human condition than is immobility. We must therefore conclude that for these natives the only positive form of existence is a *negation of nonexistence*. It is out of the question to develop this theory within the limits of the present work. But let us note in passing that it would shed new light on the *need for self-assertion*, which, in the potlatch, the feasts, the ceremonies, and the feudal rivalries, seems to be such a particular characteristic of the societies of the northwest Pacific Coast.

There is one last problem which remains to be solved: that posed by the differences between the Nass River version and those recorded on the coast, in which the action takes place on the Skeena. Up to now we have followed these latter ones. Let us now look at the Nass version.

Famine reigns in the two villages of Laxqaltsap and Gitwunksilk—it is possible to place them: the first is the present Greenville on the Nass estuary,[22] and the second is on the lower Nass, but farther upstream.[23] Two sisters, separated by marriage, each live in one of the villages. They decide to join forces, and meet half-way in a place which is named in memory of this event. They have a few provisions. The sister from down-river has only a few hawberries, the one from up-river, a small piece of spawn. They share this and bewail their plight.

One of the sisters—the one from up-river—has come with her daughter, who does not enter the story again. The one from down-river, the younger of the two, is still unmarried. A stranger visits her at night. He is called Hôux, which means "Good Luck." When he learns of the state of the women, he miraculously provides food for them, and the younger woman soon gives birth to a son, Asi-hwil, for whom his father makes a pair of snowshoes. At first they are useless; but once perfected, they bestow magic powers on their wearer. Asi-hwil's father also gives him two magic dogs, and a lance which can pass through rock. From then on the hero reveals himself to be a better hunter than other supernatural beings against whom he is matched.

Here follows the episode of Hôux's retreat from his brothers-in-law, which has been summarized above (see p. 156).

Then they carry off their sister and their nephew at Gitxaden, downstream from Nass Canyon.[24] There the hero is drawn toward the sky by the slave of a supernatural being, disguised as a white bear. But he does not succeed in reaching the heavenly abode and returns to earth having lost track of the bear.

He then goes to Tsimshian country, where he marries the sister of the sea lion hunters. He humiliates them with his superiority, is abandoned by them, visits the sea lions in their subterranean kingdom, looks after them and cures them, and gets a canoe made of their intestines which brings him back to the coast, where he kills his brothers-in-law with artificial killer whales. He finds his wife and never leaves her again (Boas 1902, pp. 225–229).

Clearly, this version is very poor. It has very few episodes, and when compared with the version by Boas and Hunt 1912, which has been our point of reference up to now, the sequence of events seems very confused. It would be quite wrong, however, to treat the Nass version simply as a weakened echo of the Skeena ones. In the best-preserved part—the initial sequence of events—it is as if the richness of detail had been preserved, but at the cost of permutations which, without any doubt, form a system. Let us therefore begin by listing them, distinguishing the elements which are common to both versions from the elements which have been transformed.

In both cases, the story begins in a river valley: that of the Skeena, that of the Nass. It is winter and famine reigns. Two related women, one living upstream and the other downstream, decide to join forces, and meet halfway.

Already, several differences are apparent:

	Nass	Skeena
Place of the action	Nass	Skeena
State of the river	?	frozen
Situation of the two villages	not far apart	"very far apart" [25]
Relationship between the women	sisters	mother and daughter
Civil status	(1 married / 1 unmarried)	2 widows

These differences, it is clear, are equivalent to a *weakening of all the oppositions* in the Nass version. This is very striking in the situations of the two villages and even more so in the relationship between the two women. In the latter there is a constant element, the relationship of elder to younger, which is manifested in the form *mother/daughter* in the one case, and *elder sister/younger sister* in the other. The first couple live *farther apart* from one another than the second and are brought together by a *more radical event* (the double simultaneous widowhood) than the second (of whom only one is married—it is not stated whether she has lost her husband).

One may also prove that the Nass version is a weakening of the Skeena version and that the Skeena version is not a strengthened form of the other. The proof lies in the vestigial survival of the original mother/daughter relationship in the form of the maternity of the elder sister, who is accompanied by her daughter. This is a detail which in every other respect has no function in the Nass version (the constant element being given by the opposition between *retrospective fertility* and *prospective fertility*), as seen in Formula a.

a. [mother:daughter] :: [(mother + daughter) : nonmother]

But these differences, which one could consider in a "more" or "less" or quantitative sense, are accompanied by others which are genuine inversions.

In the Skeena versions, the elder of the two women comes from down-river, the younger from up-river. In the Nass variant, the contrary is true, since the pair (mother and daughter) comes from Gitwunksilk, upstream of the canyon, and the unmarried sister (who will marry the supernatural protector and is therefore identical with the daughter in the Skeena version) arrives from Laxqaltsap, which is downstream.

In the Skeena version, the women are completely empty-handed, reduced to sharing a *single rotten berry*, found at their meeting place.[26] Once again, the Nass version shows a weakening, since the women bring provisions, though they are in fact very meager—a handful of berries and a piece of spawn.

	Down-river		*Up-river*
Skeena version:	o ⟶	rotten ⟵ berry	o
Nass version:	berries ⟶	⟵	spawn

It would be easy to show that on the northwest Pacific Coast and in other regions of America, decomposition is considered the borderline between food and excrement.[27] If, in the Skeena version, a single berry (*quantitatively*, the minimal food) is the bearer of decomposition (*qualitatively*, the minimal food), then it is because berries in themselves are thought of *specifically* as a weak kind of food, in contrast with strong foods.

Without any doubt, in the Skeena version the two women are deliberately associated not with any particular food but with lack of any sort of food. But this "dearth of food," though a negative category, is not an empty category, for the development of the myth gives it, in retrospect, a content. The two women represent "absence of food," but they are also bound respectively to the east and to the west, to the land and to the sea. The myth of Asdiwal tells of an opposition between two types of life, also bound up with the same cardinal points and the same elements: mountain hunters on the one side, fishermen and sea hunters on the other.[28] In the Skeena version the "alimentary" opposition is therefore double: (1) between animal food (at the extreme positions) and vegetable food (in the intermediate position); and (2) between sea animal (west) and land animal (east) as seen in Figure 10.

From this we obtain Figure 10. Formula b:

b. [land : sea] :: [(sea + land) : middle]

Its analogy with Formula a is immediately obvious.

The alimentary system of the Nass version is based on a *sim-*

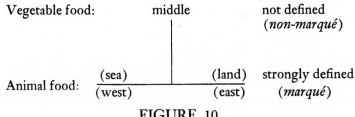

FIGURE 10

plified structure (with two terms instead of three) and on *weakened oppositions*. From not being defined at all, vegetable food moves to a state of being weakly defined. From a borderline state between food and absence of food, it becomes a positive food, both quantitatively (a handful of berries) and qualitatively (fresh berries). This vegetable food is now opposed not to animal food—a category which is strongly defined (and here distinguished by a minus sign -1)—but to the weakest imaginable manifestation of this same animal food (to which we still assign a plus sign $+1$),

and this is done in three ways:
  fish, and not meat
  fish spawn, and not fish
  a piece "as big as the finger"

Thus we have a system:

$$
\left.
\begin{array}{l}
\text{Sea} \\
\text{West} \\
\text{Vegetable food} \\
\text{(relatively} \\
\text{abundant in} \\
\text{quantity)}
\end{array}
\right\}
\;\leftarrow\;
\begin{array}{c}
\textit{weakly} \\
\textit{defined} \\
\textit{opposition}
\end{array}
\;\rightarrow\;
\left\{
\begin{array}{l}
\text{Land} \\
\text{East} \\
\text{Animal food} \\
\text{(relatively} \\
\text{weak in} \\
\text{quality)}
\end{array}
\right.
$$

FIGURE 11

From the point of view of the alimentary system, the correlation between the two variants of the myth can thus be expressed by the following formulae:

  c1. [(−meat) : (−fish)]
          :: [dx (meat + fish) : dx (vegetable food)]

or, in simplified form (ignoring the minute quantity dx):

  c2. [meat : fish]
          :: [(meat + fish) : (vegetable food)]

where the sum of (meat + fish) constitutes the category of animal food. It will be noticed, once again, that there is an analogy between the three formulae a, b, and $c_1 = c_2$.

The two types of food in the Nass version are berries (downstream) and spawn (upstream). Spawn is an animal food from the river, berries a vegetable food from the land—and, of all earth-grown foods, this (in contrast to the game that is hunted in the mountains) is the one most commonly associated with the river banks.[29]

Thus the transformation that has occurred in the process of transferring the story from the one version to the other can, from this point of view, be written as Formula d:

d.   [west : east] :: [sea : land]
          :: [water : solid ground] :: [river : bank]

But the opposition between the river and its banks is not only a weakened form of the fundamental contrasts between east and west and between solid ground and water, which are most strongly defined in the opposition sea/land. It is also a *function* of this last opposition.

In fact, the opposition river/bank is more strongly defined inland (where the element "water" is reduced to "river") than toward the coast. There the opposition is no longer so pertinent because, in the category "water," the sea takes precedence over the river; and in the category "land," the coast takes precedence over the bank. One can thus understand the logic of the reversal whereby, *up-river*, we are led again to Formula d:

d.   [water : solid ground] :: [river : bank]

where the combination (river + bank) has, by permutation, been assimilated into the category "land," this time in opposition to the category "sea"—we are led to Formula e:

e.   [water : solid ground] :: [sea : (river + bank)]

where the combination (river + bank) has, by permutation, been moved into the position originally occupied by "land."

Since d. and e. can be recast in Formula f:

f.   [land : water] :: [(river + bank) : sea]

which is analogous to formulae a, b, and c, this example shows how a mythological transformation can be expressed by a series of equivalences, such that the two extremes are radically inverted (*S.A.*, pp. 224–225).

In fact, in the last stage of the transformation, the (downstream, west) position is occupied by a vegetable food, that is, by an "earth-food"; the (upstream, east) position is occupied by an animal food, which, since it consists of fish spawn, comes from the river and is therefore a "water-food." The two women, reduced to their common denominator, which is the relationship elder/younger, have thus, in coherent fashion, had their positions exchanged with respect to the relationship upstream/downstream.[30]

Consequently, in the Skeena version, the weak opposition between river and bank is *neutralized* (this is expressed in the myth by specifying that the river is frozen and that the women walk on the ice) in favor of the strong opposition between sea and land which is, however, negatively evoked (since the women are defined by their lack of foods which are associated with their respective positions). In the Nass version it is the strong opposition which is neutralized, by weakening and inversion, in favor of the weak opposition between river and bank, which is positively evoked (since in this case the women are provided, albeit meagerly, with the appropriate foods).

Parallel transformations are to be found in the episode of the supernatural protector as related by the two versions. In that of the Skeena, he provides meat alone, in an ever-increasing quantity (in the order: little squirrel, grouse, porcupine, beaver, goat, black bear, grizzly bear, caribou). In the Nass version, he provides meat and fish at the same time in such large quantities that in that one case the hut is "full of meat and fish" but only "full of dried meat" in the other. In the Skeena version this balance between the two types of life is brought about only much later and in a transitory way: during Asdiwal's third marriage with the sister of the Gitxatla people, when, accompanied by his brothers-in-law, he is abundantly provided with "salmon and fresh meat," which they sell to the starving Tsimshian (cf. Boas 1902, pp. 225–226; Boas and Hunt 1912, pp. 74–77, 120–123).

On the other hand, Asdiwal's father gives him magic objects which are immediately effective (Skeena version). Those given to Asi-hwil have to be gradually perfected (Nass version). In each case, the hero returns from the west like the food, transported in the insides of a sea lion. But in the second case the change from stomach (Skeena) to intestines (Nass) suggests a food that is nearer to putrefaction, a theme that is final here and no longer initial (a rotten berry was the women's first food in the Skeena version). Nor must it be forgotten that, from this point of view, the candlefish—the only hope of escaping from starvation (in Tsimshian, candlefish is called: *hale-mâ'tk*, which means "saviour") —must be tolerated up to the point of decomposition; otherwise the fish would be offended and would never return.

How can a concrete content be given to this double mechanism of the *weakening of oppositions*, accompanied by a *reversal of correlations* the formal coherence of which we have now established? It should first be noted that the inversion is given in the respective geographical positions of the two populations. The Nisqa, people of the Nass, are found in the north; the Tsimshian (whose name means: "inside the river Skeena" from *K-sia'n*, "Skeena") in the south. In order to marry on (relatively speaking) foreign territory, the Nass hero goes to the land of the Tsimshian—that is to say, toward the Skeena, in the south; and the last marriage of the Skeena-born Asdiwal shows him, up to the time of the break, camping with his in-laws on the Nass and thus in the north. Each population spontaneously forms symmetrical but inverse conceptions of the same country.

But the myths bear witness to the fact that the duality Skeena valley/Nass valley—which, with the region in between, forms the Tsimshian country (in the broadest sense)—is seen as an opposition, as are also the economic activities which are respectively associated with each of the two rivers.

A young man of miraculous birth decided to go up to heaven while night reigned on earth. Changed into a leaf, he impregnated the daughter of the Master of the Sun, who bore a son called Giant. The child seized the sun, made himself master of daylight, and went down to earth where he found himself a companion, Logobola, who was master of mist, water, and marshes. The two boys had a competition, and after several undecided contests they decided to shoot arrows and play for the River Skeena against the River Nass. Giant won by a trick and was so overjoyed that he spoke in Tsimshian—in the dialect of the lower reaches of the

Skeena—to voice his feelings. And Logobola said, "You won, brother Giant. Now the candlefish will come to Nass River twice every summer." And Txamsem (Giant) said, "And the salmon of Skeena shall always be fat." Thus they divided what Txamsem had won at Nass River. . . . After which the two brothers parted.

One of the versions recorded by Boas says, "Txamsem went down to the ocean and Logobola went southward to the place he had come from" (Boas and Hunt 1916, p. 70; cf. Boas and Hunt 1912, p. 7ff.).

In any case, the symmetry of the geographical positions provides only the beginning of an explanation. We have seen that the reversal of correlations is itself the function of a general weakening of all the oppositions, which cannot be explained merely by a substitution of south for north and north for south. In passing from the Skeena to the Nass, the myth becomes distorted in two ways, which are structurally connected. First, it is reduced and, second, it is reversed. In order to be admissible, any interpretation must take account of both of these aspects.

The Skeena people and the Nass people speak similar dialects (Boas and Hunt, 1911). Their social organization is almost identical.[31] But their modes of life are profoundly different. We have described the way of life on the Skeena and on the coast, characterized by a great seasonal movement which is in fact two-phased: between the winter towns and the spring camps on one hand, and then between the spring candlefish season on the Nass and the summer fishing of the salmon on the Skeena.

As for the Nass people, it does not seem that they made periodic visits to the Skeena. The most that we are told is that those who lived very far up the Nass were called *kit'anwi'like*, "people who left their permanent villages from time to time," because they came down toward the Nass estuary each year, but only for the candlefish season (Sapir 1915, p. 3). The largest seasonal migrations of the Nisqa seem thus to have been limited to the Nass, while those of the Tsimshian were based on a much more complex Skeena-Nass system. The reason is that in March the candlefish visit the Nass, which therefore becomes the meeting place of all the groups who anxiously await the arrival of their "savior." The salmon go up both rivers much later. Thus the Nisqa lived in one valley, and the Tsimshian in two.

Since this is so, all the natives are able to conceptualize the duality Nass/Skeena as an opposition which correlates with that of candlefish/salmon. There can be no doubt about it, since the myth that lays the foundations of this opposition was recorded by Boas in two practically identical versions, one in Nass dialect, the other in Skeena dialect. But an opposition that is recognized by all need not have the same significance for each group. The Tsimshian lived through the opposition in the course of each year; the Nisqa were content to know about it. Although a grammatical construction employing couplets of antithetical terms is present in the Tsimshian tongue as a very obvious model, and probably presents itself as such quite consciously to the speaker,[32] its logical and philosophical implication would not be the same in each of the two groups. The Tsimshian use it to build up a system which is global and coherent but which is not communicable in its entirety to people whose concrete experiences are not stamped with the same duality; perhaps, also, the fact that the course of the Nass is less definitely orientated from east to west than is that of the Skeena, adds to the obscurity of the topographical schema.

Thus we arrive at a fundamental property of mythical thought, other examples of which might well be sought elsewhere. When a mythical schema is transmitted from one population to another, and there exist differences of language, social organization, or way of life that make the myth difficult to communicate, it begins to become impoverished and confused. But one can find a limiting situation in which, instead of being finally obliterated by losing all its outlines, the myth is inverted and regains part of its precision.

Similar inversions occur in optics. An image can be seen in full detail when observed through any adequately large aperture. But as the aperture is narrowed, the image becomes blurred and difficult to see. When, however, the aperture is further reduced to a pinpoint, that is to say, when *communication* is about to vanish, the image is inverted and becomes clear again. This experiment is used in schools to demonstrate the propagation of light in straight lines—in other words, to prove that rays of light are not transmitted at random but within the limits of a structured field.

This study is in its own way an experiment, since it is limited to a single case, and the elements isolated by analysis appear in several series of concomitant variations. If the experiment has helped to demonstrate that the field of mythical thought, too, is structured, then it has achieved its object.

Postscript

Fifteen years devoted to the study of American mythology have elapsed since I wrote this text, and some modifications (and notes) are called for—some of which have already been incorporated in the text. Taking too literally Boas's remark (1915, p. 793) that the 1895 and 1912 versions were practically identical, I had paid too little attention to the former, thinking it could be neglected as a "weak variant" of the latter, with only "a few minor differences" between them (Lévi-Strauss 1971b, p. 34, n. 1). But in fact there are considerable differences between the two versions.

The main one is in the respective position of the two women, which is completely reversed in the two versions. The mother comes from upstream and the daughter from downstream, which seems to weaken the above interpretation of the relation between the 1912 version in Tsimshian dialect and the 1902 version in Nisqa dialect. This would be true only if the frozen river, on which the two women are traveling in the 1895 version, were the Skeena. But, although this version is also Tsimshian in origin and does not name the river (at least not at the beginning of the myth), there are good reasons to believe that it is the Nass. In this case, our interpretation, far from being invalidated, would be further strengthened, since it links the change of river with the change in the upstream-downstream position of the women.

Why is the Nass more likely to be the river in the 1895 version? Let us first note that this version has the younger woman marrying a man from another tribe. Geographically speaking, the mother and daughter do not live far from each other, since they meet two days after leaving their respective villages on foot; but, on the other hand, they are sociologically very far apart, since the daughter's marriage affords a very clear example of exogamy. This is why, when his son Asiwa grows up, Ho (human incarnation of the bird Hadsenas) decides that Asiwa will go and live with his mother and his grandmother, in the latter's village, according to the same principle of matrilocal residence prevailing in the Nass version (see p. 156).

Settled in his maternal grandmother's village, Asiwa devotes himself to mountain hunting, to the exclusion of sea hunting (an apparently superfluous detail, since this village is far upstream, but one which becomes interesting later). He marries there and this marriage—for which he pays the young woman's brothers a high price in whole animals killed in the hunt—is very likely with a fellow countrywoman. This endogamic marriage thus precedes the one with the daughter of the Sun, here designated only as the master of the supernatural bear. Whereas in the Skeena version the episode with his countrywoman comes after the celestial marriage and the hero bears the consequence of his infidelity.

Now the 1895a version (p. 287) specifies that Asiwa lived with his wife in the mountains, but that his dwelling was near the Nass, on the bank of which first appeared to him the supernatural bear whom he pursued up river. This is not all. For when his compassionate father-in-law consented to send him back to earth, he put him down on the bank of the Nass, at the very place where Asiwa later met six brothers of the Gitxatla tribe on their way back from fishing for candlefish. They took him with them (presumably to the islands where they lived) and gave him their sister in marriage, only to abandon him later on a reef because Asiwa ("although until then he had only hunted in mountains," cf. Boas 1895a, p. 287), humiliated them by proving a better sea hunter. Thus, in this case also, the 1895 version reverses the 1912 version, in which the Gitxatla people pick up the hero on the coast, while on their way to the Nass for the seasonal fishing for candlefish. Here, on the contrary, they pick him up on the Nass at the end of that fishing season and go with him toward the coastal islands where they live.

All the previous indications thus tally to suggest that before the hero's Gitxatla marriage, the myth took place entirely on the Skeena. The 1895 version would thus become a compromise between the 1912 version, which takes place on the Skeena, and the 1902 version, which actually comes from the Nass River; whereas this 1895 version has the same origin as the Skeena version but situates the action on the Nass. In the first place, the respective positions of the women are consistent with the Nass version, but their relationship is the same as in the Skeena version. Other details in the myth coincide to give it this same character of a compromise between the other two. We have seen here that the women, instead of living near each other (or, on the contrary, very far from each other), are not far apart geographically, and since the daughter married into a foreign tribe, they are very far apart sociologically and politically. It is thus with food. Instead of bringing some supplies or—being totally deprived of food—finding on the spot only one rotten berry, they arrive without supplies. They pick some half-rotten berries which they share and, near their camp, the bark of conifers which they eat. This duality of supply would correspond to the duality between river bank and solid ground, thus overlapping that of water and solid ground in the Skeena version with that of river and bank in the Nass version (see pp. 179–180). It should be noted, by the way, that if, in the 1912 version, the single completely rotten berry found by the women cannot properly serve as food, either quantitatively or qualitatively, neither can the bark of a "rotten spruce-tree" (p. 77) which the women tear from the trunk, seemingly just to feed their fire: ". . . their fire was about to be extinguished. Then the young noble woman . . . went to get bark" (p. 73). As in the Skeena version, their supernatural protector provides the women with bigger and bigger game, although on a reduced scale, which in the 1895 version ranges from partridge to mountain goat.

Is it now possible to understand the particular position of the 1895 version, independently from the fact that, while collected like the 1912 and the 1916 versions in the Tsimshian dialect of the lower Skeena, it takes place, not on this river, but on the Nass, like the 1902 version which comes from there? In other words, why do the Tsimshian themselves feel the need of a version of their myth situated not on their land but in Nisqa country? Does this transfer possess an intrinsic function, independent from the observable changes which, as matters stand for us, are reduced to a compromise between the other versions?

Let us briefly compare the 1895 version to the corresponding passages in the Skeena version. The latter takes place at first on this river, on which the hero travels from upstream downstream. He reaches the estuary, then goes up along the coast—where he meets the Gitxatla people—to the mouth of the Nass. The itinerary described in the 1895 version is symmetrical and inverted. The hero goes up the Nass, first as far as his grandmother's village where he marries, then further on upstream in pursuit of the bear. Then he goes back down, together with the Gitxatla people, as far as their territory at the estuary of the Skeena. The two versions are very careful to respect this symmetry. The 1912 version reports, that Asdiwal, already settled downstream from his birthplace, started pursuing the white she-bear "who was going downstream" (see p. 150). The 1895 version (p. 287) tells us that Asiwa, settled and married upstream near his grandmother's village, was led by the bear still further "upstream." These differences are shown in Figure 12:

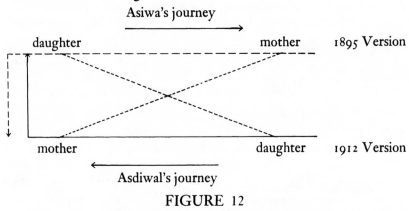

FIGURE 12

This symmetrical construction nevertheless brings about certain difficulties, judiciously passed over in silence in the 1895 version. Indeed, it implies that Asiwa was picked up by the Gitxatla people very far upstream on the Nass, without specifying how they managed to get back afterward to their territory in the islands off the Skeena estuary. A description of the downstream journey on the Nass might indeed have altered the beautiful symmetry between the spatial configurations as they emerge out of the two versions. But what can it mean?

We remember how the 1912 and 1916 versions end. In the first one, Asdiwal feels some nostalgia for the mountains where he spent his childhood. He goes back to them and his son joins him there. Asdiwal dies in the mountains, changed into a stone one day when he goes hunting without his magic snowshoes which he forgot. In the 1916 version, the forgetfulness of Waux—who duplicates the character of his father, on whose grounds he continues to hunt—is compounded with another fault: he cannot get his wife to obey him; she misunderstands all his orders. Consequently he himself is turned to stone like his father, while his wife, replete with fat, bursts and is changed into flint.

Now, how does the 1895 version end? After getting rid of his wicked brothers-in-law (with the exception of the youngest one, as in the 1912 version), Asiwa lives peacefully with his Gitxatla wife in her village (thus on the coast). But several years later, he ardently wishes to see again the sea lions who treated him so well. His son wants to know why and what the sea lions gave him to eat. At first, Asiwa refuses to answer, then, harried with questions, he reveals that he was fed rock cod (a spiny fish of the Scorpenid family, *Sebastodes ruberrimus*) and candlefish oil which, he adds, was very good. Hardly has he pronounced these words but he falls dead, while fishbones are coming out of his stomach. It is because he told what took place among the sea lions, the myth concludes, that he dies in this manner.

This ending suggests several remarks. According to the 1912 and the 1916 versions, Asdiwal and his son Waux live in the mountains (for which Asdiwal felt nostalgia). They both die while journeying deeper into them (into an unexplored region, the 1916 version specifies) on a hunting expedition, which thus presents the heroes as providers of food. On the other hand, according to the 1895 version, Asiwa, at first exclusively a mountain hunter (see p. 186), lives on the seashore, perhaps even on an island, and he dies because of the nostalgia he feels for his stay among the sea lions, on the high seas (still further out in the ocean), where (his regrets stemming largely from the sea lions' cooking) he sees himself again as receiver of food. Nostalgia for the mountains in one case (although Asdiwal has twice lived married near the estuary of the Skeena and on the coast), nostalgia for the high seas in the other case (although Asiwa has lived married upstream on the Nass, "in the mountains" (Boas 1895a, p. 287)—these endings present, between the two of them, the same strict symmetry as the respective journeys attributed to the hero in the different versions. Once more, this example confirms that mythical messages retroactively determine inverted constructions through opposition.

In relation to these two messages—death of the hero because of the nostalgia he feels for either land or sea, a death thus due to his inability to realize balance between the two elements—the Nass version (see pp. 175–176) occupies a neutral position. The attempted celestial journey of the hero fails, his subterranean stay with the sea lions does not leave him any regrets, and he ends his days peacefully on the coast where he first married. One then understands why the 1895 version can have a symmetrical relation with the 1912 and 1916 versions and also offer points of convergence with the Nass version, in which the opposition between messages is annulled. In deviating from the other Skeena versions, the 1895 version goes through the Nass version, as it were, before reaching the plane on which it presents a symmetrical and inverted image of the former. (On the tendency of the northwest Pacific Coast myths to envisage simultaneously all the possible solutions of the same problem; cf. Lévi-Strauss 1972*b*.)

The 1895 version has another aspect of considerable interest. It enables us to state precisely the semantic position of *forgetfulness* in myths. Remember that the 1912 version explains Asdiwal's death by an oversight on his part, and that the 1916 version also explains his son Waux's death by an oversight which is intensified by a misunderstanding between husband and wife, from which they both die. But the 1895 version replaces forgetfulness with another fault: Asiwa's indiscretion in revealing to his son the menu of the meal he shared with the sea lions. In the present state of our ethnographical knowledge of the Tsimshian, we do not know why this revelation constitutes a lapse. Was it forbidden to cook scorpaenids in candlefish oil? Or was the initial mistake in the eating of fish bones, which was permitted to sea lions, but may have been prohibited to men, as were salmon (see p. 174)? Or then again, had the sea lions forbidden Asiwa's revealing any of the details of his sojourn in a supernatural world where he had been admitted by special protection? The solution of this small problem is luckily not necessary to establish the point which interests us. It is enough that the 1916 version introduces not only forgetfulness but misunderstanding as a combinatory variant of the fault, and that the 1895 version replaces them both by an act of indiscretion. How, in fact, are forgetfulness, misunderstanding, and indiscretion alike, and how do they differ? And can we place them and determine their relations within a semantic field?

Let us define indiscretion, which consists in saying something to someone which should not have been said to him, as an excess of communication with others. Thus, misunderstanding—which consists in understanding in something said something other than what was meant—can be defined as a lack of communication, also with others. We can then see the place of forgetfulness in such a system. It is a lack of communication, not (in this instance) with others, but with oneself. To forget is not to say to oneself what one ought to have been able to say.[33]

	INDISCRETION	MISUNDERSTANDING	FORGETFULNESS
Excess/lack	+	–	–
Others/oneself	+	+	–

FIGURE 13

The motif of forgetfulness recurs frequently in tales and myths, but one tends too often to consider it a "gimmick" which the narrator arbitrarily uses to revive a plot. If the interpretation just proposed could be generalized, we see that it would be something quite different. Forgetfulness would appear as a true category of mythical thought or, at least, as a mode, endowed with a precise signification, of this category formed by communication.

After these considerations of the 1895 version, which had to be given its place, we would like to end with some brief remarks on another problem: that of marriage with the matrilateral cross-cousin, which we had presented as typical not only of the Tsimshian but also of the neighboring peoples (Lévi-Strauss 1971*b*, p. 27). A recent and remarkable work by Rosman and Rubel seems to establish in a convincing manner—by the comparative study of genealogies and cycles of obligations in the potlatch —that if these data confirm the preferential character of marriage with the matrilateral cousin among the Tsimshian, such is not the case for the Haida and the Tlingit, for whom the mechanism of the potlatch seems compatible only with a matrimonial preference for the patrilateral cousin.

But, whatever the practice observed at the end of the nineteenth and at the beginning of the twentieth centuries (we know that the observations available seldom go back further), among the Tlingit and the Haida as well as among the Tismshian, the myths assert the same preference for marriage with the matrilateral cross-cousin. We have summarized and commented on the Tsimshian myth of the princess who refused to marry her cousin (see pp. 168–169). As Boas pointed out, this myth also exists among the Tlingit and the Haida. The Haida version of Skidegate is of little help, as it does not say that the woman is a relative, and the whole tale takes place in Tsimshian country (Swanton 1905, p. 354). Thus it does not claim to teach us anything about neighboring peoples. On the other hand, the version from Masset (Swanton 1908, pp. 654–655), which begins among the Tlingit, is very explicit about the kinship relations between the two protagonists—respectively the father's sister's son and the mother's brother's daughter, which the informant comments on thus: "At that time they married only their uncles' children. They did not want others to take the things their uncles owned. Therefore [a man] did not allow any one else to marry his uncle's child. So thought Ga'ogal, the town-chief's son. He worked for his uncle's daughter. His uncle's daughter also wanted him."

The Tlingit version (Swanton 1909*b*, p. 243) reflects the same situation. A young Indian, the son of the "chief of a certain clan," wants to marry his cousin. However, her father (and the boy's uncle) "wanted his daughter to marry some great chief from outside." As the hero hopes to achieve his purpose by establishing his rights over his uncle's wife, mother of the girl he loves (for "in olden times when a man married a woman with a marriageable daughter he married the daughter as well"), the myth seems to refer to those high-ranking families in which, according to Swanton, Murdock, and Laguna, a man who succeeded his maternal uncle married his widow, his daughter, or both of them (Rosman and Rubel 1971, p. 40, n. 3).

An old report suggests that, among the Tlingit, the preference for marriage with the patrilateral cousin was perhaps only a consequence, applicable to the man, of a more general tendency to choose the spouse in the father's clan; a tendency which, in the case of the wife, would lead to a symmetrical and inverted marriage formula.

The relatives of the girl are very desirous, as a rule, to marry her to some one on the father's side of the family. It may be an uncle, a cousin, or a grandfather. The same principle holds true with the relatives of the young man, who seek to marry him to some girl or woman who is a near relative of his on the father's side. It may be his cousin, or aunt, or grandmother. Such marriages are not only considered very proper among the natives, but they more heartily desire them than marriages of any other connection (Jones 1914, p. 128).

We see that, if the Tlingit formulated their matrimonial preferences in this manner, these would result in the choice of a patrilateral cousin for a man, but of a patrilateral cousin for a woman who would herself be her spouse's matrilateral cousin.

A Tlingit tale speaks of a young Haida who, abandoned by his matrilateral cousin as soon as he had married her, left with his father to get married again in another village (Swanton 1909*b*, p. 242). And it is also with his father's help that he later compensates his first wife when she claims a part of his possessions. This insistence on the father's role suggests that a patrilateral marriage could have followed the matrilateral marriage of the beginning, and that the two forms were thus both permitted. If we add that a Tsimshian myth (Boas and Hunt 1916, p. 154) refers to a young man who is urged by his parents and all his maternal uncles to take a wife in his father's clan—contrary to the well-documented preference for the matrilateral cousin—we must admit that some uncertainty exists about the way these populations thought their own system through and put it into practice.

These facts in no way diminish Rosman and Rubel's demonstration, which keeps all its force. But they do at least suggest that either (1) the two modes of generalized exchange could coexist among the Tlingit and the Haida (even if one presented an exceptional character); or (2) that a certain divergence appeared between ideology and practice, manifesting in its own way this tension between the lines to which we drew attention (see p. 169). Without pretending that they were ensuring their equilibrium by the sole mechanism of matrimonial exchanges, these societies have increasingly relied on other cycles of prestations, bearing on titles and property. This is the reason why—even if the prevalence of the patrilateral marriage were definitely recognized among the Tlingit and the Haida—we do not believe that it could weaken our previous considerations on the precariousness of this formula

(Lévi-Strauss 1969*a*). For this intrinsic precariousness would be made even more manifest by the fact that the societies that have succeeded in making the formula more durable possess other mechanisms, political and economic, on which their cohesion depends to a greater extent.

NOTES

1. Hatsenas (Boas and Hunt 1912), Hadsenas (Boas 1895). It is a bird like the robin (*Turdus migratorius*) but not a robin (Boas and Hunt 1912, pp. 72–73). According to Boas, it sings "hō, hō" and its name means "luck" and describes a bird sent as a messenger from heaven (1895*a*, p. 286). One is reminded of the black bird (*Ixoreus naevius*) which is indeed a winter bird, with a strange and mysterious call (Lévi-Strauss 1971, pp. 438–439, 447).

In this work, which has no linguistic pretentions, the transcription of native terms, has been simplified to the extreme, keeping only those distinctions which are essential in avoiding ambiguities among the terms quoted.

2. The name of Asdiwal certainly has several connotations. The Nass form, *Asi-hwil*, means "crosser of mountains" (Boas and Hunt, 1902, p. 226). But cf. also "*Asdiwal*," "to be in danger" (Boas and Hunt 1912, p. 257) and *Asewaelgyet*—a different name for and special variety of the thunderbird (Barbeau 1950, Vol. I, pp. 144–145, Vol. II, p. 476).

3. The map on p. 154, more precise and more complete than the one published in the previous editions of this work, was kindly given me by Professor Wilson Duff, of the University of British Columbia in Vancouver, to whom I wish here to express my gratitude. The names of places are easily identifiable in spite of a transcription slightly different from that of Boas.

4. Swanton gives "Kinagingeeg, near Metlakatla" (1952, p. 606); cf. Krause 1956, pp. 214–215: *Kin-nach-hangik*, "on the peninsula near Fort Simpson."

5. Swanton gives *Kitkatla*, "on Porcher Island" (1952, p. 607).

6. Boas gives *Ginadâiks*, "one of the nine towns of the Tsimshian" (Boas and Hunt 1912, p. 223); cf. *Kinnatöiks* "on the Tsimshian peninsula near Fort Simpson" (Krause 1956, pp. 214–215).

7. For a summary and comparative analysis of all the texts which have been listed as referring to the greed of the demiurge, see Boas and Hunt 1916, pp. 636ff.

8. As the smallest mammal to appear in mythology, and also because in the mythology of the Northwest Coast the mouse represents the land animal at its most modest level: that of domestic life. The mouse is in fact the domestic animal of the earth. With this distinction, she is entitled to the

tiny offering of fat which drips from woolen ear ornaments when they are thrown into the fire in her honor.

9. "The love of the master of the sea lions and of his whole tribe increased very much" (Boas and Hunt 1912, p. 133).

10. The Tsimshian of the Nisqa group "look to the river (Nass) for their food supply, which consists principally of salmon and candlefish. Indeed, it is owing to the enormous numbers of the latter fish that run in to spawn in the early spring that the name Nass, meaning 'the stomach or food depot' has been given to the river" (Emmons 1910).

11. The double aspect, natural and supernatural, of the opposition between peak and valley, is already in the myth, since the hero's perilous situation results from an earthquake, caused by the gods. (Cf. pp. 165–166).

12. As we shall later see, the apparent gap in the cycle is explained by the fact that in the story of Waux, Asdiwal's son, the closure will be the result of a matrilateral marriage which ends in a terminal situation: husband and wife without children.

13. Asdiwal himself has inherited from his father the lightness and speed of a bird—qualities which are ideally suited to a hunter who, according to native thought, should be as light-footed as a bird on the wing (Boas and Hunt 1916, p. 403). Boas's informant considers Waux as Asdiwal's only child (Boas 1916, p. 243). This is a mistake, for Asdiwal also had a son by his third marriage (Boas and Hunt 1912, pp. 123, 133, 135). But this point is unimportant since the third marriage was simply a repetition of the second.

14. On this point see Volume I *Structural Anthropology*, Chapter XI, "The Structural Study of Myth."

15. Boas's informant seems to have made a mistake which Boas has only partially corrected. In Boas and Hunt 1916, the text is as follows: "Before his mother died, she wanted her son to marry one of her own cousins, and he did what his mother wanted him to do" (p. 244). Thus it would be a cousin of the mother and not of the son. The corresponding native text is to be found in Durlach (1928, p. 124) a transcription (in simplified signs) of which follows: "*na gauga* [?] *dem dzake na'ot da hasa'x a dem naksde lguolget a klâlda lgu-txaât.*"

The kinship term *txaâ* denotes the father's sister or the mother's brother's children—that is to say, cross-cousins. *Lgu-* is a diminutive. The suffix *-t* is a third-person possessive. In his summary of the story of Waux, Boas repeats the suspect phrase: "He marries one of his mother's cousins" (Boas and Hunt 1916, p. 825). But in the commentary he corrects his interpretation by placing this example quite rightly with all those he quotes of marriages with a matrilateral cross-cousin: "The normal type of marriage, as described in the traditions, is that between a young man and his mother's brother's daughter. Thus . . . a mother requests her daughter to marry her cousin (¶ 244)" (p. 440). Since ¶ 244 only mentions Waux's marriage, it is clear that this time Boas rectifies the kinship relation, but confuses the sex of the husband and wife. From this there arises a new contradiction, for this cousin would be the father's sister's daughter. The real meaning seems to be: Before dying, his mother wanted him to marry one of his own cousins.

16. Boas and Hunt 1916, p. 411, in contradiction with p. 401. We will come back later to this divergence.

17. Describing the marriage ceremonies of the Nisqa as reported by another informant, Boas explains that the fight between the two groups can become so violent that one of the slaves in the suitor's guard is killed: "This foretells that the couple will never part" (Boas 1916, p. 531).

18. Asdiwal's double visit to heaven (which contrasts with his single journey below the earth) seems to be intended to make even clearer the analogy with salmon fishing. In fact, his return to heaven takes place exactly as if it were a "catch" in a net which is let down through an opening in the heavens—just like the ritual fishing of the first salmon of spring, which is carried out, with a net, through a hole made in the ice still covering the river.

19. If our interpretation is correct, it must be admitted that the explicit opposition sky/earth is here realized in an implicit form—sky/water—which is the strongest opposition inherent in the system of the three elements as used by the myth.

This system can be represented by the following formula (read the sign : to mean "is to," the sign :: to mean "as," the sign > to mean "is above," and the sign / to mean "is opposed to"):

1. sky : earth :: earth : water
   which can also be written
2. sky > earth > water
   Then the hypothesis put forward above about the "fishing up" of Asdiwal can be verified by the following permutation:
3. sky : water :: earth : earth
   which may be said to correspond to Asdiwal's second supernatural voyage, where the opposition to water (earth) is expressed by a subterranean voyage. We are therefore perfectly entitled to put
4. sky/earth :: sky/water (where "water" stands for "beneath the sky")
5. earth/water :: earth/earth (where "/earth" stands for "below the ground")

But this duplication of the "earth" pole is only made necessary by the assimilation (in veiled terms) of the major opposition between sky and earth to the minor opposition (still implicit) between earth and water. Asdiwal is fished up like a fish off an earth which is confused with the liquid element, from the heights of a sky pictured in terrestrial terms as a "green and fertile prairie."

From the very beginning the myth seems governed by one particular opposition which is more vital than the others (even if not immediately perceptible): that between earth and water, which is also the one most closely linked with methods of production and the objective relationships between men and the world. Formal though it be, analysis of a society's myths verifies the primacy of the infrastructures.

20. See Boas's hesitation (1916, pp. 401, 411–412). Even Garfield, who gave the problem much attention cannot bring herself to admit to the existence of succession in the paternal line (Garfield, Wingert, and Barbeau, 1951, p. 17).

21. Information is lacking on the subject of other fish, especially the scropaenids. But it is apparent in Boas 1895a that, among the sea lions, the hero had eaten their fish bones, since they ultimately come out of his stomach, causing his death.

22. "Lakkulzap or Greenville"; "Gitwinksilk . . . near the mouth of the Nass River" (Swanton 1952, p. 586). However, Gitwinksilk (Gitwinksihlt) is upstream of the Canyon on the map in M. Barbeau (1950).

23. "Greenville (laxqaltsa'p) . . ." (Sapir 1915, p. 2). According to Sapir, the Gitwankcitlku," people of the place where lizards live," form the third Nisqa group, starting from downstream.

24. "Gitxate'n, people of the fish traps" (Sapir 1915, p. 3); Gitrhatin, at the mouth of the estuary, and downstream from the Canyon. It seems to be the same place as the one first called Laxqaltsap (Barbeau 1950, map).

25. That is, at any rate, what the myth emphatically affirms, but the village of the younger woman is not named.

26. "A few berries," in Boas 1895.

27. Many myths treat of the loss of salmon by mankind, thanks to men's refusing a piece of moldy fish; or to their disgust on discovering that the Mother of Salmon gives birth through her excretory canal.

28. "The sea hunter required a training quite different from that of the mountain hunter" (Boas and Hunt 1916, p. 403).

29. "Woman go out jointly by canoe or walking in the woods to gather berries" (Boas and Hunt 1916, p. 404).

30. The younger woman, representing prospective fertility, shows a markedly feminine character, in the elder woman, this is not so marked. The younger must always be in the (earth) position in the Skeena version, because she is to bear Asdiwal, master of mountains and earth-born hunter; this is true in the Nass version for the same reason, and also because of the strictly feminine character of the gatherer of berries, which stand for earth food. Cf. "While the men procure all the animal food except shellfish, the women gather berries and dig roots and shellfish" (Boas and Hunt 1916, p. 52, 404).

31. It is clear that Goddard (1935) was mistaken in attributing only two exogamic divisions to the Nisqa instead of four (cf. Sapir 1915, pp. 3–7). This mistake can probably be explained by the fact that the Nisqa, immediate neighbors of the Tlingit, find it necessary more often than the Tsimshian to apply the rule of the lowest common multiple to their social organization, so that the laws of exogamy may be respected in marriages with foreigners.

32. Boas and Hunt quote thirty-one pairs of "local particles" in oppositions of the following type: upward/downward; into/out of; forward/backward, etc. (1911, pp. 300–312).

33. Following a lecture given in February 1973 in Vancouver, where I presented this interpretation, Mrs. Hilda Thomas of the University of British Columbia, suggested that nostalgia, as the opposite of forgetfulness, could be defined as an excess of communication with the self and thus illustrate the fourth and last combination: +, −.

CHAPTER X

Four Winnebago
Myths

AMONG THE MANY TALENTS which make him
one of the great anthropologists of our time, Paul Radin has one
which gives a singular flavor to his work. He has the authentic
aesthetic touch, rather uncommon in our profession. This is what
we call in French *flair:* the gift of singling out those facts, observations, and documents which possess an especially rich meaning, sometimes undisclosed at first, but likely to become evident
as one ponders the implications woven into the material. A crop
harvested by Paul Radin—even if he should not choose to mill
the grain himself—is always capable of providing lasting nourishment for many generations of students.

Chapter X was originally published under the title "Four Winnebago Myths: A
Structural Sketch," in *Culture in History: Essays in Honor of Paul Radin* (New
York: Columbia University Press, 1960), pp. 351–362. Prepared under the direction of Professor Stanley Diamond during Paul Radin's lifetime, this book was
published after he died on February 21, 1959.

[*Translator's note:* This chapter was originally written in English and later
adapted in French by Professor Lévi-Strauss. A few minor modifications were
brought to the text in the course of this adaptation of the original English
version.]

This is the reason why I intend to pay my tribute to the work of Paul Radin by giving some thought to four myths which he has published under the title *The Culture of the Winnebago: As Described by Themselves* (1949). Radin himself pointed out in the Preface: "In publishing these texts I have only one object in view, to put at the disposal of students authentic material for the study of Winnebago culture." Despite this intention, and despite the fact that the four myths were each obtained from different informants, it seems that, on a structural level, there was good reason for making them the subject of a single publication. A deep unity underlies all four, notwithstanding the fact that one myth (as Radin has shown in his introduction and notes) appears to differ widely in content, style, and structure from the other three. My purpose will be to analyze the structural relationships among the four myths and to suggest that they can be grouped together, not only because they are part of a collection of ethnographic and linguistic data referring to one tribe (which Radin too modestly claims as his sole purpose), but also because they are of the same genre and their meanings logically complement each other.

The title of the first myth is "The Two Friends Who Became Reincarnated: The Origin of the Four Nights' Wake." This is the story of two friends, one of them a chief's son, who decide to sacrifice their lives for the welfare of the community. After their death, they undergo a series of ordeals in the underworld, and finally reach the lodge of Earthmaker, who permits them to become reincarnated and to resume their previous lives among their relatives and friends.

As explained by Radin in his commentary (p. 41, ¶32), there is a native theory underlying the myth. It is that every individual is entitled to a specific quota of years of life and experience on earth. If a person dies before his time, his relatives can ask the spirits to distribute among them the life span which he has failed to utilize.

There is more to this theory than meets the eye. The unspent life span given up by the hero, when he lets himself be killed by the enemies, will be added to the capital of life, set up in trust for the group. Nevertheless, his act of dedication is not entirely without personal profit. By becoming a hero an individual makes a choice, he exchanges a full life span for a shortened one. But while the full life span is unique, granted once and for all, the shortened one appears as the juridical cause of a kind of renewable lease taken on eternity. That is, by giving up one full life, an indefinite succession of half-lives is gained. But since all the years sacrificed by the hero will increase the life expectancy of the ordinary people, everybody gains in the process. This holds for both the ordinary people, whose average life expectancy will slowly but substantially increase generation after generation, and the warriors with shortened but indefinitely renewable lives, provided their minds remain set on self-dedication.

It is not clear, however, that Radin pays full justice to the narrator when he treats as a "secondary interpretation" the fact that the expedition is undertaken by the heroes to show their appreciation of the favors of their fellow villagers (p. 37, ¶2). My contention, based on the previous analysis, is that this motive of the heroes deserves primary emphasis, and it is supported by the fact that there are two war parties. The first is undertaken by the warriors while the heroes are still in their adolescent years, so that they are neither included in nor even informed of it. They hear about the party only as a rumor (¶11–14), and they decide to join it uninvited. We must conclude, then, that the heroes have no responsibility for the very venture wherein they distinguish themselves, since it has been instigated and led by others. Moreover, they are not responsible for the second war party, during which they are killed, since this latter foray has been initiated by the enemy in revenge for the first.

The basic idea is clear. The two friends have made good marriages and have developed into successful social beings (¶66–70). Accordingly, they feel indebted to their fellow tribesmen (¶72). As the story goes, they set out, intending to sacrifice themselves by accomplishing some useful action. They die in an ambush prepared by the enemy to revenge the former defeat. The obvious conclusion is that the heroes have willingly died for the sake of their people. They were innocent of those hostile acts that brought about their death and for which their compatriots bore the responsibility. Yet the latter will inherit the unspent portion of the heroes' lives, given up for their benefit. The heroes themselves will be permitted to return to earth and will probably behave in the same manner; thus the same process of life-transfers will be repeated all over again.

This interpretation is in agreement with information given

elsewhere by Radin. In order to pass the test of the Old Woman who rids the soul of all the recollections belonging to its earthly life, each soul must be solicitous not of its own welfare, but of the welfare of the living members of the group.

Now at the root of this myth we find—as the linguists would say—a double opposition. First, there is the opposition between *ordinary life* and *heroic life*, the former realizing the full life span, not renewable, the latter gambling with life for the benefit of the group. The second opposition is between two kinds of death, one straight and final, although it provides a type of un-earthly immortality in the villages of the dead; the other oscillating, and swinging between life and death.

Indeed, one is tempted to see the reflection of this double fate in the Winnebago symbol of the ladder of the afterworld as it is expressed in the Medicine Rite. One side is "like a frog's leg, twisted and dappled with light-and-life. The other [is] like a red cedar, blackened from frequent usage and very smooth and shiny" (p. 71, ¶91–93; cf. Radin 1945, especially the author's illuminating comments on pp. 63–65).

To sum up the meaning of the myth so far: If one wants a full life, one gets a full death; if one renounces life and seeks death, then one increases the full life of his fellow-tribesmen, and secures for oneself a state composed of an indefinite series of half-lives and half-deaths. Thus we have a triangular system, shown in Figure 14.

Reincarnation
(half-life, half-death)
Full life_____|_____Full death

FIGURE 14

The second myth, entitled "The Man Who Brought His Wife Back from Spiritland," is a variation on the same theme, although there is a significant difference involved. Here too, we find a hero—the husband—ready to sacrifice his unspent life span; not, as in the first myth, for the benefit of the group, but rather for the benefit of only one individual, his beloved wife who has been taken away from him. Indeed, the hero is not aware at first that by seeking death he will secure a new lease on life for both his dead wife and himself. Had he been so aware—and this holds equally for the protagonists in the first myth—the essential element of sacrifice would have been missing. In both cases the result is similar: An altruistic loss of life means life regained, not only for the self-appointed victim, but also for the one or more persons to whom the sacrifice was consecrated.

The third myth, "The Journey of the Ghost to Spiritland, as Told in the Medicine Rite," belongs, as the title suggests, to a religious society. It explains how the members of the Medicine Rite, after death, undergo (as do the protagonists of the other myths) several tests in Spiritland, which they overcome, thus gaining the right to become reincarnated.

At first sight this situation seems to differ from the others, since nobody sacrificed his life. However, the members of the Medicine Rite actually spend their lives in symbolic sacrifice. As Radin has shown, in *The Road of Life and Death* and elsewhere, the Medicine Rite follows the pattern familiar in North America of letting oneself be "killed" and then "revived." Thus the only departure consists in the fact that, whereas in the first and second myths the heroes are willing to die once and (so they anticipate) permanently, the heroes of the third myth (the members of the Rite) repeatedly, though symbolically, have trained themselves to self-sacrifice. They have, so to speak, mithridatized themselves against real death by renouncing a full ordinary life which is replaced, in ritual practice, by a lifelong succession of half-lives and half-deaths. Hence we are entitled to assume that, in this case too, the myth is made up of the same elements, although the individual—and not another person, nor the group as a whole—is conceived as the primary beneficiary of his sacrifice.

Let us now consider the fourth myth, "How an Orphan Restored the Chief's Daughter to Life," a tale that has given Radin some concern. This myth, he says, is not only different from the other three: its plot appears unusual relative to the rest of Winnebago mythology. After recalling that in his book *Method and Theory of Ethnology* (1933, pp. 238–245), he suggested that this myth was a version, altered almost beyond recognition, of a type which he then called village-origin myths, he proceeds to explain in *The Culture of the Winnebago* (1949, pp. 74ff.) why he can no longer support this earlier interpretation.

It is worthwhile to follow closely Radin's new line of reasoning. He begins by recapitulating the plot—such a simple plot, he says, that there is practically no need for doing so: "The daughter of a tribal chief falls in love with an orphan, dies of a broken heart, and is then restored to life by the orphan who must submit to and overcome certain tests, not in spiritland but here, on earth, in the very lodge in which the young woman died" (p. 74).

If this plot is "simplicity itself," where do the moot points lie? Radin lists three which he says every modern Winnebago would question: (1) the plot seems to refer to a highly stratified society; (2) in order to understand the plot, one should assume that in that society women occupied a high position and that, possibly, descent was reckoned in the matrilineal line; and (3) the tests which in Winnebago mythology usually take place in the land of ghosts occur, in this instance, on earth.

After considering two possible explanations and dismissing them—that we are dealing here with a borrowed European tale or that the myth was invented by some Winnebago radical—Radin concludes that the myth must belong to "a very old stratum of Winnebago history." He also suggests that two distinct types of literary tradition, divine tales and human tales, have merged with certain archaic elements and that all these disparate elements have then been reinterpreted to make them fit together.

I am certainly not going to challenge this elegant reconstruction backed by an incomparable knowledge of Winnebago culture, language, and history. The following analysis does not pretend to offer an alternative to Radin's own analysis, but to complement it. It lies on a different level, logical rather than historical, and it takes as its context the three myths already discussed—not Winnebago culture, old or recent. My purpose is to seek the structural relationship—if any—which prevails between the four myths, and to explicate it.

First, there is a theoretical problem which should be noted briefly. Since the publication of Boas' *Tsimshian Mythology*, anthropologists have often simply assumed that a full correlation exists between the myths of a given society and its culture. This, I feel, is going further than Boas intended. In the work just referred to, he did not suppose that myths automatically reflect the culture, as some of his followers always seemed to anticipate. More modestly, he tried to find out how much of the culture actually did pass into the myths, if any, and he convincingly showed that some of it does. It does not follow that whenever a social pattern is alluded to in a myth this pattern must correspond to something real and attributable to the past if, under direct scrutiny, the present fails to offer an equivalent.

There must be, and there is, a correspondence between the unconscious meaning of a myth—the problem it tries to solve—and the conscious content it makes use of to reach that end, i.e., the plot. However, this correspondence is not necessarily an exact reproduction; it can also appear as a logical transformation. If the problem is presented in straight terms—that is, in the way the social life of the group expresses and tries to solve it—the overt content of the myth, the plot, can borrow its elements from social life itself. But should the problem be formulated upside down, and its solution sought for *ad absurdo*, then the overt content can be expected to become modified accordingly to form an inverted image of the social pattern actually present in the consciousness of the natives.

If this hypothesis is true, it follows that Radin's assumption that the pattern of social life referred to in the fourth myth must belong to a past stage of Winnebago history is not inescapable. We may be confronted with the pattern of a nonexistent society, past or present—even one contrary to the Winnebago traditional pattern—only because the structure of that particular myth is itself inverted, in relation to those myths which use as overt content the traditional pattern. To put it simply, if a certain correspondence is assumed between A and B, then if A is replaced by –A, B must be replaced by –B, without implying that, since B corresponds to an external object, there should exist another external object –B, which must exist somewhere: either in another society (borrowed element) or in a past stage of the same society (survival).

Obviously, the problem remains: Why do we have three myths of the A type and one of the –A type? This could be the case because –A is older than A. But it can also be so because –A is one of the transformations A_4 of A, which is already known to us under the three guises A_1, A_2, A_3, since we have seen that the three myths of the assumed A type are not identical.

We have already established that the group of myths under consideration is based upon a fundamental opposition between the lives of ordinary people unfolding toward a natural death, followed by the banal existence of their soul in one of the spirit villages, and the lives of heroes, whose unspent life span increases the life quota for the others and gives the hero a new lease on life. The first three myths do not envisage the first term of the alternative; they are exclusively concerned with the second. But there is a secondary difference which permits us to classify these myths according to the particular end assigned to the self-sacrifice in each. In the first myth, the group is intended to be the immediate beneficiary; in the second it is another individual (the wife); and in the third it is the victim himself.

When we turn to the fourth myth, we will agree with Radin that it exhibits "unusual" features in relation to the other three. However, the difference seems to be of a logical, rather than of a sociological or historical nature. It consists in a new opposition introduced within the first pair of opposites (between "ordinary" life and "extraordinary" life). Now there are two ways in which an "extraordinary" phenomenon may be construed as such: by excess or by default, consisting in either a surplus or in a lack. While the heroes of the first three myths are all overgifted—with social dedication, conjugal love, or mystical fervor—the two heroes of the fourth myth are, if one may say so, "below standard" in at least one respect, which is not the same for each.

The chief's daughter occupies a high social position, so high, in fact, that she is cut off from the rest of the group and is therefore paralyzed when it comes to expressing her feelings. Her exalted position makes her a defective human being, lacking an essential attribute of emotional life. The boy is also defective, but socially; he is an orphan and very poor. May we say, then, that the myth reflects a stratified society? This would compel us to overlook the remarkable symmetry which prevails between our two heroes, for it would be wrong simply to say that one is high and the other low. As a matter of fact, each of them is high in one respect and low in the other, and this pair of symmetrical and inverted structures belongs to the realm of ideological constructs rather than of sociological systems. We have just seen that the girl occupies a high social position, but that, as a living creature, thus from the natural point of view, she has a low position. The boy is undoubtedly very low in the social scale. However, he is a miraculous hunter, who entertains privileged relations with the natural world, the world of animals. This is emphasized over and over again in the myth (¶10–14, 17–18, 59–60, 77–90).

May we not therefore claim that the myth actually confronts us with a polar system bringing together—and at the same time opposing—two individuals, one male, the other female, and both exceptional insofar as each of them is overgifted one way (+) and undergifted in the other (−)? (See Figure 15.)

	Nature	Culture
Boy	+	−
Girl	−	+

FIGURE 15

The plot consists in carrying this disequilibrium to its logical extreme. The girl dies a *natural* death; the boy stays alone and goes through a *social* death. Whereas during their ordinary lives the girl was overtly above and the boy overtly below, now that they have become segregated (either from the living or from society), their positions are inverted: the girl is below (in her grave), the boy above (in his lodge). This, I think, is clearly implied in a detail stated by the narrator which seems to have puzzled Radin: "On top of the grave they then piled loose dirt, placing everything in such a way that nothing could seep through" (p. 87, ¶52). Radin comments: "I do not understand why piling the dirt loosely would prevent seepage. There must be something else involved that has not been mentioned" (p. 100, n. 40). I would like to suggest that this detail be correlated with a similar detail about the building of the young man's lodge: ". . . the bottom was piled high with dirt so that, in this fashion, they could keep the lodge warm" (p. 87, ¶74). There is implied here, I think, not a reference to recent or past custom but rather a clumsy attempt to emphasize that, relative to the earth's surface, the boy is now above and the girl below.[1]

This new equilibrium, however, will be no more lasting than the first. *She who was unable to live cannot die:* her ghost "lingers on earth." In that form, she finally induces the young man to fight the ghosts and take her back among the living. With a wonderful symmetry, the boy will meet, a few years later, with a similar, although inverted, fate: "Although I am not yet old," he says to the girl (now his wife), "I have been here [lasted] on earth as long as I can. . . ." (p. 94, ¶341) *He who overcame death proves unable to live.* This recurring antithesis could develop indefinitely, and such a possibility is noted in the text (by giving the hero an only son, he too soon an orphan, he too a sharpshooter). But a different solution is finally reached. The heroes, equally unable to die or to live, will assume an intermediate identity, that of twilight creatures living under the earth but also able to come up on it. They will be neither men nor gods, but wolves; that is, ambivalent spirits combining good and evil features. So ends the myth.

If the above analysis is correct, two consequences follow. First, our myth makes up a consistent whole wherein the details balance and fit each other nicely. Secondly, the three problems raised by Radin can be analyzed in terms of the myth itself. No hypothetical past stage of Winnebago society, which could only be a conjecture, need be invoked.

Let us, then, try to solve these three problems, following the pattern of our analysis.

1. The society of the myth appears stratified, only because the two heroes are conceived as a pair of opposites, but their opposition is shown from the point of view of both nature and culture. Thus the so-called stratified society should be interpreted, not as a sociological vestige, but as a projection on some imaginary social order of a logical structure wherein all the elements are given both in opposition and in correlation.

2. The same answer can be given to the question of the assumed exalted position of the women. If I am right, our myths state three propositions, the first by implication, the second expressly stated in the myths 1, 2, and 3, the third expressly stated in myth 4.

These propositions are as follow:

a. Ordinary people live (their full lives) and die (their full deaths).
b. Extraordinary people with positive attributes die (earlier) and live (again).
c. Extraordinary people with negative attributes are able neither to live nor to die.

Obviously, proposition (c) offers an inverted demonstration of the truth of (a) and (b). Hence, it must use a plot starting with protagonists (here, man and woman) in inverted positions, so that each one may assume half of the demonstration, symmetrical to the other half incumbent to the other person. This leads us to state that a plot and its component parts should neither be interpreted by themselves nor relative to something outside the realm of the myth proper, but as substitutions given in and understandable only with reference to a group of myths.

3. We may now come to the last problem raised by Radin about the fourth myth: Why does the contest with the ghosts take place on earth instead of, as was usually the case, in Spiritland. To this query I shall suggest an answer along the same lines as the others. It is precisely because our two heroes are seen as *underliving* (one in respect to culture, the other to nature) that, in the narrative, the ghosts become a kind of *superdead*. It will be recalled that the whole myth develops and is resolved on an intermediary level, where human beings become underground animals and ghosts linger on earth. It tells about people who are, from the start, half-alive and half-dead; in the preceding myths, the opposition between life and death is strongly emphasized at the beginning and overcome only at the end. Thus, the integral meaning of the four myths is that, in order to be overcome, the opposition between life and death should be first acknowledged, or else the ambiguous state will persist indefinitely.

I hope to have shown that the four myths under consideration all belong to the same transformational group and that Radin was even more right than he supposed in publishing them together. In the first place, the four myths deal with extraordinary (in opposition to ordinary) fate. The fact that ordinary fate is illustrated here and thus is reckoned as an "empty" category, does not imply, of course, that it cannot be illustrated elsewhere. In the second place, we find an opposition between two types of extraordinary fate, by excess or by lack. This new dichotomy which permits us to distinguish myth 4 from myths 1, 2, and 3 corresponds, on a logical level, to the discrimination that Radin makes on psychological, sociological, and historical grounds. Finally, myths 1, 2, and 3 have been classified according to the purpose of the sacrifice of the hero or heroes, which is the theme of each.

Thus the myths can be organized in a dichotomous system with several levels of correlations and oppositions. But we can go even further and try to order them on a common scale. This is suggested by the curious variations which can be observed in each myth with respect to the kind of test the hero is put to by the ghosts. In myth 3 there is no test at all, so far as the ghosts are concerned. The tests consist in overcoming material obstacles, while the ghosts themselves figure as indifferent fellow travelers. In myth 1 they cease to be indifferent without yet becoming hostile; on the contrary, the hero must resist their overfriendliness by resisting inviting female spirits and the infectious good humor of male spirits who pose—to better fool him—as merrymakers. Thus, from *companions* in myth 3 they change to *seducers* in myth 1. In myth 2 they will behave as human beings, but they now act as *aggressors*, and permit themselves all kinds of rough play. This is even more evident in myth 4, but here their human appearance vanishes. It is only at the end that we know that ghosts, in the form of crawling insects, are responsible for the trials of the hero. We have thus, from one myth to the other, a twofold progression: from a peaceful attitude to an aggressive one, and from human to nonhuman behavior.

This progression can be also correlated with the kind of relationship which the hero (or heroes) of each myth entertains with the social group.

The hero of myth 3 belongs to a ritual brotherhood. He definitely assumes his privileged fate as member of a group, acting with and in his group. The two heroes of myth 1 have resolved to part from the group, but the text states repeatedly that this is in order to find an opportunity to achieve some worthy deed that will benefit their fellow tribesmen. They act, therefore, for the group. But in myth 2 the hero is only inspired by his love for his wife. There is no reference to the group. The action is undertaken independently for the sake of another individual. Finally, in myth 4 the two heroes' negative attitude toward the group is clearly revealed; the girl dies of her inability to communicate; indeed, she prefers to die rather than speak, believing death to be her final exile. As for the boy, he refuses to follow the villagers when they decide to move away and abandon the grave. The segregation is thus willfully sought by both protagonists and their actions unroll against the group.

Figure 16 summarizes our discussion. I am quite aware that the argument, in order to be fully convincing, should not be limited to the four myths considered here, but should include more of the invaluable Winnebago mythology which Radin has given

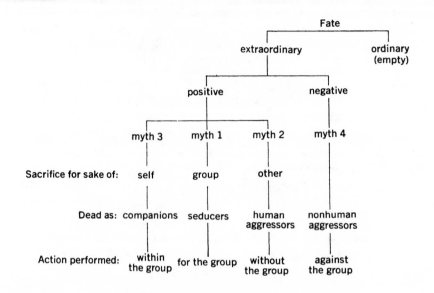

FIGURE 16

us. But I hope that by integrating more material, the basic structure outlined has, at least, become richer and more complex without being impaired. By singling out one small book which its author would perhaps consider a minor contribution, I have intended to emphasize, in an indirect way, the fecundity of the method followed by Radin, and the lasting value of the problems he posed.

NOTES

1. The interpretation is indeed a plausible one in this context. But we are not short of examples, both in North and South America, where heavy stones are piled up on a grave during funeral rites to prevent the dangerous ghost of the dead man from escaping; nor, on the contrary, do we lack examples where the dirt is kept loose to maintain communication between the dead and the living. The difficulty here is that the second proceeding seems destined for a result one would rather expect from the first.

CHAPTER XI

The Sex of the Sun
and Moon

O<small>NE OF THE FIRST</small> conversations with Roman Jakobson that I can remember was about the manner in which languages and myths proceed to mark the opposition of the moon and the sun. We were trying to pick out contrasts in the gender of the words designating the sun and the moon here and there, or in the verbal forms denoting their relative size and luminosity. We were very soon to recognize that the problem was not a simple one, and that what seemed so obviously a binary opposition to the Western observer could be expressed in singularly round-about ways in distant cultures.

To celebrate the seventieth anniversary of Roman Jakobson's birth—which is also roughly the twenty-fifth of our first meeting —I propose, in memory of these discussions, to compile some

Chapter XI was originally published under the title "Le Sexe des astres," in *To Honor Roman Jakobson: Essays on the Occasion of His Seventieth Birthday*, Janua Linguarum, Series Maiur, No. 32 (The Hague: Mouton, 1967), Vol. II, pp. 1163–1170.

notions picked up in the course of my readings. They all relate to American cultures, but, in spite of this regional character, they might prompt some researchers to take up, in a wider perspective, the study of a problem which had rightly preoccupied mythologists from the end of the nineteenth century to the beginning of the twentieth, but which since seems to have fallen into oblivion.

Both in South and North America, many languages refer to the sun and the moon by the same word. Such is the case of the Iroquois, where the term *gaä′gwa* in the Onondaga dialect, *karakwa* in the Mohawk, connote the two heavenly bodies, completed if need be by a determinant: *andá-kāgagwā*, "light of day," and *soá-kāgagwā*, "light of night." The languages of the Algonkin group, with the well-known enormity of its diffusion, proceed in the same manner. Thus, in Blackfoot: *kèsúm* "sun, moon"; in Menomini, *ké′so*, "sun"; *tipäké′so*, "last night's sun," "moon"; in Montagnais, *čišekao-pišum* and *tepeskau-pišum;* in Arapaho, *hīcīs*, "celestial light"; in Gros-Ventre, *hīsös*.

A single term is used to refer to the sun and the moon in Seminole, in Hichiti, in Choctaw, and in Cherokee. The Kutenai say *nata′ne.k!* and the Klamath *sábas* for both the sun and the moon. The Quinault call the moon by a word that means "nocturnal sun." In several languages or dialects of California—Achomawi, Northern Maidu, Karok, Patwin, western and northern Pomo, Kato, Wailaki, Lacustrine Miwok, Wappo—the sun and the moon bear the same name.

In South America, languages such as the Carib and the Tupi generally have distinct terms. However, the use of a single term is prevalent in the tribes of Tukano languages: *muhi-pun* in Uaupès Tukano, *avyá* in Cubeo. The Huitoto call the sun *hitoma* and the moon *hwibui* or *manaidé-hitoma,* "cold sun." While the Chibcha of the Andean plateau had the distinct terms *zuhé* and *chia* for the sun and the moon, which they made, respectively, male and female; on the western slope the Cayapa say *pá′ta* and *pōpá′ta* for both masculine stars; and the Waunana of the Chaco use a single word *edau*, "sun," "day," "moon."

In spite of a rich vocabulary (to which we shall later return), most of the Ge languages form the names of the moon and the sun from the same root: *put-, pud-*. Several Arawakan languages follow the same procedure. Thus, for the sun and the moon, respectively: *kamoi* and *kairi*, in Palikur; *kamu* and *kaier*, in Vapidiana; *kxami* and *kwataua* in Kustenau; and *kamai* and *kaimaré*, in Paressi.

The use of the same term to refer to the sun and the moon, or of terms formed with the same root, does not imply that the sun and moon are objectively confused or that they are attributed with the same sex. The Iroquois call the sun and the moon by the same word, and have them come out of the head and the body of a decapitated woman, respectively, or the reverse. They nevertheless depict the sun as male and the moon as female, in accordance with other origin myths which have the sun, as light, deriving from the cut-off head of a man whose body presides over diurnal warming-up; and the moon, as light, from the cut-off head of a woman whose body presides over nocturnal warming-up. The language consequently unites stars that the mythology distinguishes in two ways: by the sex of the personage from whom they originate, and by the upper or lower part of this personage's body—corresponding to two different functions, illuminating and caloric, fulfilled by each star individually.

In fact, this distinction of the illuminating and caloric functions seems often more important than that of the stars proper, which may explain that the heavenly bodies as such are referred to by the same word. With regard to this, we have seen that the Tukano languages of South America proceed like Iroquois and Algonkin. However, the Cubeo do not place the sun and the moon on the same footing. They say that the sun is nothing more than the moon dispensing light and heat during the day. In its solar aspect, the luminary *avyá* has no anthropomorphic connotation. On the other hand, the moon, a masculine divinity, has a considerable place in the religious representations.

The Warao of the Orinoco delta, who have different words for the sun and the moon, do not rank these heavenly bodies equally either. According to observers, it seems that the word *okohi* designates the hottest time of the day, and refers to the heating power of the sun, as distinct from its luminosity. Indeed, the moon and the sun have in common the power to give light, but only the latter is also able to give heat. The existence of a special name does not prevent the sun from being conceived as a mode of the moon, of which it illustrates a privileged case. Its notion has a greater intension but a lesser extension. This is what Warao mythology expresses by saying that the moon is the sun's "receptacle."

Similarly, the Sherente, who are Ge from the Central Plateau, call the sun *bdu* and the moon *wa*, but instead of the first term, they prefer to use *sdakro*, which means "light," "sun heat." In spite of the geographical distance, the ideas of the Emok Toba of the Chaco are remarkably close to those of the Cubeo. In both groups, the moon is a masculine god, deflowerer of virgins, and responsible for menstruation; he is the center of interest. The sun, *nála*, of the feminine gender, appears mostly in two aspects only: *lidàgá*, "luminous," and *n:táp*, "warming." In the mythical traditions of these Indians, the sun does not play an important part. Generally speaking, there are striking cases where the term referring to the sun is used indifferently to signify "heavenly body," "day," and a "season": *kamu*, "sun," "day," in Vapidiana; *dě'i*, "sun," "day," in Chamacoco; *bari*, "sun," "day," "summer," in Cashinahua; and *antú*, "sun," "day," "weather," in Araucanian. The examples could be multiplied. The Wintu of California, however, doubly invert the Warao's theory by seeing in the moon "the silver underside of the sun's belly."

The Surára from northern Brazil, who make the moon their demiurge, explain the secondary place of the sun in their mythology by saying that the star of the day is alone in the sky, while the star of the night enjoys the company of innumerable stars. Since the region is mountainous, the peaks, in their multiplicity, present a sort of terrestrial counterpart to the stars. They rank immediately after the moon in the hierarchy of the divinities and play, in relation to it, the part of intercessors before the solitary sun. The opposition between the plurality of nocturnal lights and the oneness of the diurnal luminary, common in tropical America, is found as far away as the Southern Guarani, who form the word designating the stars, *yacitata*, from *yaci*, ("moon") and *tata*, "fire."

However, the number of nocturnal stars would not be so remarkable if they were not contrasted with the night, much more strongly so than the sun is contrasted with the day. In the case of the night, the presence or absence of the stars has as a result a relative brightness or a total absence of light; whereas the sun, congruent rather than opposed to the day, determines only different degrees of light, whether it shines or hides behind clouds. The Amazonian Mundurucu, who pay attention to this inequality in their myths, attribute it to the existence of two distinct suns: the summer sun and the winter sun. Significantly, they give the moon to the latter as wife. The major opposition is thus not the same as ours. It is not situated between celestial bodies but between meteorological conditions. According to whether it is visible or invisible in the night register, the moon defines the opposition of light and darkness more strongly than the sun does in the day register because it only adds heat and light to a state of light; the reality of this would be attested, even in its absence, by the "moon light" opposed to the "pitch black night."

It is true that the sun, logically subordinate to the moon, proves empirically to be more efficient. Distinct genders can connote this double opposition. The sun is feminine and the moon masculine among the Déné-Peaux-de-Lièvre, the Dakota, the Maidu, the central Algonkin, the Cherokee, the Seminole, the Chimila, the Mocovi, and the Toba, about whom we have contradictory information. Among the Micmac, the Menomini, the Blackfoot, the Chibcha, the Araucanian, the Ona, the Yahgan, and the ancient Peruvians, the inverse relation prevails. It will be noted, however that, in the ideology of several populations, the sex of the sun and moon appears unstable, according to whether the language (when it distinguishes genders), the rituals, or the myths are considered, and, for the myths themselves, as a function of their popular or learned character. Thus, among the Arapaho, more or less esoteric myths preserve the masculine character of the sun, but they describe the moon sometimes in the form of a woman who can then be either (1) the sun's wife or, (2) the grandmother of the son conceived by the moon, if the moon is a masculine personage. Elsewhere, the gender of the names varies according to whether they are profane or sacred.

Within the same myth, the Thompson Indians distinguish the divine sun, who is male, from the visible sun, daughter of the former and who seeks him from east to west during her daily journey. No doubt a more thorough investigation would show that the gender rarely connotes the stars in an absolute manner.

We have suggested that the sun and the moon are commutative in function of more fundamental oppositions which they make it possible to express: light/darkness, strong/weak light, heat/cold, etc. And the sexes assigned to them also seem commutative according to the functions incumbent to each, in the context of a particular myth or ritual.

When the sun and the moon have distinct genders, they may or may not be related. In the former case, they are either brother and sister, husband and wife, or both at the same time, as happens in the myth—attested from one end of the New World to the other—of the incest of the sun and the moon. This myth assumes the masculine gender for the moon and the feminine for the sun, since its most common procedure is to explain the spots on the moon by the marks with which, in order to recognize him, a young girl soiled the face of her nocturnal and unknown lover. The Peruvians alone seem to have legitimized this incest by inverting the sexes of the couple, although the myths of the Klamath and the Plateau Salish, on the one hand, and those of several tribes in Southern California on the other hand, offer at least the outline of the same solution.

Lehmann-Nitsche, who has several times pondered this problem, has pointed out that the formula of marriage between a masculine sun and a feminine moon is spread throughout the Andes in South America, from the Cumana of Venezuela to Tierra del Fuego, through the Chibcha, the ancient Inca, the Araucanian, and reaching out into the Chaco, because of ancient indications on the mythology of the Toba. At the same time, he mentioned the presence of another axis, transversal to the previous one, on which are distributed myths of the sun and the moon as elder and younger brother, respectively.

Leaving aside Guianese and Amazonian tribes (Carib, Tukuna), for whom the astral twins do not have a marked astral character, this mythical system presents a practically continuous distribution from the eastern and central Ge of the plateau to the Puelche of the Pampas, through the tribes of the Xingu, the Bakairi, the Bororo, and the Southern Tupi-Guarani. We have noted that it reappears in Colombia and in Ecuador, on the western slope of the Andes. The opposition of the sun and the moon is expressed, no longer by the masculine or feminine gender of each, but by their unequal age—even if they are twins—and especially by their natural gifts. The sun is thoughtful, careful, efficacious. His brother moon acts without due consideration and makes all sorts of blunders, often fatal, which his elder brother must then repair.

The Ge have a wealth of terms to designate the sun and the moon, some profane, others sacred, some connoting meteorological aspects, others used to name divine personages, which could reflect a median orientation between the "fraternal" axis and the "conjugal" axis; or, more precisely, an orientation between the area of the "fraternal" axis, which would theoretically require distinct names for each brother, and the northwest region of the Amazon basin, where the merging of the sun and the moon under the same name prevails (when the former is not reduced to a simple mode of the other). Indeed, while the tribes of the Xingu and the Bororo, close neighbors of the Ge, use very distinct names—*kéri* and *kamé*, *méri* and *ari*, etc.—the Ge sometimes form these names from the same root: *pud* and *pudléré*, for the Kraho; *put* and *puduvri*, for the Timbira; *mbudti* and *mbuduvriré*, for the Apinaye.

If it were not for this example and that of the Cayapa, one would be tempted to say that geographically close populations treat the opposition of the sun and the moon in one of two manners: Either they attribute different sexes or degrees of reality to the sun and moon, although the words which designate them are identical; or they attribute the same sex to them but give them different names and characteristics. In one case, the opposition would be of a physical order; it would be moral in the other one.

The formula seems much too simple, and, in the north as well as in the south, there would be examples to contradict it, examples which one would like, however, to examine in detail to see whether they do not form particular cases. Indeed, the "fraternal" axis exists in North America (if we disregard the traditional delimitations of the specialists, who would no doubt deny that the examples are homogeneous). It presents an approximate north-west-south-east distribution, from the Salish of the Plateau to the Arapaho, through the Gros-Ventre, the Crow, the Hidatsa, and the Cheyenne. Consequently, in the boreal hemisphere also, the "fraternal" axis confirms the one of the merging of names. The position of the Cheyenne, the Gros Ventre, and the Arapaho, who are all central Algonkin, could present, from a formal point of view, some analogy with the position of the Ge. Thus, in Arapaho, *hicinicic*, "sun" and *bi'gucic* ("moon"), by contraction of *bi'ga*, "night" and *hicic*, "light." Since the Ge and the Algonkin see in the sun and the moon two brothers, the constraints of the language and those of the myths express themselves in different directions, one tending to merge in the vocabulary terms which the other builds up as a pair and must then make distinct.

All the preceding indications show that there is no automatic correspondence between linguistic oppositions and those expressed otherwise—in religious beliefs, rituals, myths, or tales. The grammatical contrast of genders does not reflect the same contrast at the semantic level, and can even contradict it. What is more, it happens that semantic contrasts, recurrent at many levels, are mutually contradictory. If, however, one gives up the impossible task of obtaining in each particular case a rigorous coherence among all the levels, and if one is satisfied with having treated casually the dissimilar facts of which we have considered only a minute number in relation to all those which ought to be listed in order to draw general conclusions, a schema can be perceived which can lead to a more thorough investigation. This schema reduces the solutions adopted by each society (and there may be several for the same) to responses, stimulated by connected alternatives. Either the stars are not distinct or they are. If they are not distinct, the sun is a mode of the moon, or vice versa. If they are distinct, the difference is either sexual or nonsexual. If sexual, it makes the sun male, the moon female, or the reverse; and in either case, the stars can be husband and wife, brother and sister, or both at the same time. If the difference is not of a sexual order, they can be two women or two men, who are then in opposition because of their character or strength. This last opposition can weaken to the point where one of the siblings loses his individuality and becomes a sort of double. In this case, the last alternative leads back to the first one, showing that the system is virtually closed. This property is particularly evident among the tribes of the Columbia River and as far as California. From one group to another, and even sometimes from one myth to the other in the same group, the sun and moon are two women or two men, one a pale copy of the other or violently contrasted.

It is obvious that some transitions exist. Far from contradicting the schema, they help to arrange its elements into series. For instance, between the formula of the two brothers and that of the incestuous siblings, the Apapocuva introduce that of a homosexual and aborted incest, a choice which forces the Southern Guarani, of whom the Apapocuva are part, to divert on a paternal aunt the heterosexual advances of the moon through which the Mbya—also the Guarani—explain the origin of the moon's spots. One can see a point of intersection of the two axes in a limited region. Another point of intersection can be observed in the basin of the Columbia River. It is significant that, here and there, the myths end with the exchange of roles between a sun at first nocturnal and a moon at first diurnal, whose ardor risked consuming the earth.

Elsewhere, the fraternal relation revolves and becomes that of sister's husband and wife's brother, of maternal uncle and nephew, even of father and son. It thus changes from horizontal to vertical. Under the influence of a neighbor, and as if it underwent its attraction from a distance, a system evolves and reorganizes itself. In a way, each is a function of all the others. To try and understand them, we must apprehend them in their totality and in their relations of reciprocal dependence.

Because of its distribution extending through and beyond the Americas, it seems normal to choose the myth of the incestuous siblings as the referential axis. Indeed, both the orientation of the axis in space and the logical structure of the myth make it better able to generate the conjugal formula and the fraternal formula through inverted variations (better than either of the two formulas would be able to generate the orientation and structure). Everywhere in America, mythical thought poses the problem of the regular alternation of day and night. This alternation implies that the two stars remain at a reasonable distance; if they got too close or too far apart, they would cause the "long day" or the "long night," evoked as a threat in other myths. In the myth of the incestuous siblings, the daily periodicity appears as the component of opposite and balanced forces. The incestuous tendency of the siblings brings them together, but the collective reprobation keeps them apart. On either side of this precarious position, the myth can attain two states of inertia: either by annulling the contrast of sexes with the fraternal formula, or by annulling the relation of proximity by the conjugal formula. But, in the first case, the physical complementarity will be replaced by the moral supplementarity; and in the second case, the poles of physical complementarity will be inverted. Each mythical transformation thus overcomes the contradiction on one axis only to rejoin it on another axis, and the number of parameters increases with each mediation attempt.

Consequently, the binary model we sketched is not enough. It permits the abstract definition of values which present a limiting character, but not the translation of concrete properties and the measure of degrees of proximity. To be able to do this, one would have to elaborate an analogical model where the initial and final positions of each myth would fit into a multidimensional space, each of these dimensions providing a parameter along which would be arranged, in the most convenient manner, the variations of the same semantic function. In terms of distance, the stars can be either conjoined, near one another, at a good distance, far apart, or disjoined. In terms of sex, they can both be male, man and woman (or hermaphrodites), woman and man, or both female. In terms of categories otherwise defined: material objects, animals, meteoric phenomena, heavenly bodies, stars, or demiurges. In relation to family ties: parents, siblings, collaterals, spouses, affines, or strangers. As the sun and moon do not always, at the outset, come under the same genre, a fifth parameter expresses their relative homogeneity of their heterogeneity; and a sixth the variations in the opposite direction of synchrony and diachrony, depending on whether each term keeps its first nature until the end or whether this nature changes in the course of the narrative.

Let us illustrate the method with an example. The Sherente myth of the bird-nester studied in *The Raw and the Cooked* (Lévi-Strauss 1969*b*) can be coded in solar and lunar terms since the heroes belong to complementary and opposite social units, each one linked to the sun or the moon. We will say that, in this myth, the personages incarnating the sun and the moon are (1) disjointed, (2) male, (3) allied through marriage, and (4) human. And as they remain such throughout the myth, the pair is homogeneous and synchronic. On the other hand, in the myth of the incest of the sun and the moon, the protagonists are (1) disjointed (2) woman and man, (3) siblings, and (4) celestial. The brother and sister, at first human, are simultaneously changed into celestial bodies; the pair is thus homogeneous in the diachrony. It would be heterogeneous in the synchrony if the sun and the moon, as it sometimes happens, had always been different.

If the model required only three parameters, each myth could be represented by a path with an equal number of coordinates defining its origins and successive moments. One could then compare the semantic distances between all these paths with the geographical and historical distances, in the hope of integrating the three aspects. But we have enumerated six parameters, and more thorough research would increase this number. In spite of its complication—which excludes the treatment of the problem by graphic processes—the method at least offers an intuitive value. It is enough to have sketched it to be persuaded that the myths do not make an isolated problem out of the sex of the heavenly bodies. They combine the notions relevant to it with many others, without ever taking into consideration their empirical origin. Of the sun and the moon, the same thing can be said as of the countless natural beings mythically manipulated: Mythical thought does not seek to give them a meaning—it expresses itself through them.

Mushrooms in Culture: Apropos of a Book by R. G. Wasson

WE KNOW that the hymns of the Rig-Veda give a considerable place to an intoxicating plant, the soma, the juice of which, squeezed and filtered and then mixed with fresh or curdled milk, was consumed by priests in the course of ritual, especially, it seems, by those who were to embody the god Indra and his driver Vayu. Among the ancient Iranians, an in-

Chapter XII was originally published under the title "Les Champignons dans la culture," in *L'Homme, revue française d'anthropologie*, X, No. 1 (1970), pp. 5–16.

[*Translator's note:* The French title is "Les Champignons dans la culture." While apologizing for only half-rendering the pun, we must point out (as Professor Lévi-Strauss does on p. 233) that the French *champignon* means both "mushroom" and "fungus." This is important because, whereas the first part of the chapter refers to the fly agaric, a mushroom, its last part refers to various types of fungi used by the Indians of North and South America.]

toxicating drink called Haoma (in the Avesta) was very likely the same thing as the soma.

Since the eighteenth century, the Indianists have proposed various hypotheses on the identity of this plant which were doomed to remain gratuitous when not based on information available. Indeed, the secret—if not the cult—of the soma was lost after the Vedic period, and later texts only mention substituted categories—*Ephedra, Sarcostemma, Periploca*—which can be identified by botanists, but are eliminated as possible candidates for representing the original plant because of their acknowledged role as substitutes for soma. Neither could the soma have been a fermented drink or alcohol. The Aryans of the Vedic era knew nothing about distilling, a medieval discovery. They saw the soma, which they conceived of as masculine, diametrically opposed to fermented drinks, of which they were not ignorant but which they considered feminine (and which the Vedic texts call by a different name, *sura*).

In a work entitled *Soma: Divine Mushroom of Immortality*, which is a bibliographical treasure on account of the beauty of the watermarked paper, the quality of printing and illustration, and the limited number of copies produced, R. G. Wasson (1968) advances a revolutionary hypothesis on the nature of the soma, the implications of which go so far that ethnologists cannot leave the responsibility for making it public to the Indianists alone. According to the author, the soma would be the fly agaric (*Amanita muscaria*), well known even in France to mushroom gatherers. We have also known since the eighteenth century that most Paleo-Asiatic peoples—Kamchadal or Itelmen, Koryak, Chukchee, Yukaghir—consumed it ritually, and sometimes had even instituted a cult for it because of its hallucinogenic properties.

The writings of Roger Heim have drawn attention, in France and around the world, to hallucinogenic mushrooms, the importance and role of which Mr. Wasson rediscovered among the Indians of Mexico. The ancient sources vaguely mentioned their use, and it was to Mr. Wasson's great credit that he rediscovered—still extant in certain native communities—the use and cult of these various mushrooms, unrelated to the amanita of the Old World, although these are also found in several regions of the New World.

As early as 1957, Mr. Wasson and the late Mrs. Wasson, who died soon afterwards, published a work in two volumes: *Mushrooms, Russia and History*, to which I was proud to draw the attention of the French public [1] because it opened for our research the new and prodigiously fertile field of ethnomycology. Wasson, who was of Anglo-Saxon stock, told how, soon after his marriage to a young woman of Russian origin, he discovered, to his astonishment, during a walk in the Catskill Mountains that they had totally opposite attitudes toward mushrooms. He ignored or feared them, she was fond of them. With this apparently superficial remark, they began their long investigation which was to reveal to them the emotional nature of the reactions to mushrooms, which can be observed among various peoples or cultural groups. These range from real revulsion on the part of Germanic or Celtic peoples, to exalted fervor among the Slavs and in most of the Mediterranean basin. Hence the distinction, first formulated by the Wassons, between mycophile and mycophobe peoples. I was recently able to verify how well-founded this distinction is under amusing circumstances worthy of being related here. During a dinner, the talk drifted to mushrooms, and I briefly told the guests of the Wasson's hypothesis about the soma, mentioning as well their now-famous distinction. A British colleague, who was also there, answered rather gruffly that it was absurd to draw such deep differences between peoples. He added that, if the English had so little interest in mushrooms, it was simply because these are scarce in their country. He was thus giving a perfect demonstration of his national mycophobia, for there are naturally as many, if not more, mushrooms in England than anywhere else.

But how can we explain these different attitudes, always surrounded by an aura of mystery, and which, in a positive or negative manner, awaken in us such impassioned reactions? In 1957, the Wassons put forth the hypothesis that these attitudes subsist as vestiges of an ancient mushroom cult, as revealed in popular beliefs and in the etymology of the names designating certain species here and there. Almost everywhere in the world, these fructifications are associated with either thunder and lightning, or the devil, or madness. Our attitudes to mushrooms would thus reflect very old traditions, going back no doubt to Neolithic or even Paleolithic times. These traditions were inhibited by Celtic and Germanic invasions wherever they took place (or exerted their influence first), then by Christianity, throughout Europe— but with varying success. Apart from the diffuse beliefs and customs, the better organized cults of the Paleo-Asiatics of Eastern Siberia and of the Indians of Mexico probably remain as isolated evidence, without there necessarily being a relation between them, according to Mr. Wasson. (We will come back to this.) There is no shortage of indications to suggest that, until a relatively recent period, the mushroom cult may have been much more widespread in Europe. It would have been even more so if (as the author maintains in his last book) the mushroom cult had been transported as far as India by the Aryans whose origins have been localized in Eurasia, somewhere between India and Siberia. In their original regions, the Aryans would then have been closer to, if not in immediate contact with, forests of birch or conifers, the only trees allowing the proliferation of *Amanita muscaria*.

Mr. Wasson bases his hypothesis first on negative considerations. None of the many plant species suggested to take the place of the soma can be seriously considered. On this point, his argumentation—backed by a historical and critical report prepared for him by Mrs. O'Flaherty and included in his book—seems to be incontrovertible. On the one hand, the Vedic texts, so prolific on the subject of the soma and containing such a wealth of metaphors to describe it, refer neither to the roots, leaves, flowers, or seeds of this plant, nor to its cultivation. On the other hand, it is said repeatedly that the soma comes from the high mountains, probably those of the Hindu Kush or the Himalaya where birch and conifers grow between about 8,000 and 18,000 feet. As it happens, these data eliminate the probable cases envisaged, except for that of the fly agaric, which the Aryans could have known in their ancestral country and could have acquired, after invading India, in a dried form from the savage and hostile peoples who occupied the mountains in the north. The texts of numerous hymns suggest that, before each preparation, the soma had to be reconstituted.

Several varieties of *Amanita muscaria* exist, their color ranging from brilliant red to yellow-gold. To describe the soma, the Rig-Veda constantly use the word *hári*, which takes in this range of colors; and when substitutes came to be used, those with red coloration were favored. In conformity with popular beliefs well documented in regard to mushrooms, the Vedic hymns make the soma the son of thunder or lightning. When we consider the phases of growth of the amanita, as well as the various appearances it can take on, all the metaphors of the Rig-Veda—or what were taken for metaphors—acquire a literal and descriptive value.

It is not just any plant, but this mushroom alone, which can be compared to the red disk of the sun or likened to Agni, the fire. Of the latter it can be said that "he sloughs off the Asurian color that is his; he abandons his envelope" (consisting, as we know, of a white veil, the fragments of which maculate the cap for a long time); that "he makes of milk his vesture-of-grand-occasion"; that "by day he appears *hári* [color of fire—"chestnut color" in L. Renou's translation], by night, silvery white"; that his "hide is of bull," his "dress of sheep"; that he is "the single eye," "the mainstay of the sky," "the navel of the world"; and that "with his thousand knobs he conquers mighty renown," etc.

And if the soma is not a mushroom, how could it be compared to a breast and to an udder—images which become clear when we think of the rounded cap and bulging stem at the base of this agaric? In the most ingenious manner, and most convincingly for the reader, Mr. Wasson has illustrated each of these images by a color photograph which reveals such and such an aspect of the fly agaric and emphasizes the often startling correspondence with the figure of rhetoric which the old hymns were believed to be using.

Still more disconcerting appears what could be called Mr. Wasson's decisive argument. Among many obscure passages, the Rig-Veda contains one over which the specialists have racked their brains. This is a sentence in the fourth line of Hymn IX, 74, which Renou renders "These lords with full bladder piss [soma] quick with movement," and Wasson, more prosaically, "The swollen men piss the flowing [soma]" (p. 29).

What can this mean, except that, as all the observers in Eastern Siberia have noted, the urine of those consuming fly agaric was highly prized? Drunk by a companion or by the intoxicated man himself, it has the power of causing or renewing that same intoxication stimulated by the eating of fresh or, more often, dried mushroom. Ethnographic documents about the Paleo-Asiatic peoples lead one to think that this urine could be preferable to the original substance because it is more powerful, according to some, or, according to others, because certain chemical compounds present in the mushroom, which cause unpleasant side effects, are eliminated in their passage through the body while the hallucinogenic alkaloid or alkaloids are preserved. Thus, the Siberians practiced two different modes of consumption: either of the mushroom itself or of the urine excreted by an intoxicated person. The Vedic texts several times set forth the existence of two forms of soma (IX, 66, lines 2, 3, 5; Wasson and Wasson 1957, pp. 25–27). And the Avesta (48:10) condemns—in a text which Mr. Wasson considers incomprehensible unless the proposed interpretation is adopted—"the people who are evilly deluded by the priests with this urine of drunkenness." Our author also cites an episode of the Mahavharata (*Asvamedha Parvan*, 14–54, 12–35), in which the god Krishna offers his favorite, as a beverage, the urine of an outcast hunter who turns out to be Indra; the urine itself is a draught of immortality.

The mention of Vedic texts of three successive filters used in the preparation of the soma appears equally coherent with the interpretation proposed. The second filter, of wool, seems to be a technical object presenting no problem. But the first, which is compared to a celestial chariot traversed by sun rays, can only suggest the mushroom itself. The plant producing soma is often compared to fire and to the sun. The young mushroom, whose brilliant red cap is still spotted in a regular pattern with fragments of netting, has a reticulated aspect quite reminiscent of a filter. As for the third filter, its nature and function remain inexplicable, unless one recognizes it as the actual body of the consumer (in this case the priest personifying Indra) through which the soma passes, becoming clear and gushing out as urine. And in fact, many verses pay a great deal of attention to the traveling of the soma through the god's stomach, belly, and entrails.[2]

The outcome of all this is that the Indo-Aryans—used to the ritual consumption of the *Amanita muscaria* in their primitive habitat—had attempted, after coming to India, to maintain some sources of supply by acquiring the dried mushroom from the primitive mountain peoples. Cut off from these sources, they maintained the traditional cult for a long period, thanks to the more or less adequate substitute plants described and discussed in Brahmanic literature. Then the ancient cult completely disappeared. Having become mycophobes, the Hindus confuse all supposedly inedible mushrooms under the one contemptuous term: "dog's urine." On the other hand, the Sikh and Moslem inhabitants of the Punjab, of Kashmir, and of the northwest provinces (i.e., the first regions occupied by the Aryans) remained mycophiles; vestiges of the old cult are retained beyond the geographical or cultural borders of Hinduism. Very probably in China—where the tradition of the *Ling chich*, "fungus of immortality" was perhaps imported from India, according to Mr. Wasson, and only in the first century B.C.—it became incarnate in a fortuitous manner in the *Ganoderma lucidum*, since then more or less faithfully reproduced in the iconography. Perhaps also, via Persia, among the Manicheans, whom St. Augustine (who shared their beliefs for a time) accused of being fond of mushrooms; this accusation is found several centuries later in the writings of a Chinese scholar against an immigrant Manichean sect. The same text also denounces the sect for using red mushrooms and urine, apparently human, as ritual water. On this subject, Mr. Wasson notes that the Parsis of the Bombay region, in keeping with the religion of Zoroaster, drink in a symbolic way the urine of a bull.

The author refers several times to this positive attitude toward urine, seeing in it a vestige of a religious nexus centered around the *Amanita muscaria,* and in which we know that the consumption of urine has an important place. He even puts forward the hypothesis that the nexus could have originated because of the proximity of reindeer, as these Cervidae eat amanita which also intoxicates them. They have a pronounced liking for human urine —increased tenfold, we may suppose, when this urine contains the mushroom alkaloids. These animals, domesticated by the Siberians, would have also been their initiators so far as the consumption of urine is concerned. The hypothesis is reasonable on the surface but fundamentally weak, since Wasson himself revealed that, elsewhere in the world, humans discovered the hallucinogenic power of other mushrooms without benefiting from any animal mediation. According to him, the psychotropic substances of the fly agaric would be the only ones known to so-called primitive peoples that are not destroyed by the organic metabolism.

Cultural attitudes about human body secretions have, like all others, an ethnocentric character. The aversion we feel for urine is not a natural phenomenon, and many peoples have had a more objective attitude than ours toward this liquid of many uses. Just as the Australians readily used blood drawn from an incision of their penis to make glue, many peoples—and so it is in the American Northwest—used urine for ritual washing or just as hair lotion. Must we then conclude that their ancestors at one time consumed amanita? It is possible, and even likely, taking into account their distant Asiatic origin, and I shall later produce an argument which could suggest a more recent usage. But it seems quite unnecessary to present it here to understand that peoples not provided with manufactured chemical products have fully exploited the properties of natural substances, often the only ones at their disposal.

On the other hand, we could deduce more from the confusion of supposedly inedible mushrooms in India (and among the Yukaghir as well, who contrasted them with the amanita, of which they were fervent consumers) under the name "dog's urine."

It would be difficult to substantiate this connection, involving a distance of several thousand miles, except through an implicit belief, warranted by experience in Siberia and whose early existence in India would provide the logical link necessary to explain the comparison of urine and mushrooms.[3] Knowing in effect that in the required conditions, the psychotropism of human urine is empirically equivalent to the hallucinogenic mushroom, we can posit:

a. [human urine → amanita]   : :   [dog's urine → ordinary
                                                  mushroom]
b. [amanita : other mushrooms]   : :   [humans : dogs]

Mr. Wasson's work establishes in a manner we consider convincing that, among all the candidates for producing the soma, the *Amanita muscaria* is by far the most likely. Indeed, it allows us to give meaning to propositions and formulae which previously seemed totally devoid of it. On the other hand, only critics moved by unconscious mycophobia could feel depressed at having to admit that, after all, the passionately lyrical outpouring of the Vedic hymns are only addressed to a mushroom. These lyrical effusions would still be recognized nowadays, hardly subdued, in the mouth of a Slav taking a walk in the woods and unexpectedly coming across some boletuses freshly emerged from the ground.

There is no doubt, however, that the proposed solution presents some problems outside of the field of Vedic studies into which I do not feel competent to venture. Even if the historical or philological objections (which the specialists will not fail to formulate) are set aside, several questions come to mind. At the time when the Vedic rituals were in full swing, according to Wasson himself, only dried mushrooms from distant sources were used any longer. If his interpretation is accurate, however, the hymns continued to describe, in an abundance of detail, the most fleeting aspects of the mushrooms' growth which they manifest only in situ. Must we then admit that some appointed priests went on location and related their observations? There is nothing to suggest it in the documents cited. We must thus conclude that the hymns preserve the memory of observations made a very long time ago by the Indo-Aryans in their original habitat, observations which, at the time of the rites, could offer no meaning to the participants (who were therefore in the same situation as the later commentators).

This is not inconceivable, for the obscurity of a ritual does not necessarily affect its prestige. But we must take into consideration this fantastic discrepancy between the ritual practice and its verbal expression. Furthermore, we cannot fool ourselves. Mr. Wasson's interpretation entails consequences which go much further than the problem of the nature of the soma. If he is right, the very spirit in which the whole of Vedic literature used to be considered will be transformed. Instead of lyrical extravagance, of unrestrained verbalism which, to the nonspecialist, often seems unbearable, one would be confronted with descriptive formulae which only use metaphors to grasp the heart of reality. But if such is true in this case, it must also be in others; and we can foresee the prospect—hardly a delight to the Indianists—of all sorts of keys to be discovered in sequence, each giving access to a hidden meaning.

If, for instance, it is not enough to invoke metaphorical use, inspired by the red color of the mushroom—to explain that the hymns often give the soma the name of the deified fire, Agni—careful attention will have to be paid to Mr. Wasson's ingenious speculations on a verbal form of the *poη* type, which he perceives in the Paleo-Asiatic languages in all those of the Uralic family, which includes Samoyed and the languages of the Finno-Ugrian group. This verbal form connotes, as may be, the mushroom, the shaman's drum, inebriation, the loss of consciousness or reason. Mr. Wasson believes it is possible to link it to the proto-Indo-European forms which, according to philologists, may have yielded the Greek *sphóngos*, the Latin *fungus*, and also—our author suggests—the English "punk," designating the wick of a lighter. Moreover, the birch, whose roots offer a favorable environment for the growth of the *Amanita muscaria*, is also the favorite host of the *Fomes fomentarius*, the tinder agaric (punk). Thus an archaic triad, formerly common to all Northern Eurasia, reconstitutes itself and associates the birch (held to be the Tree of Life by most of the early peoples of that region); the punk, known for its use as an inflammable wick since the time of Maglemose; and the amanita which procures divine illumination.

Seen in this perspective, the soma of the Rig-Veda does not constitute an isolated episode in the history of the Asiatic world, but the ultimate manifestation of a widespread Eurasian cult, perpetuated almost everywhere, by legends about the Tree of Life and the Herb of Immortality. From there one can obviously go very far. Far enough, for example, to see in the Tree of Knowledge and the Forbidden Fruit of Genesis the image—fabulous but still recognizable—of the sacred Siberian birch, the host, on its trunk, of the fire mushroom; and, at its foot, of the amanita giving access to supernatural knowledge. Wasson goes further still when he toys with the idea that the religious phenomenon itself, taken as a whole, could have its origin in the use of hallucinogenic mushrooms.

This pan-mycism—if one may so call it—would of course be fragile were it not shored up by a theoretical support. Wasson borrows one (1968, pp. 217, 220) from Mary Barnard (1966) who, in a recent book, *The Mythmakers*, seeks the genesis of myths in natural phenomena. This appears to be an extremely naïve view, since there are no natural phenomena in the raw. These do not exist for man except as conceptualizations, seemingly filtered by logical and affective norms dependent on culture. It may most certainly be concluded from the fascinating film made by Roger Heim on hallucinogenic mushrooms, that the form and the content of delirium are completely different for each subject, and that both are functions of his temperament, his personal history, his upbringing, and his occupation. Mr. Wasson's testimony is of the same order when he relates his own experiment with the *Amanita muscaria* with Japanese colleagues. Only one of their group felt a euphoria bordering on ecstasy; the others felt varying discomforts. In societies which, unlike our own, institutionalize hallucinogens, these can be expected to produce, not a definite type of delirium determined by their physicochemical nature, but the one anticipated by the group for conscious or unconscious reasons and differing for everyone. Hallucinogens do not harbor a natural message, which notion seems in itself contradictory. They release and amplify a latent discourse, which each culture holds in reserve, and the elaboration of which is made possible or easier by the drugs.

Thus it does not seem legitimate to invoke, as Wasson does, the Siberian forms of delirium triggered by *Amanita muscaria*, usually peaceful and benevolent, in order to impugn the thesis—put forward by various Scandinavian scholars—according to which this mushroom would be the cause of the *berserk* fury of the ancient Vikings. There is no direct proof of it and the hypothesis thus remains gratuitous and unfounded. But nothing permits one to exclude a priori the possibility that, in societies which differed as much as the Koryak and Viking, the same drug was sought in order to produce opposite psychic effects.

It is thus without prejudice for or against some form or other of pan-mycism that I present, in conclusion, some brief considerations on the problem posed by the apparent ignorance of hallucinogenic mushrooms in the greater part of North America; that is, the part included between Eastern Siberia and Mexico, where totally different types of agaric were used for the same purpose.

As we are dealing with a part of the world for which most of the documents come from researchers of Anglo-Saxon origin or training, one should not overlook their possible mycophobia as an explanation of the relatively small place that mushrooms seem to hold in the culture of the North American Indians. It is possible that these observers, whether out of lack of interest or unconscious repulsion, may have neglected this domain. Moreover, in the most favorable cases, the distinction between the mushroom with stem and cap on the one hand (mushroom, toadstool) and the polypores and other tree fungi on the other hand, is not always sure. Finally, we have almost never bothered finding out whether the category which French subsumes under the very inclusive term "champignon" and which English distinguishes as we have mentioned, is not subdivided more finely still in such and such a native language, so that a belief or an attitude pertaining to a mushroom might refer only, in fact, to one type or one family, and opposite beliefs or attitudes might prevail toward others.

Having made these reservations, and proceeding with all due caution, two remarks of a general nature immediately come to mind. First, fungi of the polypore type seem to occupy a greater place than mushrooms in the beliefs and myths of both South and North America, Mexico excepted. Second, and as far as North America is concerned, the information available deals with mushrooms west rather than east of the Rocky Mountains.

Of all the American populations, it would indeed be the coast and interior Salish and their neighbors, whom one would be tempted to classify as mycophiles. Like the Carrier and the Indians of the Pacific coast further north, the Salish were not above naming clans or individuals after tree fungi (Jenness 1943, p. 497; Barbeau 1929, p. 166; Teit 1900, p. 292). They also ate several ground species raw (Thompson, Sanpoil, Okanagon), barely roasted (Thompson), sun-dried (Twana), or else boiled (Okanagon) (Teit 1900, p. 233; 1930, p. 483; Ray 1954, p. 104; Cline 1938, p. 29; Elmendorf 1960, p. 131). To the south, mushrooms often appear in the meals of the Indians of northern and central California. The latter also had in common with the Salish the custom of extracting, from certain wood fungi growing on conifers, a red pigment used as body paint or ointment (Teit 1900, pp. 184, 259; Driver 1919, p. 333; Teit 1906, p. 205; Olson 1967, p. 105; Goldschmidt 1951, pp. 408, 410; Voegelin 1942, pp. 180, 197). North of the Salish area, the Kwakiutl used a ground mushroom (with a name evoking rottenness) as medicinal plaster (Boas 1932, p. 187). Some Salish groups made a kind of soap from a polypore attacked by parasitic fungi (Hill-Tout 1904, pp. 31-32). Among the Salish, too, the young Thompson men rubbed their bodies with a tree fungus called "owl wood" (*Polyporus abietinus*) to acquire strength (Teit 1930, p. 504).

Among the coast Salish, the Klallam and the Quinault attributed to fungi growing on reeds or conifers the property of a gambling talisman (Gunther 1927, p. 274; Olson 1967, p. 166). The custom of using tree fungi for target practice has been noted in the same region, as well as further north among the Athapascan (Tanana), who also lent it a ritual function, that of "purifying" a polypore of the type *Fomes* before reducing it to ashes and chewing it, mixed with tobacco (or chewing it pure), among the Eyak, the Tanaina, and some western Eskimos (Adamson 1934, p. 87; Olson 1967, p. 135; McKennan 1959, p. 166).

From the Kwakiutl in the north to the Quinault in the south, one notes on the Pacific coast the scattered association of some mushrooms (phallic in appearance among the former, undoubtedly polypores among the latter) with echoes. The Squamish believe they are caused by a tree fungus (Kuipers 1967, Vol. 2, p. 59). According to the Quinault language, the same word refers to the echo and to a white-fleshed tree fungus (Boas 1902, p. 290; Olson 1967, p. 165). An association of the same type existed much farther east among the Menomini Indians, who spoke Algonkin and lived in the region of the Great Lakes. They believed that a polypore, growing on certain conifers, appears overnight once a year toward the end of February, and on this occasion shouts loudly like a human being. Thus, it was respected as a powerful spirit (Skinner and Satterlee 1915, p. 498).

East of the Rockies, the Blackfoot, the Omaha, and several tribes of the upper Missouri ate mushrooms (Chamberlain 1892, p. 573; Gilmore 1919, pp. 61-63; Fletcher and La Flesche 1911, p. 342). The Iroquois ate at least six species—but apparently not without ambivalence, keeping in mind the deadly role attributed by the myths to cooked mushrooms (Waugh 1916, pp. 121-122; Curtin and Hewitt 1918, pp. 297, 798; Fenton 1953, p. 90). In fact, the Ojibwa, neighbors of the Iroquois, saw mushrooms as the food of the dead, and a negative attitude appears among the Tête-de-Boule and the Micmac of the Atlantic coast who, like the Cheyenne (located elsewhere but also Algonkin-speaking) classified mushrooms among famine foods (Kohl 1956, p. 223; Guinard 1936, p. 70; Rand 1894, p. 50; Dorsey 1905, p. 45). This double affinity of mushrooms with death and famine seems to have been even more widespread in South America where the mythology of the Ge, the Mundurucu, the Tukuna, and the Warao gives many examples of it (Banner 1957, p. 40; Murphy 1958, p. 123; Nimuendaju 1952, p. 148). However, the Warao prescribed an infusion made with mushrooms of the *Nidularia* type for sterile women who wanted children (Roth 1915, p. 286). In the southwest of the United States, the Jicarilla Apache conceived of a different relationship between mushrooms and the supernatural world. They burned the mushrooms so that the smoke would chase away evil spirits (Opler 1960, p. 152).

In America there exists a counterpart of the beliefs of the ancient world, according to which mushrooms are spawned from celestial or meteorological events. The Blackfoot and the tribes of the upper Missouri associated mushrooms with the stars. The Nez-Percé of the Western slopes of the Rockies and some coast Salish attributed their origin to thunder and the Toba of the Argentinian Chaco to the rainbow (Gilmore 1919, p. 62; Wissler and Duvall 1908, pp. 19, 40 42, 44, 60; Walker 1968, p. 23; Métraux 1946, pp. 39–40). And so it is in the Old World for the frequent association of mushrooms with body excrements (cf. "dog's urine," "wolf's fart," noted in South America among the Toba ("rainbow's excrements") and the Matako ("excrement of the fox"); and in North America, among the Quinault ("cougar's dung") and the Siciatl or Seechelt ("thunder-excrement"). (Métraux 1939, p. 122; Olson 1967, p. 166; Hill-Tout 1904, pp. 31–32).

On the other hand, indications of any physiotropic or psychotropic function of mushrooms are extremely rare outside of Mexico. At most, we can cite, in South America, the Yurimagua in the northwest of the Amazon, who prepared a strong inebriating drink from an unidentified tree fungus; and the Kanaima of Guyana, who ate a white fungus growing on dead wood, to feel light and run faster (Chantre y Herrera 1901, L. II, p. 85; Gillin 1936, p. 150). As for North America, I have already mentioned, among some Eskimo and Athapascan in the northwest of the continent, the custom of chewing, alone or with tobacco (thus made stronger, apparently) the ashes of a fungus growing on birch trees.[4] We must also mention a curious belief of the Tewa, who are eastern Pueblo. When they ate mushrooms, they were careful to place a stick across the pot for fear of losing their memory if they neglected this precaution (Robbins et al. 1916, p. 66). Conversely, the Arapaho dancers, called "crazy dancers," wore mushrooms as earrings (Kroeber 1904, p. 195). As the Arapaho are separated from the Tewa only by the Jicarilla Apache, among whom we saw that mushrooms ward off evil, that part of the continent may be particularly important from the point of view of ethnomycology.

On the other hand, we know that the Arapaho form a separate, southern branch of the great Algonkin linguistic family, and that their original habitat was much further north. In view of this, what should one think of the Reverend Charles Lallemand's report on the Algonkin-speaking Indians (or some of them) who live in the region of Quebec? "They believe," he wrote in 1626, "in the immortality of our souls, and thus are sure that after death they go to Heaven, where they [the souls] eat mushrooms and communicate with one another." [5]

If we were not here the victims of a whim of ethnographic literature, which, like the whims attributed to nature, seems to suggest something quite different from what is actually meant, the temptation would be strong to see in Lallemand's report the memory of customs similar to those of the Siberian peoples. For the fact remains that we know other cases (cf. Lévi-Strauss 1968, pp. 219–224, 325) where native thought transfers to the supernatural order beings, objects, or knowledge formerly real but for which that society, for historical or geographical reasons, no longer have a practical use; yet, that society keeps on trying to reconcile in its ideology the memory of their past with their bygone usefulness.

NOTES

1. "Dis-moi quels champignons . . ." *L'Express*, April 10, 1958.
2. In a recent publication ("Soma and the Fly Agaric: Mr. Wasson's Rejoinder to Professor Brough," in *Ethno-Mycological Studies*, No. 2

(Cambridge: Botanical Museum of Harvard University, 1972), Wasson quotes the last two sentences of this paragraph in support of his thesis. But, here, as in the previous paragraphs, I was only attempting to interpret his work, before starting to discuss it.

3. In the course of a recent conversation, Mr. Wasson observed that an empirical connection exists between urine and some mushrooms. Thus it seems established that urine—human or animal—encourages the growth of the *Coprinus*. This phenomenon would have been observed in the Bois de Boulogne.

4. But the Eskimo of northern Alaska used to fear mushrooms (or certain species?) which they called "hard on the hand." Just touching them, you risk being poisoned and having your hands wither up. (Spencer 1959, p. 375).

5. Lallemand's report was published in a three-volume work entitled *Relations des jésuites: Contenant ce qui c'est passé de plus remarkable dans les missions de Jésus dans La Nouvelle France* (Quebec, 1858).

Relations of Symmetry Between Rituals and Myths of Neighboring Peoples

THE UNIQUE PLACE OCCUPIED by Evans-Pritchard's works in ethnological literature is due, it seems to me, to the harmonious meeting of the two main trends in our research. Our colleague's well-known liking for history has never deterred him from formal analysis. Undoubtedly, no one has more soberly and more elegantly defined the essential lines of a system of beliefs and practices, exposed its skeleton, and worked the mechanism of its articulations. At the same time, Evans-Pritchard always re-

Chapter XIII was originally published under the title "Rapports de symétrie entre rites et mythes de peuples voisins," in *The Translation of Culture: Essays to E. E. Evans-Pritchard*, ed. T. O. Beidelman (London: Tavistock Publications, 1971), pp. 161–178.

mained attentive to the arbitrary paths which events took in fashioning the particular physiognomy of a society and giving it a unique character at each stage of its development. No method can better show up than his the false affirmation that structures can only be studied in depth, at the expense of history. In him, the meeting of vast erudition, an acute sense of human values, deep psychological insight, and incomparable writing talent has brought together for a single purpose the two currents which, from the start, have too often pulled ethnological thought in opposite directions.

This is why I thought it fitting to choose, as a tribute to him, a theme which illustrates the solidarity of history and structure and throws light on their mutual reciprocal influence. Two tribes of the Central Plains in North America lend themselves very well to this attempt. Recent progress made in archaeology has yielded a lot of information on their past. At the same time, thanks to A. W. Bowers's two excellent volumes complementing older observations, we now have at our disposal detailed analyses of their myths, rituals, and ceremonial cycles.

At the beginning of the eighteenth century, when the white race arrived on the upper Missouri, the "village" tribes established in the valleys across the plains had a common culture. The Arikara, speaking the Caddo language, the Mandan and the Hidatsa, speaking Sioux, occupied neighboring territories corresponding to the present states of North and South Dakota. During the summer, they lived in huts covered by clumps of grass, grouped in villages on terraces, jutting out over the rivers. They cultivated their fields below and, while the crops were ripening, they hunted buffalo in the plains. With the coming of winter, they transported themselves to more sheltered villages at the bottom of the wooded valleys.

But this state of affairs was of recent origin. We shall leave aside the Arikara, who came from the south toward the beginning of the eighteenth century. Although belonging to the same linguistic group, the Mandan and the Hidatsa did not constitute homogeneous groups either. A very ancient Mandan settlement, originating from the eastern and southern regions, has no doubt continuously occupied the middle valley of the Missouri since at least the seventh or eighth century, a thousand years before the beginning of the historical period. Other groups arrived later, and replaced the rectangular, half-buried lodges with the rounded constructions that then became the rule. Concerning the Hidatsa, things seem even more complex. One group from the northwest, the Awatixa, reached the Missouri in the fifteenth or sixteenth century, and lived near the Mandan, from whom they borrowed their style of life and their beliefs. Two other groups, in turn, left the wooded lands west of the Great Lakes at the beginning of the eighteenth century to settle in the plains. Like the Awatixa, the Awaxawi were already agricultural people. But the Hidatsa proper lived mostly from hunting and gathering, even in historical times, when these differences were noticed by the first travelers. The traditions of the Mandan and the Hidatsa treat these diverse origins. The Hidatsa relate how the two northern groups split up to become the Crow who settled further west. Mandan legends preserve the memory of successive migrations and the arrival of the oldest Hidatsa group on the eastern bank of the Missouri. The European penetration, followed by devastating epidemics at the end of the eighteenth and the beginning of the nineteenth centuries, obliged the decimated population to relocate its villages several times. The rapport between the tribes tended to a still greater solidarity. These upheavals ended when the last survivors were brought together in the Fort Berthold reservation by the authorities.

Yet, during the years from 1929 to 1933, the period of Bowers's investigations, the information gathered from old Mandan and Hidatsa informants still differed substantially, depending on their original group or village: their myths, legendary traditions, rules of transmission of charges, and offices were different. And yet, in spite of these divergences (which concur with archaeology in attesting to the still-active influence of a historical past very complex and loaded with heterogeneous factors), everything transpires as if the Mandan and the Hidatsa had succeeded in organizing the differences in their beliefs and practices into a system. One could almost believe that each tribe—aware of the corresponding effort of the other tribe—has made the effort to preserve and cultivate the oppositions and to combine the antagonistic forces in order to form a balanced whole. This is what we would like to show now.

We have seen that the village tribes lived in a double seasonal economy. This is an understatement, for the summer season was itself twofold. It comprised a period of agricultural labor in the sheltered flats at the foot of the villages and, when the corn was knee high, a period of nomadic hunting, which for a month took the population far into the plains in pursuit of the buffalo herds. Whereas the summer villages, surrounded by ramparts and stockades, were practically inpregnable, the hunting expeditions appeared to be—and sometimes acted as if they were—war expeditions, for it happened that hunters ran into enemy parties. Thus summer labors had antithetical natures: sedentary life in protected villages and nomadic runs in exposed territories; agriculture, on the one hand, hunting and warfare, on the other. The two latter are intimately associated in spatial contiguity and moral affinity, since they are violent types of activity, pregnant with dangers and spilled blood; from this point of view, they vary mostly in degree.

This system, which brings into play complex oppositions, is in turn wholly in opposition to the winter economy. The people seldom went out of the winter villages, although accumulated food supplies were not sufficient to secure the population against famine. All hope rested then on an increase in the cold and on blizzards which would chase the buffaloes from the plains and make them seek refuge near the winter villages, in the sheltered valleys where some pasture land still remained free of snow. When the approach of the herd was signaled, a reign of absolute silence was necessary and the police corps watched over the village. People locked themselves in their huts with their dogs; they refrained from cutting wood and extinguished their fires. An overzealous hunter, a careless housekeeper, a child laughing or crying would have been severely punished. Even if one of the animals ventured into the village and skirted the buildings, the starving Indians were not allowed to kill it for fear of scaring away most of the herd. Hence, the contrasting ways of life which the summer economy juxtaposed without merging, acquired during the winter a synthetic unity. The Indians still depended on hunting, as in the summer, but this winter hunt was in opposition to the other, since it was sedentary, not nomadic, and in this way, more related to agriculture which, during the summer, was in opposition to hunting. That is not all. The summer hunt took the men away from the village and led them far into the west as they followed the buffaloes. In winter, all these relations were inverted. Instead of the Indian leaving the valleys and venturing into the plains, the wild animals left the plains and ventured into the valleys. Instead of the hunt drawing the Indians outside their villages, it took place sometimes right in the village, or at least very near, when the game came quite close. And, since hunting was related to war, everything took place during the winter, as if, in order not to starve to death, the village had to open itself wide to the buffaloes—animals which native thought compares to enemies in the summer, but which the winter transforms into allies. For the time being, restricting ourselves to the two types of hunting, it does not seem far-fetched to say that they are opposed in the manner of what we could call an "exo-hunt" for the summer, and an "endo-hunt" for the winter.

Let us first consider the summer hunting myths and rituals. Unlike their Hidatsa neighbors and other plains tribes, the Mandan did not celebrate the Sun Dance in the summer. They had instead a complex ceremony, spread over several days, which they called *okipa*, or "imitation." This ceremony, the founding myth of which was almost the same as that of the agricultural labors, fulfilled a double function: it commemorated mythical events and stimulated the fertility of the buffaloes. Thus it presented a syncretic character, and had to exert is influence over several months —as long as the gestation period lasted. Although the *okipa* always took place in the middle of the hot season, it was not particularly linked to the summer hunt, but with the hunt as a whole, winter or summer.

On the other hand, the ritual of the Small Hawk served for warfare at any time of the year, but for hunting only from June to August. The founding myth (Beckwith 1938, pp. 63–76; Bowers 1950, pp. 270–281) tells that a wild virgin named Corn Silk, offended by her parents who reproached her for remaining unmarried, left for the end of the world to marry an ogre. She successfully overcame all the trials he imposed on her and made him docile. But the ogre recovered his original nature and abandoned her with her son, with whom she fell in love after he grew up. The young man rejected his mother's incestuous advances. His name was Look-Down-to-Hunt, and he was master of hunting, because his father had passed on to him his bird-of-prey nature.

At this time two women came into his life. One, who was dark-haired, came from the north and brought dried meat with her; she was called Buffalo Cow.[1] The other, called Corn Silk, like the hero's mother, was blond, came from the south, and brought corn-flour patties with her. He married them both. But while Corn Silk was patient and generous, Buffalo Cow's jealousy and irritability compromised the harmony of the household. The two women quarreled about the services which each rendered to human beings. Offended, Buffalo Cow left with her young son.

Corn Silk talked her husband into going after the vanished wife. She was strong enough to bear his absence and would remain faithful to him and protect him from afar. At last, the hero arrived among the buffaloes, his in-laws, who did their best to destroy him. But he overcame their trials and obtained from them the promise that, from then on, they would serve as food for human beings. Famine was reigning in the village when he came back, because game was scarce and drought threatened the crops. The hero brought back the buffaloes, givers of food, and the fertile rains.

There is hardly need to interpret this myth, so explicit is it on all points. From the beginning, the heroine, Corn Silk, defines the sociological references, for her conduct correlates and contrasts two extreme types of marriage: an exogamous one with an ogre who lives at the end of the world, and an endogamous one with her own son. But she embodies agriculture, as indicated both by her name and the avowed function of her homonym, whereas her husband, and later her son, are masters of hunting. Consequently, the exogamous marriage would have exported agriculture out of the village, and the endogamous union would have imported hunting into the village. Neither eventuality is conceivable, as is proved by the incompatible natures of the two wives who personify these forms of economic activity. In order to follow Buffalo Cow, Corn Silk must be abandoned. But whereas the former is demanding and jealous and makes successful warfare—the *sine qua non* condition of successful hunting—the latter's tolerance and generosity insure that the successful hunt will also—into the bargain, as it were—bring about abundant crops. And this is indeed what happened in reality. As soon as the corn was high, the Indians abandoned their fields and villages for a nomadic life of hunting. During their absence, the plants kept on growing. Upon their return all they had to do was to harvest the corn. Thus the myth superposes terms grouped in pairs, of which it affirms the homology, although they are on different planes, ranging from the forms of technico-economic activity to domestic ethics and including the rules of social life. Agriculture implies hunting as hunting implies warfare. Agriculture is from the economic point of view what endogamy is from the sociological point of view, since they are both within the village. On the other hand, both hunting and exogamy are outward-looking. Finally, faithfulness is the opposite of conjugal infidelity (the origin of which the myth claims to explain cf. Bowers 1950, p. 281: "This was also the beginning of the custom of a man parting with his wife and child and thinking little about it"), for they are in the same relation as endogamy and exogamy, or agriculture, on the one hand, and hunting and warfare, on the other.

After the problems of summer hunting, let us now consider those of winter hunting. The ceremony of the Red Stick served to draw the buffaloes near to the villages from December to March. We know that it essentially consisted in the handing over by the young men of their naked wives, wrapped in fur coats, to the elders, personifying the buffaloes. During the ceremonial coupling which followed in real or symbolic fashion, the elders transmitted their supernatural power to the young men through the intermediary of their wives, thus ensuring their success in hunting and warfare. The Mandan and the Hidatsa celebrated this ritual in the same manner.

On the other hand, the founding myths differed from one tribe to the other, for each reserved the principal role to only one of the two women associated, as the hero's wives, with the founding myth of the summer rite. And, as could be expected from the contrasting characteristics of summer and winter hunting, the sociological functions of the women are reversed in passing from one to the other. In the Mandan myth of the Red Stick, Corn Silk is nothing but a temperamental and eccentric girl. In the homologous Hidatsa myth, Buffalo Cow has become a national heroine.

This is not all. Indeed, whereas the Mandan myth of the Red Stick (Bowers 1950, pp. 319–323) starts out like that of the Small Hawk, with the story of a virgin unamenable to marriage, who falls into the power of an ogre, it continues in a different way. The heroine escapes from her kidnapper. On the way back she adopts a very beautiful little girl, First Pretty Woman, whom she brings back to the village. The baby proves to be an ogress, personification of famine, who devours all the inhabitants. Helpful buffaloes denounce her, and she is burned at the stake. Henceforth, when famine threatens the village during the winter, the buffaloes come and offer themselves as food, in exchange for women who have been delivered to them.

In this myth, consequently, Corn Silk brings famine into the village. But the Hidatsa versions (Bowers 1965, pp. 452–454) reverse the whole system. They replace Corn Silk, taken out of the village, with Buffalo Cow, settled inside. Instead of Corn Silk, a foolhardy heroine bringing back famine from her distant journey, Buffalo Cow, a wise heroine, brings in the buffaloes in winter; and so the Indians (now her fellow villagers) escape from famine.

In the founding myth of the Mandan rite of summer hunting, the hero succeeds in rejoining his wife Buffalo Cow and in escaping from his in-laws' persecutions, thanks to the complicity of his young son, who thus proves to be the opposite of an ogre. The beautiful child of the Mandan myth of winter hunting, an adopted daughter instead of a legitimate son, and manifesting the killing absence of the buffaloes, the cause of famine (instead of neutralizing their killing presence, since at this point the buffaloes behave like enemies), is the reverse of the young helpful buffalo as he appears in the myth of summer hunting. Now, a third reversal affects the same character, White Buffalo Cow, in another winter hunting ritual celebrated from December to March by a society of women. Indeed, the founding myth (Bowers 1950, pp. 325–326) relates the capture of two buffalo children, one of whom is successfully detained in the village, and thus the cows have to come and visit it every winter, bringing the herds closer. This girl (the passive cause of the abundance of buffaloes) is thus opposed to the little ogress (who actively manifests their absence as the incarnation of famine) whose buffalo son (frustrating the cannibalistic plans of her family) is the opposite.

In adopting a formal point of view, we can perceive other relations between the myths and the rituals as they related to winter or summer hunting. Both the myth and the ritual of the cycle of the White Buffalo Cow were common to the Mandan and the Hidatsa, the latter, it is thought, having obtained it from the former (Bowers 1965, p. 205). We cannot say as much for the cycle of the Red Stick, of which only the ritual is common to both tribes, but of which, as we have seen, the founding myths differ for each tribe to the point that they present an invested image of each other. The same relationship prevails between the cycle of the Red Stick and that of the White Buffalo Cow; but this time at the level of the ritual, of which young and desirable women were the occasion in one case, and of which, when old and past the age of menopause, they are the agents in the other case. Moreover, when we compare the arrangement of the officiants in the ceremonial hut at the performance of each ritual (Bowers 1950, pp. 317, 327), we can pick out several contrasts. The participants in the White Buffalo Cow ritual were women. In the Red Stick ritual, they were both men and women. To this bisexual opposition corresponded a division of the members of the unisexual group in the other ritual into priestesses and assistants, the former active, the latter passive. In both cases, the owner of the hut and his wife played a part, but the place assigned to them was in the circle of the officiants, or outside.

Let us recapitulate: The winter ceremony of the White Buffalo Cow was common to the Mandan and the Hidatsa, both in the ritual and the myth. The other major ceremony for the winter hunt, the Red Stick, had a rite common to both, but the myths differed. Finally, at the ritual level, the two great winter ceremonies were an inverted reflection of each other.

The Hidatsa knew some weak variants of the myth of Small Hawk (cf. Beckwith 1938, pp. 77–78) (which, we remember, deals with summer hunting) but seemingly without celebrating the corresponding ritual. To complete the system of relations between the myths and rituals of the two tribes, one would thus have to find among the Hidatsa an equivalent of, or a substitute for, the summer-hunting rituals.

The Hidatsa hunting rites are linked to a mythology of the buttes, rising from the ground here and there above the plains. One of them sheltered two guardian spirits: Swallow and Hawk, who gave good hunting to unlucky Indians (Beckwith 1938, pp. 234–

238; Bowers 1965, pp. 433–436). Now, the Mandan hero of the summer hunting myth is a hawk and he has a predilection for buttes: ". . . during his leisure, he would sit on a pile of rocks on the hill back of the village" (Bowers 1950, p. 275). Like the protégé of the guardian birds in the Hidatsa myth, he also scorns the winter village and prefers to camp with his own people at the head of the valleys. Finally, the Hidatsa related all these beliefs to the summer hunt (Bowers 1965, pp. 436–437).

Thus we have converging indications which suggest that these rites, called Earthnaming, corresponded among the Hidatsa to the Small Hawk rites of the Mandan. However, according to the Hidatsa, the master of the buttes was an owl, the character who gives his name—Snow Owl—to one of the Mandan winter-hunting rites. Consequently, everything transpires as if this latter rite, reserved for winter hunting by the Mandan, had become a summer rite among the Hidatsa.

In these conditions, it seems significant that the Mandan associate the Snow Owl, not with buttes rising above the ground, but with a symbolic valley: the trapping pit where the eagle hunter hides. The hero of the myth was imprisoned in a similar pit by a fallen rock; it is by journeying underground that he arrived at the owl's lair (Beckwith 1938, p. 149; Bowers 1950, p. 286). This hero was called Black Wolf. And although the Mandan celebrated the Snow Owl rites for the winter hunt between December and March (i.e., during the coldest months), the Hidatsa celebrated the rites honoring the guardian wolves only during the hottest months (Bowers 1965, p. 148). The inversion of winter and summer is confirmed from this angle.

We have noted that summer hunting and warfare afford a double analogy, both by their resemblance and their contiguity: ". . . when on the buffalo hunt there were instances of death of Indians from enemies or from injuries inflicted by the buffaloes" (Bowers 1950, p. 277). This similarity explains that the Mandan and the Hidatsa conceive war itself as a cannibalistic hunt, in which men become game for the Sun and his sisters, celestial ogres who feed on abandoned corpses. Since the founding myths of the winter hunt present inverted characteristics in each tribe, and since the winter hunt is itself the inverse of the summer hunt, it follows that symmetrical inversions must appear, on the one hand between the Mandan and Hidatsa myths relative to the People Above, and on the other hand, between the war myths of one group and the winter hunting myths in the other group.

Let us begin with this second point. Without necessarily going into details of long and complicated myths, at first glance a parallel is evident between the Mandan myth of the People Above, from which the war rituals stem, and the Hidatsa myth of the Red Stick, from which the winter hunt rituals stem. Both refer to a quarrel between the brothers Sun and Moon either about a Cheyenne cannibal woman, who *eats* human beings, or a buffalo woman, representing a species *eaten* by human beings. Each time also, the myths relate the origin of games of chance (conceived by the Indians as a type of war) and of war itself with its supreme purpose: head hunting (cf. Bowers 1950, pp. 299–302; 1965, pp. 452–454).

The parallel relation between alternate myths can be illustrated in two ways. First, indirectly: Like the Hidatsa myth of the People Above, the Hidatsa myth of the Red Stick relates a conflict between celestial cannibals and human beings, which gives rise to games of chance, war, and war rites. This identical framework does not preclude differences, to which we will later return. For the time being, it is sufficient to remember that the Mandan myth of the Red Stick reverses the Hidatsa founding myth for the same rite and, as a consequence, the Hidatsa myth of the People Above, which has the same framework. This inversion is also confirmed directly: the Hidatsa myth of the People Above refers to a celestial nursling who is reborn as the legitimate son of an Indian woman and becomes responsible for the Hidatsa defeat at the hands of the enemies they attack. What the myth says here in the "war key"—if we are permitted the expression—is what the Mandan myth of the Red Stick expresses in the "hunt key." There, in effect, an earth-born nursling, a baby girl, adopted by a Indian woman, proves to be an ogre who devours the Mandan and who symbolizes winter famine, which results from the fact that the buffaloes do not come into the villages or their vicinity.

How far have we come? We have noted that the Mandan and Hidatsa hunting rituals each formed a system; also that these two systems afforded a symmetrical image of each other, so that the network of their reciprocal relations can be shown as in Figure 17:

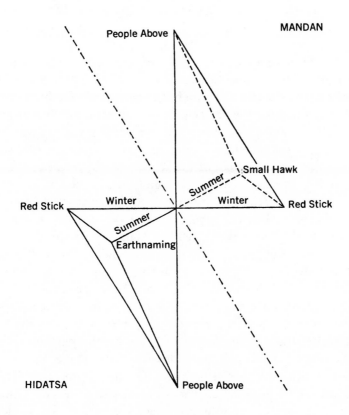

FIGURE 17

For each tribe, the main hunting myths occupy the apexes of a triangular pyramid. From one tribe to the other, they are found on corresponding opposite apexes. Thus the symmetrical relations link two by two the myths of the People Above (included as cannibal hunters); those of the Red Stick, everywhere a winter ritual; that of Earthnaming for the Hidatsa; and that of the Small Hawk for the Mandan, which both belong to summer. But Figure 17 calls for further explanations.

1. The two axes crossing in the center of the diagram which form the horizontal plane correspond to winter and summer, respectively. At the two ends of the winter axis are found the Red Stick ritual, identical in both tribes but at opposite apexes because of the inversion of the founding myths.

2. Similarly, the Mandan myth of the Small Hawk and the Hidatsa myth of Earthnaming are found located at the extremities of the summer axis. We can see that these rituals correspond to each other in several ways: duality of the heroes (Swallow and Hawk) or heroines (Corn Silk and Buffalo Cow); presence in both cases of a hero called Hawk who has a predilection for high terrain; and finally, association of the two rituals with summer hunting.

3. The myths of the People Above occupy the extremities of a third axis, perpendicular to the other two at their point of intersection. Whereas the rituals of the Red Stick, the Small Hawk, and Earthnaming presented a seasonal and periodical character, the rituals of the People Above, which could be celebrated from January to January (Bowers 1950, p. 108; 1965, p. 326), did not; in other words, they were performed aperiodically, at any time of the year. It becomes apparent from several of their features that these myths are diametrically opposed between the Mandan and the Hidatsa. In the Mandan version (Bowers 1950, pp. 229–302), two earth women who are not sisters go to heaven to become sisters-in-law by marrying celestial brothers. One, who belongs to the Mandan tribe, separates from an ogre, Sun, with the help of a string which enables her to come back down to her village. In revenge, Sun places his legitimate son at the head of the enemies of the Mandan, upon whom he declares war. In the Hidatsa version (Bowers 1965, pp. 327–329), everything is exactly reversed. Two celestial brothers come down to earth to be conceived by human beings and born as children. Sun's sister, an ogress, is joined with an earthborn character, by means of a string. She makes him her adopted son and puts him at the head of the enemies of the Hidatsa. Consequently, the war the Hidatsa declared threatens to take a bad turn for them. In one version, Moon and Thunderbirds fight side by side with the Mandan and bring them victory. The Moon's son, now chief of the Mandan, likes to sit on the tops of the buttes. In the other version, the heroes, Swallow and Hawk, which we know to be the masters of the buttes, turn back the fortunes of war in favor of the Hidatsa.

4. The preceding shows that a direct link exists, among the Hidatsa, between the myth of the People Above, founders of the rites of war, and that of Earthnaming which founds the rituals of the summer hunt. The Guardian Spirits are the same in both myths.

The Hidatsa informants state that the events related in the myth of the People Above take place at the beginning of a tale which is continued in the Earthnaming myth. Moreover, a direct link also exists between the Hidatsa myth of the Red Stick and that of the People Above. They both refer to a visit made by celestial brothers among human beings, with the intention of conceiving in one case (since the stars are reborn as Indians) and of copulating in the other (the purpose of the visit being, in this case, to become the lovers and not the children of Indian women). A war follows, but one which is declared against the Hidatsa and not by them, and in which Sun, and not his sister, fights along with the Hidatsa's enemies.

5. Connections of the same order can be observed in the Mandan myths. In the myth of the People Above and in that of the Red Stick, a heroine (also a fellow countrywoman), called Corn Silk each time, having gone to marry an ogre who lives at the end of the world, either very high up (vertical axis) or very far away (horizontal axis), either kidnaps her legitimate son to prevent him from becoming a cannibal (Bowers 1950, pp. 300–301) or adopts a little girl although she is a cannibal (p. 321). Corn Silk is also the heroine of the myth of the Small Hawk in which, as a vegetarian, she is paired with a cannibal woman who has brothers with the same appetite. The buffaloes of the first myth reverse hunting into warfare, the cannibals of the second reverse warfare into hunting, since the enemies are eaten (p. 301).

Our scheme offers two remarkable characteristics: on the one hand, the extreme symmetry of the whole; on the other, the tenuousness of the link uniting the two subsystems which seem to be joined only by a thread. But, in effect, our previous remarks show that they are strongly linked in other ways.

In the first place, the winter axis is doubled to the limits of its extension by the cycle of the White Buffalo Cow common in full to the Mandan and to the Hidatsa, in both myth and ritual (see p. 246).

Another dynamic link is added to this static one. For the cycle of the Snow Owl, present in both tribes, fulfills its function alternately in winter and summer, linked sometimes to valleys, sometimes to rising ground. So, if the cycle of the White Buffalo Cow ignores the opposition of the two subsystems, thus strengthening their solidarity, the cycle of the Snow Owl makes manifest their symmetry and plays the same role, although in different ways.

In support of this interpretation, let us emphasize that at the formal level the two cycles are found in a clear opposition. Of all the hunting rites, that of the White Buffalo Cow affords the most strongly accentuated periodic character. It was forbidden to talk about it out of season, for fear (even in August) of the cold weather coming and ruining the gardens. Its celebration could take place only during the winter solstice, on the shortest days of the year (Bowers 1950, pp. 324–327; 1965, p. 206). Moreover, the ritual had a single purpose: to make the winter cold enough to chase the buffaloes into the vicinity of the villages. On the other hand, the rites of the Snow Owl were eclectic in nature. They served for the winter hunt, for the spring and summer rains, and for war at any time of the year (Bowers 1950, p. 108). The rituals of the White Buffalo Cow precluded all other forms of activity and were not compatible with anything. But the Snow Owl rituals were compatible with everything (Bowers 1950, p. 282; 1965, pp. 433–434).

Thus it seems that the rituals which could be called "white" (*White* Buffalo Cow, *Snow* Owl) did succeed in binding together in two different ways, one passive, the other active, the "red" rituals (*Red* Stick) which the myths could only unite precariously on account of their divergent characteristics. On this subject, let us note that one version of the Hidatsa myth of the Red Stick specifies that the guardian buffaloes used this color for body painting, to the exclusion of white or black (Bowers 1965, p. 452), which suggests that the opposition of rituals through color was relevant.

Let us remembered that the predilection of the hero or heroes for the buttes served as a link-up between the Mandan myth of the People above and the Hidatsa myth of Earthnaming. In effect, the buttes rising above the plain constitute an appropriate symbol of the mediation between the myths occupying symmetrically opposed positions in the schema, i.e., the People Above for the Hidatsa and the Small Hawk for the Mandan. This hypothetical consequence is completely verified by a detail of the second myth. In order to escape from the attacks of the celestial ogre (a bird) which she intends to win over and marry, the heroine, helped by the moles (chthonic animals), stretches out in a ditch, so that her body is level with the ground and offers no hold for the claws of birds of prey. In other words, it reconstructs an approximate equivalent of the eagle hunter's pit, in which we recognized a symbol of the valley, in opposition to the butte.

Consequently, in one case the buttes play the role of a positive mediator between high and low; in the other a dell, inverse of the buttes, plays the role of negative mediator. A threefold trans-formation can thus be traced, from the imaginary level to the em-pirical level, by way of the symbolic level:

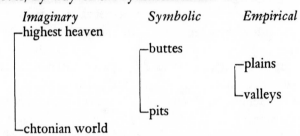

Imaginary	*Symbolic*	*Empirical*
┌highest heaven		
	┌buttes	
		┌plains
		└valleys
	└pits	
└chtonian world		

The second proof of a coherent system would be found in the code of ethics. We noted several times that the myths contrast, at one and the same time, forms of economic activity, types of social and political relations, and behavior related to domestic ethics. The myth of the Small Hawk explained the origin of unfaithfulness (Bowers 1950, p. 281); while the myth of the Snow Owl explains the origin of jealousy (p. 294). The ritual of the White Buffalo Cow was neutral, since the women who celebrated it had passed menopause. The myths of the Red Stick persuaded the men to overcome their jealousy in delivering their young wives to the elders. There remains the Hidatsa myth of Earthnaming, and it too should afford a moral connotation.

This being posited in a hypothetico-deductive manner, what, then, does the myth say? It tells the story (Bowers 1965, pp. 434–435) of an adopted stranger who risks his life to free his "sisters" kidnapped from the Hidatsa by his own people. Thus, there is praise of fraternal loyalty, which transcends the two planes of sexual life and tribal borders, as opposed to the myth of the Small Hawk, which excuses sexual infidelity, also practiced beyond tribal borders; whereas the sexual infidelity advocated in the myths of the Red Stick takes place within the tribe and even within the village.

How conscious were the Mandan and the Hidatsa of these complex relations of correlation and opposition, of symmetry and antisymmetry among their respective myths? To conclude, in an attempt at answering this question, it must first be stressed that the mythology of the two peoples presented all sorts of common points, in addition to the differences we have noted. They knew each other's myths and knew how to relate them in the same or similar terms. Thus the objection cannot be made that some, almost identical tales exist in both cases. We only wanted to show that, from a patrimony which has become common, each tribe tended to choose opposite or complementary variants when it came to founding similar rites (or rites fulfilling the same functions).

Thus, at the origin of the differences introduced into the mythical systems, there are acknowledged resemblances at the level of rituals which, as it were, lock the forms of technical and economic activity into the ideology. The Mandan and Hidatsa rituals are alike, because in arriving on the Missouri, the latter borrowed from the former their rituals, along with a type of life the problems of which these rituals help to circumvent and the contradictions of which they help to veil. In a sense, then, the manner in which the founding myths of the rituals are mutually contrasted from one tribe to the other, reflects the double evidence of a distinct historical origin for each tribe, anxious to preserve its individuality, and of a practice that history itself led the two peoples to share.

But is it not always true, even among us, that neighborliness requires of the parties that they become alike to a certain extent, while remaining different? Native philosophy was aware of this dialectical necessity, although formulating it in terms of history rather than structure. The Mandan called *Minnetaree*, a word which in their language means "they crossed the river," the oldest Hidatsa group which arrived on the Missouri from the northeast at the end of prehistoric times and learned corn growing from them. But, according to their own traditions, the Mandan did not wish this cohabitation to continue and expressed their point of view to their guests in these terms:

> It would be better if you went upstream and built your own village, for our customs are somewhat different from yours. Not knowing each other's ways, the young men might have differ-

ences and there would be wars. Do not go too far away, for people who live far apart are like strangers and wars break out between them. Travel north only until you cannot see the smoke from our lodges and there build your village. Then we will be close enough to be friends and not far enough away to be enemies (Maximilian 1843, p. 368; Bowers 1965, p. 15).

This high lesson of political philosophy, repeated almost in the same terms a century later, defines in terms of geography and history the structural configuration which was to result from its being put into practice, and which our retrospective analysis simply picked up again. Does not symmetry offer to those it both unites and opposes the most elegant and simplest means of seeing themselves as similar and different—near and distant, friends although enemies after a fashion, and enemies while remaining friends? One's own image, seen in a mirror, seems so close and one could touch it with a finger. And yet nothing is further from one than this other self, because a body, imitated in the least details, reflects them all backward; and two forms which recognize themselves in each other each retain the original orientation given them by destiny. Finally, if the customs of neighboring peoples exhibit symmetrical relations, the cause for it should be sought not only in some mysterious laws of nature or mind. This geometrical perfection also sums up in the present mode the innumerable efforts, more or less conscious, accumulated by history, all aiming in the same direction: to reach the threshold, undoubtedly the most profitable to human societies, of a just equilibrium between their unity and their diversity; and to maintain an equal balance between communication, favoring reciprocal illuminations—and absence of communication, also beneficial—since the fragile flowers of difference need half-light in order to exist.

NOTES

[1. *Translator's note:* The names used in the myths told to Beckwith and Bowers vary in their English translation. Professor Lévi-Strauss chose Bowers's name for the boy: "Looks-Down-To-Hunt" ("Looks-Down-on-the-Ground-from-Above" in Beckwith). He did not indicate his preference for the name of the dark wife who came from the north: "Buffalo Cow" in Beckwith 1938, or "Buffalo Woman" in Bowers 1950. The latter sounds more elegant, but we chose "Buffalo Cow" because of the "White Buffalo Cow" which comes later in the text.]

CHAPTER XIV

How Myths Die

WE WILL BE CONCERNED here with the death of myths, not in time, but in space. We know that myths transform themselves. These transformations—from one variant to another of the same myth, from one myth to another, from one society to another for the same myth or for different myths—bear sometimes on the framework, sometimes on the code, sometimes on the message of the myth, but without its ceasing to exist as such. Thus these transformations respect a sort of principle of conservation of mythical material, by which any myth could always come from another myth.

However, the integrity of the original formula may itself deteriorate in the course of this process. This formula degenerates or evolves, as you will, beyond the stage where the distinctive characteristics of the myth are still recognizable and where the myth retains what a musician might call its "lilt." In such cases, what does the myth become? This is what we now propose to examine with an example.

Chapter XIV was originally published under the title "Comment meurent les mythes," in *Science et conscience de la société: Mélanges en l'honneur de Raymond Aron* (Paris: Calmann-Lévy, 1971), Vol. 1, pp. 131–143.

The peoples of the Salish linguistic family, together with their Sahaptin neighbors to the South, occupied in historical times an area stretching almost without a break from the Rocky Mountains to the Pacific Ocean, and roughly covering the basins of the Columbia River in the south and the Frazer River in the north. In this vast territory numerous variants were collected of a complex of myths organized around the tale of a poor, sick, and despised old man, usually called Lynx. By a trick, he makes the daughter of the village chief pregnant. People wonder at this unexplainable pregnancy. A child is born, who points out Lynx as its father; the indignant villagers abandon the couple without fire or food. By himself, or with his wife's help, Lynx recovers his true nature, that of a beautiful young man and expert hunter. Thanks to him, his family lives in plenty, while the villagers who have gone away are starving. At last, they resign themselves to coming back and they ask his forgiveness. Those who did not persist in too harshly maltreating and trying to disfigure the hero are forgiven and receive food supplies (Boas 1895a pp. 9–10; 1901, p. 287; 1917, pp. 109–116; Phinney 1934, pp. 465–488; Jacobs 1934, pp. 27–30; Adamson 1934, pp. 193–195; Reichard 1947, pp. 109–116; Teit 1898, pp. 36–40; 1909, p. 684; Ray 1933, pp. 138–142; Hoffman 1884, p. 28–29; Haeberlin 1924, pp. 414–417; Hill-Tout 1899, pp. 534–540; 1900, p. 549; 1907, pp. 228–242).

Reduced to its essential outline, the myth is widely diffused, since one meets with it as far as tropical America, among the ancient Tupinamba of the east coast of Brazil, and also in Peru. The originality of the Salish is to have developed it in two parallel forms. In one, Lynx's son, kidnapped by an owl, then freed by his people, puts on the sanious skin of an old man; when burned, this skin will give birth to fog. In the other, a child, adventurous or out of favor (depending on the version), becomes master of the wind which in those days laid waste to the earth. Having captured and tamed it, he then exposes himself to dangers from which he escapes with the help of a character named Coyote. The fact that this second form has liberally borrowed from old French folklore disseminated in the eighteenth century by Canadian *coureurs-des-bois*, presents a problem which we have tried to solve elsewhere (see our teaching reports, *Annuaire du Collège de France*, 1969–1970, pp. 285–289) and which must not affect us here. In order to illustrate the symmetry of the two forms, it will suffice to point out that in the beliefs of the region we are dealing with (and beyond, as far as the eastern Pueblo), lynx and coyote constitute a pair of terms in correlation and opposition. This is also the case for fog and wind, to the origin of which each series of myths is, respectively, linked. They are two types of atmospheric phenomena, but one is exclusive of the other.

Moreover, the heroes of each series, the son of Lynx or the protegé of Coyote, reproduce characters (with whom sometimes they are even identified) bearing very similar names: Tsaauz, Ntsaâz, Snánaz, depending on the dialect, and among whom the native informants see as being related (Boas and Hunt 1917, p. 26). But even when the boy kidnapped by the owl is not the son of Lynx, he retains a metaphorical affinity with him. Both are master of the fog, and at different points in the narrative each camouflages himself in the ulcerated skin of an old man. Whereas the relation between them is one of resemblance, in the symmetrical series a relation of contiguity prevails between Coyote and the young hero master of wind: their collaboration is the result of a simple meeting. Finally, the first hero's capture by an owl is echoed back by the name of the second hero. He is called Snánaz which means "owl" in Shuswap, according to the informants (Teit 1909, pp. 698–699, 702–707; 1898, pp. 63–64, 87–89; 1912, pp. 265–268, 393–394; Boas and Hunt, 1917, pp. 26–30; Hill-Tout 1904, pp. 347–352; Reichard 1947, p. 146; Farrand 1900, p. 36–37, 42–43).

It is among the Thompson River Indians, who occupy a central position within the Salish linguistic area, that the two series are met with in their most articulate form. Already, the whole has been allowed to disintegrate among their Shuswap neighbors to the north, also Salish-speaking. According to J. Teit, who was the great expert on these Indians, they commonly divided their version of the myth of Snánaz, master of wind, into two separate stories. As for the symmetrical myth, about the whimpering unbearable little boy, threatened by the owl, then kidnapped by him, it fades out and tends toward what we could call a minimal expression. This process is quantitative first, as the plot is reduced to the kidnapping of the hero, his subsequent deliverance, and the transformation of the owl-man into an ordinary bird, the harbinger of death (a function attributed to the owl by all the interior Salish and many other Indians). It is also qualitative (for instance among the Kutenai, an isolated linguistic group immediately to the east of the Salish; Boas and Hunt 1918, pp. 20, 37, 50) in that the owl of the Shuswap myth is turned from an ogre into a wise and powerful magician who, far from reducing the young hero to bondage, transmits his knowledge to him and makes him even superior to himself.

Consequently, in following the same myth from the south to the north, we first observe a diminishing which affects the length and richness of the narrative, on the one hand, and the dramatic intensity of the motifs on the other, as though the plot were collapsing and contracting at the same time.

The Shuswap, both by language and culture the northernmost of the interior Salish, still show a marked affinity with their neighbors to the south. But if we pursue the investigation beyond them, we cross over a double threshold. In the northwest, the Shuswap lived next to the Chilcotin, the first representatives of the great Athapascan linguistic family, which spread continuously to the north and the northwest up to the Eskimo territories. From the cultural point of view, the Chilcotin had moved away from the amorphous sociological model, typical of the interior Salish, and had drawn nearer to the neighboring native cultures on the coast of the Pacific Ocean. These cultures, including those of the Kwakiutl, Bella Coola, and Tsimshian, were characterized as we know by a complex social organization with division into clans and phratries; by a class system distinguishing between nobles, common people, and slaves, founded on birth, primogeniture and wealth; and finally, by a prodigious flowering of graphic and plastic arts, of which the richly sculptured totem poles and ceremonial masks are the best known examples.

These linguistic and cultural characteristics are proof of the different historical pasts of the Salish, who apparently occupied the same territory for several thousand years, and the more recently arrived Athapascan. The threshold formed by the northern frontier of the Salish area must have presented an appreciable obstacle to communication. One often observes, in this type of case, that mythological systems, after passing through a minimal expression, recover their original fullness on the other side of the threshold. But their reflection is inverted, a bit like a bundle of light rays entering into a *camera obscura* through a pin-point opening and forced by this obstacle to cross over each other. The same image, seen rightside-up outside, is reflected upside-down in the camera (see p. 184). True to this model, the Chilcotin version of the myth about the boy kidnapped by an owl reinstates as rich and developed a plot as the one existing among the Salish groups south of the Shuswap. But, significantly, several essential propositions topple over and undergo transformations which sometimes result in the meaning being turned inside out.

So how do the Chilcotin tell the myth? They say that, under the pretext of feeding him, an owl enticed and kidnapped a little boy who cried without stopping. He brought him up, made him grow very fast through magic operations, and adorned him with a shell (*dentalia*) necklace. The parents set out to look for their son and meet him. But the child, who liked living with the owl, first refused to follow them. Finally he was convinced and the small group left hurriedly after burning the owl's hut. The bird-man pursued the fugitives who hid near a footbridge that he had to pass on. Frightened by the hero who was waving about his hooked fingers (he had armed them with goat's horns which gave him dangerous claws), the owl fell into the water, swam ashore and gave up the chase. The village received the hero with open arms. He appeared adorned from head to foot with the shells he had taken away, and distributed them around. Since then, the Indians have ornaments made of *dentalia*.

One day, the hero's mother found him dirty and ordered him to take a bath. He refused and she forced him. He dove into the water and disappeared. The sorrowing mother remained on the lake shore and refused to move from there. Winter came. The village women came to the lake to make holes in the ice and draw water. The hero, still living in the depths, amused himself by breaking the pails. Two sisters caught him, using as bait an elaborately decorated pail. He was so softened up and weakened by his stay in the water that he could no longer walk. The sisters tried in vain to scrape off the mud with which he was covered and which gave him a sort of second skin. They carried him to their hut where he warmed up by the fire, and they took care of him.

That winter was unusually severe. The food supplies became scarce and the men could not get the wood they needed to make snowshoes and go hunting. Although a convalescent, the hero dragged himself outside, gathered just enough wood for one pair of snowshoes, and asked a woman to bring the wood inside and shake it when she was halfway down the ladder leading into the hut (which, among these Indians, is partly underground and entered through the roof). Shaken that way, the wood multiplied and filled the hut. The hunters could make snowshoes and go out. But they found no game, and famine set in.

Then the hero asked the village people to give him arrows, and he too went hunting. He took off his silt skin in secret and hid it. In his original appearance, he killed many caribou and—once more covered with silt—distributed them among the people who had given him good arrows. But Raven had given him a weak arrow and received as his share only a coyote, which is poor game. So he spied on the hero and found the silt skin caught in the fork of a tree. Raven hid it. He saw the hero return young, beautiful, adorned with shells. Unmasked, the hero remained as he was and married the two sisters who had cured him (Farrand 1900, pp. 36–37).

To make apparent all the transformations or inversions which appear in this Athapascan version of a myth more widely known among the Salish, it would no doubt be desirable to quote other variants. But this would lead us too far afield, and so we will resign ourselves to proceeding by allusion. Instead of the usual sequence of the owl going into the hut to kidnap the child, he lures him outside. The Shuswap version, summarized above, had already proceeded to transform the owl, cannibalistic monster for the Kutenai, into a benefactor. The Chilcotin account pursues the transformation in the same direction. But it reverses the function of the bird-man, who among the Shuswap grants spiritual powers, and who becomes the custodian of material wealth (*dentalia*) which the hero gets hold of before running away. It is to this event that the myth traces back the origin of these jewels, thus attributing both an exotic and supernatural character to them. The Chilcotin had good reasons for fostering the mystery in relation to the minds of the Interior Salish, their inland neighbors, who could only obtain these shells by their intermediary (indeed they call the Chilcotin by a name which means "People of the *Dentalia*"). But the reality was quite different. The Chilcotin were the only ones able to communicate with the Bella Coola, through the passes in the coastal ranges situated in their territory, and they bought the shells from these fishermen. Thus they held a veritable monopoly as regards to the plateau Salish. The latter, especially the Thompson and the Coeur d'Alène, explained how they lost the origin (formerly a local one) of the *dentalia* shells through a series of myths symmetrical to the one under discussion. This puts their myth in diametrical opposition to that by which the Chilcotin claim to explain how they acquired the exotic source of these ornaments.

No less revealing is the episode in the Chilcotin myth in which the hero's mother wants to force him to bathe. If we list all the variants of this episode along a southeast-northwest axis, on which the Coeur d'Alène, the Thompson and the Chilcotin follow one another, we can in fact observe a triple transformation. In the Coeur d'Alène version, the thirsty mother asks her son for some water, which he refuses her. In the Thompson version, the son, feeling the heat, takes a bath in spite of his mother's forbidding it, which is the opposite of the Chilcotin episode (Reichard 1947, pp. 169–170; Boas 1917, pp. 26–30; Teit 1912, pp. 265–268). Therefore the semantic function of water ranges from drink to bath, i.e., from body content to body recipient, for drinking water goes into the body just as the body goes into the bath water. At the same time, the negative son reverses to the negative mother, who is in turn inverted to positive mother:

	COEUR D'ALÈNE	THOMPSON	CHILCOTIN
Water	content	recipient	recipient
Protagonists	son (−)	mother (−)	mother (+)

All the versions include the winter sequence, but whereas in the interior Salish versions the villagers lack firewood, in the Chilcotin version they start by lacking water, which the hero prevents the women from drawing when he amuses himself by breaking their pails. No doubt the wood plays a role in this version, but as lumber, thus in opposition to the other function wood may fill in feeding the fire. Furthermore, this opposition is redoubled by the manner, different in each case, in which the hero makes a small quantity of wood multiply: shaken halfway down the ladder or dumped directly from the top to the bottom. This latter method—the only one remembered in the Salish versions—certainly alludes to that used by the character called Lynx, of whom we spoke at the beginning of this chapter, to make the chief's daughter pregnant (by spitting or urinating from the top of the ladder on the young woman sleeping at the foot of it). All the more certainly that, in some of these versions, the boy captured by the owl is the son of Lynx and that, in the Chilcotin's myth where he is not his son, he still puts on a silt skin which makes him weak and sick, exactly like Lynx wearing the ulcerated skin of an old man; and Lynx's son who, barely freed from his captivity by the owl, voluntarily adopts the same dress. Remember that this skin, stolen from the hero and burned, gives rise to fog, in perfect symmetry with the silt which makes water opaque as fog makes the air opaque, and whose aquatic affinity is the counterpart of the affinity conceived between fog, smoke, and fire in the Salish myths.

Finally, the relation with the mythical series in which the hero makes himself master of wind—faintly attested among the Chilcotin—results from the appearance of coyote in a reverse position in the other myth: as poor game, the passive instrument of the hero's revenge against the raven who did not help him. In the strong versions about the origin of the mastered wind, we saw that the coyote actively provides aid for the hero, enabling him to escape from a perilous situation.

A priori, nothing seems to prevent the myth from passing other thresholds, beyond the Chilcotin. This passage would be marked by a contraction and an attenuation of the plot, beyond which the original image would be recovered and differently inverted along a new axis. But it is also conceivable that in crossing successive thresholds, the creative momentum may lessen and the semantic field of transformations, easily exploitable at first, may afford a diminishing return. Becoming less and less plausible as they beget one another, the last states of the system would impose such distortions to the mythical framework, putting so much stress on its resistance, that it would end up by disintegrating. Then the myth would cease to exist as such. Either it would vanish, making way for other myths, typical of other cultures or regions; or, in order to survive, it would undergo alterations affecting not only its form, but the very essence of myth.

We believe that this can be observed in the particular case under consideration. North of the Chilcotin lived the Carrier, also members of the Athapascan linguistic family but very different in their culture. Indeed the Carrier owed their name to their distinctive customs. Widows were subjected to particularly rigorous constraints, like the duty of constantly wearing the bones of their dead husbands for a prolonged period of time. Now we rediscover among them the generative cell of our mythological ensemble such as it existed, in the south, among the Sahaptin and the Salish, but singularly transformed. The Carrier tell the story of a poor orphan boy whose whole wardrobe consisted of a lynx fur. In the course of a walk, he came upon the chief's daughter naked. She did not see him at all, but later recognized him by the contact of his rough hands which had grazed her body. To escape dishonor, she married him. The chief graciously accepted this son-in-law, hardly worthy of him, bestowing gifts of clothing and ornaments on him, and thereby "washing" his poverty off. He was well advised to do so, as the young man turned out to be an expert hunter and killer of the monsters who persecuted the Indians. One day, however, he died tackling a gigantic man-killing lynx. His disconsolate wife killed herself over her husband's body (Jenness 1934, pp. 114–121).

When this account is compared with the story of Lynx as we summarized it at the beginning according to the Sahaptin and Salish versions, several types of changes are observed. Some appear as inversions. Instead of being old, the hero is young; he sees the chief's daughter outside the village and not inside (or very near) the hut. Moreover, everything transpires as if the Carrier version systematically replaced literal expressions with their metaphorical equivalents. A garment made of lynx fur characterizes a protagonist named Lynx elsewhere; symbolic contact with the young woman's body replaces her actual impregnation. There is a no less symbolic correlation of poverty ("washed" off the hero by the chief's presents) with the silt skin of the Chilcotin version, which the two sisters try in vain to wash off; and with the ulcerated skin of an old man in the Salish versions in which the hero, after getting rid of it, appears adorned with the riches he already owned. Finally, instead of a story inspired by the concept of a distributive justice and ending with the separation of the protagonists in two camps—

the wicked who are punished, the good who are forgiven—we have here a plot evolving to a tragic and inescapable end. These features all show that, with the Carrier version, a decisive passage occurs from a formula mythical until then to a romantic formula within which the initial myth (which was—do not forget—the "story of Lynx") appears as its own metaphor: the monstrous lynx looming up without motivation at the end, and castigating, not so much the hero adorned with all the virtues, as the narrative itself for having forgotten or failed to recognize its original nature and disowning itself as a myth.

Let us now consider another threshold: that which separated the Athapascan of the interior from the tribes of the Pacific coast on their northwest, whose social and cultural characteristics we evoked briefly on p. 259, and to which we should add the linguistic ones. Established at the mouth of the Nass and the Skeena Rivers, the Tsimshian, who speak a separate language and were perhaps related to the great Penutian family, were divided into clans bearing animal names. The Bear clan of the Nisqa subtribe justified, by a legend, its exclusive title to the wearing of a ceremonial headdress of carved and painted wood, inlaid with abalone shell and portraying the face of an owl surrounded by little manlike figures with claws. They tell how a chief had a young son who cried incessantly. He was threatened with the owl, who indeed appeared. But instead of kidnapping the insufferable little boy, the owl flew off with his sister, whom he planted at the top of a tree, from which no one could get her down in spite of her complaints. At last, she resigned herself, stopped lamenting, and married the owl. She soon gave birth to a son and when he had grown up, she asked her husband's permission to send him back among men. The owl agreed to this, composed a song for the occasion, and carved a headdress in his image. He took his wife and son to their village. After the mother had certified the identity of her son for her people, she went back with her husband, leaving the child who later bequeathed to his clan of origin the headdress carved by the owl and the song he had taught him: "O my brother! White Owl gave me this tree as my seat."

To make the discussion simpler, we will leave aside the character of the sister. Her presence in the plot is in fact explained by a transformation, the reason and origin of which must be sought in the Salish versions found in the Frazer, especially among the Stseelis or the Chehalis which this is not the place to examine here (Hill-Tout 1904, pp. 347–352).

Let us be content to show how this Tsimshian version differs from those of the Chilcotin and the interior Salish. Whereas the Carrier referred to these latter versions by a play of metaphors, it is clear that the Tsimshian narrative, exclusively, brings into play relations of contiguity. In particular, it does not present itself as a myth, but as a legend relating supposedly historical events and meant to fill a precise and restricted purpose, that is the founding of certain clan privileges. And yet, it is without question the same myth because the carved headdress, published by Boas (1897, pp. 324–325 and plate 1; 1895b, p. 572), represents characters thrusting hands with threatening claws toward the owl they have surrounded. This is a motif which the Tsimshian legend, as collected by Boas, does not explain, but of which the informants were nevertheless knowledgeable, since they called these characters "claw men," who are mentioned in the Chilcotin myth we summarized p. 262

But, from there, one can go back much further. These claws made of goat's horns, by means of which the Chilcotin hero caused the owl's downfall, transform the basket bristling with awls on the inside, where the Shuswap and the Kutenai owls deposited the hero after kidnapping him. These awls in turn transform the vermin, the owl's food, which line the basket in the more southern Salish versions in which the kidnapper bird has the role of a loathsome master and not an ogre (Kutenai version) or a shaman presiding over initiation tests (Shuswap version). At the end of this regressive process, we rediscover among the Sanpoil, who lived in the southeast part of the Salish area (thus at the opposite end from the Tsimshian), an implicit reference to the central theme of their narrative and the ritual song that goes with it. Indeed, the Sanpoil called the fork in the central pole of their huts, used for dances in honor of guardian spirits, the "owl's perch" (Ray 1939, p. 129).

Thus, a myth of Salish origin is first inverted as a myth when it passes the linguistic and cultural threshold separating the Salish from the Athapascan; it then becomes a romantic tale when it passes from the Chilcotin to the Carrier. When passing another threshold, it undergoes a different transformation, this time to the order of legendary tradition, as a means of founding certain modalities of an ancestral system. In one case, it swings toward the novel, and in the other toward what is certainly not history but has some pretensions to it.

To finish this survey, let us turn to the east, the geographical direction opposite to that of the Tsimshian. This will enable us to perceive a third type of transformation, beyond the cultural and linguistic threshold separating the Athapascan from the tribes of the great Algonkin linguistic family stretching to the shores of the Atlantic Ocean. Its westernmost representatives in the north were the Cree, adjacent to the Athapascan. About the year 1880, the people of the Poule-d'Eau lake region related that there was in olden times a village where a child mysteriously disappeared every night. In another corner of the village lived a little boy who cried and wept all the time. One day, his mother, annoyed, shook him roughly. The child slipped out of his skin "like a butterfly coming out of its chrysalis" and flew away in the shape of a big white owl.

The woman watched for her son's return and discovered that it was he who, changed into an owl at night, stole the other children to eat them, and who reassumed his human appearance at daybreak. She brought the villagers together and accused this son, whom she had conceived with a white man. The little ogre was condemned to death, but he pleaded with his fellow villagers and promised great wonders in return for his life. Finally, he was locked up alive, with some food supplies, in a wooden box propped on stakes, and the whole population moved away.

When the people came back three years later, they were astounded to see on the deserted site a large village of wooden houses, inhabited by white men whose language the Indians did not understand. It was a trading post. The owl-child lived there. They recognized him and questioned him. He explained that these new people were born of the children he had kidnapped and devoured. "But he, having become a great white chief, gave them Cree weapons, clothes, implements. And, from then on, the two peoples lived very harmoniously" (Petitot 1886, pp. 462–465).

It is a fact that the Cree—so named as an abbreviation of

Kristineaux (from Kenistenoa, one of the names by which they called themselves)—appeared as early as 1640 in the Jesuits' reports; and that, very early, they established friendly relations with the French and the English. Toward the end of the seventeenth century, they already served the fur trade as hunters and guides, and their subsequent history remains closely associated with that of the Hudson Bay Company and of the Northwest Fur Company. Their version of the myth of the child kidnapped by an owl obviously results from a manipulation meant to make the myth fit an aspect of their history by which the Cree differed from their neighbors, who were more reserved or even hostile to the whites.

But we also see that we are not dealing with the same type of story as the one the Tsimshian legend referred to, at the price of another manipulation of the myth. Not only because it is tribal in one case and clannish in the other, but for more profound reasons. The Tsimshian were trying to justify an order they wished to retain unchanged by a tradition the origin of which they dismissed as lost in the dawn of time. The Cree adapted the same myth to recent history, with the manifest intention of justifying a development in the making and of validating one of its possible orientations —collaboration with the white man—among others left open to them. The story of the Tsimshian legend is imaginary, because no woman ever married an owl. That of the Cree myth refers to real events, because the white men did marry Indian women and the Indians had visited a trading post for the first time. At the time when the myth was collected, their friendly relations with the white men still were part of their actual experience.

Thus, a myth which is transformed in passing from tribe to tribe finally exhausts itself—without disappearing, for all of that. Two paths still remain open: that of fictional elaboration, and that of reactivation with a view to legitimizing history. This history, in its turn, may be of two types: retrospective, to found a traditional order on a distant past; or prospective, to make this past the beginning of a future which is starting to take shape. By emphasizing with an example this organic contiguity apparent among mythology, legendary tradition, and what we must call politics, we wish to pay tribute to a scholar and philosopher who has never consented to make history a privileged domain in which man would be sure of finding his truth.

PART FOUR

Humanism
and the Humanities

Answers to Some Investigations

The Three Humanisms

To MOST OF US, ethnology appears to be a new science, a result of the subtlety and inquisitiveness of modern man. Primitive objects took their place in our aesthetics less than fifty years ago. And if our interest in the customs and beliefs of savages goes back a little farther, the first works systematically devoted to them hardly predate 1860. This was the time when Darwin posed the problem of biological evolutionism, which corresponded, in the minds of his contemporaries, to the problem of man's social and intellectual evolution.

Yet, therein lies a dangerous illusion, insofar as it deceives us

Chapter XV includes several essays that were originally published in the following journals: "Les trois humanismes," *Demain*, No. 35 (1956); "Structuralisme et critique littéraire," *Paragone, Nuova Serie-2* (Milan: Arnoldo Mondadori, 1965); *Letteratura*, No. 182, pp. 125–133; "A propos d'une rétrospective," *Arts*, No. 60, November 16–22, 1966; "L'Art en 1985," *Arts*, April 7–13, 1965; "Civilisation urbaine et santé mentale," *Les Cahiers de l'Institut de la vie*, No. 4 (April 1965), pp. 31–36; "Témoins de notre temps," *Le Figaro littéraire*, November 25, 1965.

about the real place occupied in our view of the world by the knowledge of distant peoples. Ethnology is neither a separate science, nor a new one. It is the most ancient, most general form of what we designate by the name of humanism.

When, at the end of the Middle Ages and the beginning of the Renaissance, Greco-Roman antiquity was rediscovered, and when the Jesuits made Greek and Latin the basis of intellectual training, was that not a first form of ethnology? They recognized that no civilization can define itself if it does not have at its disposal some other civilizations for comparison. The Renaissance rediscovered in ancient literature forgotten notions and methods. But more important still, it realized the means of putting its own culture in perspective—by confronting contemporary concepts with those of other times and other places.

Those who criticize the teaching of classics should not be mistaken about it. Were the working knowledge of Greek and Latin confined to the short-lived acquisition of some rudiments of dead languages, there would not be much point in it. But—as secondary school teachers well know—through the language and the texts, the student is initiated into an intellectual method which is the same as ethnography, and which I would willingly call the technique of estrangement.

The only difference between classical culture and ethnographic culture resides in the dimensions of the known world in their respective epochs. At the beginning of the Renaissance, to Western man, the human universe was circumscribed by the limits of the Mediterranean basin. As for the rest, one barely suspected its existence. But it was already known that no fraction of humanity could aspire to understand itself without reference to all the other human beings.

In the eighteenth and nineteenth centuries, humanism broadens out with the progress of geographical exploration. Rousseau and Diderot lay claims only on the most distant civilizations. But China and India already fit into the picture. Our university terminology which designates their study as nonclassical philology, acknowledges by its inability to create an original term that we are indeed dealing with the same humanistic movement, only encroaching on new territory; just as, for the ancients, metaphysics was what came after physics. By concerning itself today with those last, still disregarded civilizations—the so-called primitive societies—

ethnology has humanism traveling through its third stage. It will undoubtedly be the last, since after that man will no longer have anything of himself to discover—at least from the outside (for another research exists, this one in-depth, the end of which we are not close to seeing).

But the problem presents another aspect. The first two humanisms—classical and nonclassical—saw their extension limited not only in area but also in quality. The classical civilizations had disappeared and could only be reached through texts and monuments. As for the Middle and Far East, for which this difficulty did not exist, the method remained the same because it was believed that such distant civilizations merited our interest only by their most scholarly and refined productions.

The domain of ethnology consists of new civilizations which also pose new problems. These civilizations without writing do not furnish written documents, and as their technological level is usually quite low, most of them have not left figurative monuments. Hence the need for ethnology to provide humanism with new tools of investigation.

The modes of understanding that the ethnologist utilizes are at the same time more exterior and more interior (one could also say coarser and more precise) than those of his predecessors, the philologists and historians. In order to penetrate into societies of particularly difficult access, he must place himself very much outside them (physical anthropology, prehistory, technology), and also very much inside them by the identification of the ethnologist with the group whose existence he shares and the extreme importance he must attach—for lack of other components of information—to the slightest nuances of the natives' psychic life.

Ethnology, always this side of traditional humanism or even going beyond it, surpasses it in every way. Its field takes in the whole of the inhabited world, while its method brings together procedures characteristic of all spheres of knowledge: including both the human sciences and natural sciences.

In succeeding one another, the three humanisms thus combine with each other and enable our understanding about man to progress in three directions. First, on the surface; undoubtedly, this is the most "superficial" aspect, both literally and figuratively. Secondly, through the wealth of its means of investigation, since we are gradually realizing that ethnology has to invent new modes of understanding in relation to the particular characteristics of the "residual" societies it inherited. These modes of understanding can be fruitfully applied to other societies, including our own.

But there is more. Classical humanism was not only restricted in its object but also in its beneficiaries, who formed the privileged class. The exotic humanism of the nineteenth century found itself tied to the industrial and commercial interests which supported it and to which it owed its existence. After the aristocratic humanism of the Renaissance and the bourgeois humanism of the nineteenth century, ethnology marks the advent, for the finite world which our planet has become, of a doubly universal humanism.

Seeking its inspiration in the midst of the most humble and despised societies, it proclaims that nothing human can be strange to man, and thus founds a democratic humanism in opposition to those preceding it and created from privileged civilizations for the privileged classes. By bringing together methods and techniques borrowed from all the sciences to serve in the understanding of man, it calls for the reconciliation of man and nature in a generalized humanism.

Structuralism and Literary Criticism [1]

Both in linguistics and anthropology, the structural method consists in perceiving invariant forms within different contents. But the structural analysis that certain critics and historians of literature unduly claim to apply consists, on the contrary, in seeking recurring contents under variable forms. Thus we already see evidence of a double misunderstanding regarding content and form, and regarding the relation between notions as distinct as recurrence and invariance (the former still open to contingency, the latter appealing to necessity).

Moreover, structural hypotheses can be verified from without. In principle if not always in reality, they can be compared with independent, well-defined systems, each in its own right enjoying a certain degree of objectivity, which test the validity of the theoretical constructs.

In linguistics, these objective controls are of two types. The physical and acoustical analysis of articulated language (done with the help of machines which now also make possible its synthesis) shows immediately the relevant features postulated by the phonological hypotheses. In the second place, the requirements of communication supply a criticism in a fundamental way, since a speaker's every verbal emission exists in order to be understood. Thus, its meaning is not only intentional. It takes its real final form only after flowing into that mold, the other half of which is always filled by the interlocutor or, more precisely, the social group.

In anthropology, these two types of control also exist—for example, in the study of marriage rules or myths. Beyond the structures which can be formalized, the investigation includes the exploration of autonomous levels on which these structures must engage: on the one hand, the techno-economic infrastructure and, on the other, the particular conditions revealed by sociological study in which life occurs in society. Consequently there are also brought together the factors of a double external critique, one which reintroduces in the human sciences a system equivalent to the means of experimentation in the natural sciences.

The fundamental vice of literary criticism with structuralist pretensions stems from its too often being limited to a play of mirrors, in which it becomes impossible to distinguish the object from its symbolic image in the subject's consciousness. The work studied and the analyst's thought reflect each other, and we are deprived of any means of sorting out what is simply received from the one and what the other puts into it. One thus becomes locked into a reciprocal relativism, which can be subjectively attractive but which does not seem to refer to any type of external evidence. This criticism—visionary and spell-binding—is structural to the extent that it makes use of a combinative system to support its reconstructions. But in so doing, it obviously presents structural analysis with raw material rather than a finished contribution. As a particular manifestation of the mythology of our time, it lends itself very well to analysis, but in the same way that one could, for example, structurally interpret the reading of tarot cards, tea leaves, or palms, i.e., to the extent that these are coherent deliriums.

Thus, it will only happen that literary criticism and the history of ideas are able to become truly structural, if they find outside themselves the means of a double objective verification. It is not difficult to see from where these means should be borrowed.

On the one hand, at the level of linguistic and even phonological analysis, where verifications can be made independently from the conscious elaborations of the author and his analyst; on the other, at the level of ethnographic investigation—i.e., that of external history in the case of societies like ours. Hence, "the introduction of structuralist methods into a critical tradition proceeding essentially from historicism" is far from presenting a problem. It is the existence of this historical tradition which can alone provide a basis for structural undertakings. To be so convinced, one has only to refer, in the domain of art criticism, to a work as full and thoroughly structuralist as that of Erwin Panofsky. If this author is a great structuralist, it is because he is first a great historian, and because history affords him both a source of irreplaceable information and a combinatory field where the accuracy of the interpretations can be tested in a thousand ways. Thus, it is history, in conjunction with sociology and semiology, which will enable the analyst to break the circle of timeless confrontation, where it is never known (as a pseudo-dialogue unfolds between the critic and the work) whether the critic is a faithful observer or the unconscious animator of a play which he acts out for himself. The audience will always wonder whether the text of the play is spoken by flesh-and-blood characters or by a clever ventriloquist through puppets he himself invented. Because structural analyses are often positioned at the level of synchrony, they do not turn their backs on history. Wherever history is found it cannot be ignored since, on the one hand, it multiplies the quantity of available synchronic levels by the time dimension; on the other hand, the past levels—precisely because they are completed—are placed out of reach of subjective illusions, and can therefore serve to check the uncertainties of intuitive perception and the illusions of a mutual fascination which, however tempting, always risks generating complicity at the expense of veracity.

Apropos of a Retrospective [2]

Whatever reticence one may feel today about certain aspects of Picasso's work, he is a painter whose genius must be acknowledged. And when one aspires, even in a very modest way, to be creative, it is wise to beware of what one may say about, or of the way one may react toward, Picasso, for this reaction risks being mixed up with a certain feeling of jealousy.

It seems to me that if any bona fide creator were asked who he would have liked to be, he would not fail to answer "Picasso." This because he is an outstanding example in our century of a man who has done everything he wanted, who has followed his whims, has done just what he pleased, and obtained the greatest fame, immense fortune, and fabulous prestige. And that, in itself, commands admiration.

The problem posed by Picasso—and by cubism and painting in general beyond cubism—is to know to what extent the work itself accomplished a structural analysis of reality. In other words, is it for us a medium of knowledge? This is a work which, rather than contributing an original message, gives itself over to a sort of breaking down of the code of painting, a secondhand interpretation, much more an admirable discourse on pictorial discourse than a discourse about the world. So much for the synchronic point of view.

Now, looking at it from the diachronic point of view, I apologize for resorting to my personal history by recalling the revelations brought to me, during my adolescence, by the works of Picasso. When I went on my regular Thursday morning pilgrimage to the rue de la Boétie—this was between 1924 and 1928 —I looked forward to see Picasso's painting in the window at Rosenberg's—was it really there? (It was one of those monumental still lifes he painted in those days—a veritable metaphysical understanding.) Nowadays, I cannot find myself in this state of grace again, neither in front of Picasso nor in front of contemporary painting. I feel a sort of rancor toward cubism and modern painting, because I have the impression—and it is probably of my own doing much more than its own—that it has not kept its past promises to me.

What, in the years of my adolescence, held for me a metaphysical meaning, finds itself reduced to the level of what the Americans call "interior decorating," a sort of accessory to the furnishings. But I note that this is not true of all paintings. Going back to the Louvre, for example, I feel in the presence of Mantegna the same emotion which I experienced in seeing *The Parnassus* for the first time at the age of seven or eight. Concerning the painting of the last half-century, I will therefore say that its message has been vehement but brief.

Cubism hoped to recover a truer image of reality behind the world, no matter what means it used.

Anyway, among my structuralist colleagues, some consider that cubism and other aspects of modern painting have had a determining influence on them, by inciting them to seek behind tangible appearances a more solid organization of reality at a deeper level.

In my case, the decisive influence came from the natural sciences. What made me a structuralist was less a viewing of the work of Picasso, Braque, Leger, or Kandinsky, than the sight of stones, flowers, butterflies, or birds. There are then, at the origin of structuralist thought, two very different stimulations: the former more humanist—as I would put it—the latter oriented toward nature.

The work of Picasso irritates me, and it is in this sense that I am concerned with it. Because it brings to bear one piece of evidence (among many which would, no doubt, be found in literature and music) of the deeply rhetorical nature of contemporary art. Picasso often seems to think that since there are laws accounting for the nature and structure of the work of art, works of art can be created by applying or imitating laws, or by borrowing recipes from them. It seems to me that the real problem posed by artistic creation lies in the impossibility of thinking through the outcome ahead of time.

Something similar occurred with the rhetoricians of the Renaissance who elaborated a very profound theory of the poetic work, in which the act of creation proceeded to imprison itself. By a sort of paradox, structuralism—as I conceive it—which has been reproached for its abstractness and formalism, only finds a real satisfaction in art at the cost of much freshness and innocence.

The problem of cubism is that its nature is a nature once removed, a nature such as emerges from previous interpretations or manipulations. The future of art—if it has one—requires rather a getting in touch with nature again, in its raw state, which is, strictly speaking, impossible; but there can at least be, let us say, an effort in that direction.

What does nature mean to the supposedly cultured people of

our time, who admire the works of Picasso? I shall attempt to answer by an analogy.

A recent film, which gave me much food for thought, was Wyler's *The Collector* (*L'Obsédé*, in French). It is about a young man depicted as uncultured, asocial, and morally perverse because he devotes his time to collecting first butterflies and then a beautiful girl whom he sequesters and who gets to play the role of a heroine. She embodies the culture that really dominates contemporary society. She belongs to a higher social class; she has read books and seen paintings about which the young man knows nothing; this makes communication impossible between them. She tries in vain to redeem him by attempting to interest him in art books in which we see reproductions of Picasso which, as it happens, shock the young man. For the film maker, this is the real criterion which demonstrates his inferiority.

And yet, it seems to me that we have here a complete reversal of an authentic value system, and that the healthy attitude—forgetting about legality—is rather that of the hero who reserves his passion for real objects, butterflies, or natural beauties, be they insects or a pretty girl. Whereas the very symbol of the artificial contemporary taste is illustrated by the heroine who, for her part, lives only through art books. For these are not even original works—an important point on the relationship between Picasso and contemporary society. These paintings cannot be owned, they are much too expensive. Yet, the element of possession which partakes of sensuality is also an essential aspect of our relationship to the beautiful.

Thus, does not the false taste which the film vindicates first consist in getting one's pleasure out of reproductions instead of realities; and through the former, out of works of art which offer second- or third-level reinterpretations of nature—this in the presence of someone who seeks precisely this "immediacy" to nature through means that may not be very orthodox from the legal point of view, but which basically partake of a more correct sense of beauty and truth?

It is not genius which is in the wrong, it is the times. I was amazed to find out, last week, that while some paintings—let us not mention any names—sell for tens, hundreds, millions of francs, butterflies belonging to a fabulous collection put up for sale (with the exception of one or two specimens, which were not so much more beautiful than others but which happened to be rare or unique, that reached 10,000 francs) went by the box at prices ranging from 200 to 500 francs [approximately forty to one hundred dollars]. I indeed maintain, like the hero of the film, that as great or equal an aesthetic pleasure can be found in the contemplation of exotic butterflies as in a master's canvas.

If there is madness or injustice somewhere, it does not lie with the famous painter who profits from a state of affairs that he did not create. It lies in a sort of growing stupidity of man in front of himself; as though nothing except what he himself created could have any value whatsoever, be it intellectual or monetary, while so many marvels, untouched by market value, remain inaccessible.

Alas, we are all witnesses of our time, and so is Picasso, simply because he lived and produced in a particular time. Yet he is this in a unique way. Not only does he bear witness through his works. They, too, convey the taste of our times by their immense success. And, more significantly, Picasso is a witness of our time because it is largely he himself who created this taste. He has always been ahead of the taste of his times. For him, I would not use the term "witness," but rather that of "support," and, needless to say, the major supporting document of the history of our times.

Picasso conveyed very well the deep spirit of his era. Were I to make reservations, one would be that he conveyed it too well and that his works make up one testimony among many to this type of imprisonment which man increasingly imposes on himself from within his own human nature; in short, that he contributed to narrowing down this kind of shut-up world where man, in tête-à-tête with his own works, imagines that he suffices to himself; a sort of ideal prison and a rather bleak one.

We record the extreme manifestations of this great, supposedly humanist current which claimed to set up mankind as a separate kingdom. This current seems to me to represent one of the greatest obstacles in the way of the progress of philosophical thought and perhaps of the renewing of aesthetic creation.

I do not think that I would any longer feel at ease in the company of a masterpiece of cubism or abstract art. With Max Ernst, and also Paul Delvaux, yes—because in spite of their learn-

ing, one finds a freshness in them. And, if not with them, with
the unsophisticated painters, or such masterpieces of *bricolage*
with which an art gallery may open tomorrow.

To trickery, however genial, what other antidote can one
imagine?

Art in 1985

By his vocation, the ethnologist attributes value and meaning only
to those changes perceptible to a very distant observer situated
in another culture, since, studying cultures very different from
his own, he is himself submitted to the same limitations. This may
be a privilege, and any change worthy of being recorded as a
contribution to the understanding of the human mind is to be a
change seen as such in a generalized perspective: a change true
for all possible observers, not only for him who occupies a privileged position in relation to this change.

This explains why the ethnologist almost always feels dis-
armed when confronted with short-term expectations. In twenty
years' time, our painting, literature, and music have undoubtedly
undergone a noticeable evolution, from the point of view of an
observer in the society in which they are generated. But it is
doubtful that an observer more distant in time or space will make
the same observations. The works of 1985 and of today will appear to him as belonging to the same form of civilization. The
gross divergences handled by ethnologists are useless within these
narrow limits. The variations are too fine and too numerous and,
even supposing that prognostications were theoretically and practically possible, only computers would allow one to integrate
them, to delineate a trend and make an extrapolation.

This further implies that, in our midst, the arts enjoy a peaceful and healthy existence and that their present condition pre-
figures something of their future. All reasonable forecasts would
naturally be precluded if we had to admit that the works which
we accept today testify to a crisis, whose outcome it would then
be impossible to predict. This outcome might well consist in the
birth of another type of art, the shape of which we cannot
yet guess. It might also result in the consciously and resolutely

professed renunciation of all art by a society which—it would then be obvious—has increasingly, for a good many years, mystified itself with its high regard for an art that is merely the form of an art, suited only to foster the illusion of having an art.

But it is not inevitable that the crisis will resolve itself. Perhaps it will only spring back up, with more unsubstantial nourishment offered to the appetite of illusion. For the problem of art's future in Western society (and, by a predictable extension, in tomorrow's world) is not one which can be answered, even partially, in twenty years or so, or by invoking historical precedents. This problem, presenting itself for the first time in the life of mankind, merges with another: What can art become in a civilization which, cutting the individual off from nature and constraining him to live in a fabricated environment, dissociates consumption from production, and drains the latter of the creative feeling? Whether the cult of art takes the form of smug contemplation or greedy consumption, it tends to make culture a transcendental object, from whose distant existence man collectively draws a vainglory made all the more idiotic because, as an individual, he confesses his importance to create it.

Even restricted to the near future, predictions depend on the answer—which it is impossible to give—to an interlocutory question: Is our civilization homogeneous with all the others, and may one draw conclusions from what happened and is still happening in the former in order to predict what will happen in the latter? Or else: Are we dealing with entirely different forms, and, in this case, how will their relationship be defined? At first glance, viruses, intermediate organisms between life and inert matter, represent a particularly humble form of the former. And yet, they need other living beings in order to reproduce themselves. Thus, far from being able to precede them in evolution, viruses presuppose other beings and exemplify a relatively advanced state. On the other hand, the reality of a virus is almost of an intellectual order. In effect, its organism is reduced practically to the genetic formula that it injects into simple or complex beings, thus forcing their cells to betray their characteristic formula in order to obey its own and to manufacture beings like itself.

In order for our civilization to appear, the previous and simultaneous existence of other civilizations was necessary. And we know, since Descartes, that its originality consists essentially of a method which, because of its intellectual nature, is not suited to generating other civilizations of flesh and blood, but one which can impose its formula on them and force them to become like it. In comparison with these civilizations—whose living art expresses their corporeal quality because it relates to very intense beliefs and, in its conception as much as in its execution, to a certain state of equilibrium between man and nature—does our own civilization correspond to an animal or viral type? Had one to choose in favor of the latter hypothesis, it could be foretold that in twenty years the morbid hunger which drives us to gulp down all forms of past and present art in order to elaborate our own will experience a growing difficulty in satisfying itself.

Faced with those already three-quarters-dried-up, soon-to-be-polluted wellsprings still provided by the flesh-and-blood societies in our museums and exhibitions, a lack of appetite will replace competition. Without any great change on the surface, it will be understood better than today perhaps that a society bears its art like a tree its flowers, as a function of their being rooted in a world which neither one nor the other claims to make entirely its own.

Urban Civilization and Mental Health

The contrast is not so much between urban and rural life, which each allow of very diverse modalities (as among several forms of urban life). Actually, fatigue resulting from distances, the separation of generations, the instability of couples, the dispersion of family work, the discontinuity brought about by the cessation of activity, are encountered, together or separately, in a great many nonurban societies, even among those studied by ethnologists. Conversely, urban life can be intense while remaining concrete and lively, as in the suq towns of the Orient, or compatible with rural life, as in the small peasant cities of Italy. Even in Paris, a certain equilibrium was preserved until the end of the nineteenth century: the real country started right before its gates. Living in the heart of the city, Rousseau hardly needed an hour's walk to find the peace of fields and woods.

The real dangers appear later when the city stops being an

urban site enclosed within its boundaries, even if these boundaries periodically widen out to become a sort of fast-growing organism that, at its periphery and to an ever-increasing depth, secretes a destructive virus; a virus which gnaws at all the life forms except those by-products of its activity, which it scatters outside by expelling them. City man then finds himself cut off from that nature, the contact with which can alone regulate and regenerate his psychic and biological rhythms. The proof that this lack is cruelly felt is obvious in the importance of weekend outings; in the preference now for a fourth week of holidays rather than an increase in the hourly wage; in the obsessive desire for a house in the country and for a garden. All the solutions are condemned to remain lame anyway, since the increase in population inevitably imposes a collective nature on them, and excludes the silence and solitude which are essential elements of the state that is to be recovered.

This segregation of man outside the natural environment—of which he is morally as well as physically an inseparable part—his being forced by the modern forms of urban life to live almost entirely inside an artifice, constitutes a major threat to the mental health of the species.

So much the more because this perversion of urban civilization, due to industrialization, has transformed itself on the ideological plane into a philosophy and an ethic which lightheartedly come to terms with the emergence of a humanity destructive of everything but itself—then, inevitably, of itself also, as soon as it does not possess any more "glacis" to protect it from its own attacks. This philosophy, this ethic have gone so far as to glorify the breach between man and the other forms of life in the name of humanism, leaving man only self-love as a principle of thought and action.

Without playing on words, but taking them in their ethnological meaning, one may indeed wonder whether "culture" can grow and spread in "maisons"—which by assumption would not open wide onto something else, and thus first of all on nature, of which culture itself is a manifestation.

This is the same as saying that the *Maisons de la culture* [3] will not be able to bring forward a solution to the crisis of urban civilization so long as the latter is not *completely* permeated with the conviction that culture is not everything and that it must

first be inspired by a feeling of deference toward *given reality*—
not only nature but history also—and must finally force on itself
the limitations and the discipline implied by this state of mind.
For, if nature is not actively lived by the general society, the
rituals which claim to celebrate it in some specialized precincts
(be they museums, lecture or theatre halls, or a "Maison de la
culture") will serve at best as alibis.

Let us begin by proclaiming that respect for life—even human
life—does not exist in a society determined to destroy irreplaceable
forms of life, whether animal or vegetable; that love for the
past is a lie in cities where the need for growth has caused men
to massacre all the vestiges of what they once were and of those
who made them; and that the cult of beauty and truth is incompatible with seashores being turned into shanty towns and ghettoes
and with the sides of "national" roads turned into garbage dumps.

If we admit this, it follows that the "maisons de la culture"
cannot treat culture as a closed world, nor develop themselves
as closed worlds. In the terms of the inquiry, this double principle
entails three consequences:

1. *Priority given to "active culture" over "passive culture."*
Whether the latter actually takes the form of a smug contemplation or an avid consumption, it proceeds from the same attitude
which sees in culture a transcendental object. Thus, in a shocking
paradox, man feels collectively toward culture a vainglory which
is all the more idiotic because, as an individual, he confesses his
impotence to create it.

One of the great evils of urban civilization is, as we know,
that it dissociates consumption from production; it exacerbates
the former and drains the latter of its creative feeling.

Man will be helped to feel more closely bound to the system
of beings and things before which the creative mind feels singular
modesty and respect. This will be done by making the best use
of all the opportunities that industrial society leaves for the individual to test himself as creator, and by revealing to him those
in which he is indeed, unknown to himself, a creator (for instance, as a speaking subject).

2. *Priority to the sciences,* such as history and archaeology, and
all the natural sciences that can be practiced *empirically and
on a small scale,* while also already productive, and which study
beings or objects perceived both as beautiful and true. They help

man to rebuild the network of his relationships with the world, thus suggesting to him multiple "anchorages" in the nature of mineral, vegetable, and animal life, or of man himself, objectified by the past.

3. Inclusion of the *Maisons de la culture* in a general policy of creating and expanding the means required by this program, i.e., zoological and botanical gardens, natural reserves, archaeological and prehistorical sites, preservation of city quarters or restoration of ancient villages.

If, as is foreseeable, the development of urban life (especially in France) must be accompanied by the modernization of agricultural production and by the movement toward urban centers by a part of the rural population, the lands—having become tenantless—could be entrusted to departments responsible for transforming them into natural reserves. In this way, many small biological or archaeological stations could be created in the vicinity of cities. The *Maisons de la culture* would thus be closely associated with their management, under the supervision of those civil servants who, in well-organized societies, ought to enjoy a prestige at least equal to that of the civil engineer, the military man, and the business manager. I mean the director of the prehistorical division, the architect of historical monuments, the forester.

These reserves might instill among the *Maisons de la culture* an *emulation* based on the taste for knowledge and love of and respect for life in all its forms. Other methods could be conceived—alas no less precarious and having the same limitations. But, in multiplying the attempts, one would always tend toward the same goal: the establishment of a counterbalance system which, hopefully, may establish a better balance between present and past, change and stability, the uprooted city man and the lasting truths of the world.

Witnesses of our Time [4]

Dear Sir,
    I will put in your time-vault documents relative to the last "primitive" societies, on the verge of disappearance: specimens of vegetable and animal species soon to be destroyed by man; samples of air and water not yet polluted by industrial wastes;

notices and illustrations of sites soon to be ravaged by civil or military installations.

Twenty-five compartments will certainly not suffice! But in deciding what, of the artistic and literary production of the last twenty years, deserves to survive for a millennium, one would be bound to be mistaken. It would be presumptuous and futile to draw to the attention of our distant successors scientific theories and apparatuses which they will judge obsolete.

Better to leave them some evidence of so many things that the misdeeds of our generation and the next will have forever deprived them of knowing: the purity of the elements, the diversity of beings, the grace of nature, and the decency of men.

NOTES

1. The journal had asked various people the following questions: Artistic and literary criticism have shown lately a strong interest for procedures of the structural type, particularly those elaborated by post-Saussurian glottology.
   a. Do you feel that these procedures can provide efficient tools for criticism? If so, which of the various conceptions of structuralism do you have in mind?
   b. Do you feel that structuralist methods can be introduced into a tradition of criticism which proceeds essentially from historicism?

2. The following is an abridged version of an interview with André Parinaud. It was published in this form in *Arts* on the occasion of the opening of the exhibition "Homage to Picasso," at the Grand Palais and at the Petit Palais, Paris, November 1966–February 1967.

[3. *Translator's note:* Literally, the "Houses of Culture" are centers established in the 1960s by the Minister for Cultural Affairs in France. They aim at promoting cultural manifestations of all kinds (art exhibitions, concerts, films, etc.) and are found in many French cities.]

4. Jean Prasteau had asked various people to cite facts, discoveries, inventions, books, pictures of the last twenty years, which they would enclose, or of which they would enclose evidence, in the twenty-five compartments of a coffer, buried somewhere in Paris, for the benefit of archaeologists in the year 3000.

Scientific Criteria in the Social and Human Disciplines

T HE AUTHOR of the present text hopes he will
not be out of line in confessing to an uneasy feeling, even to a
malaise, caused by the announcement of the investigation decided
on by the General Conference of UNESCO. It seems to him that
the contrast is too great between the interest shown for "the
principal trends of research in the field of social and human sciences" and the utter neglect of which those sciences are the victims, in the very place where the greatest enthusiasm was shown
in favor of this project.

Chapter XVI was originally published under the title "Criteria of Science in the
Social and Human Disciplines." Reprinted by permission of UNESCO from the
International Social Science Journal, XVI, No. 4 (1964), pp. 579–597. © UNESCO
1964. This text was written in answer to a preliminary investigation following the
decision of the General Conference of UNESCO to extend to the social and
human sciences the investigation on the principal trends of research, which had
already explored the physical sciences.

Less spectacular than this unexpected show of good will (actually of an impractical nature, since it takes place on an international level where there are no means of immediate intervention), how much more efficient it would have been if, at the national level, there were the granting of a place of work to scattered researchers, who are most often demoralized by the lack of a chair, a table, and the few square yards indispensable for the decent exercise of their work; by the nonexistence or insufficiency of libraries, and the lack of funds. As long as we have not been freed from these troublesome preoccupations, we cannot help feeling that the problem of the place given to the social and human sciences in contemporary society has, once more, been approached the wrong way. We have chosen to satisfy them in principle rather than in reality and to comfort ourselves with the illusion that they exist, rather than to grapple with the real task, which would be to give them the means of existence.

The drawback would be less serious and would be, after all, simply another missed opportunity, if the national and international authorities did not intend to have the researchers themselves share responsibility in an investigation of which they will doubly bear the burden. First, because it has mainly the value of an excuse, so that the superfluity promised to them will take the place of what they really need; and secondly because it calls for their active participation, so that—unless they wish to face being reproached with a lack of good citizenship—they will have to spend their time (already eaten up by the material difficulties in which they are left to fend for themselves), as ordered, on an undertaking whose theoretical value is in no way determined.

One would not have expressed these doubts about the previous investigation on the trends of research in the domain of the hard sciences. But the situation was different there. These sciences have been in existence for so long and they have provided such numerous and convincing proofs of their value that the fact of their reality can be taken for granted. They present no interlocutory problem. Since they exist, it is legitimate to ask what they do, and to describe how they do it.

One will also admit that it was easy to introduce into the structure of national and international institutions some parallel between the hard sciences and a different type of research—named "social and human sciences" for the sake of the cause. The nomenclature was thus simplified and, because of this, the teachers, researchers, and administrators, who spend comparable time and effort in either of these two areas are assured of being treated, materially and morally, in an equal manner.

A doubt seeps in when reasons of a practical order (we must never lose sight of the fact that they proceed from an administrative convention) are exploited to their utmost consequences for the profit of professional interests, unless we are more simply dealing with intellectual laziness. The author of the present text has devoted his entire life to the practice of social and human sciences. But he feels no embarrassment in recognizing that between them and the hard sciences one could not pretend to a true equality; the latter are sciences, the former are not. If, however, they are designated by the same term, it is through a semantic fiction and a philosophical hope for which confirmation is still lacking. Consequently, the parallel implied by the two investigations—even at the level of a statement—betrays an imaginary vision of reality.

Let us then first attempt to define more precisely the differences in principle attached to the use of the term "science" in the two cases. No one doubts that the hard sciences are actually sciences. Of course, not all that is done in their name shows equal quality: there are great scientists, others are mediocre. But the common connotation to all the activities performed under the cover of the hard sciences cannot be questioned. Logicians would say that, in the case of the hard sciences, their definition "in extension" corresponds to their definition "in intention." The characteristics that make a science deserve this name also belong, on the whole, to the totality of those concrete activities which include, empirically, the domain of the hard sciences.

But, when we pass on to the social and the human sciences, the definitions in extension and in intention cease to coincide. The term "science" is then only a fictitious name designating a great many activities, totally varied, only a small number of which offer a scientific character (provided that one wanted to define the notion of science in the same manner). In fact, many of the specialists in those disciplines arbitrarily listed under the label of social and human sciences would be the first to deny all pretention to scientific work (at least in the same sense and in the same spirit as their colleagues in the hard sciences). Doubtful distinctions, such as the one between *l'esprit de finesse* and *l'esprit de géométrie* have for a long time helped them plead this case.

Under these circumstances, a preliminary question must be asked. Since one is pretending to define "the principal trends of research in the social and human sciences," what do we want to talk about first? If one wishes to show oneself faithful to that ideal of symmetry implicitly indicated between the two investigations, one will have, now as then, to envisage the object "in extension." But then, one is faced with a double difficulty. Since it is impossible to offer a satisfactory definition of the totality of the subjects taught in the arts and social sciences faculties, one will not be able validly to restrict oneself to such a definition. Whatever does not pertain to the hard sciences will, through this alone, claim to pertain to sciences of another type, and their field will thus become unlimited. Moreover, as the very criterion of science becomes confused with that of disinterested research, one will be unable to reach any conclusion as to the goal of the UNESCO investigation. Without a term which can be practically assigned, the investigation will theoretically remain without an object.

To guard against this danger—in a field whose limits vary according to whether one chooses to define it by its empirical content or by the notion one has of it—it will be necessary to start by isolating this restricted zone where the two meanings approximately coincide. The investigations will then be theoretically comparable, but they will cease to be empirically homogeneous, since it will become evident that only a small part of the social and human sciences can be treated in that manner deemed appropriate for all the hard sciences.

To our way of thinking, the dilemma does not lend itself to resolution. But, before attempting to seek a solution which will inevitably be lame, one may rapidly review certain secondary causes of the disparity manifested between the physical and the human sciences.

First, it seems to us that, through the history of societies, the physical sciences have benefited from the start from a preferential treatment. Paradoxically, this treatment was due to the fact that for centuries—not to say millennia—scientists were dealing with questions which were of no concern to the population at large. The obscurity in which they pursued their research was the providential mantle which sheltered it and allowed it to remain for so long unhindered—at least in part, if not (as it would have been preferable) in its totality. Thanks to this, the early scientists were at leisure to address themselves first to the things they thought they could explain, instead of being asked endlessly to explain what other people were interested in.

From this point of view, the misfortune of the human sciences lies in the fact that man cannot help but be interested in himself. In the name of this preoccupation, he first refused to offer himself to science as an object of investigation, because this concession would have forced him to moderate and limit his impatience. The situation was reversed some years ago because of the effect of the prodigious results obtained by the hard sciences. An increasing demand is noticeable, that urges the social and human sciences to decide, in their turn, to give proof of their usefulness. We apologize for seeing in the recent resolution of the General Conference of UNESCO a sign of this suspicious eagerness which, for our sciences, constitutes yet another danger. For we forget that they are still in their infancy. Even supposing that they may one day be put to the service of practical action, they have, for the time being, nothing or almost nothing to offer. The best way to allow them to exist is to give them much, but above all to ask them nothing.

In the second place, all scientific research postulated a dualism of the observer and his object. In the case of the natural sciences, man plays the part of the observer and has the world as his object. The field within which this dualism exists is certainly not unlimited, as contemporary physics and biology have discovered, but it is wide enough for the body of hard sciences to have freely unfolded in it.

If the social and human sciences are really sciences, they must preserve this dualism, which they shift only to locate it within man himself; so that the cut-off line passes between the man who observes and the man or men who are observed. But, in so doing, these sciences do not go beyond their respect for a principle. Because, if they had to model themselves entirely on the hard sciences, they would experiment not only on those men whom they are content to observe (which is theoretically conceivable, though difficult to put into practice and morally unacceptable). It would also be vital for those men to be unaware that they are being experimented upon, since their awareness of it would modify in an unforeseeable manner the process of experimentation. Thus awareness appears as the secret enemy of the sciences of man in the double form of a spontaneous awareness (inherent to the object of the observation) and of a reflective awareness—an awareness of awareness—in the scientist.

To be sure, the human sciences are not entirely lacking the means to get around this difficulty. The thousands of phonological and grammatical systems offered to the linguist's examination, the variety of social structures spread out in time or in space, which feeds the curiosity of the historian and the ethnologist constitute, it has often been said, so many "ready-made" experiments. Unlike positivists, we recognize today that their irreversible character does not at all weaken their value, since the function of science is not so much to predict as to explain. More precisely, the explanation implies in itself a sort of prediction. It is predicted that, in some other "ready-made" experiment which the observer must discover in situ and which the scientist must interpret, the presence of certain properties will necessarily bring about their relationship with others.

The fundamental difference between the physical sciences and the human sciences is thus not—as it is often maintained—that the former alone has the ability to make experiments and to repeat them identically at other times and in other places. The human sciences can also do this; if not all of them, at least those (such as linguistics and, to a lesser extent, ethnology) which are able to grasp a few recurrent elements variously combined in a great many systems, beneath the temporal and local peculiarity of each of them.

Does it not mean that the ability to experiment, whether a priori or a posteriori, is essentially due to the manner of defining and isolating what we have agreed to understand as scientific fact? If the physical sciences were to define their scientific facts in the same whimsical and careless manner as most of the human sciences, they, too, would be imprisoned in a present which would never be reproduced.

If, from this point of view, the human sciences exhibit a sort of impotence (which often simply hides their lack of good will), it is because a paradox lies in wait for them and they confusedly perceive its threat. Any exact definition of the scientific fact results in the impoverishment of sensible reality and thus in its dehumanization. Consequently, insofar as the human sciences succeed in producing truly scientific work, the distinction between the human and the natural must decrease for them. If ever they become sciences in their own right, they will cease to differ from the others. Hence the dilemma that the human sciences have not yet dared face: either to keep their originality and accept the insurmountable paradox between awareness and experiment, or pretend to transcend it. But then, they must renounce their own separate place in the system of sciences and accept falling back, as it were, "in the ranks."

Even in the case of the hard sciences, there is no automatic link between the prediction and the explanation. It cannot be denied, however, that their forward progress has been strongly served by the combined effect of these two beacons. It happens that science explains phenomena that it does not predict—this is the case with Darwinian theory. It also happens, as in the case of meteorology, that it can predict phenomena which it is unable to explain. Nevertheless, each aim can, theoretically at least, find its rectification or its verification in the other. The physical sciences would certainly not be what they are if an occurrence or a coincidence had not happened in a considerable number of cases.

If the human sciences seem doomed to follow a mediocre and stumbling path, it is because this path does not allow a kind of navigational fixation (one would like to say by triangulation) which permits a traveler to calculate at each moment his movement in relation to fixed points and to draw information from them. Until now, the human sciences have been content with hazy and rough explanations which almost always lacked strict criteria. Although they seem predisposed by vocation to cultivate the predictions continuously and avidly demanded of them, it may be said—without being unjustly harsh—that making mistakes is a customary occurrence.

In truth, the function of the human sciences seems to be

situated halfway between explanation and prediction, as if they were unable to proceed resolutely one way or the other. This does not mean that these sciences are theoretically and practically useless, but rather that their use is measured by a proportioning of the two orientations, which never admits either one completely, but, by keeping a little of each, creates an original attitude in which is concentrated the proper mission of the human sciences. They never explain—or they rarely do—right to the end. They never predict with any certainty. But, understanding a quarter or a half, and correctly predicting once out of two or four times, they are nonetheless able, by the close interdependence which they set up between these half-measures, to bring to their practitioners something between pure knowledge and efficacy: a wisdom, or at least a certain form of wisdom, which enables one to act a little less badly because one understands a little better, but without ever being able to sort out exactly what one owes to either of the two aspects. For wisdom is an equivocal virtue, made up partly of knowledge and partly of action, yet totally different from either one taken separately.

We have seen that, for the social and human sciences, a preliminary question exists. Their denomination does not correspond—or corresponds only imperfectly—to their reality. Thus, one must first attempt to introduce some order into that confused mass offered to the observer under the name of social and human sciences. Then, one must determine what within it deserves to be qualified as "scientific" and why.

At the first glance, the difficulty is due to the association of disciplines labeled social and human sciences although they do not, logically, belong to the same level, moreover, the levels to which they belong are numerous, complex, and sometimes difficult to define. Some of our sciences study empirical entities which are both *realia* and *tota*, societies which are or were real, and which could be localized in a determined portion of space or time and envisaged each in its totality. We recognize ethnology and history.

Others are devoted to the study of entities which are no less real but correspond to only one part or one aspect of the entities previously mentioned. Thus linguistics studies language; law, juridical forms; economics, systems of production and exchange;

political science, institutions of an equally special type. But these categories of phenomena have nothing in common, except to illustrate this fragmented condition which separates them from whole societies. Take language, for example. Although it is the object of a science like the others, it permeates them all; in the order of social phenomena, nothing can exist without it. Thus one could not put linguistic facts on the same level as economic or juridical facts; the former are possible without the latter, but not vice versa.

On the other hand, if language is a part of society, it is coextensive with social reality. This cannot be said of the other partial phenomena which we have considered. Economics has for a long time dealt only with two or three centuries of human history, law with about twenty (which is also very little). Even supposing that it is theoretically possible for these sciences to loosen their categories and lay claim to a greater competence, it is not at all certain that, they would not, as distinct branches of knowledge, succumb to the rigor of the treatment they would have to inflict upon themselves.

Even the parallel which we have summarily drawn between history and ethnology cannot withstand criticism. For if, theoretically at least, all human societies can be studied ethnographically (although many of them have not been, and never will be since they have ceased to exist), not all of them can be studied historically—because of a lack of written documents for the vast majority of them. And yet, considered from another angle, all the disciplines dealing with a concrete subject—be this subject total or partial—are grouped in the same category if we want to distinguish them from other branches of the social and human sciences, which seek to reach less *realia* than *generalia*. For example, social psychology, and no doubt sociology also—if we want to assign to it a specific aim and style which would clearly isolate it from ethnography.

If demography enters the picture, the whole thing is even more complicated. From the point of view of the absolute generality and the immanence of all the other aspects of social life, the subject of demography, which is statistical, is situated at the same level as language. For this reason, perhaps, demography and linguistics are the two sciences of man which have been successful in going further along the way of rigor and universality. But, curiously, they diverge the most from the point of view of the humanity and inhumanity of their subject, since language is a specifically human attribute whereas numbers belong, as a constitutive mode, to any type of population.

Since Aristotle, logicians have periodically tackled the problem of the classification of sciences; and although their tables must be revised as new branches of knowledge appear and old ones are transformed, they provide an acceptable working basis. The most recent of these tables do not ignore the human sciences. But, as a general rule, they deal summarily with the question of their place in relation with the hard sciences, and they consider them globally by grouping them under two or three headings.

In truth, this problem of the classification of the social and human sciences has never been treated seriously.

But the brief recapitulation which we have presented in order to point out the ambiguities, confusions, and contradictions in nomenclature, shows that nothing can be attempted on the basis of recognized divisions. We must first start with an epistemological criticism of our sciences, in the hope that, in spite of their empirical diversity and heterogeneity, a small number of fundamental attitudes will emerge. Their presence, absence, or combination will make the peculiarity or the complementarity of each one clearer than its goal, openly and confusedly proclaimed.

In Volume 1 of *Structural Anthropology*, (pp. 280–288), I made an outline of what such an analysis of the social and human sciences could be, depending on their situation in relation to two pairs of oppositions; on the one hand, the opposition between empirical observation and model building; and on the other, an opposition based on the nature of these models, which may be either mechanical or statistical, depending on whether their elements are or are not of the same magnitude or on the same scale as the phenomena which they are meant to represent:

Empirical observation	Model building
Statistical models	Mechanical models

This schema immediately makes much clearer—in spite (or maybe because) of its simplicity—than an inventory of their works would have been able to do, the respective positions of the four branches of the human sciences—among which one has often sought to sow the seeds of polemics.

If indeed we agree to give arbitrarily a positive sign to the first term of each pair of oppositions and a negative sign to the second, we obtain the following table:

	HISTORY	SOCIOLOGY	ETHNOGRAPHY	ETHNOLOGY
Empirical observation vs. model building	+	–	+	–
Mechanical models vs. statistical models	–	–	+	+

This shows that ethnography and history differ from ethnology and sociology, inasmuch as the first two are founded on the collection and organization of documents and the latter two study the models built from or through these documents. On the other hand, ethnography and ethnology both correspond, respectively, to the two stages of a research finally leading to mechanical models, whereas history (with its so-called auxiliary sciences) and sociology lead to statistical models, although each proceeds in its own way.

I finally suggested that by bringing in other pairs of opposites: between observation and experimentation, the conscious and the unconscious, structure and measure, mechanical and reversible time versus statistical and irreversible time—one could make these relations deeper and richer, and could apply the same method of analysis to the classification of sciences other than those taken as examples.

The comparisons outlined above promote the intervention of a new set of opposites: between total perspective and partial perspective (in time, space, or both together); between the objects of the study apprehended as *realia* or *generalia;* between measurable and nonmeasurable empirical facts, and so forth. It would then be seen that in relation to all these opposites, the disciplines have their place well marked, positively or negatively; and that in a multidimensional space (for this reason unsuited to intuitive representations) to each one there corresponds an original path which sometimes crosses, sometimes goes along other paths, and sometimes parts from them. This does not preclude the possibility that some disciplines submitted to this critical test lose their traditional unity and burst into two or several subdisciplines meant to remain isolated, or else link up with other research with which they would then merge. Finally, one may discover logically possible paths (i.e., not proceeding by leaps and bounds) which would set the course of those sciences yet unborn or already existing in a latent stage among scattered researches, their unity not yet perceived. The unsuspected presence of these missing elements would explain the difficulty we experience in discerning the lineaments —some are indeed missing—of a systematic organization of our knowledge.

Finally, this would perhaps be one way to understand why certain choices, certain combinations are, de facto or de jure, compatible or not with the exacting demands of scientific explanation, so that the first stage would quite naturally lead to the second, which we would then be able to tackle. At this second stage, the problem will be to "skim," as it were, the confused mass of the social sciences as they appear at a first glance, and to extract, if not the disciplines themselves, at least certain problems and the way of treating them which would permit the comparison between the sciences of man and the sciences of nature.

From the outset, we must establish in the most absolute manner that, of all the social and human sciences, linguistics alone can be put on an equal footing with the hard sciences. And this for three reasons: (a) it has a universal subject, the articulated language of which no human group is lacking; (b) its method is homogeneous (in other words, it remains the same, whatever the particular language to which it is applied, modern or archaic, "primitive" or civilized); and (c) this method is based on some fundamental principles, the validity of which is unanimously recognized by specialists in spite of some minor divergences.

No other social or human science exists which can totally fulfill these conditions. Let us restrict ourselves to the three disciplines which are the closest to linguistics because of their ability to bring out necessary relations between phenomena. The subject of economics is not universal, but narrowly restricted to a small portion of the development of man. The method of demography is not homogeneous, outside of the particular case presented by great numbers; and the ethnologists are far from having achieved among themselves this unanimity about principles, which is already taken for granted by the linguists.

I thus believe that linguistics alone can be rightfully set within the conditions of the investigation planned by UNESCO, perhaps adding to it some of the "spearhead" research one can note here and there in the field of the social and human sciences, and which is obviously a transposition of the linguistic method.

What is to be done about the rest? The most reasonable method would seem to be a preliminary inquiry among the specialists of all the disciplines, asking for an answer in principle. Do they or do they not feel that the results obtained in their particular fields conform to the same criteria of validity as those taken for granted by the hard sciences? If they feel they do, these specialists will then be asked to list such results.

We can foresee that we will then be faced with a list of questions and problems for which it will be maintained that a certain "amount of comparability" exists, from the point of view of scientific methodology conceived at the most general level. These samples will be very disparate and it is very likely that we will notice two things.

In the first place, we see that the points of contact linking the social or the human sciences, on the one hand, and the natural or hard sciences, on the other, do not always occur in those disciplines of those two which one would have been inclined to compare. It is sometimes the most "literary" among the human sciences which prove to be in the forefront.

Very traditional branches of the classical humanities, such as rhetoric, poetics, and stylistics already know how to take recourse to mechanical or statistical models which enable them to treat certain problems by methods derived from algebra. Through their use of computers, stylistics and textual criticism can be said to be attaining the level of exact sciences. In the race to scientific exactness, we must reserve the rights of numerous outsiders. One would indeed be greatly mistaken in thinking that the sciences called "social" benefit at the start from advantage over some of the sciences more simply called "human."

Much will be learned from the study of these apparent anomalies. It will indeed establish that those disciplines which are the closest to a truly scientific ideal are also the ones which know best how to restrict themselves to considering a subject easily isolated, well delimited, the different states of which can be observed and analyzed with the help of only a few variables. Undoubtedly, the variables are always more numerous in the sciences of man than is generally the case in the physical sciences. Thus we will attempt to compare them at the level where the discrepancy is relatively minimal—for example, between the physical sciences in which the variables are the most numerous and the human sciences in which their number is the lowest. Because the former must resort to the use of reduced models (such as the ones tested by aerodynamics in their wind tunnels), we will better understand the use that the human sciences must make of models and better appreciate the fruitfulness of the method called "structural." Indeed, they consist in systematically reducing the number of variables, considering, on the one hand, that for the sake of the argument, the object under study forms a closed system; and seeking, on the other, to consider together variables of the same type only, even if the operation has to be done again from different angles.

In the second place, the list of samples will be surprising not only in its diversity. It will also be much too numerous, since those who will have been trusted to choose them have the best reasons to show themselves indulgent. We will except the case (and we will come back to this) of those specialists who deliberately put themselves out of the race because they feel that their research pertains to art and not to science, or to a type of science which cannot be reduced to the kind illustrated by the hard sciences.

We can anticipate however that the examples will be many and their value quite unequal. They will have to be sorted; only some will be kept, others will be rejected. Who will be the judge? We are dealing with a delicate question, since the problem is to bring out certain properties held in common by research in the social and human sciences, but with reference to norms pertaining, if not exclusively to hard sciences, at least to a scientific epistemology formulated at the most general level. The problem is thus to obtain a *consensus* on what is scientific and what is not scientific—not only within the social and human sciences (which are not qualified to decide, since, in the final analysis, it is on their own scientific maturity that we will have to make pronouncement) but also by calling upon the representatives of the hard sciences also.

Our conception thus tends to give the UNESCO investigation an unsteady basis. It looks as if its instigators had simply wanted to superimpose one investigation onto another (the second investigation into the social and human sciences, the first investigation into the hard sciences), whereas we actually propose to replace this horizontal section with a vertical one—the second investigation being meant to prolong the first one while integrating its purpose and a part of its results. On the other hand, the first investigation was total, whereas the second can only be selective. Adding the two will form a whole, but one which will taper to a point.

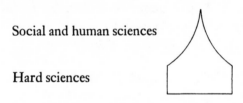

Social and human sciences

Hard sciences

FIGURE 18

Figure 18 is not an arbitrary one. We intend to show that it faithfully reflects an evolution which has been taking place in the social and human sciences during the last few years.

The distinction between social and human sciences corresponds to ancient preoccupations. Perhaps it is already implied in the organization of the *Institut de France*, a century and a half old, where the specialists in the study of man are separated into two academies: the *Académie des sciences morales et politiques*, and the *Académie des inscriptions et belles-lettres* dealing with epigraphy and literature. But nothing is more difficult to grasp than the criterion on which this distinction was based. For the founders of the *Institut de France* it seemed to have been of an historical order; all those dealing with pre-Renaissance human works in one academy, the moderns in the other. This distinction ceases to be applicable to exotic civilizations in which these temporal categories do not have the same meaning or even disappear entirely (as is the case with societies studied by ethnology), and one has not yet gone so far as splitting up the philosophers between the two academies, and making a distinction between those who study the history of ancient doctrines and those who meditate on present concerns.

Will it be said that the human sciences are more inclined toward theory, erudition, and pure research, and the social sciences toward practice, observation, and applied research? Then it is each individual science which one will see blossom forth, according to its type of research and the temperament of its scientists. One would also seek to distinguish them by their phenomena, taking into consideration that those studied by the social sciences emerge directly from the group, whereas the human sciences tend rather to consider works individually conceived and produced. But besides the fact that this would prove to be untrue in a great many cases, the second attempt points directly to an inherent contradiction in the distinction itself. All that is human is social. It is the very expression "social sciences" which conceals a pleonasm and must be held as redundant. For, in calling themselves "social," they already imply that they deal with man, and it goes without saying that being first "human," they must automatically be "social."

And actually, what science is not? As I wrote several years ago:

> Even the biologist and the physicist are becoming more and more aware of the social implications of their discoveries, or, better still, of their anthropological meaning. Man is no longer satisfied with knowing; as he knows more, he sees himself knowing, and the true object of his research becomes more and more, every day, this indivisible coupling of humanity transforming the world and transforming itself in the process.[1]

This is also true from a methodological point of view. The biological method must make increasing use of models of a linguistic type (genetic code and information) and a sociological one (since we now speak of a truly cellular sociology). As to the physicist, the phenomenon of interference between the observer and the object of his observation has become for him much more than a practical inconvenience affecting laboratory work. It is an intrinsic mode of positive knowledge, which brings it very much closer to some branches of the social and human sciences, such as ethnology, which knows itself to be restricted by such a relativism and accepts it. The social and human sciences also have their uncertain relationships between structure and process; for instance, one can be perceived while the other is ignored, and vice versa (which, by the way, provides a convenient means of explaining the complementarity between history and ethnology).

We cannot pretend that the distinction between social sciences and human sciences is not actually erupting everywhere. It first appeared and spread in the United States less than half a century ago. It still subsists in some institutions (as well as in the great national research councils); and it was still vigorous enough to impose itself on UNESCO at the time of its creation. But, beside the fact that some countries have never accepted it (such as France, where it is not impossible that the French will rally to it but, hopefully, will give it a totally different meaning), nothing is more striking than the criticism which it soon met in the Anglo-Saxon countries, from men as different as the late Robert Redfield in the United States and E. E. Evans-Pritchard in England. Indeed, it was enough for anthropology to be removed from the human sciences and ranked among the social sciences to feel at once that it was being exiled.

As if to bring a better solution to this old problem, we see presently in the United States the emergence of a new terminology which regroups the sciences according to other criteria. Such is, we believe, the meaning of the emergence of the "behavioral sciences," which study human behavior. Contrary to what is often believed, this term does not at all designate the social sciences. It stems on the contrary from the increasing conviction, in the United States and elsewhere, that the term "social sciences" is a mongrel expression and best avoided.

The term "behavioral sciences" was obviously formed from the word "behavior," which, for reasons peculiar to the history of thought in the United States (and this alone would preclude its being exported), implies the notion of a rigorous treatment of human phenomena. In fact, we could say that the behavioral sciences cover a domain situated at the intersection of the human sciences and the hard sciences. They bring together all the human problems which permit or demand a close collaboration with biology, physics, and mathematics.

This comes out clearly in an interesting document titled "Strengthening the Behavioral Sciences," produced by a subcommittee of the President's Science Advisory Committee whose role, in relation to the American Government, is comparable to the one filled in France by the *Délégation générale à la recherche scientifique et technique*. This document was published several times, especially by the journals *Science* and *Behavioral Science*.[2] This shows how important it was felt to be.

The document stresses five types of research "illustrating . . . both successes already attained and challenging problems that can be attacked now or in the near future." [3] They are, in succession: a theory of communication between individuals and groups, founded on the use of mathematical models; the biological and psychological mechanisms of personality development; brain neurophysiology; and the study of individual psychism and intellectual activity, based on animal psychology and on computer theory.

Thus, in the five cases considered, we are dealing with a research which implies a close collaboration between certain social and human sciences (linguistics, ethnology, psychology, logic, philosophy) and some of the hard sciences (mathematics, human anatomy and physiology, zoology). This manner of defining problems is fruitful, since it enables us to regroup, from the double point of view of theory and methodology, all the most progressive researches. At the same time, this perspective is obviously not compatible with the traditional distinction between the physical sciences and the human sciences which neglects the essential. Whereas the physical sciences are today fully established sciences, of which one can very well ask that they publicize their "trends," this is not true of the human sciences, about which one must first question their scientific capability. In wanting to maintain at all cost the fiction of their parallel position, one risks forcing them into a hypocritical and phony position.

We fear that, once more, the consideration shown the social and human sciences, the flattering place set aside for them among all the others, is really no more than a diversion. One can legitimately ask the hard sciences what they are. But the social and human sciences are not yet in a position to account for themselves. If such a demand is made of them—or if it is thought politically clever to pretend to make one—then we must not be surprised if we receive falsified accounts.

After this return to concerns expressed at the beginning of this chapter, let us now revert to the case of behavioral sciences, or more exactly to the original area which the term implies. We can already see how it confirms and strengthens our suggestions. In fact, it postulates a resolutely selective attitude toward the social and human sciences through which it succeeds in rebuilding a bridge toward the hard sciences. Experience justifies this double orientation. Indeed we believe we shall not meet with much opposition if we maintain that, right now, the linguist and the ethnologist can more easily find mutually profitable topics of conversation with the specialist in cerebral neurology or animal ethology than with the jurist, the economist, or the specialist in political science.

If we had to proceed to a new distribution of the social and human sciences, a division into three groups would be preferable to this implicit dualism. One would first reserve the rights, already mentioned, of those who are not filled with desire or nostalgia by the word "science"; that is, those who see in the specific type of "human science" they practice a research pertaining more to erudition, moral reflection, or aesthetic creation. We do not consider that they are left behind since—as there is no possible human science which does not call upon this type of research, and even perhaps which does not begin with it—many fields in our sciences are either too complex, or too close, or too remote from the observer to be approached in any other manner. The title "arts and literature" would suit them rather well.

The other two faculties would then be called "social sciences" and "human sciences," but with the condition that at last something precise be put into this distinction. On the whole, the faculty of social sciences would include all legal studies, such as they are presently being taught in law schools. To them would be added (this is only partly realized in the French system) economics and political science, and some branches of sociology and social psychology. On the side of the human sciences would be grouped prehistory, archaeology, history, anthropology, linguistics, philosophy, logic, and psychology.

Henceforth, the sole conceivable principle in the distinction between the social and human sciences would be clearly apparent. This will not be willingly accepted. Under the shelter of the social sciences are found all those sciences which agree without reluctance to settle down in the very midst of their society, with all that this implies about the preparation of students for a professional activity and the consideration of problems from a practical angle. We do not say that these concerns exclude others, but that they exist and are frankly acknowledged.

On the other hand, the human sciences are those which put themselves outside each particular society. Either they seek to adopt the point of view of some society or that of an individual within any society, or finally, aiming to grasp a reality immanent in man, they place themselves beyond any individual and any society.

Between the social sciences and the human sciences, a relationship (which from then on seems to be one of opposition rather than one of correlation) is established between a centripetal attitude and a centrifugal one. The former sometimes leaves the outside, but only to return inside. The latter follows the inverse process. If, sometimes, they are set within the society of the observer, it is only to get away from it quickly and insert specific observations into a whole of more general range.

By the same token, one discovers the nature of the affinity which the behavioral sciences insist they have with the hard sciences, one which is far more valid for the human than for the social sciences. In fact, those sciences for which we reserve the term "human sciences" can have as their subject one which brings them closer to the social sciences. From a methodological point of view they are closer to the hard sciences, so long as they reject any complicity with this area (which does not belong to them). To put it plainly, let us say that, unlike the social sciences, they are never "in cahoots" with it.

By denying themselves any complacency, even if an epistemological order, toward their subject, the human sciences adopt the point of view of immanence; whereas the social sciences, by their particular stress on the observer's society, give it a transcendental value. This is very obvious in the case of economists who do not hesitate to proclaim (in order to justify the narrowness of their goal) that economic rationality constitutes a privileged condition of human nature, one which made its appearance at a certain moment of history and in a certain part of the world. It is no less clear in the case of jurists, who treat an artificial system as if it were real, and who, in order to describe it, start from the postulate that it does not contain any contradictions. In this regard, they have often been compared to theologians. Undoubtedly, that transcendance to which the social sciences refer themselves implicitly or explicitly is not of a supernatural order. Yet one could call it "supercultural." It isolates a particular culture, puts it above the others, treats it as a separate, legitimately self-contained universe.

These remarks are not meant to be critical. After all, the politician, the administrator, the diplomat fulfilling an essential social function, the judge or the lawyer cannot reexamine at each moment the particular order of their activity. Neither can they take those ideological and practical risks (which are common enough in the history of the hard sciences) inherent to a truly fundamental research when this research brings about the destruction of a certain world representation; the upheaval of a body of hypotheses and the replacement of a system of axioms and postulates. Such an adamant position implies being aloof from action. The difference between the social sciences and the human sciences is not only a matter of method. It is also a matter of temperament.

But, in whichever way this difference is to be interpreted, the conclusion is the same. There are not, on one side, the hard sciences, and on the other, the social and human sciences. There are two approaches, one of which alone is scientific in spirit: that of the hard sciences, which study the world, and from which the human sciences draw their inspiration when they study man as a part of the world. The other approach, illustrated by the social sciences, undoubtedly makes use of techniques borrowed from the hard sciences. But their relationships thus established with the latter are extrinsic, not intrinsic. In relation to the hard sciences, the social sciences stand as dependents, while the human sciences hope to become their disciples.

This gives us the opportunity to express our opinion on a delicate matter, which has already caused much turmoil: Must the "trends" (the object of this investigation) be those of a contemporary Western society or should they include all the reflections on man which have come to light in other times and in other places? From a theoretical point of view, it is difficult to conceive why one should decide in favor of the former. But the latter would raise almost insuperable difficulties. Western knowledge is doubly accessible, since it exists in a written form and in languages known by most of the specialists, whereas a considerable fraction of the other only lives in oral tradition and the rest of it would first have to be translated.

The formula we have suggested makes it possible to get around this dilemma. We have suggested that only those researches which satisfy an external criterion be used as a basis for the investigation. This criterion should be a conformity to the norms of scientific knowledge as they are generally acknowledged, not only by the specialists of the social and human sciences (as this would result in a vicious circle), but also by those of the hard sciences.

On this basis, a very large consensus could be achieved. But it will at once be noticed that whereas the criterion of scientific knowledge can only be defined by reference to Western science (which is apparently not challenged by any society), the social and human researches which can best lay claim to it are not all Western—far from it. Contemporary linguists willingly acknowledge that grammarians from India made certain fundamental discoveries several centuries ahead of them; and this is certainly not the only area in which the knowledge of the Orient and the Far East will have proved to be superior. In the same order of ideas, ethnologists today are convinced that societies without writing, with even a very low technical and economic level, have sometimes been able to endow their political or social institutions with a conscious and reflective character which gives them a scientific aspect.

If, after considering the results, we now consider the subject and the method, we notice among the physical sciences, the social sciences, and the human sciences relationships which are no longer quantitative and which need to be carefully placed. It is clear that the social sciences and the human sciences both make use of the same subject: man. But beyond that point they are no longer related. Because, as far as their method is concerned, two remarks must be made: The social sciences, as well as the human sciences, attempt to define themselves in relation to the hard sciences, possessors of the mysteries of the scientific method. But our sciences maintain inverted relations with their canonical counterparts. Secondly, the human sciences have borrowed from the hard sciences the lesson that one must begin by challenging appearances if one aspires to understand the world; whereas the social sciences have adopted the symmetrical lesson; namely, that one must accept the world if one aims at changing it.

It all seems as if the false unity of the social and human sciences, animated by the same desire to test themselves by the touchstone of scientific knowledge, could not withstand a contact with the physical sciences. They split from each other, succeeding only in assimilating opposite aspects of their method. When they fall short of prediction, the social sciences regress to a rather low form of technology (which, for this reason no doubt, is given the ungracious name of technocracy). When they go beyond explanation, the human sciences tend to lose themselves in vague philosophical speculations.

This is not the place to inquire why a double-sided method has been practiced with well-known success by the hard sciences, while each of the social and the human sciences have only been able to use one half of it—which they actually do their best to distort at once. After all, this inequality is not surprising. There only exists—there has ever only existed—a single physical world, the properties of which have remained the same at all times and in all places; whereas throughout the millennia, here and there, thousands of human worlds continuously appeared and died, like a short-lived fluttering. Of all these worlds, which is the right one? And if all are (or none is), where is the subject of the social and human sciences located, behind or in front of them? The difference between these sciences reflects the alternatives which torment them (unlike the hard sciences which feel no uncertainty about their subject): either to favor one of these worlds in order to gain a hold over it; or to call them into question for the benefit of a common essence which remains to be discovered; or of a single universe which, if it is really unique, will unfailingly come to merge with the one of the hard sciences.

In the preceding pages, we have done nothing to conceal this divergence, which some people may even accuse us of having willingly accentuated. We feel, in fact, that it is not in the interest of the social sciences and the human sciences to hide what divides them, and that it is even to the advantage of both to pursue for a while their separate ways. If the progress of knowledge is one day to demonstrate that the social and human sciences deserve to be called sciences, the proof will be provided by experiment, that is, by verifying that the earth of scientific knowledge is round; and that—believing they are going away from each other to attain the status of a positive science (although through different means)—the social sciences and the human sciences, without even noticing it, will merge with the hard sciences from which they will cease to be distinguishable.

Thus the new relation must give the word "trend" its richest and fullest meaning. It must attempt to be a vigorous meditation on something that does not exist yet—rather than a falsified balance sheet to avoid the embarrassment of exposing the lack of achieved results. At the cost of a constructive effort where imagination will play its part, this new relation must seek to guess at latent gestations, to sketch the outlines of vague evolutions. It must seek less to describe the present state of our sciences than to anticipate the paths along which (and perhaps thanks to it), the sciences of tomorrow may be able to proceed.

NOTES

1. *Les Sciences sociales dams l'enseignement superieur: sociologie, psychologie sociale et anthropologie culturelle* (Paris: UNESCO, 1954), p. 275. (The teaching of social sciences).

2. See *Science*, CXXXVI, No. 3512 (April 20, 1962), pp. 230–241; *Behavioral Science*, VII, No. 3 (July 1962), pp. 275–288.

3. *Behavioral Science*, p. 277.

Cultural Discontinuity and Economic and Social Development

The Problem of Cultural Discontinuity
Confronting Ethnography and History

IT WAS in the sixteenth century that the problem of cultural discontinuity first presented itself to the Western conscience, in a sudden and dramatic manner, with the discovery of the New World. At that time, the alternatives seemed simple: Either the American natives were men, and thus had to be, willy-

Chapter XVII was originally published as a communication to *Table ronde sur les prémisses sociales de l'industrialisation*, organized by the International Social Science Council in September 1961, in *Information sur les sciences sociales*, Vol. II, No. 2 (The Hague: Mouton, June 1963), pp. 7-15. Reprinted by permission of the International Social Science Council.

nilly, integrated into the Christian civilization, or their humanity was debatable and they belonged to the animal world. But it was not until the eighteenth century that the problem was set in truly historical and sociological terms. Yet, we must note that whatever the solution proposed, all the authors agreed on the premises; that is to say, that it is possible to compare those societies which would today be called primitive with Western civilization. Whether the former are placed, as Condorcet believes, at the very beginning of a progressive and ascending evolution; or, as Diderot sometimes liked to suggest, whether they constitute a summit whence humanity has known nothing but continuous decadence; or, again, in Rousseau's more modern and subtle thought, whether a distinction must be made between a state of nature, the notion of which is purely theoretical, and a condition of humanity still illustrated today by savage peoples, which would represent a sort of optimum equilibrium between man and nature—none of these conceptions has ever doubted that cultural discontinuity exists as the apparent witness and last vestige of a once-common development.

It was above all Auguste Comte who denounced the weakness of this vision of the unified development of humanity, conceived sometimes as a progression, sometimes as a regression, and yet again as a complex mixture of the two formulae. In the Fifty-second lesson of the *Cours de philosophie positive*, Comte, in effect, criticizes the perils of the theory of unified social and cultural development. According to him, one must study this development as a specific property of Western civilization, possibly having to adjust the conclusions thus obtained to the transformation, from the outside, of different societies. Marxism confirms this specificity of particular evolutions: "Whoever would want to reduce to the same laws the political economy of Tierra del Fuego and that of England would surely bring to light no more than the most commonplace banality" (Engels 1954). Agreeing on this point with positivism, Marxism sees in development an intrinsic property of Western civilization: "The old primitive communities can exist for millennia before commerce with the outside world produces in their midst such differences of fortune as to lead to their dissolution" (Engels 1954).

But Marxist thought introduces two points of major importance for the problem which we are considering here. In the first place, it credits the old primitive civilizations with discoveries without which Western development would be inconceivable and in relation to which the breadth of this development, as it could be envisaged in the nineteenth century, is reduced to modest proportions: "The most distant antiquity . . . has, for a point of departure, man struggling away from the animal kingdom, and, for its content, the victory over such difficulties as will never again be met by organized men in the future" (Engels 1954). In the second place, and more important, Marx reverses the perspective by which the processes of industrialization and development are generally considered. For him, industrialization is not an autonomous phenomenon which must be introduced from the outside into the midst of passive civilizations. On the contrary, it is a function, and an indirect result, of the condition of societies called "primitive" or, more precisely, of the historical relationship between them and the Western world.

The fundamental problem of Marxism is to know why and how labor produces a surplus. It has not been observed often enough that Marx's answer to this problem is of an ethnographic nature. Primitive man was sufficiently limited in number to be established only in those regions of the world where natural conditions ensured a positive return for his labor. On the other hand, it is an intrinsic property of culture—in the sense given to that term by ethnologists—to establish between surplus and labor a relationship such that the former is always added to the latter. For these two reasons, one logical and the other historical, it can be postulated at the outset that all labor necessarily produces surplus. The exploitation of man by man comes later, and it appears concretely in history in the form of an exploitation of the colonized by the colonizer; in other words, through the appropriation, for the exploiters' profit, of the extra surplus which, we have seen, the primitive has the full right to dispose of. "Let us suppose that one of these islanders needs twelve hours' work to satisfy all his needs. We can see that the first favor granted to him by nature is a great deal of leisure. In order to use it productively for himself, a succession of historical influences is required; in order to spend it in overwork for other men, he must be constrained by force" (Marx 1967, Vol. 2).

Thus, colonization historically and logically precedes capitalism, and the capitalist regime consists in treating Western people as Western people had previously treated native populations. For Marx, the relationship between capitalist and proletarian is thus only another particular case of the relationship between colonizer and colonized. From this point of view, one could almost maintain that, in Marxist thought, economics and sociology first appear as offshoots of ethnography. It is in *Das Kapital* that the thesis is put forward with perfect clarity. The origins of the capitalist regime go back to the discovery of gold and silver regions in America; then on to the enslaving of the natives; then to the conquest and looting of the East Indies; finally to the transformation of Africa into "a sort of commercial preserve for the hunting of black skins. Such are the idyllic means of primitive accumulation which announce the dawn on the capitalist era." Immediately afterward the mercantile war is declared. "The mute slavery of the New World was needed as a cornerstone on which the covert slavery of Europe's wage earners was built."

Whether one accepts or rejects the Marxist position, these considerations are important because they draw one's attention back to two aspects of the problem of development so often neglected by contemporary thinkers.

In the first place, those societies which today we call "underdeveloped" are not such through their own doing, and one would be wrong to conceive of them as exterior to Western development or indifferent to it. In truth, they are the very societies whose direct or indirect destruction between the sixteenth and the nineteenth centuries have made possible the development of the Western world. Between them there is a complementary relationship. That same development and its greedy requirements have made these societies such as they are today. Thus we are not dealing with the contact between two processes each pursued in isolation. The relationship of estrangement between the so-called underdeveloped societies and the mechanized civilization consists mainly in the fact that this mechanized civilization finds in them its own creation; or, more precisely, the counterpart of those destructions it committed upon them in order to found its own reality.

In the second place, this relationship cannot be conceived in the abstract. One cannot possibly overlook that, for several centuries, it has manifested itself concretely in violence, oppression, and extermination. From this point of view also, the problem of the development is not a purely speculative matter. The analysis which can be made of it and the solutions which can be suggested for it must necessarily take into account irreversible historical conditions and a moral climate which together form what one could call the dynamic explosiveness of the colonial situation.

Consequently, the development can never be considered as Malinowski did: "the result of an impact of a higher and more active culture on a simpler and more passive one" (1945, *The Dynamic of Culture Change*). "Simplicity" and "passivity" are not intrinsic properties of these societies, but the result of the development's action upon them from its very beginnings; a situation created by brutality, pillage, and violence, without which the historical conditions of this very development would not have been brought together. (If they had been brought together differently, the kind of contact would have been quite different and such as we can in no way imagine.) There is not, there cannot be, a "point zero of change" (Mair 1969), unless we could agree to place it at the only moment when it really existed: in 1492, on the eve of the discovery of the New World. The historical conditions of that development which was to benefit the Western world were brought together by the destruction first of the New World itself and then of several others. This destruction enabled the development to happen in the first place, before it could return to impose itself from the outside on the very societies it had destroyed in order for it to be born and grow from their ruins.

What is true at the level of official history is equally true at the level of its sidelights. Grappling with the problems of the industrialization of underdeveloped countries, Western civilization first meets with the deformed image, as if unchanged through centuries, of the destruction which it first had to perpetrate in order to exist. In the same manner, although on a more reduced scale, we would be wrong to believe that the coming into contact of mechanized civilization with those populations which had remained the most alien to it takes place in the abstract. In fact, long before an acknowledged contact took place, some anticipated effects had been felt for many years, in two ways: either in the form of a second destruction from a distance, or in that of an absorption, which is also the equivalent of a destruction.

The ravages of epidemics introduced by the white man among populations who had not yet developed any immunity against them have been too often described to make it necessary to recall the extermination of whole societies by diseases, started in the sixteenth century, the desperate effects of which we are still witnessing today. In a similar manner, the horse, spreading out across the plains of North America much faster than Western civilization penetrated into them, upset the native cultures by anticipation as it were, in the same way that pathogenic germs travel with surprising speed. Even in the most remote regions of the earth, where the presence of untouched societies could be assumed, their ravages are felt several years—and sometimes several dozens of years—before the contact proper had been made.

The same can be said of raw materials and techniques. In an article "La révolution de la hache" Alfred Métraux (1959) has shown how the adoption of iron axes, while making technical and economic activities simpler and easier, may lead to a real destruction of the native civilizations. The Yir Yoront of Northern Australia, studied by Lauriston Sharp, have lost, with their adoption of metal implements, the whole of their economic, social, and religious institutions which were linked to the possession, utilization, and transmission of stone axes. The adoption of more advanced machinery has led to the breakdown of social organization and the disruption of the group. Yet, in the form of worn-out or damaged tools, sometimes even of indescribable fragments, iron travels faster and farther than men, through wars, marriages, or commercial exchanges.

This destruction from afar can also take the form of a real absorption of native group, by a civilization which has barely touched them yet. Stanner has recently described an old misadventure, experienced in similar manner by other ethnologists in Australia, South America, and elsewhere. Around 1930, alerted by official and informal reports that indicated the existence of tribes still in an entirely savage state in a remote region of Australia, he was to discover, once there, that precarious settlements maintained by Europeans or Chinese in succession for some fifty years had succeeded in creating a vacuum in the midst of a native population which had become wanderers in search of metal tools, tobacco, tea, sugar, and clothing. The so-called "savages" were simply the last peoples, already socially and morally degenerated, of the Australian interior who had been drawn toward the pioneer frontier like their predecessors. So that, in the unexplored territories, there was no one left (Stanner 1960).

The Three Sources of the Resistance to Development

Once we have defined the concrete historical framework within which cultural discontinuity manifests itself, we can attempt, with fewer risks, to bring out the deep causes of the resistance to development.

But we must first of all give a special place to those cases, however exceptional, where the native culture succeeds in taking a partial refuge in a sort of cultural "niche" provided for it by the industrial civilization.

The most famous example is that of the Iroquois of New York State, who for more than a century have provided the best teams specialized in the building of metallic structures, such as bridges, skyscrapers, etc. This vocation is partly explained by their traditional training in the crossing of torrents and precipices, and also perhaps because here Indians may have found in an activity fraught with danger, full of prestige, and highly lucrative—as well as intermittent, which implies a certain measure of nomadism—a substitute for their ancient war parties.

Less durable, but just as striking, was the extraordinary flourishing of plastic and graphic arts on the northwest coast of Canada and Alaska after the settlement of fur-trading posts. Increased leisure, combined with the introduction of iron tools and a new wealth favorable to speculation, forcibly stimulated for about fifty years a latent orientation toward struggles for prestige, in which the possession, exhibition, and destruction of precious objects played an important part. In this case it is true that due to the introduction of European diseases, the demographic breakdown acted momentarily in the same way, since many aristocratic titles were left without heirs and became coveted as a means of social climbing for a class of "nouveaux riches." But these two examples, and the few others which might have been added to them, are nothing but odd occurrences.

Generally speaking, there seem to be three deep causes for the resistance to development. First, a tendency on the part of most of the societies called primitive to prefer unity to change; in the second place, a deep respect for the forces of nature; and finally, their reluctance to becoming involved in a historical development.

The Desire for Unity

The noncompetitive nature of some of the societies we call primitive has often been invoked to explain their resistance to development and industrialization. Yet, on this point, we must keep in mind that the passivity and indifference which have struck the observers may be a consequence of the traumatic contact, and not an initially given condition. Nevertheless, one can not insist too much on the fact that this absence of a spirit of competition does not very often result from a state induced from outside or from a previous passive conditioning, but rather from a deliberate progress, corresponding to a certain conception of the relationships between man and the world and of men among themselves. The extent to which attitudes so different from those of the Western world can be deeply anchored may be seen, rather amusingly, in an observation recently made in New Guinea among the Gahuku-Kama. These natives have learned from the missionaries how to play soccer, but instead of seeking victory for one of the teams, they multiply the number of games until the defeats and victories are equally balanced. The match is ended not when one team is victorious, as among us, but when there is no loser (Read 1959, p. 429).

In other societies, completely opposite observations can be made, but they are equally incompatible with a true spirit of competition. Thus when traditional games are played between two teams, representing the living and the dead respectively, the former must necessarily end up being the winners.

It is actually the same Gahuku-Kama who, as so often in New Guinea, divide the political responsibilities between the chief and the orator. The latter's role is to express all conflicts openly and aggressively while the chief intervenes to appease, pacify, and bring about mediated solutions. From this point of view, it is rather striking that in most so-called "primitive" societies, the idea of taking a majority vote is inconceivable, as the social cohesion and the good will within the group are held preferable to any innovation. Consequently, only unanimous decisions are taken among them. Sometimes—and this is verified in several parts of the world—the deliberations are preceded by simulated fights in the course of conditions of an indispensable unanimity.

The Respect for Nature

The conception of many primitive societies about the relationship between nature and culture can also explain some of the resistance to development. Development implies the unconditional priority of culture over nature, which is almost never admitted outside the area of industrial civilization. The discontinuity between the two rules is undoubtedly universally recognized, and there is no society—be it ever so humble—which does not place high value on the arts of civilization, through the discovery and usage of which man differs from animals. Among the peoples called "primitive," however, the notion of nature always offers an ambiguous character. Nature is preculture and it is also subculture. But it is by and large the means through which man may hope to enter into contact with ancestors, spirits, and gods. Thus, there is in the notion of nature a "supernatural" component, and this "supernature" is as undeniably above culture as nature itself is below it.

Under these conditions, it is not surprising that techniques and manufactured objects are afflicted in native thought by a sort of devaluation, as soon as such thought deals with essentials: the relationship between man and the supernatural world. Innumerable examples of the proscription of locally manufactured objects, or recently introduced ones, for all ceremonial acts and various moments of ritual, are to be found in classical and nonclassical antiquity as well as in Western folklore and in contemporary native societies. As was the case with the prohibition of usury by the Fathers of the Church and by Islam, we find here a very deep resistance to what could be called "instrumentality," which fashions attitudes much beyond the avowed goal of such and such a prohibition.

It is in this same manner that we must interpret the aversion toward property transactions, rather than seeing it as an immediate consequence of the economic administration or the collective ownership of the land. If, for instance, some poor native communities in the United States, barely a few dozen families strong, rebel against the prospect of expropriation compensated by several hundred thousands of dollars, sometimes even several millions of dollars, it is because—in the words of these people themselves—certain territory is conceived by them as a "mother," so that they may neither let it go nor exchange it. Taking this reasoning further still, we know of populations of wild-grain collectors (the Menomini of the Great Lakes region) perfectly aware of the agricultural techniques of their neighbors (the Iroquois), yet refusing to apply them to the production of their basic food (wild rice), although it is well suited to cultivation, for the reason that they are forbidden to "wound their mother the earth." In such cases, this is indeed a priority given to nature over culture, which our civilization has also known in the past and which resurfaces sometimes in times of doubt and crisis, but which in the societies called "primitive" acts as a firmly constructed system of beliefs and practices.

It is indeed the same opposition which gives a theoretical basis to the division of labor according to sex. As variable as this division may seem to be when we compare societies among themselves, it possesses constant elements which are variously interpreted and the applications of which only differ here and there. Thus the homology between the opposition *nature/culture* and the opposition *female/male*, by virtue of which are reserved for women those forms of activity which are conceived of as being of the order of nature (such as gardening); or as putting the artisan in direct contact with natural products or objects (handmade pottery, weaving-braiding), while men tend to appropriate the same types of activity when they require the intervention of culture in the form of tools and machinery whose fabrication has reached a certain level of complexity (relative to the societies).

The Rejection of History

In this double perspective, it is obviously futile to pose the problem of societies "without history." The question is not knowing whether the societies called "primitive" have or do not have a history in the sense we give this term. These societies exist in time like all the others, and with the same title to it, but unlike us, they refuse to belong to history and they try very hard to inhibit, within themselves, whatever would constitute the faint promise of a historical development. As one proverb of the Lovedu of South Africa says in such a nostalgic and significant way: "The ideal is to come back home, since no one will ever leave the bosom of his mother again."

Our Western societies are made for change; it is the principle of their structure and of their organization. The societies called "primitive" appear to us to be such mostly because they have been conceived by their members to endure. Their opening to the outside is very narrow, and what we would call "l'esprit de clocher" (village chauvinism) dominates them. The stranger, even when he is a close neighbor, is thought of as dirty and uncouth; one often goes so far as to deny him a human quality. Conversely, the internal social structure has a tighter weave, a richer decor, than complex civilizations. Nothing is left to chance in them, and the double principle that there is a place for everything, that everything must be in its place, permeates moral and social life. It also explains how societies with a very low techno-economic level can experience a feeling of well-being and plenitude, and how each of them believes it offers its members the only life worth living. Thus perhaps they give these members more happiness. But because this happiness sees itself as complete, each form is inevitably separated from the others and is fixed de jure, if not always de facto.

CHAPTER XVIII

Race and History

Race and Culture

To SPEAK of the contribution of human races to world civilization might seem surprising in a collection of articles meant to fight racial prejudice. It would be pointless to have devoted so much talent and so much effort to prove that nothing in the present state of science allows us to affirm the intellectual superiority or inferiority of one race with regard to another, only to then, surreptitiously, restore substance to the notion of race by seeming to demonstrate that the great ethnic groups which make up humanity, have individually brought their specific contributions to the common patrimony.

But nothing is further from our intention than such an enterprise, which would only lead to the formulation of a reversed racist doctrine. When attempting to characterize the biological

Chapter XVIII was originally published under the title "Race et Histoire," in *La Question raciale devant la science moderne* (Paris: UNESCO, 1952). The text has been revised and corrected in places.

races by specific psychological properties, one strays just as much from scientific truth in defining them positively as negatively. We must not forget that Gobineau, whom history has made the father of racist theories, did not conceive of the "inequality of the human races" in a quantitative manner, but qualitatively. For him, the great races which contributed to the formation of contemporary mankind without being called primitive—white, yellow, black—were not so much unequal in real value as different in their particular aptitudes. He considered that the stigma of degeneration is more related to the phenomenon of crossbreeding than to the position of each race in a scale of values common to all; it was thus meant to stike at the whole of humanity, condemned without racial distinction to a greater mixing of blood. But anthropology's original sin lies in the confusion between the purely biological notion of race (supposing that even in this limited field such a notion might pretend to a measure of objectivity, which modern genetics denies) and the sociological and psychological products of human cultures. It is enough for Gobineau to have committed this sin, to find himself locked in this infernal circle which, from an intellectual error not devoid of good faith, leads to the involuntary legitimization of all the attempts of discrimination and oppression.

Thus, when we speak in this study, of the contribution of the human races to civilization, we do not mean that cultural contributions from Asia or Europe, from Africa or America, draw some originality from the fact that these continents are on the whole inhabited by peoples of different racial origins. If this originality exists—and there is no doubt about it—it is due to geographical, historical, and sociological circumstances, and not to distinct aptitudes related to the anatomical or physiological constitution of black, yellow, and white races. But we feel that, to the very extent that this series of articles attempts to render justice to this negative point of view, it runs at the same time the risk of relegating to the background an equally important aspect of the life of mankind. It does not develop in a monotonously uniform manner, but through extraordinarily diversified types of societies and civilizations. This intellectual, aesthetic, sociological diversity is not linked by any cause-and-effect relation to the biological diversity which exists among certain observable aspects of human groups. It only parallels it in another way. At the same time, it differs from it in two important characteristics. First, it takes place at another order of magnitude. There are many more human cultures than there are human races, since the former are numbered in the thousands and the latter in mere units. Indeed, two cultures developed by men belonging to the same race may differ as much, or more, than two cultures belonging to racially distant groups. In the second place, unlike the diversity among races, whose main interest lies in their historical origin and their distribution, the diversity among cultures presents many problems, and one may wonder whether it constitutes for mankind an advantage or a handicap, a general question which is naturally broken down into many.

Finally, and most important, we must ask ourselves what makes this diversity, at the risk of seeing racial prejudices, barely extracted from their biological roots, reshaping themselves on another plane. It would be useless to have obtained from the average man the assurance that he cease attributing an intellectual or moral significance to one's skin being black or white, one's hair smooth or kinky, only to have him remain silent when he is confronted with another question which, as experience shows, he elaborates on at once: If no innate racial aptitudes exist, how do we explain that the civilization developed by the white man has made the immense progress we know, while those of colored peoples have remained behind—some halfway, others some thousands or ten thousands years behind? One should not assume to have thus settled in a negative way the problem of the inequality of human *races*, if one considers at the same time the problem of the inequality—or diversity—of human *cultures* which—de facto if not de jure—is closely linked to it in public opinion.

Diversity of Cultures

To understand how, and to what extent, human cultures differ among themselves, whether these differences cancel each other out or contradict one another, or whether they form a harmonious whole, we must first try to draw up a list of them. But here the difficulties start, since we must realize that human cultures do not differ among themselves in the same ways, nor on the same levels. We are first faced with societies juxtaposed in space, some near, others distant, but on the whole contemporary. Next, we must take into account forms of social life which have succeeded one another in time and which we are prevented from knowing through direct experience. Any man can turn himself into an ethnographer and go and share on the spot the life of a society in which he is interested; on the other hand, even if he becomes a historian or an archaeologist, he will never enter directly into contact with a vanished civilization, but will only do so through the written documents or figurative monuments which this society—or others —have left. Finally, we must not forget that the contemporary societies which have remained without writing, such as the ones we call "savage" or "primitive," were themselves preceded by other forms, which it is practically impossible to know, even indirectly. A conscientious inventory would have to reserve blank spaces for them—in an undoubtedly greater number than the number of spaces in which we feel able to inscribe something. An initial observation must obviously be made: The diversity of human cultures is (de facto for the present, de facto and also de jure for the past) much greater and much richer than we shall ever be able to know.

But even as we are filled with humility and convinced of these limitations, we face other problems. What must we understand by different cultures? Some appear to be different, but if they stem from a common tree, they do not differ in the same manner as two societies which did not come into contact at any stage of their development. Thus the ancient empires of the Incas in Peru and of Dahomey in Africa present more absolute differences than, let us say, contemporary England and the United States, although these latter two societies must also be treated as distinct. Conversely, some societies recently brought together in close contact seem to present the image of the same civilization, although they reached it by different paths which must not be neglected. There are in human societies forces which work simultaneously in opposite directions: those leaning toward the preservation, and even the accentuation of particularities, and those working toward convergence and affinity. The study of language presents striking examples of such phenomena. For example, whereas languages of the same origin tend to differentiate themselves (such as Russian, French, and English), languages of varied origins, but spoken in adjacent territories, develop common characteristics. Russian, for example, differentiated itself in some ways from other Slavic languages and adopted some features, phonetic at least, of the Finno-Ugrian and Turkish languages spoken in its immediate geographic vicinity.

When studying these facts (other features of civilization such as social institutions, art, and religion would easily provide similar examples), one ends up wondering whether human societies are not defined (with regard to their mutual relationships) by a certain *optimum* diversity beyond which they could not go, but below which they should not go either without endangering themselves. This optimum would vary as a function of the number of societies, their numerical importance, geographical remoteness, and of the material and intellectual means of communication at their disposal. Indeed, the problem of diversity occurs not only with regard to cultures considered in their reciprocal relationships; it also exists within each society, and in all the groups that constitute it—castes, classes, professional or religious milieux, etc., developing some differences to which each attaches an extreme importance. We can wonder if this *internal diversification* does not tend to increase when the society becomes, in other ways, larger and more homogeneous. Such was perhaps the case of ancient India, with its system of castes which flourished after the establishment of the Aryan hegemony.

So we see that the notion of the diversity of human cultures cannot be conceived in a static manner. This diversity is not that of an inert sampling or a dried-up catalogue. Men have undoubtedly built different cultures because of their geographical remoteness, the peculiar properties of their environment, and their ignorance of the rest of humanity. But this would be strictly true only if each culture or each society were born or had developed in total isolation from the others. However, this is never the case, except perhaps in exceptional examples such as that of the Tasmanians (and here again, for a limited period). Human societies are never alone; when they seem the most isolated, it is still in the form of groups or bundles. For instance, it is not an exaggeration to suppose that the North American and the South American cultures have been cut off from almost all contact with the rest of the world during several thousands of years. But this large portion of detached humanity consisted of a multitude of small and large societies, in close contact with one another. Beside these differences due to isolation, there are those (just as important) due to proximity, that is, the desire to differ, to stand out, to be oneself. Many customs were not born from some inner need or through some favorable accident, but from the sole desire not to remain behind a neighboring group which submitted a domain of thought or activity to precise rules that had not been thought of by the first group. Consequently, the diversity of human cultures must not lead us to an observation which both divides and is divided. Diversity is less a function of the isolation of groups than of the relationships which unite them.

Ethnocentricity

And yet, it seems that the diversity of cultures has rarely appeared to men for what it is: a natural phenomenon, resulting from the direct or indirect relationships between societies. They rather tended to see in it a sort of monstrosity or scandal. In these matters, the progress of knowledge did not so much consist in dissipating this illusion in favor of a more accurate view point, as in accepting it and finding the means of becoming resigned to it.

The most ancient attitude, resting no doubt on a solid psychological basis (since it tends to reappear in each of us when we find ourselves in an unexpected situation), consists in the pure and simple repudiation of cultural forms (moral, religious, social, and aesthetic) which are the most removed from those with which we identify. "Savages' customs," "this is not done among us," "that should not have been allowed," etc.—all are coarse reactions which translate the same tremor, the same repulsion when faced with ways of living, believing, and thinking alien to us. Antiquity confused all that was not part of the Greek (and later Greco-Roman) culture under the same word "barbarous"; Western civilization later used the term savage in the same sense. Under these terms the same judgment is concealed. The origin of the word "barbarous" probably refers to the confusion of inarticulated bird songs as opposed to the meaningful value of human language; and the word "savage," which means "of the forest," also evokes a type of animal life, as opposed to human culture. In both cases, one refuses to admit the very fact of cultural diversity, and prefers to reject as outside of culture, back into nature, all that does not conform to the norm regulating our life.

This simplistic point of view, which is deeply anchored in the minds of most men, need not be discussed, since this article—as well as the others in the same collection—serves precisely to refute it. It will suffice to note here that it conceals a rather significant paradox. This mode of thought by which the "savages" (or all those one chooses to qualify as such) are rejected outside mankind, is precisely the most marked and characteristic of these very savages themselves. We know, in effect, that the notion of humanity, which includes without distinction of race or civilization all the forms of the human species, appeared very late and in a limited way. In the very place where it seems to have reached its highest development, it is not at all certain—and recent history proves this —that it is protected from ambiguities and regressions. But for huge portions of the human species, and during tens of millennia, this notion seems to have been totally lacking. Mankind stops at the frontiers of the tribe, of the linguistic group, and sometimes even of the village, to the extent that a great many of the peoples called primitive call themselves by a name which means "men" (or sometimes—shall we say with more discretion—the "good ones," the "excellent ones," the "complete ones," thus implying that the other tribes, groups, and villages have no part in human virtues or even human nature, but are at the most made up of "bad people," "nasty people," "land monkeys," or "lice eggs." One often goes so far as to deprive the stranger of this last shred of reality by making him a "ghost" or an "apparition." Thus curious situations are created in which two interlocutors proceed to cruel exchanges. In the Greater Antilles, some years after the discovery of America, while the Spaniards sent out investigating commissions to ascertain whether or not the natives had a soul, the latter were engaged in the drowning of white prisoners in order to verify, through prolonged watching, whether or not their corpses were subject to putrefaction.

This anecdote, at once baroque and tragic, illustrates well the paradox of cultural relativism (which we will see elsewhere in other forms). It is by the very manner in which one attempts to establish a discrimination between cultures and customs that one identifies most thoroughly with those one tries to refute. By refusing to see as human those members of humanity who appear as the most "savage" or "barbaric," one only borrows from them one of their characteristic attitudes. The barbarian is first of all the man who believes in barbarism.[1]

Undoubtedly, humanity's great philosophical and religious systems—be they Buddhism, Christianity, or Islam; Stoic, Kantian, or Marxist doctrines—have constantly attacked this aberration. But a simple proclamation of the natural equality of all men, and of the brotherhood which must unite them without distinction of race or culture, is somewhat disappointing for the mind because it overlooks a real diversity which can be readily observed. And it is not enough to say that this diversity does not affect the root of the problem to make it possible for one to pretend, both theoretically and practically, that the problem does not exist. Thus the preamble to the second declaration of UNESCO on the problem of race makes the judicious remark that "the man in the street" is convinced of the existence of races "through the immediate evidence of his senses when he sees together an African, a European, an Asiatic, and an American Indian."

The great declarations of human rights also have the strength and the weakness that they enunciate an ideal which forgets, too often, the fact that a man does not realize his nature in an abstract humanity, but in traditional cultures whose most revolutionary changes still retain whole sections and are themselves explained as a function of a situation strictly defined in time and in space. Caught between the double temptation to condemn experiences which give him an emotional shock and to deny differences which he cannot understand intellectually, modern man gave free rein to a hundred philosophical and sociological speculations in order to establish futile compromises between these contradictory poles and to account for the diversity of cultures, while seeking to suppress that which seems to him scandalous and shocking.

But, as different and, at times, strange as the speculations might be, they can in fact all be reduced to a single formula which the term "false evolutionism" seems to render best. What does it consist of? Very precisely, it is an attempt at suppressing the diversity of cultures while pretending to recognize it fully. If one treats the different states of human societies, both ancient and distant, as *stages* or *steps* of a single development which, starting from the same point, must have them all converge toward the same goal, it is quite evident that diversity is only apparent. Humanity becomes one and the same; but this unity and this identity can only be realized progressively, and the variety of cultures illustrates the moments of a process that conceals a deeper reality or delays its manifestation.

This definition may seem succinct when one thinks of the immense conquests made by Darwinism. But we are not concerned with the latter, since the biological evolutionism and the pseudoevolutionism which we are considering here are two very different doctrines. The former comes to light as a vast working hypothesis, based on observations in which the part left to interpretation is minimal. For example, the different types constituting the genealogy of the horse can be put in an evolutive series for two reasons. The first is that a horse is necessary to generate a horse; the second is that superimposed layers of soil (thus historically more and more ancient) contain skeletons which gradually range from the most recent form to the most archaic one. Thus it becomes highly likely that *Hipparion* is the real ancestor of *Equus caballus*. The same type of reasoning no doubt applies to human species and its races. But in passing from biological features to cultural facts, things become a lot more complicated. One can pick up material objects from the ground and notice that, depending on the depth of the geological layers, the shape or manufacturing technique of a certain type of object is progressively modified. And yet an axe does not physically give birth to another axe in the way an animal reproduces. Thus, in this case, to say that one axe has evolved from another constitutes a metaphorical and approximate formula, devoid of the scientific exactness attached to the same expression when applied to biological phenomena. What is true of material objects, physically present in the ground and belonging to recognizable eras, is even more true of the institutions, the beliefs, the tastes of a past generally unknown to us. The notion of a biological evolution corresponds to a hypothesis to which has been attributed the highest coefficient of probability found in the social sciences. On the other hand, the notion of a social or cultural evolution only contributes at the most an attractive, but dangerously convenient means of presentation of the facts.

Moreover, the too-often-neglected difference between true and false evolutionism is explained by their respective dates of appearance. Undoubtedly, sociological evolutionism was to receive a seminal impetus from biological evolutionism; but it precedes it in time. Without going back to the conceptions of antiquity (taken up again by Pascal), which assimilate humanity to a living being passing through the successive stages of childhood, adolescence, and maturity, it is in the eighteenth century that we see the fundamental schemata flourishing which will later on be the object of so many manipulations: Vico's "spirals," his "three ages" anticipating Comte's "three states," and Condorcet's "ladders." The two founders of social evolutionism, Spencer and Tylor, elaborated and published their doctrine before *The Origin of Species* was published and without having read it. Preceding biological evolutionism, as a scientific theory, social evolutionism is, too often, no more than the falsely scientific covering up of an old philosophical problem, to which it is not at all certain that observation and induction may one day provide the key.

Archaic Cultures and Primitive Cultures

We have suggested that each society is able to divide its own culture into three categories: those which are contemporary but located in other parts of the world; those which appeared approximately in the same place but preceded it in time; and finally, those which existed both in a previous time and in a different place from the present one.

We have seen that access to the knowledge about the three groups equally varies. In the case of the third, and when dealing with those cultures without writing, without architecture, and with only rudimentary techniques (as is the case for half of the inhabited part of the world and for 90 to 99 percent—according to the region —of the time elapsed since the beginnings of civilization), it may be said that we can know nothing and that all we try to imagine about them is the product of gratuitous hypotheses.

Nevertheless, it is extremely tempting to try to establish, among the cultures of the first group, relations comparable to an order of succession in time. How could comtemporary societies, still ignorant of electricity and the steam engine, not evoke the corresponding phase of the development of Western civilization? How can we fail to compare the native tribes, which are without writing or metallurgy but which draw figures on rocky walls and manufacture stone tools, with the archaic forms of that same civilization, whose similarity is evident in the vestiges found in the caves of France and Spain? This is mostly where false evolutionism ran wild. And yet this attractive game in which we almost irresistibly engage each time we have the opportunity of doing so (the Western traveler is only too pleased to recognize the "Middle Ages" in the Orient, the "century of Louis XIV" in Peking before World War I, the "Stone Age" among the natives of Australia and New Guinea) is an extraordinarily pernicious one. Of vanished civilizations, we only know certain aspects—and these known aspects are less numerous as the civilization is more ancient, since they are the only ones to have withstood the destruction of time. The process consists in taking the part for the whole, concluding —because *some* aspects of both the present and the vanished civilizations present similarities—with the analogy of *all* their aspects. Not only is this reasoning logically indefensible, but in a great number of cases it is proven wrong by the facts.

Until a relatively recent period, the Tasmanians and the Patagonians possessed flint implements, and some Australian and American tribes still manufacture them. But the study of these tools is of little help in understanding how tools were used during the Paleolithic Age. How did one use those famous "hand axes," which must have been used in so precise a manner that their shape and technique of manufacture have remained the same for one or two hundred thousand years, in an area spreading from England to South Africa, from France to China? What was the use of these extraordinary Levalloisian pieces, triangular and flattened, which are found by the hundreds in archaeological sites and of which no hypothesis has given a satisfactory account? What were the so-called "command staffs" that were made of reindeer bone? What could have been the technology of the Tardenoisian cultures who left behind them an incredible number of minute pieces of flint with infinitely diversified geometrical shapes, but very few tools scaled to the human hand? All these uncertainties show that between the Paleolithic societies and some contemporary native societies, a resemblance no doubt exists: They both used implements made of cut stone. But even at the technological level, it is difficult to go further: the way the material was used, the types of tools and their purpose were different; and so the latter teach us little about the former. How then could they instruct us on the language, the social institutions, or the religious beliefs?

One of the most popular interpretations among those inspired by cultural evolutionism treats the cave paintings left by Neolithic societies as magical configurations linked to hunting rites. The reasoning goes as follows: Contemporary primitive peoples have rituals, which often seem to us devoid of practical value; the prehistoric cave paintings, by their number as much as by their location in the deepest part of the caves, seem to us to be without practical value; their authors were hunters: consequently, they were used for hunting rituals. It is enough simply to pronounce this implicit argument in order to see how inconsistent it is. Moreover, it is mostly the nonspecialists who use it, since the ethnographers (with firsthand knowledge of these primitive peoples so easily put to every kind of work by a pseudoscientific cannibalism showing little respect for the integrity of human cultures) agree in saying that nothing in the observed facts allows one to formulate any hypothesis about the documents in question. And since we are speaking of cave paintings, we must stress the fact that, apart from South African cave paintings (considered by some to be recent native works), the "primitive" arts are as remote from Magdalenian and Aurignacian art as they are from contemporary European art. These arts are characterized by a very high degree of stylization, going as far as the most extreme deformations, whereas prehistoric art offers a startling realism. It would be tempting to see in this latter trait the origin of European art; but even this would be inaccurate since, in the same area, Paleolithic art was followed by other forms which did not have the same characteristics. The continuity of geographical location makes no difference to the fact that different populations followed one another, ignorant of or uninterested in the works of their predecessors, and each bringing along contrary beliefs, techniques, and styles.

The state of civilization in pre-Columbian America on the eve of its discovery, evokes the European Neolithic period. But this comparison does not withstand close examination either. In Europe, agriculture and animal domestication go together, while in America an exceptional development of the former goes along with an almost complete—or at least an extremely limited—ignorance of the latter. In America, lithic implements survive in an agricultural economy which, in Europe, is associated with the beginning of metallurgy.

It is not necessary to multiply the examples. The attempts made to discover the wealth and originality of human cultures, and to reduce them to variously backward replicas of Western civilization, are confronted with another, much deeper difficulty. On the whole (with the exception of America, to which we will return), all human societies have behind them a past which is probably of the same order of magnitude. In order to treat some societies as "stages" in the development of others, one would then have to admit that in these latter societies something was happening, and nothing (or very little) was happening in the former. And indeed, one willingly speaks of "peoples without history" (to say sometimes that they are the happiest). This elliptic formula only means that their history is and will remain unknown—not that it does not exist. For dozens or even hundreds of millennia, there were men who also loved, hated, suffered, invented, and fought in these places. In truth, there are no peoples still in their childhood. They are all adult, even those who have not kept the diary of their infancy and their adolescence.

It could no doubt be said that human societies have differently used their "times past," times which for some of them may even have been wasted. It could be said that some hurried on while others dawdled along the way. In this manner, one would come to distinguish between two types of history: a progressive, acquisitive history, which accumulates discoveries and inventions in order to construct great civilizations; and another history, perhaps equally active and as talented, but from which is lacking the synthetic gift that is the privilege of the former. Each innovation, instead of adding itself to previous innovations with the same orientation, would dissolve in a sort of undulating flux which would never permit it to escape for long from the primitive way.

This conception seems to us much more flexible and subtle than the simplistic views we dealt with in the previous paragraphs. We can reserve for it a place in our attempt at interpreting the diversity of cultures, without being unfair to any of them. But before getting to it we must examine several points.

The Notion of Progress

We must first consider the cultures belonging to the second group we distinguished, that is, those which historically preceded the culture (whatever it is) from that point of view in which we place ourselves. Their situation is much more complicated than in the previously considered cases, since the hypothesis of an evolution, which seems so uncertain and so fragile when used to organize distant contemporary societies into a hierarchy, may appear in this case not only difficult to controvert but even directly confirmed by the facts. We know, by the corroborating testimony of archaeology, prehistory, and paleontology, that modern Europe was first inhabited by various species of the *Homo* type, using tools made of roughly cut silex. Those first cultures were followed by others, whose stone cutting becomes more refined. Then, polishing came along as well as the carving of bone and ivory; pottery, weaving, agriculture, and animal breeding later appeared, progressively associated with metallurgy, the various stages of which we can also distinguish. These successive forms are thus organized in the sense of an evolution and a progress; some are superior and others are inferior. But if all this is true, how would these distinctions not inevitably react upon the way we treat contemporary forms, which present similar differences? Our previous conclusions thus run the danger of being reconsidered through this new bias.

The forward steps accomplished by mankind since its origins are so obvious and startling that all attempt to discuss them would be reduced to a rhetorical exercise. And yet, it is not so easy as one believes to order them in a continuous and regular series. Some fifty years ago, scholars used schemata of an admirable simplicity to represent them: Paleolithic Age, Neolithic Age, the Copper, Bronze, and Iron ages. This is all too convenient. Today we suspect that the polishing and the cutting of stone have sometimes existed side by side; when the second technique completely overshadows the first one, it is not as the result of a technical progress spontaneously sprung from the previous stage, but rather as an attempt to copy, in stone, the metal weapons and implements owned by civilizations undoubtedly more "advanced," but in fact contemporaneous with their imitators. Conversely, the pottery believed to be linked with the "age of polished stone" is associated with the cutting of stone in some regions of Northern Europe.

To consider only that period of stone cutting called the "Paleolithic age," it was still thought some time ago that the different forms of this technique—characterizing the "nuclei," the "flake," and the "blade" industries, respectively—corresponded to a historical progress in three stages called Lower Paleolithic, Middle Paleolithic, and Upper Paleolithic. Today it is admitted that these three forms have coexisted, forming not a one-way progress, but aspects—or, as we say, facets—of a reality undoubtedly not static but submitted to very complex variations and transformations. In fact, the Levalloisian already mentioned, who flourished between the two hundred-fiftieth and the seventieth millennium B.C., attained a perfection in flint cutting which was only to be found again at the end of the Neolithic Age, 245 to 65,000 years later, and which we would find very difficult to reproduce today.

What is true of cultures is also true at the level of races, without it being possible (because of the different orders of magnitude) to establish any correlation between the two processes. In Europe, Neanderthal man did not make an earlier appearance than the more ancient forms of *Homo sapiens;* the latter were their contemporaries, perhaps even their predecessors. And it is not impossible that the most various types of hominids coexisted in time, such as the "pygmies" of South Africa and the "giants" of China and Indonesia; and that, in some parts of Africa, they even coexisted.

Once more, none of this aims at denying the reality of a progress of mankind, but it invites us to consider it with greater care. The development of prehistoric and archaeological knowledge tends to *spread out in space* those forms of civilization which we imagined as *spread out in time*. This means two things: First, that "progress" (if this term is still suitable to designate a very different reality from the one to which it was first applied) is neither necessary nor continuous; it proceeds by leaps and bounds, or, as the biologists would say, by mutations. Secondly, these leaps and bounds do not always go in the same direction; they go together with changes in orientation, a little like a chess knight that can always avail itself of several progressions but never in the same direction. Humanity in progress hardly ressembles a man climbing up a flight of stairs, with each of his movements adding a new step to all those he has passed. It is rather like a player whose luck is resting on several dice and who, each time he throws, sees them scattered on the table, with a variety of combinations. What one wins on one throw is always liable to be lost on another. It is only from time to time that history is cumulative—in other words, that the numbers can be added up to form a favorable combination.

The example of America shows convincingly enough that this cumulative history is not the exclusive privilege of one civilization or one period of history. This immense continent doubtlessly saw man arrive in small groups of nomads moving over the Behring strait in the course of the last ice age, at a date which modern archaeological knowledge tentatively sets around the twentieth millennium B.C. During this period, these men achieved one of the world's most astonishing demonstrations of cumulative history. They explored thoroughly the resources of a new natural environment. Besides the domestication of some animal species, they cultivated the most diverse vegetable forms for their food, their remedies, and their poisons. And—something unequaled anywhere else—they adapted such poisonous substances as cassava plants to the role of basic food; they used other plants as stimulants or anesthetics; they collected certain poisons or narcotics according to the way they affected certain animal species; finally, they perfected to the highest degree certain industries such as weaving, ceramics, and the working of precious metals. In order to appreciate this immense accomplishment, it is enough to measure the contribution of America against the civilizations of the Old World. In the first place, there are potatoes, rubber, tobacco, and coca (the basis of modern anesthetics) which, in various ways, constitute four pillars of Western culture; there are corn and ground nuts, which were to completely transform the African economy before becoming widespread in the alimentary diet of Europe; then cocoa, vanilla, tomatoes, pineapples, pimentos, several types of beans, cotton, and gourds. Finally, the zero, basis of arithmetic (and, indirectly, of modern mathematics), was known and used by the Mayas at least half a millennium before being discovered by Indian scholars, from whom Europe received it through the Arabs. For this reason perhaps, their calendar was then more accurate than that of the Old World. Much ink has been spilled about the question whether the political regime of the Incas was socialist or totalitarian. In any case it fell within the most modern formulae and was many centuries ahead of European phenomena of the same type. The recent revival of interest in curare should call to mind, if necessary, that the scientific knowledge of the native Americans, applied to so many vegetable substances unused in the rest of the world, can still provide the latter with important contributions.

Static History and Cumulative History

The preceding discussion of the American example should urge us to push on further with our reflection on the difference between "static history" and "cumulative history." If we have granted America the privilege of cumulative history, is it not only in effect because we recognize it as the birthplace of a certain number of contributions we have borrowed from it or which resemble ours? But what would be our position before a civilization which had tended to develop its own values, none of which were liable to be of interest to the observer's civilization? Would he not be inclined to see this civilization as static? In other words, does the distinction between the two forms of history depend on the intrinsic nature of cultures to which it is applied, or does it not result from the ethnocentric perspective in which we always put ourselves to evaluate a different culture? We would thus see as cumulative any culture which developed in a way analogous to ours—in other words, whose development would have a *meaning* for us. Whereas the other cultures would seem to us static—not necessarily because they are so, but because the line of their development means nothing to us and cannot be measured in terms of the system of references which we use.

That this is obviously the case is shown by even a summary examination of the conditions in which we apply the distinction between the two histories—to characterize not those societies different from ours but those within the very midst of our own. This application is more frequent than one would believe. Older people generally consider as static the history unfolding during their old age, as opposed to the cumulative history which they witnessed in their younger days. An era in which the old people are no longer active, in which they no longer play a part, has no more meaning; nothing happens in it, or they only see a negative character in whatever happens. On the other hand, their grand-children live this period with all that fervor their elders have lost. The enemies of a political regime do not willingly recognize that it evolves; they condemn it in its totality and place it outside of history, as a sort of monstrous intermission only at the end of which life will start again. Very different is the conception of the regime's partisans and all the more so, we must observe, as they participate closely at a high level in the functioning of the apparatus. Historicity, or more precisely the wealth of events in a culture or a cultural process, are functions not of their intrinsic properties but of the situation in which we find ourselves in relation to them, of the number and the diversity of the interests we have secured in them. The opposition between progressive cultures and static cultures thus seems to result, first, from a difference of focus. For the observer at the microscope, who has set the focus at a certain measured distance from the object, the bodies located before and beyond it—even if the distance is only a few hundredths of a millimeter—appear confused and unclear or do not even appear at all; we see through them.

Another comparison permits us to reveal the same illusion: the one used to explain the first rudiments of the theory of relativity. In order to demonstrate that the dimension and speed of the displacement of bodies are not absolute values, but functions of the observer's position, we are reminded that, for a passenger sitting by the window of a train, the speed and length of the other trains vary according to whether they move in the same direction or the opposite way. And every member of a culture is as closely linked to that culture as the imaginary passenger is to his train. From the day we are born, our environment penetrates us through a thousand conscious or unconscious processes, with a complex system of references consisting in value judgements, motivations, and centers of interest (including the reflexive view of the historical development of our civilization imposed upon us by our education), without all of which this civilization would become unthinkable or would appear to be in contradiction with real behavior. We literally move along this system of references, and the exterior cultural realities can only be observed through the deformation imposed by it (when it does not go so far as to make it impossible for us to perceive any of it).

To a very large degree, the distinction between "mobile cultures" and "immobile cultures" is explained by the same changes in perspective which make a moving train seem mobile or immobile to our passenger. All the same, it is true that there will be a difference whose full impact will appear on that day—as yet far away, but surely coming—when we shall seek to formulate a theory of relativity generalized quite differently from Einstein's —one that is applicable at the same time to physical sciences and social sciences (in both, everything seems to happen in a symmetrical but inverted manner). To the observer of the physical world, as the example of the passenger in the train shows, it is those systems evolving in the same direction as his own which seem immobile, while the fastest ones are those which evolve in different directions. It is the other way around for cultures, since they seem to us all the more active as they go in the same direction as ours, and stationary when their direction diverges. But in the case of the sciences of man, the *speed* factor has only a metaphorical value. To make the comparison valid, the speed factor must be replaced by *information* and *meaning*. We know that it is possible to accumulate far more information about a train moving along a parallel path at a speed similar to ours (one can see the faces of the passengers, count them, etc.) than about a train which passes us, or which we pass at very great speed, or which seems to us to get shorter because it goes in another direction. At the limit, it goes so fast that we can only keep a confused impression of it from which the very signs of speed are absent; it is reduced to a temporary blurring of the field of vision. It is no longer a train, it *signifies* nothing anymore. It seems to me that a relation exists between the physical notion of *apparent movement* and another notion that equally pertains to physics, psychology, and sociology: that of the *quantity of information* able to "pass" between two individuals or groups, as a function of the greater or lesser diversity of their respective cultures. Each time we tend to classify a human culture as inert or static, we must ask ourselves if this apparent lack of mobility does not result from our ignorance of its true interests, conscious or unconscious; and if, possessing criteria different from our own, this culture is not—as far as we are concerned—victim of the same illusion. In other words, we would appear to each other as devoid of interest, quite simply because we do not resemble one another.

Western civilization has been entirely devoted, for the last two or three centuries, to putting more and more powerful mechanical means at the disposition of man. If this criterion is adopted, the quantity of energy available per inhabitant will become the greater and lesser scale of measuring the development of human societies. Western civilization in its North American form will occupy the top place, the European, Soviet, and Japanese societies coming next, and trailing behind, a mass of Asiatic and African societies which will soon become indistinguishable. Yet, these hundreds or even thousands of societies we call "underdeveloped" and "primitive" are not really identical, although they are merged in a confused whole when they are considered in the manner we just mentioned (which is hardly a suitable way to classify them, since this line of development is entirely lacking among them or occupies quite a secondary place). From other perspectives, they are situated at opposite ends from one another, so we would end up with different classifications, depending on the point of view elected.

If the criterion used were the degree of ability to triumph over the most hostile geographical environment, there is hardly any doubt that the Eskimo on the one hand, the Bedouin on the other, would be the great winners. India, better than any other civilization, has been able to develop a philosophical and religious system, and China a way of life, both of which are able to reduce the psychological consequences of demographic disequilibrium. Already thirteen centuries ago, Islam formulated a theory of the solidarity of all forms of human life—technical, economic, social, and spiritual—which the Western world was to rediscover only quite recently with certain aspects of Marxist thought and the beginnings of modern ethnology. One knows the prominent place this prophetic vision gave to the Arabs in the intellectual life of the Middle Ages. The Western world, master of machinery, shows a very elementary knowledge of the use and resource of that supreme piece of machinery which is the human body. Conversely, in this domain as in the related area of the connection between the physical and the moral, the Orient and the Far East are several millennia ahead of the West. They have produced vast theoretical and practical totalities, like the yoga of India, the breathing techniques of the Chinese, or the visceral gymnastics of the ancient Maori. The agriculture without soil, so recently made fashionable, was practiced for several centuries by some Polynesian peoples who could also have taught the world the art of navigation, and deeply disturbed the eighteenth century by revealing to it a type of social and moral life more generous and free than anything one could suspect.

In everything which concerns family organization and the harmonious relationships between familial and social groups, the Australians, who are backward on the economic level, are so far ahead of the rest of humanity that it is necessary, in order to understand the systems of rules they elaborated in a conscious and thoughtful manner, to call upon certain forms of modern mathematics. They are the ones who have really discovered that marriage rules form the canvas on which the other social institutions are only the embroidery. For even in modern societies, where the role of the family tends to be reduced, the intensity of family ties is not smaller; it is only confined in a tighter circle, at the limits of which other links, related to other families, immediately come to take over. The articulation of families through intermarriages may lead to the formation of broad bonds between a few entities or of small bonds between numerous groupings; but, small or large, it is these hinges which keep the whole social structure together and give it its flexibility. In a manner often very lucid, the Australians have made up the theory of this mechanism and listed the principal methods which make it possible, with the advantages and disadvantages of each. They have also gone beyond the level of empirical observation and proceeded to the knowledge of certain laws regulating the system. Thus, it is no exaggeration to see them, not only as the precursors of all familial sociology, but also as the ones who really first applied speculative strictness to the study of social facts.

The wealth and daring of aesthetic invention among the Melanesians—the talent they show for integrating into social life the most obscure products of the mind's inconscious activity—constitute one of the highest peaks achieved by man in that direction. The contribution of Africa is more complex, but also more obscure, since it is only recently that one has started to suspect the importance of its role as a cultural "melting pot" of the ancient world: a place where all the influences have merged, either to leave again or be kept in reserve, but always to be transformed. The Egyptian civilization, whose importance for humanity we know, is only intelligible as a common work of Asia and Africa. The great political systems of ancient Africa, its juridical constructions, its philosophical doctrines long concealed from Western minds, and its plastic arts and music—which methodically explore all the possibilities afforded by each means of expression—are so many clues to an extraordinarily fertile past. Moreover, the latter is directly confirmed by the perfection of the ancient techniques of working bronze and ivory, which go so far beyond everything the Western world was producing at the same period. We have already mentioned the American contribution, and it is not necessary to come back to it.

Furthermore, it is not so much these scattered contributions which ought to retain our attention, for they would risk giving us the doubly erroneous idea of a world civilization tailored like a Harlequin's suit. Too much has been made of all the discoverers: the Phoenicians for writing; the Chinese for paper, gun powder, and the compass; the Indians for glass and steel. These elements are less important than the way in which each culture groups them, retains them, or rejects them. The originality of each culture consists rather in its specific application to the solving of problems, it giving a certain perspective to its values, which are approximately the same for all men. For all men, without exception, have a language, technical skills, art, positive knowledge, religious beliefs, and a social, economic, and political organization. Yet, the composite mixture of these is never exactly the same for each culture, and modern ethnology seeks more and more to uncover the secret origin of these selections rather than to make an inventory of the separate features.

The Place of Western Civilization

One may formulate some objections against such an argument because of its theoretical nature. It may be said, at the level of abstract logic, that one culture is unable to hold a true judgment about another; since a culture cannot get away from itself, its judgment remains caught in a relativism without appeal. But look around you. Pay attention to what has been happening in the world for a century, and all your speculations will collapse. Far from remaining locked within themselves, all civilizations, one after another, recognize the superiority of one among them: the Western civilization. Do we not see the whole world progressively borrowing its techniques, its way of life, its entertainments, and even its clothing? Just as Diogenes proved motion by walking, so it is the very march of human cultures (from the huge masses of Asia to the tribes lost in the Brazilian and African jungles) which proves by a unanimous rallying, unprecedented in history, that one form of human civilization is superior to all others. What the "underdeveloped" countries reproach the others with in international assemblies is not that they westernize them, but that they do not provide the means for becoming westernized fast enough.

We touch here the most sensitive point of our discussion. It would be useless to want to defend the originality of human cultures against themselves. Moreover, it is extremely difficult for the ethnologist to judge accurately a phenomenon such as the universalization of Western culture, and this for several reasons. First of all, the existence of a world civilization is probably a unique fact in history; at least, its precedents would have to be sought in a remote prehistory about which we know almost nothing. Next, a great uncertainty reigns over the consistency of the phenomenon in question. It is a fact that for a century and a half Western civilization has tended, either in its totality or through some of its key elements (such as industrialization) to spread throughout the world. It is also true that, to the extent that other cultures try to preserve some of their traditional heritage, their attempt is generally reduced to the superstructures, that is, the most fragile aspects will presumably be swept away by the profound transformations taking place. But this phenomenon is in progress and we do not yet know how it will end. Will it end up in a total westernization of the planet, with Russian and American variants? Will syncretic forms appear, as one perceives the possibility of westernization for the Islamic world, India, and China? Or, finally, is the tide already at its peak, and will it diminish to the point where the Western world is close to succumbing (like the prehistoric monsters) to a physical expansion incompatible with the internal mechanisms ensuring its existence? It is with all these reservations in mind that we will attempt to evaluate the process unfolding under our eyes and of which we are the conscious or unconscious agents, accomplices, or victims.

We will begin by noting that this adoption of the Western way of life (or of some of its aspects) is far from being as spontaneous as Western people would like to think. It is less the result of a free decision than of a lack of choice. Western civilization has established its soldiers, its trading posts, its plantations, and its missionaries throughout the entire world. It has directly or indirectly intervened in the life of colored populations. It has thoroughly upset other traditional ways of life, either by imposing its own in their stead or by establishing such conditions that cause the disappearance of existing frameworks without replacing them by something else. Thus, conquered or disorganized peoples could only accept the substitute solutions which were offered to them; or, if they were unwilling to do so, they could only hope to get sufficiently close to the substitutes that they could fight them on their own ground. In the absence of this inequality in the proportions of the forces, societies do not surrender all that easily. Their *Weltanschauung* is closer to that of those poor tribes of Eastern Brazil by whom the ethnographer Curt Nimuendaju was able to make himself adopted. Every time he would come back to them after a sojourn in civilized parts, the natives would weep with pity at the thought of the sufferings he must have undergone away from the only place—their village—where they felt life was worth living.

However, by making this reservation, we have only shifted the question. If Western superiority does not rest on consent, is it not then due to its greater energy, which precisely enabled it to force consent? Here we reach the core of the argument because this inequality of force no longer pertains to collective subjectivity, as the adhesion we mentioned earlier. It is an objective phenomenon which can only be explained by calling upon objective causes.

We do not intend to attempt here a philosophical study of civilizations. While we could discuss for whole volumes the nature of those values professed by Western civilization, we will only mention the most obvious ones, those least subject to controversy. They seem to be reduced to two: Western civilization seeks, on the one hand, according to Leslie White's expression, to increase continuously the quantity of energy available per inhabitant, and on the other hand, to protect and prolong human life. If one wants to be brief, the second aspect will be considered as a modality of the first since the quantity of available energy increases—in absolute value—with the length and the integrity of individual life.

To avoid any arguments, we will also admit, to begin with, that these characteristics can go together with compensating phenomena, acting as a braking device, in a way. Thus the great massacres of world wars, and the inequality which rules the distribution of available energy between individuals and between classes.

This being established, we immediately note that if Western civilization has in fact given itself entirely to these tasks in the exclusive manner in which, perhaps, lies its weakness, it is certainly not the only civilization to have done so. All human societies, since the most remote times, have acted in the same way; and it is those very distant and very archaic societies, which we would willingly equate to today's "savage" peoples, that have accomplished the most decisive progress in that direction. At the present time, this progress still constitutes the greater part of what we call civilization. We still depend on these enormous discoveries which have marked what was called, without the slightest exaggeration, "the Neolithic revolution," namely, agriculture, animal breeding, pottery, and weaving. To all these "arts of civilization," we have brought only some improvements over the last eight or ten thousand years.

It is true that certain minds have the unfortunate tendency to reserve the privilege of effort, intelligence, and imagination to recent discoveries, and to assume that those accomplished by humanity during its "barbarian" period were due only to chance and thus invited no praise. This aberration seems so serious and so widespread, and it is so profoundly likely to prevent us from acquiring an accurate view of the relationship between cultures, that we believe it is vitally necessary to dispel it entirely.

Chance and Civilization

We read in ethnology manuals—and not in the lesser ones—that man owes his knowledge of fire to some accidental lightning or brush fire; that finding game accidentally roasted under these conditions revealed to him the cooking of food; that the invention of pottery is the result of some lump of clay being forgotten near a fire. It would seem as if man had first lived in a sort of technological golden age, in which one picked inventions as easily as fruits and flowers. To modern man would be reserved the toils of labor and the illuminations of genius.

This naïve view stems from a total ignorance of the complexity and the diversity of the operations implied in the most elementary techniques. To fashion an efficient flint tool, it is not enough to pound a stone until it bursts—that became very obvious the day we tried to reproduce the principal types of prehistoric tools. In this way—and also by observing the same technique among people who still practice it—was discovered the complexity of the necessary processes involved, sometimes entailing the preliminary manufacture of true "cutting tools," such as balanced hammers to control the impact and its direction, and damping devices to prevent the vibration from splitting the flint. What is also necessary is a vast accumulation of knowledge on the local origin, the processes of extraction, the resistance and the structure of the materials used, and adequate physical training, the knowledge of the "tricks of the trade," etc., in a word a true "liturgy" corresponding, *mutatis mutandis*, to the various chapters of metallurgy.

In the same manner, natural fires may sometimes grill or roast. But it is very difficult to imagine (outside of volcanic phenomena, which have a restricted geographical distribution) that they cook by boiling or steaming. Yet, these cooking methods are no less universal than the others. Thus there is no reason to exclude the inventiveness that is certainly required for the latter methods, when one wants to explain the former.

Pottery offers an excellent example, because of a widespread belief that nothing is easier than to fashion a lump of clay and harden it in fire. Just try and do it. First, the right type of clay must be found for firing. And, if a great number of natural conditions are necessary for this purpose, none is sufficient, for clay has to be mixed with some inert matter, chosen with regard to its specific characteristics in order to produce a usable container after firing. Modeling techniques must be elaborated in order to realize this feat of keeping in balance for quite some time, and to modify at the same time, a plastic substance which does not "hold." Finally, there are the special types of heating material, the shape of the kiln, the type of heat, and the duration of firing, all of which serve, despite the possible mishaps—cracks, crumbling, deformations—to make it strong and waterproof. The examples could be multiplied.

All these operations are far too numerous and complex to be accounted for by sheer luck. Each one of them taken separately means nothing. It is only their combination, imagined, willed, and sought by experiment, which allowed success. Chance undoubtedly exists, but it produces no result by itself. For some two and a half millennia the Western world has known of the existence of electricity—discovered by chance no doubt—but this chance was to remain fruitless until the purposeful experimentation of such people as Ampère and Faraday. Nor did chance play any greater part in the invention of the bow, the boomerang, or the blowgun (or in the emergence of agriculture and animal breeding) than it did in the discovery of penicillin. Thus one must carefully distinguish between the transmission of a technique from one generation to another (which always occurs relatively easily thanks to observation and daily practice) and the creation or the improvement of techniques within each generation. The latter always presupposes the same power of imagination and the same determined efforts on the part of some individuals, whatever the particular technique considered. Those societies we call primitive are no less rich in Pasteurs and Palissys than the others (Lévi-Strauss, 1966).

Later we will return to chance and probability, but in another place and with another function. We will not lazily use them to explain the appearance of ready-made inventions, but to interpret a phenomenon at another level of reality. In spite of a proportion of imagination, of invention, and creative effort (which we may assume remains more or less constant throughout the history of humanity), this combination only produces important cultural mutations at certain times and in certain environments. Purely psychological factors are not sufficient to achieve this result. They must first be present, with a similar orientation, among a sufficient number of individuals for the creator to be at once assured of a public; and this itself depends on the combination of a great number of other factors—historical, economic, and sociological. Thus, in order to explain differences in the course of civilizations, one would be forced to invoke combinations of causes so complex and so discontinuous that they would be impossible to understand, either for practical reasons, or even for such theoretical reasons as the unavoidable complications inherent to the techniques of observation. In fact, to unravel a skein composed of so many tenuous threads, one would at least have to submit the society in question (and also the world around it) to a total and continuous ethnographic study. Even without mentioning the enormity of the enterprise, we know that ethnographers, although working on a much reduced scale, are often limited in their observations by the subtle changes that their presence alone is enough to introduce into the human group, the object of their study. With modern societies, we also know that public opinion polls modify the orientation of opinion by the very fact of their use, by creating among people a factor of self-awareness which did not exist before.

This situation justifies the introduction into the social sciences of the notion of probability, which has for a long time existed in certain branches of physics (in thermodynamics, for example). We will come back to this later. For the time being, it is enough to remember that the complexity of modern discoveries does not result from a greater frequency or a greater availability of genius among our contemporaries. Quite the contrary, since we have recognized that through the centuries each generation has only to add a constant interest to the capital bequeathed by the previous generations in order to progress. We owe them nine-tenths of our wealth, and even more if—as someone calculated for fun—one evaluates the appearance date of the principal discoveries in relation to the approximate beginnings of civilization. We note that agriculture appeared in the course of a recent phase corresponding to 2 percent of this period; metallurgy to 0.7 percent; the alphabet to 0.35 percent; Galileo's physics to 0.035 percent and Darwinism to 0.009 percent (White 1949, p. 350). The scientific and industrial revolution of the West is totally included in a period equal to about one-half of a thousandth part of the life span of humanity. Thus one should exercise some caution before maintaining that this revolution is destined to change entirely the meaning of humanity.

It is nonetheless true—and this, we believe, is the definitive formulation which can be given to our problem—that, from the point of view of technical inventions (and of the scientific thought which makes them possible), Western civilization has proved to be more cumulative than others; and that after having disposed of the same initial Neolithic capital, it knew how to bring about certain improvements (alphabetic writing, arithmetic, and geometry) some of which were rapidly forgotten. But after a stagnation that spread, over two or two and a half millennia (from the first millennium B.C. until about the eighteenth century), the West suddenly showed itself as the center of an industrial revolution which equalled the Neolithic revolution by its magnitude, its universal character, and the importance of its results.

Consequently, twice in its history, and in a span of some ten thousand years, humanity was able to accumulate a multiplicity of inventions orientated in the same direction. This multiplicity, on the one hand, and the continuity on the other, are concentrated in a period of time short enough for the operation of highly technical syntheses. These have led to significant changes in relationships that man has with nature and which, in turn, have made other changes possible. The image of a chain reaction, started by catalytic bodies, permits the illustration of this process which, until now, has taken place twice, and twice only, in the history of mankind. How did this happen?

First, we must not forget that other revolutions, presenting the same cumulative characteristics, have happened elsewhere and at other times, but in different fields of human activity. We explained above why our own industrial revolution together with the Neolithic revolution (which preceded it in time but which stems from the same preoccupations) are the only ones which can appear to us as such, because our system of references enables us to measure them. All the other changes which certainly took place only reveal themselves in the form of fragments, or as thoroughly distorted. They cannot *make sense* for modern Western man (in any case not all their importance). For him, they might just as well not exist.

In the second place, the example of the Neolithic revolution (the only one which modern Western man succeeds in understanding clearly enough) must inspire him with some humility about the preeminence he might feel tempted to claim for one race, one region, or one country. The industrial revolution was born in Western Europe; then it appeared in the United States, and next in Japan. Since 1917, it has increased in the Soviet Union, and tomorrow it will no doubt spring up somewhere else. From one half-century to another, it shines with a more or less bright light in one or another of its centers. On the scale of millennia, what becomes of those questions of priority of which we are so vain?

Give or take one or two millennia, the Neolithic revolution started simultaneously in the Aegean basin, in Egypt, in the Near East, in the Indus valley, and in China. And since the discovery of radioactive carbon to determine archaeological periods, we suspect that the American Neolithic period was more ancient than was once believed, it is very likely that it did not start much later than in the Old World. It is likely that three or four little valleys could even claim to have been a few centuries ahead in this contest of priority. What do we know about it today? In any case, we are sure that the question of priority is not important—precisely because the simultaneous appearance of the same technological upheavals (closely followed by social upheavals) in such vast territories and in such remote regions makes it obvious that it did not depend on the genius of a race or a culture, but on conditions so general that they are outside the consciousness of men. Let us then be assured that if the Industrial Revolution had not made its first appearance in Western and Northern Europe, it would have appeared one day in some other part of the world. And if, as is likely, it has to spread to the whole of the inhabited world, each culture will introduce into it so many particular contributions that the historian of the distant future will legitimately hold as futile the questions of knowing who, within one or two centuries, may claim to have been the first.

This established, we must introduce a new limitation, if not so much as to the validity, at least about the exactness of the distinction between static and cumulative history. Not only is this distinction related to our interests, as we have already shown, but it never succeeds in being quite clear-cut. In the case of technical inventions, it is plain that no period, no culture is absolutely static. All peoples own and transform, improve or forget techniques complex enough to enable them to dominate their environment; without these techniques they would have disappeared a long time ago. So the difference is never between cumulative and noncumulative history—all history is cumulative in various degrees. We know for example that the ancient Chinese and the Eskimos had advanced the art of mechanics very far, and developments had gone extremely close to starting a "chain reaction" which would determine the passage of one type of civilization to another. We know the example of gun powder: the Chinese had solved, technically speaking, all the problems it posed, except the one of its usage with a view to great results. The ancient Mexicans did not ignore the wheel, as it is often said. They knew it well enough to manufacture toys on wheels for children; only one further step would have been required to give them the cart.

Under these conditions, the problem of the relative rarity (for each system of references) of "more cumulative" cultures in relation to "less cumulative" cultures is reduced to the well-known problem of the theory of probability. The same problem consists in determining the relative probability of a complex combination in relation to other, less complex combinations of the same type. In roulette for instance, a sequence of two consecutive numbers (e.g., 7 and 8, 12 and 13, 30 and 31) is fairly common. A sequence of three consecutive numbers is already rare, one of four, much more so. And it is only once out of an extremely high number of throws that a sequence of six, seven, or eight numbers might perhaps occur in a consecutive order. If we fix our attention exclusively on the long sequences (for instance, if we bet on a sequence of five consecutive numbers), the shorter series will become for us equivalent to nonconsecutive sequences. This is to forget that they only differ from ours by a fraction and that, considered from another angle, they may present equally strong regularities. Let us take our comparison still further. A player who would transfer all his winnings to longer and longer sequences could become discouraged, after thousands or millions of throws, in never seeing the sequence of nine consecutive numbers appear, and think that he would have been better off to stop sooner. Yet, there is nothing to prove that another player, following the same betting formula but on another type of sequence (for instance, a certain rhythm of alternation between red and black, or between odd and even), would not see as significant combinations what the first player would only perceive as disorder. Mankind does not evolve in one way. If, at a certain point, his development seems stationary or even regressive, this does not mean that, from another point of view, there are not important transformations.

David Hume, the great English philosopher of the eighteenth century, one day decided to solve the imaginary problem that perplexes many people who wonder why instead of all women being pretty, only a small minority of them are. He easily demonstrated that the question is meaningless. If all women were at least as pretty as the most beautiful one among them, we would find them ordinary and would only call pretty that small minority who would surpass the common model. In the same manner, when a certain type of progress interests us, we give credit for it to those cultures in which it is most perfected, and we remain indifferent to the others. Thus progress is nothing but the maximum of progress, predetermined, in a sense, by everyone's taste.

The Collaboration of Cultures

Let us now consider our problem from a final point of view. A player such as the one mentioned before, who would only bet on the longest sequences (in whatever way these sequences may be conceived) would be most likely to lose all his money. But such would not be the case with a coalition of gamblers playing on the same sequences of absolute value—but also on several roulette tables, thereby giving themselves the advantage of putting together the favorable results of each player's combinations. For if, having alone drawn 21 and 22, I need 23 to continue my sequence, there are of course more chances for that number to appear among ten tables than on a single one.

This situation is very much like that of cultures that have succeeded in realizing the most cumulative forms of history. These extreme forms have never been isolated cultures, but rather cultures which willy-nilly combined their respective games and realized through various means (migrations, borrowings, commercial exchanges, wars) those *coalitions* of which we have just imagined the model. And this is where we touch upon the absurdity of declaring one culture superior to another. Indeed, if a culture were alone, it could never be "superior." Like the isolated gambler, it could only make a success of small sequences of a few elements, and the probability of a long sequence "coming out" in its history would be so small (without being theoretically excluded) that one would have to include an infinitely longer time than the one during which the total development of mankind takes place to ever hope to see it realized. But, as we have mentioned above, no culture is isolated. It is always in coalition with other cultures, and this is what enables it to build cumulative sequences. The probability that, among these sequences, one longer than the others might appear naturally depends on the range, the duration, and the variation of the coalition regime.

Two consequences emerge from these remarks. In the course of this study, we wondered several times how humanity could have remained stationary during nine-tenths of its history, and even longer. The first civilizations are from two to five hundred thousand years old, yet the conditions of life only transformed themselves during the last ten thousand years. If our analysis is accurate, it is not because Paleolithic man was less intelligent, less gifted than his Neolithic successor. It is simply because, in human history, a combination (to the degree n) has taken a time of duration (t) to emerge; it could have happened much earlier, or much later. The fact is no more significant than the number of throws a player must wait for to see a given combination occur. This combination can happen on the first throw, or the thousandth, or the millionth, or never. But during all that time, humanity, like the player, does not stop speculating. Without always wanting to, and without ever being quite aware of it, humanity "sets up cultural business," throws itself into civilizing "operations" which are not always crowned with success. Sometimes it comes close to succeeding, sometimes it compromises previous acquisitions. The great simplifications allowed by our ignorance of most aspects of prehistoric societies permit one to illustrate this uncertain and ramified progress, since nothing is more striking than these second thoughts leading from the Levalloisian zenith to the Mousterian mediocrity, from the Aurignacian and Solutrian splendors to the Magdalenian coarseness, then to the extreme contrasts afforded by the various aspects of the Mesolithic.

What is true in time is no less true in space, but it must be expressed in another manner. The chance that a culture has to put together this complex totality of inventions of all orders which we call a civilization is a function of the number and the diversity of the cultures with which it participates in the elaboration—most often involuntary—of a common strategy. We speak of number and diversity. The comparison between the Old World and the New World on the eve of the discovery illustrates this double necessity very well.

At the beginning of the Renaissance, Europe was a place where the most varied influences met and merged, such as the Greek, Roman, Germanic, and Anglo-Saxon traditions, and the

Arabic and Chinese influences. Pre-Columbian America did not enjoy, quantitatively speaking, fewer cultural contacts, for the American cultures enjoyed relationships, and together the two Americas formed an immense continent. But whereas the cultures which fertilized one another in Europe are the product of a differentiation several millennia old, those of America, more recently populated, have had less time to diverge, and they present a more homogeneous aspect. Thus, although one cannot say that the cultural level of Mexico or Peru was, at the time of discovery, inferior to that of Europe (we have even seen that in many regards it was superior to it), the various aspects of culture were perhaps also less well formulated. Side by side with amazing successes, the pre-Columbian civilizations are full of failures; they have, as it were, "blanks" in them. They also offer the sight, less contradictory than we may think, of the coexistence of precarious forms and abortive forms. Their rather stiff and weakly diversified organization very likely explains their total collapse in front of a handful of conquerors. The deep cause of it may be sought in the fact that the American cultural "coalition" was established between partners who differed less among themselves than those of the Old World.

Thus, there is no cumulative society in itself and by itself. Cumulative history is not the property of certain races or certain cultures which would thus be distinguishable from others. It results from their *behavior* rather than from their *nature*. It expresses a certain way of life of cultures which is nothing other than their *manner of being together*. In this sense, it can be said that cumulative history is that form of history which characterizes those social superorganisms made up of groups of societies, whereas static history—if it really existed—would be the mark of that type of inferior life which pertains to isolated societies.

The exclusive fatality, the unique fault which can afflict a human group and prevent it from completely fulfilling its nature, is to be alone.

Thus one often distinguishes what is awkward and unsatisfying for the mind in those attempts, which are usually deemed sufficient, to justify the contribution of the human races and cultures to civilization. Features are enumerated, questions of origin are carefully examined, priorities are perceived. As well meant as these efforts may be, they are futile because they fail in three ways. First, the credit for an invention attributed to such or such a culture is never certain. Secondly, cultural contributions can always be split into groups. On the one side, we have features, isolated acquisitions, whose importance is easy to evaluate and which also present a limited character. Tobacco came from America; this is a fact. But after all, and despite all the good intentions of the international institutions to this end, we cannot melt with gratitude toward the American Indians every time we smoke a cigarette. Tobacco is a delightful adjunct to the art of living, as others are useful ones (rubber, for instance). We owe them additional pleasure and convenience, but if they did not exist the roots of our civilization would not be shaken up. And so far as a serious need for them is concerned, we would have known how to find them or to put something else in their place.

At the opposite pole (with, naturally, a whole series of intermediate forms) are the contributions offering the character of a system, that is, those corresponding to the specific manner in which each society has chosen to express and satisfy the totality of human aspirations. The originality and irreplaceable nature of these life styles (or "patterns" as the Anglo-Saxons put it) cannot be denied, but they represent so many exclusive choices and one does not easily recognize how one civilization could hope to benefit from the life style of another, unless by renouncing being itself. In fact, the attempts at compromise are only likely to lead to two results: either the disorganization or collapse of the system of one of the groups; or an original synthesis, but one which then consists in the emergence of a third system which cannot be reduced to the other two. Actually, the problem is not even to know whether a society can or cannot derive profit from the life style of its neighbors, but whether and to what extent it can succeed in understanding them and even in knowing them. We saw that this question offers no definite answer.

Finally, there is no contribution without a beneficiary. But if there are actual cultures which can be located in space and time, and of which it can be said that they have made a "contribution" and are still doing so, what is this "world civilization," the supposed beneficiary of all these contributions? It is not a civilization distinct from all the others, enjoying a same coefficient of reality. When we speak of world civilization, we do not mean an era of history, or a group of men. We are thinking of an abstract notion, to which we attribute either a moral or logical value: moral in the case of a goal we have proposed for existing societies; logical if we mean to group under the same term the common elements which can be drawn from the different cultures by analysis. In both cases, we must acknowledge the fact that the notion of a world civilization is a poor one, schematic and with little intellectual and emotional content. A desire to evaluate cultural contributions heavy with thousands of years of history and with all the weight of thoughts, sufferings, desires, and labors of the men who brought them to life, and exclusively to measure them against the standard of a world civilization which is still a hollow form—such a desire would be to impoverish them considerably, to empty them of their substance, and to keep nothing of them but a body without flesh.

On the contrary, we have tried to show that the real contribution of cultures does not consist in a list of their particular inventions but in the *contrastive features* which exist between them. The feeling of gratitude and humility which each member of a given culture can and should feel toward all the others can only be based on a single conviction: that the other cultures differ from his own in the most varied manner—this, even if the ultimate nature of these differences escapes him or if (despite all his efforts) he only succeeds in imperfectly understanding it.

We have considered the notion of a world civilization as a sort of extreme idea or as an abridged way of designating a complex process. If our demonstration is valid, there is not—there cannot be—a world civilization in the absolute sense which is sometimes given this term. For civilization implies the coexistence of cultures offering among themselves the maximum of diversity, and even consists in this very coexistence. World civilization could not be anything on the world scale except the coalition of cultures, each preserving its originality.

The Double Meaning of Progress

Are we not then finding ourselves confronted with a strange paradox? Taking the terms with the meaning we gave them, we say that all cultural *progress* is a function of a *coalition* among the cultures. This coalition consists in putting together (in a manner conscious or unconscious, voluntary or involuntary, intentional or accidental, sought for or constrained) the *chances* which are met by each culture in its historical development. Finally, we have admitted that this coalition is all the more fruitful when it exists among more diversified cultures. This established, it seems that we are faced with contradictory conditions. For this *common game*, from which all progress results, must sooner or later result in the *homogenization* of the resources of each player. And if diversity is an initial condition, we will see that the chances of winning become less as the game is prolonged.

For this inescapable consequence, there only seem to be two remedies. One consists in each player provoking contrasting features in his game. This is possible, since each society (i.e., the "player" of our theoretical model) is composed of a coalition of groups—religious, professional, and economic—and the social stake is made up of the stakes of all these elements. Social inequalities are the most striking examples of this solution. The great revolutions which we have chosen as an illustration, the Neolithic and the industrial, came along with not only a diversification of the social body (as Spencer had seen so well) but also the institution of contrasting statuses among the groups, especially from the economic point of view. We have long observed that the Neolithic discoveries quickly led to social differentiation, with the emergence in the ancient Orient of great urban concentrations and the appearance of states, castes, and classes. The same observation can be made about the Industrial Revolution, conditioned by the appearance of a proletariat and leading to new and more advanced forms of exploitation of human labor. Until now, one tended to treat these social transformations as the consequence of technical transformations, and to establish between them a relationship of cause and effect. If our interpretation is accurate, the causal relation (with the temporal succession it implies) must be abandoned (and this is actually the general tendency of modern science) in favor of a functional correlation between the two phenomena. Let us note in passing that acknowledgment of the fact that technical progress has had the development of the exploitation of man by man as an historical corrective may incite us to a certain discretion in the manifestations of pride which the first of these phenomena so willingly inspires in us.

The second remedy is largely conditioned by the first. It consists of introducing, willy-nilly, into the coalition new partners, external this time, whose "stakes" would be very different from those characterized by the initial association. This solution was also tried out and if the term "capitalism" permits identification with the first one on the whole, "imperialism" or "colonialism" will help to illustrate the second. The colonial expansion of the nineteenth century largely enabled industrial Europe to renew—certainly not for its exclusive benefit—a forward thrust which, if the enslaved peoples had been introduced into the process, would have risked a much faster depletion.

We see that in both cases the remedy consists in enlarging the coalition, either by internal diversification or through the inclusion of new partners. In the final analysis, the problem is always to increase the number of players; in other words, to come back to the complexity and the diversity of the initial situation. But we also see that these solutions can only slow down the process temporarily. Exploitation can exist only within a coalition. Between dominating and dominated groups, contacts exist and exchanges are produced. In their turn, and in spite of the unilateral relationship which apparently links them, they must, consciously or unconsciously, put together their "stakes"; and the differences which oppose them tend to be reduced progressively. Social improvements, on the one hand, and the gradual accession of colonized peoples to independence, on the other, present us with the unfolding of this phenomenon. Although there is still a long way to go in both directions, we know that things will inevitably go that way. Perhaps, indeed, we must interpret as a third solution the appearance of antagonistic political and social regimes in the world. It is conceivable that a diversification, every time renewing itself at another level, could make it possible to maintain indefinitely—through variable forms which will never cease to surprise men—this state of disequilibrium on which the biological and cultural survival of mankind depend.

Anyway, it is difficult to conceive of as anything but contradictory a process which can be summarized in the following manner: In order to progress, men must collaborate; and in the course of this collaboration they see the gradual pooling of their contributions whose initial diversity was precisely what made their collaboration fecund and necessary.

But even if the contradiction is to remain without a solution, humanity must hold it as a sacred duty to keep the two terms of this contradiction in mind. It must never to lose sight of one to the exclusive benefit of the other. It must, naturally, avoid a blind particularism which would tend to reserve human status for one race, one culture, or one society; but it must also never forget that no fraction of humanity should dispose of formulae which could be applied to all, and that a humanity merged into a single way of life is inconceivable, because it would be an ossified humanity.

In this regard, the international institutions have an immense task ahead of them and they bear heavy responsibilities. They are more complex than we think. For the mission of international institutions is twofold: It consists partly in a liquidation and partly in an awakening. Institutions must first assist humanity and make the reabsorption of these defunct diversities as painless and safe as possible. These diversities are the valueless residues of modes of collaboration which exist as putrefied vestiges and constitute a permanent risk of infecting the international body. They must be pruned, amputated, if need be, to facilitate the birth of other forms of adaptation.

But at the same time, the international institutions must be passionately sensitive to the fact that, in order to have the same functional value as previous ones, these new modes cannot simply reproduce them or be conceived in the same pattern without being reduced to more and more insipid—and finally useless—solutions. On the contrary, they have to know that humanity is rich in unforeseen possibilities, each of which will, when it appears, always strike men with astonishment; that progress is not made after the comfortable image of this "improved similitude" wherein we seek of ourselves a leisurely repose, but rather is full of adventure, ruptures, and scandals. Humanity is constantly struggling with two contradictory processes. One of these tends to promote unification, while the other aims at maintaining or reestablishing diversification. The position of each era or of each culture in the system (the orientation in which it finds itself engaged) is such that only one of the two processes seems to have a meaning. The latter is seemingly the negation of the former. But to say—as one might well feel like saying—that humanity defeats itself at the same time as it makes itself would still stem from an incomplete vision. For, on both planes and at two opposite levels, we are dealing with two different manners of *making oneself*.

The necessity of preserving the diversity of cultures, in a world threatened by monotony and uniformity, has certainly not remained unnoticed by international institutions. They must also understand that, to reach this goal, it will not be enough to favor local traditions and to allow some respite to times gone by. It is the fact of diversity which must be saved, not the historical content given to it by each era (and which no era could perpetuate beyond itself). We must listen to the wheat growing, encourage secret potentialities, awaken all the vocations to live together that history holds in reserve. One must also be ready to consider without surprise, repulsion, or revolt whatever unusual aspect all these new social forms of expression cannot fail to present. Tolerance is not a contemplative position, dispensing indulgence to what was and to what is. It is a dynamic attitude consisting in the foresight, the understanding, and the promotion of what wants to be. The diversity of human cultures is behind us, around us, and ahead of us. The only demand we may make upon it (creating for each individual corresponding duties) is that it realize itself in forms such that each is a contribution to the greater generosity of the others.

NOTES

1. See Raymond Aron's interesting discussion of this passage, "Le Paradoxe du même de de l'autre," in *Échanges et communications*, ed. J. Pouillon and P. Maranda, *Studies in General Anthropology*, V (The Hague, 1970), Vol. II, pp. 943-952.

Bibliography

Adamson, T. (1934). *Folk-Tales of the Coast Salish*, Memoirs of the American Folklore Society, Vol. XXVIII. Philadelphia.

Adler, A. and Cartry, M. (1971). "La Transgression et sa dérision," *L'Homme, Revue française d'anthropologie*, XI, No. 3.

Albisetti, C. (1948). "Estudos complementares sôbre os Bororós orientais," *Contribuições missionárias*. Publicaçoes da Sociedade brasileira de anthropologia e etnologia, Nos. 2–3, Rio de Janeiro.

Albisetti, C. and Venturelli, A. J. (1962–1969). *Enciclopédia Bororo*, Vols. I–II, Campo Grande.

Banner, H. (1957). "Mitos dos Indios Kayapo," *Revista de Antropologia*, Vol. 5, No. 1. São Paulo.

Barbeau, M. (1929). *Totem Poles of the Gitskan*. National Museum of Canada, Bulletins of the Canada Department of Mines, Geological Survey, LXI. Ottawa.

———. (1950). *Totem Poles*. National Museum of Canada, *Anthropological Series 30*, Bulletin No. 114, 2 vols. Ottawa.

Barnard, M. (1966). *The Mythmakers*. Athens, Ohio.

Beckwith, M. W. (1938). *Mandan-Hidatsa Myths and Ceremonies*. Memoirs of the American Folklore Society, XXXII. Philadelphia.

363

———. (1962). "Strengthening the Behavioral Sciences," *Science*, CXXXVI, No. 3512; *Behavioral Science*, VII, No. 3.

Beynon, W. (1941). "The Tsimshians of Metlakatla," *American Anthropologist*, n.s., XXXXIII.

Boas, F. (1891). "Dissemination of Tales among the Natives of North America," *Journal of American Folklore*, IV.

———. (1895a). "Indianische Sagen von der Nord-Pacifischen Küste Amerikas," in *Sonder-Abdruck aus den Verhandlungen der Berliner Gesellschaft für Anthropologie, Ethnologie und Urgeschichte, 1891–1895*. Berlin.

———. (1895b). *Fifth Report on the Indians of British Columbia*. Reports of the British Association for the Advancement of Science No. 65. London.

———. (1897). *The Social Organization and the Secret Societies of the Kwakiutl Indians*. U.S. National Museum Annual Report 1895. Washington, D.C.

———. (1902). *Tsimshian Texts*. Smithsonian Institution, Bureau of American Ethnology Bulletin No. 27. Washington, D.C.

———, ed. (1911). *Handbook of American Indian Languages*. Smithsonian Institution, Bureau of American Ethnology Bulletin No. 40, 2 vols. Washington, D.C.

———. ed. (1917). *Folk-Tales of Salishan and Sahaptin Tribes*. Memoirs of the American Folklore Society, XI. Philadelphia.

Boas, F. and Hunt, G. (1902). *Kwakiutl Texts* II, Memoirs of the American Museum of Natural History. Leyden–New York.

———. (1912). *Tsimshian Texts*. Publications of the American Ethnological Society, n.s., III. Leyden.

———. (1916). *Tsimshian Mythology*. Smithsonian Institution, Bureau of American Ethnology, 31st Annual Report, 1909–1910. Washington, D.C.

———. (1918). *Kutenai Tales*. Smithsonian Institution, Bureau of American Ethnology Bulletin No. 59. Washington, D.C.

———. (1925). "Stylistic Aspects of Primitive Literature," *Journal of American Folklore*, XXXVIII.

———. (1932). "Current Beliefs of the Kwakiutl," *Journal of American Folklore*, XLV.

Bowers, A. W. (1950). *Mandan Social and Ceremonial Organization*. Chicago.

———. (1965). *Hidatsa Social and Ceremonial Organization*. Smithsonian Institution, Bureau of American Ethnology. Bulletin No. 194. Washington, D.C.

Braudel, F. (1958). "La Longue Durée," *Annales*, IV.

———. (1959). "Histoire et sociologie," in *Traité de sociologie*, ed. G. Gurvitch. Paris.

Casagrande, J. B., ed. (1960). *In the Company of Man: Twenty Portraits by Anthropologists*. New York.

Chamberlain, A. F. (1892). *Report on the Kootenay Indians*. Reports of the British Association for the Advancement of Science, No. 62. London.

Chantre y Herrera, J. 1901. *Historia de las misiones de la Compañia de Jesús en el Moroñón español: (1637–1767).* Madrid.

Cline, W., ed. (1938). *The Sinkaietk or Southern Okanagon of Washington.* General Series in Anthropology No. 6. Menasha, Wisc.

Colbacchini, A. A. (1919). *A Tribu dos Boróros.* Rio de Janeiro.

———. (1925). *I Boróros Orientali "Orarimugudoge" del Matto Grosso, Brasile.* Contributi Scientifici delle Missioni Salesiane del Venerabile Don Bosco No. 1. Turin.

Colbacchini, A. and Albisetti, C. (1942). *Os Boróros Orientais.* São Paulo–Rio de Janeiro.

Comte, A. (1893). *Positive Philosophy,* trans. H. Martineau. London.

Crocker, J. C. (1969). "Reciprocity and Hierarchy among the Eastern Bororo," *Man,* n.s., IV, No. 1.

Curtin, J. and Hewitt, J. N. B. (1911). *Seneca Fiction, Legends, and Myths.* Smithsonian Institution, Bureau of American Enthnology, 32d Annual Report. Washington, D.C.

Deacon, A. B. (1934). *Malekula: A Vanishing People in the New Hebrides.* ed. C. H. Wedgwood. London.

Demeunier, M. (1776). *L'Esprit des usages et des coutumes des différents peuples, ou Observations tirées des voyageurs et des historiens,* 3 vols. London.

Diamond, S., ed. (1960). *Culture in History: Essays in Honor of Paul Radin.* New York.

Dorsey, G. A. (1905). *The Cheyenne.* Field Columbian Museum, Anthropological Series No. 9. Chicago.

Dorsey, G. A. and Kroeber, A. L. (1903). *Traditions of the Arapaho.* Field Columbian Museum Anthropological Series No. 5. Chicago.

Douglas, M. (1952). "Alternate Generations Among the Lele of the Kasai, Southwest Congo," *Africa,* XXII, No. 1.

———. (1963). *The Lele of the Kasai.* London.

Driver, H. E. (1939). "Culture Element Distributions X: Northwest California," *Anthropological Records,* I, No. 6.

Drucker, P. (1965). *Cultures of the North Pacific Coast.* San Francisco.

Durkheim, E. (1896–1897). "La Prohibition de l'inceste et ses origines," *Année sociologique,* I.

———. (1900). "La Sociologia ed il sua dominio scientifico," *Rivista italiana di Sociologia,* IV (French translation in: A. Cuvillier, *Où va la sociologie française?,* appendix. Paris, 1953).

———. (1963). *Incest: The Nature and Origin of the Taboo.* New York. (Original French ed., 1897).

———. (1964). *The Rules of Sociological Method,* trans. S. A. Solovay and J. H. Mueller. New York. (Original French ed., 1895.)

———. (1968). *The Elementary Forms of the Religious Life,* trans. by J. W. Swain. New York. (Original French ed., 1912).

Durkheim E. and Mauss, M. (1963). *Primitive Classification,* trans. by R. Needham. Chicago. (Original French ed., 1901–1902).

Durlach, T. M. (1928). *Relationship Systems of the Tlingit, Haida and*

Tsimshian. Publications of the American Ethnological Society, XI. New York.

Elmendorf, W. W. (1960). "The Structure of Twana Culture [with] Comparative Notes on the Structure of Yurok Culture [by] A. L. Kroeber," *Research Studies, Monographic Supplement* 2.

Emmons, G. T. (1910). "Niska," in *Handbook of American Indians North of Mexico*. Smithsonian Institution, Bureau of American Ethnology Bulletin No. 30, 2 vols. Washington, D.C.

Engels, F. (1954). *Anti-Dühring*. Moscow. (Original German ed., 1878).

Espinas, A. (1901). "Etre ou ne pas être, ou du postulat de la sociologie," *Revue philosophique*.

Étienne, P. (1970). "Essai de représentation graphique de l'alliance matrimoniale," *L'Homme, Revue française d'anthropologie*, X, No. 4.

Evans-Pritchard, E. E. (1951). *Social Anthropology*. London.

———. (1961). *Anthropology and History*. Manchester.

Farrand, L. (1900). *Traditions of the Chilcotin*. Memoirs of the American Museum of Natural History, IV. Leyden–New York.

Fenton, W. N. (1953). *The Iroquois Dance: An Offshoot of the Calumet Dance*. Smithsonian Institution, Bureau of American Ethnology Bulletin No. 156. Washington, D.C.

Fewkes, J. W. (1903). *Hopi Katcinas, Drawn by Native Artists*. Smithsonian Institution, Bureau of American Ethnology 21st Annual Report, 1899–1900. Washington, D.C.

Fletcher, A. C. and La Flesche, F. (1911). *The Omaha Tribe*. Smithsonian Institution, Bureau of American Ethnology, 27th Annual Report, 1905–1906. Washington, D.C.

Fortes, M. (1949). "Time and Social Structure: An Ashanti Case Study," in *Social Structure: Studies Presented to A. R. Radcliffe-Brown*, ed. Meyer Fortes. Oxford.

Fortune, R. F. (1963). *Sorcerers of Dobu*. New York. (1st edition, 1932.)

Foster, G. M. (1959). "The Potter's Wheel: An Analysis of Idea and Artifact in Invention," *Southwestern Journal of Anthropology*, XV, No. 2.

Frazer, Sir J. G. (1911–1915). *The Golden Bough: A Study in Magic and Religion*, 12 vols. London.

Garfield, V. E. (1939). *Tsimshian Clan and Society*. University of Washington Publications in Anthropology, VII, No. 3. Seattle.

Garfield, V. E. and Wingert, P. S. (1966). *The Tsimshian Indians and their Arts*. Seattle.

Garfield, V. E., Wingert, P. S., Barbeau, M. (1951). *The Tsimshian: Their Arts and Music*. Publications of the American Ethnological Society, XVIII. New York.

Gillin, J. (1936). "The Barama River Carib of British Guiana." Papers of the Peabody Museum, XIV, No. 2. Cambridge, Mass.

Gilmore, M. R. (1919). *Uses of Plants by the Indians of the Missouri River Region*. Smithsonian Institution, Bureau of American Ethnology, 33d Annual Report, 1911–1912. Washington, D.C.

Gobineau, A. de (1853–1855). *Essai sur l'inégalité des races humaines*. Paris.

Goddard, P. E. (1935). *Indians of the Northwest Coast.* The American Museum of Natural History, Handbook Series No. 10. New York.

Godel, R. (1957). *Les Sources manucristes du Cours de linguistique générale de Ferdinand de Saussure.* Geneva.

Goethe, J. W. von (1946). *The Metamorphosis of Plants,* trans. Agnes Arber. Waltham, Mass. (Original German ed., 1790.)

Goldschmidt, W. (1951). *Nomlaki Ethnography.* University of California Publications in American Archaeology and Ethnology, XLII, No. 4. Berkeley.

Guiart, J. (1958). "Espiritu Santo (Nouvelles-Hébrides)," *L'Homme, Cahiers d'ethnologie, de géographie et de linguistique.*

———. (1963). *Structure de la chefferie en Mélanésie du sud.* Paris.

Guinard, J. E. (1930). "Witiko among Tête-de-Boule," *Primitive Man,* III, No. 3.

Gunther, E. (1927). *Klallam Ethnography.* University of Washington Publications in Anthropology I, No. 5. Seattle.

Haeberlin, H. K. (1924). "Mythology of Puget Sound," *Journal of American Folklore,* XXXVII.

Heim, R. (1963). *Les Champignons toxiques et hallucinogènes.* Paris.

———. (1967). *Nouvelles Investigations sur les champignons hallucinogènes.* Paris.

Heim, R. and Wasson, R. G. (1958). *Les Champignons hallucinogènes du Mexique.* Paris.

Heusch, L. de (1958). *Essai sur le symbolisme de l'inceste royal en Afrique.* Brussels.

———. (1971). *Pourquoi l'épouser? et autres essais.* Paris.

Hiatt, L. R. (1965). *Kinship and Conflict: A Study of an Aboriginal Community in Northern Arnhem Land.* Canberra.

Hill-Tout, C. (1899). *Notes on the N'tlakápamu of British Columbia, a Branch of the Great Salish Stock of North America.* Reports of the British Association for the Advancement of Science No. 69. London.

———. (1904a). "Report on the Ethnology of the Siciatl of British Columbia, a Coast Division of the Salish Stock," *Journal of the Royal Anthropological Institute,* XXXIV.

———. (1904b). "Ethnological Reports on the Stseélis and Sk.aúlits tribes of the Halōkmēlem Division of the Salish of British Columbia," *Journal of the Royal Anthropological Institute,* XXXIV.

———. (1907). *The Natives of British North America.* London.

Hodge, F. W. (1910). *Handbook of American Indians North of Mexico.* Smithsonian Institution, Bureau of American Ethnology, Bulletin No. 30, 2 vols. Washington, D.C.

Hoffman, W. J. (1884). *Selish Myths.* Essex Institute Bulletin No. 15. Salem, Mass.

Hubert, H. and Mauss, M. (1929). *Mélanges d'histoire des religions,* 2nd ed. Paris.

———. (1964). *Sacrifice: Its Nature and Function,* trans. W. D. Halls. Chicago. (Original French ed., 1899.)

Hume, D. (1748). *Essays, Moral and Political*. London.

Jacobs, M. (1934). *Northwest Sahaptin Texts*. Columbia University Contributions to Anthropology, XIX, Nos. 1–2.

Jenness, D. (1934). "Myths of the Carrier Indians," *Journal of American Folklore*, XLVII.

———. (1943). *The Carrier Indians of the Buljley River*. Smithsonian Institution, Bureau of American Ethnology Bulletin No. 133. Washington, D.C.

Jones, J. F. (1914). *A Study of the Thlingets of Alaska*. New York.

Kohl, J.-G. (1956). *Kitchi Gami: Wanderings Round Lake Superior*. Minneapolis.

Krause, A. (1956). *The Tlingit Indians: Results of a Trip to the Northwest Coast of America and the Bering Straits*, trans. E. Gunther. Seattle.

Kroeber, A. L. (1904). *The Arapaho. III, Ceremonial Organization*. Bulletin of the American Museum of Natural History, XVIII, No. 2. New York.

Kuipers, A. H. (1967). "The Squamish Language," *Janua Linguarum. Series practica*, LXXIII, Nos. 1–2.

Leach, E. R. (1961). *Rethinking Anthropology*, London.

———. (1970). *Lévi-Strauss*, London.

Lehmann-Nitsche, R. (1919). "El Diluvio según los Araucanos de la Pampa: La Cosmogonia según los Puelche de la Patagonia. Mitologia sudamericana, I, II," *Revista del Museo de la Plata*, XXIV, *segunda parte*, 2d. s., XI.

Levy-Bruhl, L. (1949). *Les Carnets de Levy-Bruhl*. Preface by Maurice Leenhardt. Paris.

Lévi-Strauss, C. (1958). "Dis-moi quels champignons . . . ," *L'Express*, 10 April.

———. (1963). *Structural Anthropology*, trans. C. Jacobson and B. G. Schoepf. New York. (Original French ed., 1958.)

———. (1964). *Totemism*. London. (Original French ed., 1962.)

———. (1966). *The Savage Mind*. London. (Original French ed., 1962.)

———. (1968). *L'Origine des manières de table*. Paris.

———. (1969a). *The Elementary Structures of Kinship*, trans. J. H. Belle and J. R. von Sturmer, ed. R. Needham. Boston. (Original French ed., 1949.)

———. (1969b). *The Raw and the Cooked*, trans. J. and D. Weightman. New York. (Original French ed., 1964.)

———. (1971a). *Mythologique IV: L'Homme nu*. Paris.

———. (1971b). "The Story of Asdiwal," in *The Structural Study of Myth and Totemism*, ed. E. Leach. London. (Original French ed., 1958.)

———. (1972a). "Compte rendu d'enseignement," *Annuaire du College de France, 72e année*. Paris.

———. (1972b). "Compte rendu de M. Detienne: Les Jardins d'Adonis," *L'Homme, Revue française d'anthropologie*, XII, No. 4.

Lienhardt, G. (1964). *Social Anthropology*. Oxford.

Livingstone, F. B. (1958). "Anthropological Implications of Sickle Cell Gene Distribution in West Africa," *American Anthropologist*, n.s., LX, No. 3.

McKennan, R. A. (1959). *The Upper Tanana*. Yale University Publications in Anthropology, LV. New Haven.

Mair, L. (1965). "How Small Scale Societies Change," in *Penguin Survey of the Social Sciences*. London.

———. (1969). *Anthropology and Social Change*. London.

Malinowski, B. (1922). *The Sexual Life of Savages in North-Western Melanesia*, 2 vols. New York.

———. (1945). *The Dynamic of Culture Change*. New Haven.

Mallery G. (1893). *Picture-Writing of the American Indians*. Smithsonian Institution, Bureau of American Ethnology, 10th Annual Report, 1888–1889. Washington, D.C.

Marx, K. (1967). *Das Kapital*, ed. Frederick Engels. New York. (Original German ed., 1890.)

Matthews, W. (1887). *The Mountain Chant: A Navajo Ceremony*. Smithsonian Institution, Bureau of American Ethnology, 5th Annual Report, 1883–1884. Washington, D.C.

Mauss, M. (1969). *The Gift: Forms and Functions of Exchange in Archaic Societies*, trans. I. Cunnison. Introduction by E. E. Evans-Pritchard. London. (Original French ed., 1923–1924.)

Maximilian, Prince of Wied (1843). *Travels in the Interior of North America*. trans. H. E. Lloyd. London.

Maybury-Lewis, D. (1960). "The Analysis of Dual Organizations: A Methodological Critique," *Anthropologica. Bijdragen tot de Taal-, Land-, en Volkenkunde*, CXVI, No. 1.

Mead, M. (1950). *Sex and Temperament in Three Primitive Societies*. New York. (1st ed., 1935.)

Meggitt, M. J. (1962). *Desert People: A Study of the Walbiri Aborigines of Central Australia*. Sydney.

Merleau-Ponty, M. (1960). *Signes*. Paris.

Métraux, A. (1939). "Myths and Tales of the Matako Indians," *Ethnological Studies*, IX.

———. (1946). *Myths of the Toba and Pilagá Indians of the Gran Chaco*. Memoirs of the American Folklore Society, XL. Philadelphia.

———. (1959). "La Révolution de la hache," *Diogène*, XXV.

Murphy, R. F. (1958). *Mundurucú Religion*. University of California Publications in American Archaeology and Ethnology, XLIX, No. 1. Berkeley.

Nimuendaju, C. (1939). *The Apinayé*. The Catholic University of America, Anthropological Series, No. 8. Washington, D.C.

———. (1942). *The Sherente*. Publications of the Frederick Webb Hodge Anniversary Publication Fund No. 4. Los Angeles.

———. (1946). *The Eastern Timbira*. University of California Publications in American Archaeology and Ethnology, XLI. Berkeley.

———. (1952). *The Tukuna.* University of California Publications in American Archaeology and Ethnology, XLV. Berkeley.

Olson, R. L. (1967). *The Quinault Indians and Adze, Canoe and House Types of the Northwest Coast.* Seattle.

Opler, M. E. (1960). "Myth and Practice in Jicarilla Apache Eschatology," *Journal of American Folklore* LXXIII.

Petitot, E. (1886). *Traditions indiennes du Canada nord-ouest.* Paris.

Phinney, A. (1934). *Nez Percé Texts.* Columbia University Contributions to Anthropology, XXV. No. 25. New York.

Pospisil, L. (1959–1960). "The Kapauku Papuans and their Kinship Organization," *Oceania,* XXX, No. 3.

Pouillon, J. and Maranda, P. (1970). *Echanges et communications: Mélanges offers à Claude Lévi-Strauss à l'occasion de son 60e anniversaire,* 2 vols. Paris–The Hague.

Radcliffe-Brown, A. R. (1958). *Method in Social Anthropology: Selected Essays,* ed. M. N. Srinivas. Chicago.

Radin, P. (1923). *The Winnebago Tribe.* Smithsonian Institution, Bureau of American Ethnology, 37th Annual Report, 1915–1916. Washington, D.C.

———. (1933). *Method and Theory of Ethnology.* New York.

———. (1945). *The Road of Life and Death.* Bollingen Series, V. New York.

———. (1949). *The Culture of the Winnebago: As Described by Themselves.* Special Publications of the Bollingen Foundation. New York. (Also issued as International Journal of American Linguistics Memoir 2. Baltimore.)

Rand, S. T. (1894). *Legends of the Micmacs.* New York.

Ray, V. F. (1933). "Sanpoil Folk Tales," *Journal of American Folklore,* XLVI.

———. (1939). *Cultural Relations in the Plateau of Northwestern America.* Publications of the F. W. Hodge Anniversary Publication Fund, III. Los Angeles.

———. (1954). *The Sanpoil and Nespelem.* Human Relations Area Files. New Haven.

Read, K. E. (1959). "Leadership and Consensus in a New Guinea Society," *American Anthropologist,* n.s., LXI, No. 3.

Redfield, R. (1950). "Social Science among the Humanities," *Measure,* I.

———. (1953). "Relations of Anthropology to the Social Sciences and to the Humanities," in: *Anthropology Today,* ed. A. L. Kroeber. Chicago.

Reichard, G. A. (1947). *An Analysis of Coeur d'Alene Indian Myths.* Memoirs of the American Folklore Society, XLI. Philadelphia.

Richards, J. F. (1914). "Cross Cousin Marriage in South India," *Man,* XIV.

Robbins, W. W., Harrington, J. P., and Freire-Marreco, B. (1916). "Ethnobotany of the Tewa Indians," Smithsonian Institution, Bureau of American Ethnology Bulletin No. 55. Washington, D.C.

Rosman, A. and Rubel, P. (1971). *Feasting with Mine Enemy.* New York.

———. (1972). "The Potlatch: A Structural Analysis," *American Anthropologist,* n.e., LXXIV, No. 3.

Roth, W. E. (1915). *An Inquiry into the Animism and Folklore of the Guiana Indians,* Smithsonian Institution, Bureau of American Ethnology, 30th Annual Report, 1908–1909. Washington, D.C.

————. (1924). *An Introductory Study of the Arts, Crafts and Customs of the Guiana Indians.* Smithsonian Institution, Bureau of American Ethnology, 38th Annual Report, 1916–1917. Washington, D.C.

Rousseau, J.-J. (1774–1783). *Collection complète des oeuvres de Jean-Jacques Rousseau,* 12 vols. London.

Sapir, E. (1915). *A Sketch of the Social Organization of the Nass River Indians.* National Museum of Canada, Bulletins of the Canada Department of Mines, Geological Survey, XIX, Ottawa.

Saussure, F. de (1959). *Course in General Linguistics,* trans. W. Baskin, C. A. Sechehaye, with A. Reidlinger. New York.

Shapiro, W. (1969). "Asymetric Marriage in Australia and Southeast Asia," *Bijdragen tot de taal-, land- en Volkenkunde,* CXXV.

Sharp, L. (1952). "Steel Axes for Stone Age Australians," *Human Organization,* XI.

Skinner, A. and Satterlee, J. V. (1915). *Folklore of the Menomini Indians.* American Museum of National History, Anthropological Papers, XIII, No. 3. New York.

Spencer, R. F. (1959). *The North Alaskan Eskimo.* Smithsonian Institution, Bureau of American Ethnology, Bulletin No. 171. Washington, D.C.

Stanner, W. E. H. (1960). "Durmugam, a Nangiomeri [Australia]," in *In the Company of Men: Twenty Portraits by Anthropologists,* ed. J. B. Casagrande. New York.

Stevenson, M. C. (1904). *The Zuni Indians: Their Mythology, Esoteric Fraternities and Ceremonies.* Smithsonian Institution, Bureau of American Ethnology, 23rd Annual Report, 1901–1902. Washington, D.C.

Swanton, J. R. (1905). *Haida Texts and Myths.* Smithsonian Institution, Bureau of American Ethnology, Bulletin No. 29. Washington, D.C.

————. (1908). *Haida Texts.* Memoirs of the American Museum of Natural History, XIV. New York.

————. (1909a). *Contribution to the Ethnology of the Haida.* Memoirs of the American Museum of Natural History, VIII. New York.

————. (1909b). *Tlingit Myths and Texts.* Smithsonian Institution, Bureau of American Ethnology, Bulletin No. 39. Washington, D.C.

————. (1952). *Indian Tribes of North America,* Smithsonian Institution, Bureau of American Ethnology. Bulletin No. 145. Washington, D.C.

Teit, J. A. (1898). *Traditions of the Thompson Indians.* Memoirs of the American Folklore Society, VI. Philadelphia.

————. (1900). *The Thompson Indians of British Columbia.* Memoirs of the American Museum of Natural History, II. New York.

————. (1906). *The Lilloet Indians.* Memoirs of the American Museum of Natural History, IV. New York.

————. (1909). *The Shuswap.* Memoirs of the American Museum of Natural History, IV. New York.

————. (1912). *Mythology of the Thompson Indian*. Memoirs of the American Museum of Natural History, XII. New York.

————. (1930). *Ethnobotany of the Thompson Indians of British Columbia*, ed. E. V. Steedman. Smithsonian Institution, Bureau of American Ethnology, 45th Annual Report. Washington, D.C.

Turner, T. S. (1966). "Social Structure and Political Organization among the Northern Cayapo" (mimeographed). Cambridge: Harvard University.

Voegelin, E. W. (1942). "Culture Element Distributions XX: Northeast California," *Anthropological Records*, VII, No. 2.

Walker, D. E., Jr. (1968). *Conflict and Schism in Nez Percé Acculturation*. Seattle.

Wasson, R. G. (1968). *Soma, Divine Mushroom of Immortality*. New York.

Wasson, V. P. and R. G. (1957). *Mushrooms, Russia and History*, 2 vols. New York.

Waugh, F. W. (1916). *Iroquois Foods and Food Preparation*. Canada Department of Mines, Geological Survey, Memoir 86. Ottawa.

Wedgewood, C. H. (1928). "Cousin Marriage" in *Encyclopaedia Britannica*.

White, L. A. (1949). *The Science of Culture*. New York.

Williams, F. E. (1932). "Sex Affiliation and Its Implications," *Journal of the Royal Anthropological Institute*, LXII.

Wissler, C. and Duvall, D. C. (1908). *Mythology of the Blackfoot Indians*. Anthropological Papers of the American Museum of Natural History, II. New York.

Index